19.95

NONVERBAL BEHAVIOR
AND COMMUNICATION

NONVERBAL BEHAVIOR AND COMMUNICATION

Edited by
ARON W. SIEGMAN
STANLEY FELDSTEIN
UNIVERSITY OF MARYLAND BALTIMORE COUNTY

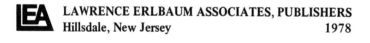 LAWRENCE ERLBAUM ASSOCIATES, PUBLISHERS
Hillsdale, New Jersey   1978

DISTRIBUTED BY THE HALSTED PRESS DIVISION OF

JOHN WILEY & SONS

New York   Toronto   London   Sydney

Lawrence Erlbaum Associates, Inc., Publishers
62 Maria Drive
Hillsdale, New Jersey 07642

Distributed solely by Halsted Press Division
John Wiley & Sons, Inc., New York

Library of Congress Cataloging in Publication Data

Main entry under title:

Nonverbal behavior and communication.

    1. Nonverbal communication.   I. Siegman, Aron Wolfe.
II. Feldstein, Stanley, 1930-
BF637.C45N62   152.3'84   77-15566
ISBN 0-470-99344-8

Printed in the United States of America

**To Our Wives
and Children**

Contents

Preface

For a number of years now, the senior editor of this book has been teaching a course on nonverbal communication to intermediate-level and upper-level undergraduates. When this course was first offered, the only books on the market that dealt with this topic in a comprehensive manner were of the popular literature variety, some with a frank sensationalist appeal; i.e., here is a new and easy method with which to "read" other people's innermost thoughts and desires, especially those of a sexual nature. Notwithstanding this put-down of the pop-literature on nonverbal communication, it probably helped generate the widespread interest on college campuses for courses on nonverbal communication in which attempts were made to separate fact from fancy, and it may even have stimulated some serious research in the area. Lest the above give rise to a misunderstanding, it should be pointed out that serious research on nonverbal communication antedates popular interest in the subject, as will be shown later on; nevertheless, until recently, such research was restricted in scope.

This situation has changed dramatically over the past decade. Research is burgeoning and a number of scholarly books devoted to nonverbal communication are now available. Many of these books represent discussions and summaries of the authors' own research on fairly restricted aspects of nonverbal communication, and hence they tend to be both too specialized and too advanced for general classroom use. There are a few textbooks dealing with nonverbal communication in a comprehensive fashion, but these tend to be on a rather elementary level. Thus, the need for a comprehensive text written for an audience of advanced undergraduate and graduate students is still very much with us.

It is this need that provided the impetus for the present volume. We approached a number of scholars known for their contributions to different areas of nonverbal communication and invited them to contribute a chapter summarizing the state of the art in their respective areas of expertise. They were specifically instructed to be comprehensive, not to restrict themselves to their own research (unless, of course, theirs preempts the field, which is, in fact, true in at least several cases), and to pitch the level of their contributions to the audience identified earlier. We are aware, of course, that in an edited book, such goals are not likely to be uniformly implemented, if only for the obvious reason that people's standards of what is elementary, intermediary, and advanced vary considerably. Indeed, the result of our effort is a quite heterogeneous set of chapters. Some are addressed to general, basic issues, whereas others present a comprehensive, integrated review of the research literature. They vary also in both length and readability. It seems to us, however, that the heterogeneity makes the book as a whole more readable than it might otherwise be.

The chapters are divided into four sections on the basis of their primary concerns. The first section views nonverbal communication from the perspectives of animal behavior and the neurophysiological structure of the human brain. The second section reviews some of the major findings with regard to the roles of the body, the face, and the eyes, and delineates the basic issues involved. The third section is devoted to the behavior of the vocal channel, and the final section examines the uses of space and time in nonverbal behavior and communication.

We believe that the book will prove useful not only as a text in courses about nonverbal communication, but also as supplementary reading for courses about interviewing theory and techniques and about the psychology of language.

We should like to note, in closing, that we were fortunate to have several individuals critically read various chapters of the book. Two, Drs. Donald S. Boomer and Allen T. Dittmann, are also contributors. The others were Drs. Bernard Baumrin, Sherry R. Rochester, and Marilyn Wang. We are grateful for their comments.

ARON W. SIEGMAN
STANLEY FELDSTEIN

NONVERBAL BEHAVIOR
AND COMMUNICATION

Introduction

An attractive feature of nonverbal communication as a research area is that it has captured the interest of scholars of different disciplinary backgrounds—psychologists, linguists, anthropologists, psychiatrists, and sociologists—with each discipline bringing to the area its peculiar theoretical and methodological perspectives and biases. Each of these disciplines also tends to have a favorite topic or problem area within the general domain of nonverbal communication. For example, for fairly obvious reasons, psychiatrists have been primarily interested in the expressive correlates of affective experiences, especially anxiety, and anthropologists have done most of the early work on proxemics. Along with the varying yet overlapping topical concerns that the different disciplines bring to the area of nonverbal communication are major differences in methodology.

Methodological Issues

Psychologists who are very much concerned with objectivity, measurement, and quantification have brought nonverbal communication into the laboratory. The advantages of this approach are obvious, but there are disadvantages as well. Typical of the experimental method is the manipulation of one variable, and the monitoring of the effects of this manipulation on the dependent variable. It is, of course, possible to manipulate more than one independent variable at a time, but even in such increasingly popular multivariate designs, the experimenter tends to look at the effects of the manipulations, individually and in combination, upon a single dependent variable. The reason for this is that while researchers are becoming familiar with statistical procedures that assess the interaction of several *independent* variables, few of them are familiar with procedures that assess the interaction of several *dependent* variables. This methodological constraint may account for the fact that psychological research concerned with nonverbal communication tends to focus on a single channel, be it eye contact, body movements, or some vocal characteristic of speech. This approach is reflected in the very organization of this book, which is primarily, although not exclusively, in terms of identifiable single channels of communication. One problem with the single-channel approach is that different people may use different channels for the same message. Thus, some individuals may express their liking for other persons via the vocal channel, while some may do so via the visual channel. To the extent that there is such functional equivalence between channels, the single-channel paradigm is clearly an inappropriate one. By way of contrast, social scientists less concerned with quantification and tests of significance tend to look at functionally organized behavioral domains, such as courtship behavior or greeting behavior, and to monitor an individual's nonverbal communications in a variety of channels. The latter approach, however, tends to be descriptive and, therefore, does not allow for causal statements about the observed relationships.

It should be stressed that although the examination of a single-channel versus multiple-channels of communication may be related to methodological preferences, it is not an inevitable consequence of such preferences. It is possible to manipulate experimentally behavior that is functionally meaningful, such as approval seeking, and to monitor the effects of the manipulation on a variety of channels, as has in fact been done by Rosenfeld (1966a,b). The important point is that the particular organization of this book notwithstanding, there is a clear recognition, even on the part of psychologists who use the experimental method, that communication is multi-channeled and that different channels may be used by different people for the same message; it is a recognition that any general model of interpersonal communication must take into account.

Another problem with the usual experimental paradigm is that it fails to consider the interactional, reciprocal nature of interpersonal communication. Typically, in experimental studies of nonverbal communication, the behavior of one of the participants, usually a confederate of the experimenter, is controlled. For example, if the experimentally manipulated variable is eye contact, one of the participants in an interaction is trained to behave in a uniform and consistent manner with all his partners, except in relation to eye contact, which is controlled according to a predetermined schedule (e.g., it may be withheld all the time from some subjects in a between-subjects design, or some of the time from all subjects in a within-subjects design). Thus, the continuous feedback and readjustment that characterizes dyadic communication is not taken into consideration. By way of contrast, naturalistic studies of conversation can capture the cybernetic nature of interpersonal communication. Clearly, then, the use of the experimental rather than the naturalistic paradigm involves a trade-off between level of control and appropriateness of the model.

Definitional Issues

A major concern in the area of nonverbal communication is that of definition. For the author in this field, as well as the teacher, the problem—which may appear to be a fairly abstract one—has a very practical implication: what to include and what to exclude from his book or course. Some topics, such as proxemics or the facial, vocal, and bodily expressions of emotion, are included in most textbooks on nonverbal communication. Then there are topics, such as dress codes, which are included by some authors and excluded by most others. Some implicitly held definitions of nonverbal communication are broad enough so that any behavior would qualify. Of course, definitions that are broad enough to include almost any behavior, as long as it is not verbal, are not very useful. Wiener, Devoe, Rubinow, and Geller (1972) have suggested a definition which takes as its starting point the term "communication." For them, communication implies that one person (an encoder) is actively making his experience known to some other person (a decoder) by means of a shared code. The difficulty with this definition is that it may be too restrictive. The difficulty is caused by the term "code," which implies an *arbitrary* relationship between the elements which make up the code and their referents. This definition excludes from the domain of nonverbal communication any behavior that bears a direct, nonarbitrary relationship to that which it signifies. Potential candidates for exclusion are the facial, vocal, and bodily correlates of affective experiences, the various hesitation phenomena which appear to signify cognitive processing and at least certain aspects of proxemics. Indeed, the definition excludes much of what is included in this book!

Wiener *et al.* (1972) are quite explicit about the assumption that nonverbal communication must be in the form of a code which bears an arbitrary relationship to its referents. "To find invariance of behavioral form and referent across cultures would to us be prima facie evidence that the behavior is not part of a coding system. We could agree that some forms of behavior (e.g., facial variations) might be more likely than others to be used in making public some sets of experience (e.g., mood state). However, a behavior whose significance is found to be invariant across cultures (i.e., observers attribute the same significance to the behavior in all cultures) would be difficult to include as a code component, which for us involves an assumption of an arbitrary relationship between symbol and referent" (Wiener *et al.*, 1972, p. 203). In effect, then, these authors argue that communication can take place only via symbols (which have an arbitrary relationship to their referents) and not via signs (which have a nonarbitrary relationship to their referents).

The distinction between signs and symbols is an old one, but the argument that communication should be limited to symbols seems unnecessarily restrictive. In making their argument, Wiener and his associates explicitly state that language, which is a system of *mostly* arbitrary symbols, provided them with their criteria for their definition of nonverbal communication. In other words, their limited definition of communication is clearly a consequence of viewing language as the prototype of all communication. But the concern with nonverbal communication is precisely a result of the increasing realization that there is more to communication than language. Infants communicate before they have even the rudimentary form of language, and it is not unreasonable to assume that nonverbal communication predated verbal communication in the history of mankind as well. It simply will not do, therefore, to formulate a model of nonverbal communication based on verbal communication. What we need, instead, is a model of communication which includes the essential features of both verbal and nonverbal communication.

Some of the difficulties associated with the definition offered by Wiener and his associates can be avoided by simply defining communication as the act of making one's experiences known to another person, whether it is via symbols or via signs. The emphasis here is on the *act* rather than on the *medium*. Nonverbal communication, then, could include all nonverbal behaviors that are involved in the transmission of experiences or information from one person to another (or others). This definition includes all behaviors which are part of an individual's communicative act and excludes those which are not. The definition, however, has its own difficulties, not the least of which is that it involves us in the issue of intent. Nevertheless, it should be pointed out that even the adoption of a more restrictive definition does not necessarily exclude topics such as the facial expressions of emotion from consideration, as long as they are considered under the rubric of nonverbal behavior rather than communication.

Substantive Issues

The sections into which the book is divided roughly organize the chapters in terms of their concerns with the bodily structures and zones that are involved in nonverbal behavior and with the patterning of such behavior in space and time. To begin with, it is clearly traditional to approach the examination of almost any sort of behavior by paying some attention to relevant biological considerations. It is also usually helpful to do so, even if only to raise questions about probable sources and built-in constaints. Much has been said about the biological foundations of human language. Although the extent to which it is innately programmed remains an issue of continuing controversy, most investigators are likely to agree with Cherry's (1961) succinct assertion that "... *human language is vastly more than a complicated system of clucking*" (p. 4, original italics). The implied distinction between human and infrahuman communication is explicitly discussed by Petrovich and Hess (Chapter 1), although against a broader emphasis on the role of the chemical and acoustical channels of animal communication. Their perspective is ethological and they offer no resolutions of the arguments for and against the distinction. They do point out, however, that the discontinuity theory of the evolution of language that is implied in the distinction itself implies the assumption that the biological evolution of communication is continuous.

Jaffe (Chapter 2) is concerned with a quite different level of biological constraint. He speculates that the neurophysiology of the brain, particularly the asymmetrical specialization of its hemispheres, can account for much of the structure and efficiency of face-to-face conversation. His primary interest is in the alternation of speakers in a conversation and he argues that ". . . *cerebral hemispheric specialization in man has evolved under the selective pressure of efficient face-to-face conversations*" (original italics). In amassing evidence for his position, he provocatively probes such issues as the differential lateralization of linguistic and nonlinguistic behavior, the role of interjections, and the implications of delayed auditory feedback and speech-linked gestures. Moreover, he suggests, and explores in some detail, the possibility that the "mutual illumination of physiology and ordinary conversation" provides a clearer interpretation and understanding of aphasic disorders. The chapter is richly suggestive of a neurophysiological perspective from which to view many of the behaviors discussed in subsequent chapters.

There is little doubt that face-to-face human communication involves more than the exchange of verbal messages. It includes patterns of visual interactions, facial expressions, gestures, body postures and movements, and tone of voice. The chapters in the second section are devoted to various kinds of nonverbal, nonvocal behavior. Taken together, they provide the reader with a comprehensive, non-parochial view of the basic issues and findings in the area of gestural, facial, and visual behavior.

Dittmann's chapter (10) is used as the introductory chapter for this section, because it addresses itself to some fundamental issues of definition and classification. The term "body language," a term frequently used in the early popular literature on nonverbal communication, leads Dittmann to raise the question: What are the criteria of a language? Dittmann concludes "that language is a code . . . [an] agreed upon system in which: (1) The thoughts and ideas we wish to convey are simplified and grouped into categories. (2) These categories are organized so that the relationships among the categories can be clear. (3) The results of these processes are restructured into symbols of a form that can be communicated from one person to another. To the extent that any communication system is a code in this sense, a great deal of information can be transmitted from sender to receiver in a short period of time with great dependability" (p. 73). According to Dittmann, then, efficiency and reliability are the two hallmarks of language as a code. The author then examines in detail two nonverbal codes, American Sign Language and Indian Sign Language, and concludes that they are codes in the same sense that spoken languages are codes.

With American Sign Language as the prototype of a true body *language,*

Dittmann examines the body movements which accompany speech. According to Dittmann, there are only few discrete body movements that behave like coded material in that they are easily understood by most members of the community. These include the hitchhiker's movement for thumbing a ride, whirling the ear with the index finger to say, "He's crazy," the index finger to the lips for "shhh," and the airman sign for "A-OK." These discrete and categorical emblems have meanings that everyone in the language community can agree upon. "Most movements are not of that type, however, and they take as their organizing principles either the rhythmical structure of the concurrent speech, or their association with the state of being of the person, either long-term or situationally influenced. We use these less specific behaviors as cues to make inferences about those states in the person and the success of those inferences varies with a number of factors. Extended discourse in body language, parallel to that possible in spoken language or ASL (American Sign Language) does not seem to occur" (p. 93).

For the reader who is acquainted with Ekman's work on the facial expression of emotions, a good deal of what will be found in his chapter (4) is likely to be familiar. As far as research on the facial expression of emotion is concerned, Ekman and his associates have pretty much preempted the field which, of course, makes him an ideal author for a chapter devoted to this topic. On the other hand, being a prolific writer who has reported his findings in many scientific and lay journals and in several books in great detail, some duplication with what has already appeared in print under his name is inevitable.

Ekman begins his chapter with a summary of his cross-cultural studies, which leads him to conclude—as did Charles Darwin over 100 years ago—that there are universal facial expressions associated with the basic emotions such as fear, anger, and happiness. These universal expressions could, of course, derive from species-constant learning experiences, but Ekman is of the opinion that at least some of these expressions are genetically determined.

It should be stressed that according to Ekman there are both universal and culture-specific elements in the facial expression of emotion, with the latter reflecting cultural differences in the conditions which *elicit* a specific emotion and cultural differences in *display rules.* "While the appearance of the face for each of the primary emotions is common to all peoples, facial expressions do vary across cultures in at least two respects. What elicits or calls forth an emotion will usually differ; people may become disgusted or afraid in response to different things in different cultures. Also, cultures differ in the conventions people follow about attempting to control or manage the appearance of their face in given social situations. People in two different cultures may feel sadness at the death of a loved one, but one culture may prescribe that the chief mourners must mask their facial expression with a mildly happy countenance" (p. 105–106).

Ekman then proceeds to summarize the research related to his development of an atlas for the scoring of emotional expressions in the face, based on muscular movements in the brow/forehead area of the face, the eyes/lids and root of the nose area, and the lower face.

In the last part of his chapter, Ekman addresses himself to an important yet frequently neglected issue: that of individual differences in the encoding and the decoding of emotions. Although Ekman's focus is on the facial expression of affect, his conceptual framework can be readily applied to some of the other nonverbal channels of communication as well. An example is the concept of frozen affect, first described by Silvan Tomkins. This concept refers to the fact that in some people, after a particular expression, the face, instead of returning to a neutral countenance, returns to a slight version of one or another affect. Thus, the person always looks just slightly disgusted—or amused or angry—etc. The same can, of course, be said of people's voices. Similarly, Ekman's concepts of *frozen affect* and *blends* can be readily transferred to the vocal channel. It is hoped that the bringing together of the various contributions in a single volume will encourage this kind of interchannel fertilization.

Just as Ekman's name is associated with research on facial expression of emotion, Exline's is associated with research on visual interaction. This research has been summarized in an earlier review article (Exline, 1972). The purpose of Chapter 5, which is co-authored by B. J. Fehr, is to integrate the research done by others with the research done in Exline's laboratory, including several recently completed and as yet unpublished studies, and to present a conceptual framework. The authors use Charles Morris' theory of signs primarily as a convenient framework for ordering and bringing some structure to the amorphous field of visual interaction, rather than as a theoretical framework with which to explain and make sense of the data. The findings stand in their own right, and there is no implication that they support Morris' theory of signs, or that they are inconsistent with competing philosophical formulations.

As do several other authors in this book, Exline and Fehr begin their chapter with a definition of communication. They acknowledge that some authors consider communication to have occurred only when the sender consciously intends a given message to be received by another. This position, of course, excludes most nonverbal behavior from the category of communication. "People are typically not aware of what they do with their hands, feet, or other parts of their body when they talk with others." This narrow definition of communication is rejected by Exline and Fehr. "It is our contention . . . that these subsidiary behaviors are more than secondarily informative; they are a fully integrated part of the total message one transmits to another. The message itself would be different were they not present" (p. 121).

Next, the authors take up another recurrent theme in this book, that of reliability and validity. Can the frequency, direction, and duration of gazes be reliably and validly measured, and are they reliably and validly perceived? In relation to the perception of gaze direction, some investigators feel that the ability of humans to tell when they are looked at is very limited. The authors, however, conclude "... it seems likely that humans will be found capable of accurately determining the direction of the look" (p. 126). That there is no agreement on such a basic issue illustrates the fact that in the area of nonverbal communication, as in other newly developing areas of psychology, we have frequently proceeded to investigate complex substantive questions before having established the reliability and validity of our measuring instruments. The detailed discussion of these issues by Exline and Fehr is, therefore, a most welcome contribution.

The authors next proceed to tackle the crux of the chapter: the different meanings that can be attributed to the various kinds of visual interaction, and their impact on the participants' behavior. The authors delineate three different functions of visual interaction in dyadic communication. First, there is the regulatory function; visual cues help regulate, among others, the orderly alternation of speaker-listener roles. Second, as pointed out earlier, visual cues contribute meaning to the messages which are exchanged between the communicants. And third, visual cues contain messages about the relationship that exists between the communicants. In a very basic sense, to look at another person, whatever the function of the look, means to pay attention to the other person; it means engagement or the desire to engage the other. The precise nature of this involvement—whether, for example, it is friendly or hostile—depends on the context, on the participants' roles, on the direction and duration of the gaze, and on other nonverbal cues. Precisely how these parameters, singly and in interaction, determine the meaning of visual contact is the "meat" of the Exline and Fehr chapter.

It is the construct of attention which provides the authors with a conceptual framework for interpreting the numerous studies in the area of visual contact. In the absence of other cues, visual contact between communicants, or the lack thereof, communicates very little beyond their mutual attentiveness, or desire for it. It may very well be the case that all nonverbal signals, when considered in isolation, are inherently ambiguous. Consequently, what we need to know much more about is how specific nonverbal cues combine within and especially across channels to provide specific meanings—an almost unexplored area of research.

In addition to the communication afforded by eye-to-eye contact, Hess and Petrovich (Chapter 6) make a case for "pupil-to-pupil communication." They present a broad survey of the studies concerned with the role of pupillary behavior in interpersonal communication. Such behavior is limited; the pupil can expand, contract, or remain the same. The majority of studies suggest that pupillary dilation conveys interest, presumably positive interest. Negative stimuli appear to elicit pupillary constriction. The authors review in detail the studies Hess and others have conducted which relate changes in pupil size to heterosexual and homosexual interest (Don Juans display the same pupillary response to women as do homosexual men) and preferences of children for peers and parents. They also point out that pupil size is inversely related to age and suggest that the relationship is a result of evolutionary selection because of the greater appeal that children with larger pupils appear to have for adults. Other research has demonstrated that even schematically drawn eyes ("eyespots") can elicit pupillary responses in viewers. Paired eyespots elicited pupillary dilation whereas sets of single and triple eyespots elicited constriction. Such findings, the authors propose, suggest an "innate schema for two eyespots." It also seems to be the case that the lack of a change in pupil size is perceived as an indication of disinterest. It is the evidence that individuals appear to respond to changes in pupil size on the parts of those with whom they interact that entitles pupillary behavior to be considered a nonverbal channel of communication.

Although they do so briefly, the authors carefully review the methodological problems that have attended the investigations of pupillary behavior. Moreover, they suggest areas that still need to be explored and issues that need to be faced.

The third section of this book is devoted to the vocal channel. Unlike many authors who write about nonverbal communication as if it were a field *sui generis,* independent of verbal communication, we view nonverbal communication as very much related to the verbal message, not subordinate to it but rather as an integral part of the total communicative act. In addition to summarizing the empirical literature on the vocal channel, the two chapters in this section attempt to spell out some of the relationships between the encoding and production of language on the one hand, and vocal (but nonverbal) behavior on the other.

Siegman's contribution (Chapter 7), "The Telltale Voice: Nonverbal Messages of Verbal Communication," is divided into five parts. In the introduction, which is devoted to a definition of terms, he proposes a typology of vocal cues in terms of their functions, which is reminiscent of that proposed by Exline and Fehr for the visual domain. Siegman distinguishes between vocal cues which impart meaning to the verbal message, those which regulate the flow of verbal interaction between the participants, and those which are expressive of the speaker's background, his affective states, his attitudes and feelings toward the person being addressed, and of speech production and information processing. It is this third category of vocal cues with which the chapter is mostly concerned.

The second part is an historical and critical review of "personality and speech" research, an area which generated much research during an earlier period, subsequently went out of fashion, and is now showing signs of new life. Until recently, common wisdom had it that although people attribute specific personality traits to certain vocal qualities, these attributions, while quite reliable, lack validity. Siegman suggests that a variety of methodological problems may account for the lack of validity. Furthermore, he argues that at least as far as extroversion is concerned, there is objective evidence for specific vocal correlates. Finally, he argues that such personality attributions, whether valid or not, are an important basis for person perception, and that they influence our reactions to other people. The section concludes with a discussion of two alternative models for speech-personality attributions.

The third part of the chapter deals extensively with the effects of anxiety, and, briefly, with the effects of depression and anger on some vocal parameters of speech: tempo, speech disruptions, indices of hesitation, and verbal productiveity. Although much of this research was prompted by clinical concerns, Siegman argues for the value of conceptualizing these issues in terms of general psychological principles.

The fourth part summarizes studies about how the *relationship* between two or more communicants is expressed in the vocal channel, an area about which there are interesting speculations, but precious little solid empirical data.

In the fifth and last part, Siegman cites numerous studies which demonstrate that most, if not all, of the vocal indices (pauses, filled and unfilled, and speech disturbances) which have been identified as vocal correlates of affective experiences, are also affected by speech production and other cognitive processes. These findings cast considerable doubt on the frequently cited proposition that the nonverbal channels of communication are primarily devoted to the encoding of affect. Siegman argues that a given hesitation phenomenon, such as silent pauses, can serve different functions, cognitive or affective, and, conversely, that different hesitations, such as pauses and speech disruptions, can serve the same function, depending on the context in which they occur. This, of course, enormously complicates the decoding task, a point which was made earlier in relation to visual contact cues, and it buttresses the proposition that the nonverbal channels of communication are inherently ambiguous.

Boomer, in Chapter 8, contends that the *phonemic clause* is the "natural" unit of spontaneous speech. Unlike the clause of written language, the phonemic clause is identified by a characteristic patterning of pitch contour, rhythm, and loudness, and *not* by words. The thrust of the chapter is that the clause is not simply a linguistic unit; indeed, it is that, even though it is distinguished by its paralinguistic features. The point is that the clause has a behavioral reality as well. In Boomer's words, "Pause production and perception, tongue slips, and two kinds of listener responses were shown to be lawfully ordered to this unit" (p. 260). His work and that of others lead him to suggest that the phonemic clause may serve as the functional unit that will allow for the integration of verbal and nonverbal channels of communication.

In view of the increasing attention being paid to two-person interactions, it seems fair to wonder about the role of phonemic clause in conversational speech. That it may have such a role is suggested by the finding that listener responses tend to cluster about its boundaries. Rosenfeld (Chapter 10) raises the possibility of considering it to be a minimal information unit in conversational speech. However, another unit that has been viewed as basic is the speaking turn. Duncan (1972) made use of a unit which ". . . in size lay between the phonemic clause and the speaking turn" (p. 288), and La France (1974) apparently used a similar unit. It is not yet clear how the phonemic clause and speaking turn are related.

Boomer also calls attention to the neurophysiological problem of temporal integration. The latter "... refers to the brain's capacity to initiate, maintain, and control an extended behavior sequence ..." (p. 260). The phonemic clause is such a sequence and it is speech behavior. It was Lashley who suggested that the study of speech may yield important information about the functioning of the brain, although the speech unit he discussed was the "sentence." Boomer offers the phonemic clause as the more appropriate unit for investigation and asserts that some of the research findings he describes provide support for Lashley's speculations about the neurophysiological function in temporal integration.

Space and time are fundamental dimensions of existence, and it is hardly surprising to find that they may serve communicative functions. The final section presents three chapters that explore these dimensions.

Patterson (Chapter 9) examines the role of space in social interactions and distinguishes two issues: territoriality and personal space. Territoriality is, of course, an old established concept in the ethological and animal behavior literature where it refers to the demarcation and defense of a geographical area. As applied to human behavior, however, the term has come to include the claim to or the "marking" of objects, such as chairs and tables in public places. Territoriality is undoubtedly a major souce of aggressive or agonistic behavior in many lower animal species and, according to some authors (e.g., Audrey, 1966), it is the major biological basis of human aggression as well. The latter hypothesis has gained widespread popular acceptance, probably because wars between nations frequently do involve territorial disputes. It is not at all certain, however, that territoriality is in fact the major or even a major instigator of interpersonal impulsive aggressive behavior, nor is it clear that individual aggressive impulses trigger wars between nations. According to Patterson, territoriality is not nearly as pervasive a concern for social interaction as is personal space, which he defines as the "limiting distance which separates individuals when interacting with one another."

As do most other contributors to this book, Patterson addresses himself to the twin issues of reliability and validity. Personal space, when measured directly, is an impressively reliable phenomenon, although people are frequently unaware of their precise personal preferences. Some investigators, however, have used indirect indices, but they do not correlate very well with each other. This, of course, makes comparisons across studies difficult, which is a common methodological problem in the area of nonverbal communication.

Patterson also summarizes the effects of gender, racial and ethnic background, personality (as measured by standard personality tests), and various situational factors on interactional space. Gender is clearly important in personal space preferences. Females move closer to each other than do males, but these preferences change when they interact with a member of the opposite sex. With regard to personality, several social approach-avoidance variables, such as intro-version-extroversion, social anxiety, and the need for affiliation, are identified by Patterson as possibly related to personal space. He concludes, however, that "the evidence relating the role of any one of these personality variables to spatial behavior is certainly not so compelling as to generate unqualified confidence" (p. 274), a conclusion similar to that reached by other contributors to this book who have looked at the role of personality in nonverbal communication.

Patterson concludes with a discussion of the distance-equilibrium versus the distance-matching hypothesis. According to the latter hypothesis, changes in distance, or any other intimacy cue, initiated by one of two members in a dyadic interaction, tends to be reciprocated by the other partner. According to the equilibrium hypothesis, however, such changes produce compensatory responses in order to restore the original relationship. There is evidence for each of these phenomena, but we need to know much more about the precise conditions which produce the one rather than the other.

Rosenfeld (Chapter 10) and Feldstein and Welkowitz (Chapter 11) are con-cerned, in various ways, with the functions of time. Rosenfeld's concern with time is indirect in the sense that he is interested in the flow of conversation. His principal concern is with the ". . . problem of how conversants use nonverbal behavior to regulate the flow of information throughout the main body of their interaction" (p. 292). It is the regulatory aspect of nonverbal behavior that he calls its "conversational control function" and his general goal in the chapter is to provide a unified conceptualization of the process and to evaluate the research that relates to it.

Rosenfeld's basic assumption is that conversation is an information exchange process. The assumption raises a number of issues that Rosenfeld attempts to clarify. He recognizes at the start that the analysis of conversational control functions demands that a conversational sequence be segmented into units. The segmentation is initially obvious; each participant in a conversation takes turns speaking and the turns of the two participants alternate. Thus, the first segmen-tation of the conversation is into complementary speaker-listener roles. The second level of segmentation occurs within the role periods and consists of "informational units." Further segmentation becomes more complex. The infor-mational units are separable into two classes: those that anticipate a shift of the speaker-listener roles, and those that indicate a continuation of the roles as they are. The listener signals that accompany the speaker's informational units are also differentially classifiable.

If role alternation is the behavior that grossly structures the exchange of information, there must be regulatory signals—conversational control mecha-nisms—that render the alternation relatively smooth and predictable. How do we identify the signals? But first, how do we decide whether a role shift has occurred, that is, whether a remark made by the person who was presumably listening represents his acquisition of the speaker role or a "listener response"?

And how do we define "information"? Rosenfeld is aware that these are urgent questions in need of careful answers. He thoughtfully reviews the range of criteria that might be helpful in formulating the answers. He also examines at length the potential answers offered by research concerned with the various dimensions of nonverbal and vocal behavior and concludes that progress has been made in identifying some of the nonverbal control mechanisms and in determining where they occur in the conversational stream. Rosenfeld anticipates, however, that further progress will depend upon the correction of certain methodological problems that limit much of the existing research.

Time is of central importance for Feldstein and Welkowitz (Chapter 11). Indeed, it is the temporal organization of conversation with which they are concerned. Within the context of their analysis, the speaking turn is primarily a temporal unit. It is also the unit that most adequately characterizes conversational interaction in that it implies the participation of more than one person. Their definition of the turn is empirical and objective and wholly dependent upon the sound-silence sequence of a conversation. Thus, it is in keeping with their contention that the temporal parameters of a conversation ought not to be defined in terms of any other verbal or nonverbal channel of communication. The chapter briefly reviews the research that initiated the area of conversation chronography and presents the classification of conversational time patterns preferred by the authors. However, a major portion of the chapter describes the frequency and durational characteristics of speaking turns and simultaneous speech (that is, when both participants in a conversation talk at the same time). It also discusses the differences between the authors' definition of turns and simultaneous speech and those of other investigators. Another major part of the chapter begins with a discussion of what Feldstein and Welkowitz call conversational "congruence," or ". . . the occurrence, within the span of one or more conversations, of similar intensity, frequency, or durational values for the participants on one or more of the parameters that characterize temporal patterning" (p. 358). The authors then review in detail the studies that relate the occurrence of congruence to such psychological constructs and issues as interpersonal perception, psychological differentiation, social contact, social desirability, interpersonal warmth, and level of socialization.

A point made by the chapter, one important enough to be implied by its title, is that prior to investigating the interaction of several channels, or dimensions, or nonverbal communication, each dimension ought be delineated and examined separately as objectively and thoroughly as possible.

Closing Comments

The contributors bring different theoretical and methodological perspectives to their respective chapters. On the other hand, they also hold certain important views in common. They regard nonverbal behavior as an integral part of the total communication act. They are aware of the close relationship between verbal and nonverbal communication and, as a consequence, there is a greater recognition among the contributors to this volume of the cognitive factors in nonverbal communication than is usually the case. Many contributors resort to general psychological models and principles, such as general learning principles, attribution theory, etc., in order to obtain a handle on the phenomena they deal with. More importantly, perhaps, they are all psychologists who are committed to the proposition that empirical verification is the ultimate test of any hypothesis or theory about nonverbal behavior.

Many contributors bemoan the lack of reliability of many of the indices used in nonverbal communication research and the lack of comparability between indices even when they are reliable. Clearly, much remains to be done in developing reliable and valid measuring instruments.

Several authors—Dittmann in relation to body movement, Exline in relation to visual interaction, and Siegman in relation to vocal cues—argue that nonverbal behavior is inherently ambiguous in the sense that any one cue could communicate a variety of specific messages, depending on the context, etc. It is generally agreed that this ambiguity can be reduced by looking at a multiplicity of cues, which we may very well do when we decipher nonverbal cues in everyday communication. Our research paradigms, however, have yet to take this into consideration. In this context, it should be pointed out that in real life both the encoding and decoding of nonverbal communication are dynamic processes with continuous feedback and readjustments between the communicants. Few, if any, of our experimental paradigms have taken this cybernetic dimension of nonverbal communication into consideration.

REFERENCES

Audrey, R. *The territorial imperative.* New York: Atheneum, 1966.

Cherry, C. *On human communication: A review, a survey, and a criticism.* New York: Science Editions, 1961.

Duncan, S., Jr. Some signals and rules for taking speaking turns in conversations. *Journal of Personality and Social Psychology,* 1972, **73**, 283–292.

Exline, R. V. The glances of power and preference. In J. K. Cole (Ed.), *The Nebraska Symposium of Motivation,* 1971, Vol. 19, Lincoln, Nebraska: Nebraska University Press, 1972. Pp. 163–206.

La France, M. Nonverbal cues to conversational turn-taking between black speakers. Paper read at the annual meeting of the American Psychological Association, New Orleans, August, 1974.

Rosenfeld, H. M. Instrumental affiliative functions of facial and gestural expressions. *Journal of Personality and Social Psychology,* 1966, **4**, 65–71. (a)

Rosenfeld, H. M. Approval-seeking and approval-inducing functions of verbal and nonverbal responses in the dyad. *Journal of Personality and Social Psychology,* 1966, **4**, 597–605. (b)

Wiener, M., Devoe, S., Rubinow, S., & Geller, Y. Nonverbal behavior and nonverbal communication. *Psychological Review,* 1972, **79**, 185–214.

Part I

BIOLOGICAL CONSIDERATIONS

1

An Introduction
to Animal Communication

Slobodan B. Petrovich

University of Maryland Baltimore County

Eckhard H. Hess

The University of Chicago

INTRODUCTION

Animal Communication: Interdisciplinary View

Ethology has been described as the biology of behavior (Eibl-Eibesfeldt, 1970; Tinbergen, 1963). The expansion of ethology in the last decade and its embrace by neighboring disciplines provides a strong testimony to the significance of the biological approach to the study of behavior. While ethology has a relatively long and interesting history (Burghardt, 1973; Hess, 1973; Jaynes, 1969; Klopfer & Hailman, 1967; Lockard, 1971), for its more recent rise and impetus, it owes much to the provocative, insightful, creative ideas of Konrad Lorenz (1965, 1969, 1970, 1971) and ingenious contributions of K. von Frisch (1967) and N. Tinbergen (1951, 1953, 1959, 1960). Today, the study of behavior is considered to be a new frontier in the biological sciences.

The biological approach is having a major impact on psychology. Hebb (1974) in a thoughtful paper entitled "What psychology is about" comes to the conclusion that "psychology is a biological science." Many behavioral scientists, perhaps belatedly, share in Lockard's (1971) observations, which convincingly articulate that comparative psychology has been overrun by a "biological revolution." An overview of "new" theoretical interpretations of human development (Ainsworth, 1969; Bowlby, 1969, 1973; Freedman, 1974; Nash, 1970; Piaget,

1968; Piaget & Inhelder, 1969; White, 1974) indicates the impetus and vigor of a scientific movement deeply rooted in biological principles.

The arbitrary, territorial borders between many disciplines are deteriorating. Moreover, in many specific areas of inquiry, the evolutionary link between man and animal is too well-established to allow the perpetuation of unwarranted and untenable aspects of a human–infrahuman dichotomy. In anthropology and sociology, ethological findings and attitudes are receiving recognition (Eisenberg & Dillon, 1971), and their impact can be observed in the writings of Callan (1970), Chapple (1970), Count (1973), Fox (1967), Jolly, 1972), Tiger (1969), and Tiger and Fox (1966, 1971).

In her presidential address at the Annual Meeting of the American Anthropological Association, Margaret Mead (1961) stated:

> There is one adjacent science, which has developed enormously during the last three decades and now can provide us with highly variegated and well established information about the behavior of living creatures that could be of the greatest fruitfulness for our own studies. This is the discipline called ethology . . . (p. 479].

From a similar perspective, Sebeok, a student of language and the diversity of other means of communication, in describing the interdisciplinary approach characteristic of the comparative study of animal communication–zoosemiotics, observed the following:

> A rapidly developing behavioral science has lately crystallized at the intersection of semiotics, the general theory of signs, and ethology, the biological study of behavior. Its subject matter is the ways whereby living things, chiefly animals, communicate with each other, a full understanding of which requires the cooperative attack of an exceptionally wide variety of disciplines, ranging from genetics through anatomy to sensory physiology and neurophysiology and from comparative psychology and zoology to anthropology, especially physical, social and linguistic [p. 122].

Thus, a survey of the literature on animal communication crystallizes a theme that permeates some of the recently published works (Hinde, 1972; Sebeok, 1968, 1972), and is lucidly articulated in the words of H-L. Teuber (1967): "It has become clear . . . that linguists are ethologists, working with man as their species for study, and ethologists, linguists, working with non-verbalizing species [p. 205]"

Scope

The pertinent literature on the various aspects of animal communication is so voluminous that even a limited presentation is beyond the scope of any single text. A cursory analysis leads to a deep appreciation, respect and recognition of the dimensions and complexities of the problem. Peters and Ploog (1973), while circumscribing their review to infrahuman primates and 169 references, surveyed some 400 papers covering the literature from September 1967 to May 1972. To write about insect communication would be a gargantuan task when one considers that in all probability there are hundreds of species possessing an elaborate communication system. Frings and Frings (1960) listed 1752 references on communication pertaining only to the acoustic channel in insects; there have been many publications in the interim.

This chapter makes no pretense of being a comprehensive treatise. On the contrary, it is meant only to serve as an appetizer comprised of some aspects of animal communication and provocative enough to arouse the reader's appetite for a more substantial meal.[1]

TAXONOMIC CONSIDERATIONS

Definitions of Animal Communication

As suggested by Marler (1967, 1968) the pursuit of an exclusive definition of animal communication might not be profitable. We might agree, however, that the essence of communication seems to lie in the evolution of synergistic interplay between participants, committed to maximizing the efficiency of interchange. Such relationships can be interspecific (across species boundaries), but more characteristically they are intraspecific.

The uninitiated reader may be tempted to question the inclusive scope of our remarks; from the ethological point of view, attempts to construct a taxonomic

[1] Given the limitations of this chapter, the reader is referred to the following sources, covering mostly the literature through 1973, for more extensive treatment of various aspects of animal communication: Alexander (1967); Altmann (1967); Andrew (1963a, 1963b); Ardrey (1966, 1970); Armstrong (1963); Barker (1968); Beer (1970); Birdwhistell (1970); Burkhardt, Schleidt, and Altner (1967); Burton (1970); Busnel (1963); Chauvin (1968, 1970); Count (1973); Crook (1970); Dart (1959); Darwin (1872); Davitz (1964); DeVore (1965); Dröschler (1969); DuBrul (1958); Duncan (1969); Ebling and Highnam (1970); Eibl-Eibesfeldt (1970); Eisenberg and Kleiman (1972); Esser (1971); Etkin (1964); Evans (1968); Ewer (1968); Frank (1957); Frings and Frings (1960, 1964); Frisch (1967); Gardner and Gardner (1969); Gibson (1962); Gilbert (1966); Goffman (1963, 1967); Gottlieb (1971); Graham (1965); Greenwalt (1968); Griffin (1958); Hafez (1969); Hall (1966); Haskell (1961); Hediger (1969); Hess (1973); Hinde (1969, 1970, 1972); Hockett (1960); Hockett and Altmann (1968); Huxley and Kroch (1964); Jacobson (1972); Jarrard (1971); Johnston, Moulton, and Turk (1970); Jolly (1972); Klopfer (1969); Knapp (1972); Krames, Pliner and Alloway (1974); Kummer (1971); Lancaster (1968); Lanyon and Tavolga (1960); Lenneberg (1964, 1967, 1969, 1971); Lilly (1967); Lindauer (1967); Lorenz (1969, 1970, 1971); Lorenz and Leyhausen (1973); Manning (1972); Marler (1961, 1967, 1969); Marler and Hamilton (1966); Masters (1970); Matthews and Knight (1963); McNeill (1970); Mehrabian (1969, 1972); Moltz (1971); Moncrieff (1967); Montagu (1971); Morris (1967, 1971); Nelson (1973); Norris (1966); Nottebohm (1970, 1972); Peters and Ploog (1973); Pfaffmann (1969); Premack (1970); Ralls (1971); Reynolds (1968); Sarles (1969); Sebeok (1965, 1968, 1972); Sebeok and Ramsay (1969); Shorey, (1973); Simpson (1973); Smith and Miller (1966); Smith (1969); Sommer (1969); Sparks (1967); Tavolga (1964, 1967, 1970); Tembrock (1968); Thorpe (1961); Tinbergen (1960); Watson (1970); Wickler (1968); Wilson (1965, 1971, 1975); Wood-Gush (1971); Wynne-Edwards (1962).

chart of animal communication face theoretical, methodological, and empirical difficulties, which often appear insurmountable. Consider the following questions: Is reintroduction of a human–infrahuman dichotomy justified in the contextual analysis of another heuristic labeled as verbal and nonverbal communication? How satisfactory is it to invoke a biological–synthetic theory of evolution as an explanatory model for aspects of infrahuman communication, while at the other end of a hypothetical continuum from innate to acquired, we stand behind cultural evolution as an explanatory device of "ethnic gestures"? If we are willing to consider the possibility (and we are) that "communication" is a behavioral property of all matter, living and inert, then what is not communication? Of course, we can somewhat limit the scope of our inquiry to living systems only and decide that communication is one of the manifestations of life! If one ponders the ramifications of such statements one begins to appreciate the taxonomic difficulties, for a more attractive definition is too inclusive to be useful: ". . . we may define communication as a type of behavior between living creatures of the same or different species, characterized by mutuality, rooted in biological heredity, and constituting one of the general manifestations of life (Révész, 1944, p. 117). Perhaps, in order to be somewhat exclusive, we can agree that communication is more than exteroreception or enteroreception on the one side and the response itself on the other side; it is the dynamic relationship generally characterized by intent and set up by the transmission of specific stimuli and the resultant evocation of specific responses. Faced with a similar problem, Frings and Frings (1964) stated that "communication between animals involves the giving off by one individual of some chemical or physical signal, that, on being received by another, influences its behavior [p. 3]." They made their definition even more restrictive by requiring that the sender, (i.e., the source of the message) use some specialized structure or behavior to produce the signal for the receiver, a member of the same species. This definition is too exclusive (Burghardt, 1970; Tavolga, 1970). On the other hand, discussion of communication in terms of a "social unit" is also unduly restrictive. Cherry (1957) defines communication as "the establishment of a social unit from individuals by the use of language or signs [p. 303]" and Scheflen (1964) proposes that "communication includes all behaviors by which a group forms, sustains, mediates, corrects and integrates its relationships [p. 318]."

Burghardt (1970) is aware of the limitations of the various definitions of animal communication. He concedes that, to the behavioral scientist who appreciates the complexities of social interactions existing in nature, defining a "group" is not an easy matter. His tentative "probabilistic" thesis suggests that "Communication is the phenomenon of one organism producing a signal that, when responded to by another organism, confers some advantage (or the statistical probability of it) to the signaler or his group" (Burghardt, 1970, p. 16).

Levels of Interaction and Animal Communication

Organisms differ greatly in their morphological, physiological, and behavioral characteristics and offer, thereby, covert and overt evidence of their ontogenic and evolutionary history. Organisms must also be viewed in the context of their ecosystems, which are based on organic alliances that presuppose communications of various kinds with many degrees of complexity. After stating some of these often neglected truisms, how do we relate them to animal communication? Tavolga (1968, 1970), influenced by Schneirla's (1953) conceptualizations dealing with hierarchical levels of behavioral integration, introduced a tentative schema, ". . . an approach to the study of communication that is based on the concept of qualitatively different phyletic levels, expressed as levels of behavioral organization . . ." (Tavolga, 1970, p. 282).

Vegetative level. On the vegetative level, one organism influences another merely by its growth, tropism, physical presence. The relationship is characteristic of plants, some protozoans, and sponges.

Tonic level. The tonic level of interaction includes metabolic processes, physiological byproducts, chemical exudates, basic locomotor patterns, taxis and kinesis, symbiotic relationships, mutualism, commensalism and parasitism, mimicry, primitive types of trophollactic and trail-following behavior. This level of interaction is mainly observed in protozoa and primitive metazoa.

Phasic level. Interactions on the phasic level invalue broad, multichannel energy outputs with some specialization of emitter and receiver capable of responding in a discriminatory fashion. Included would be behaviors ranging from sex recognition in lower vertebrates, schooling in fishes, hive dances of returning forager bees (which stimulated by food, emit stimuli affecting visual, olfactory, gustatory, acoustic, and tactual channels), to feeding responses of predatory insects, fishes, and anuran amphibians. Phasic interactions are observed in many invertebrates above a coelenterate level and in some primitive vertebrates.

Signal level. On the signal level of development, organisms possess specialized structures producing specific narrow channel signals. There are two components to a signal level:

1. A biosocial signal involves *communication* within social situations in which organic processes control the development of behavior. This component describes complex encounters of social insects (particularly those of the Order Hymenoptera), much of reproductive—parental behavior of some lower vertebrates, fishes, amphibians, and reptiles, and particularly the development of pairing and other reproduction-related behavior of birds.

2. A psychosocial signal involves complex patterns of signals, with an increasing role of experiential and social factors. Examples include lower mammals (with the possible exception of higher primates), bird songs, with songs of passerine birds representing a special form of signal development on a psychosocial level.

Symbolic level. The symbolic level is exemplified by vocalizations, responses, gestures, and facial expressions contributing to a complex and diversified form of psychosocial communication strongly dependent upon social interactions for its development. In addition, there is a primitive utilization of symbolism (pointing behavior and other gestures of a chimpanzee). Symbolic levels of interaction have been described in infrahuman primates, especially anthropoids (Altmann, 1967; Darwin, 1872; DeVore, 1965; Jay, 1968; Jolly, 1972). It should be noted that perhaps today Tavolga might reconsider some aspects of his classification in light of the current evidence emphasizing the cognitive processes of nonhuman primates (Jarrard, 1971; Rumbaugh, Gill, & Glasersfeld, 1973).

Language level. Communication on the language level is characterized by abstract ideas, speech, metalanguage, and metasymbolism. It is restricted to man.

According to Tavolga, the last three levels of behavioral organization—signal, symbolic, and language—comprise communication. His definition of communication, however, appears to be a more restricted version of Frings and Frings' previously presented description:

> For communication to take place, the emitter must possess a specialized stimulus-producing mechanism (chemical, morphological, or behavioral). The stimulus must occupy a narrow portion of the available spectrum of the channel (frequency, range, duration, patterning, chemical specificity). The receiver must possess specialized receptors and respond in a specific manner [Tavolga, 1968, pp. 275–276].

Heuristically, the schema of levels of communication is not without shortcomings. The so-called qualitative levels are not easy to discriminate and, as Tavolga has pointed out, the emitter and the receiver need not necessarily operate on the same level and communication could include any one or more levels in the hierarchy. However, there is much in Tavolga's conceptualizations that comparative psychologists and ethologists find useful. For example, by taking into account the evolutionary and ontogenetic history of the species, our conceptualizations about various kinds and degrees of communication may be less susceptible to sweeping comparisons and generalizations that have little regard for the differences in phyletic and contextual levels or ecological niches among the organisms compared. Thus, according to Tavolga, human language and "animal language" are only remotely comparable since such assessments involve comparisons between qualitatively different levels of biobehavioral organization.

At the same time, it is important to note that classificatory models, derived from some of the existing observational data and capable not only of assimilating new observations but also of accommodating themselves to new evidence, provide a framework for the insigntful and enlightening cross-phyletic comparisons (Andrew, 1963a, b, 1972; Eibl-Eibesfeldt, 1970, 1972; Marler, 1961, 1967, 1969; Thorpe, 1967, 1972a; Wilson, 1965; Wilson & Bossert, 1963) that allow for the study of communication homologues (behavioral similarities in organisms having a common ancertral origin) as well as communication analogues (behavioral similarities based upon considerations of commonality of function rather than structure). It should be emphasized that investigators sensitive to these issues have provided us with provocative and penetrating analyses of various aspects of animal communication (e.g., Altmann, 1967; Hinde, 1972; Lorenz & Leyhausen, 1973; Sebeok, 1968).

The Evolution of Language: On the Continuity between Human Language and Infrahuman Communication

Charles Darwin (1871) wrote, "My object in this chapter is to shew that there is no fundamental difference between man and the higher animals in their mental faculties [p. 446]." The weight of that statement generated philosophical and biological revolution, and launched comparative psychology and ethology. But that statement and Darwin's other speculations on the origin of language also planted the seeds of today's dilemma: Should we study human language within the framework of animal communication, or does human language have properties that warrant the reintroduction of the man–brute dichotomy?

Until the last decade, most linguists have not been compelled to concern themselves with the origin of language since there was no persuasive evidence supporting the principle of phylogenetic relatedness with regard to the evolution of language. Anthropological linguists had been concerned with problems involving the relation of language to ideas, values, mores, perceptions, and beliefs rather than to the study of language universals. American psychology had been trying to make language behavior conform to the prevailing *Zeitgeist*—"behaviorism" (Gewirtz, 1969; Skinner, 1957; Staats, 1968)—with an emphasis on functional analyses of language learning rather than on language ontongeny. During the past decade, the propositions of Noam Chomsky (1968) and Jean Piaget (1955) have stimulated vigorous reassessments of these concerns. Although Chomsky and Piaget often disagree, they share a biological, structuralistic, rationalistic conception of language.

The publications of Lenneberg (1964, 1967, 1969, 1971), however, present a formidable challenge to the ethologist interested in demonstrating the applicability of Darwin's statement to the ontogeny and evolution of language. Lenneberg (1967) attempts to provide the biological foundation for Chomsky's innate linguistic structures. After reviewing a vast array of evidence pertaining to the morphological, psychological, neurological, and genetic aspects of language, language development, and language pathology, he concludes that the capacity for development of language is species specific; it is, in other words, a uniquely human capacity. Lenneberg proposes a discontinuity theory and argues that it is biologically more acceptable and more in line with present theoretical positions in developmental and evolutionary biology. (We shall reconsider the issue of acceptability in our concluding remarks.)

The alternative can be illustrated by the writings of Hockett and Altmann (1968), who have introduced design features applicable to the comparative study of human and animal communication (Table 3 in this chapter). Particularly provocative and penetrating are the analyses of Hockett and Ascher (1964), Marler (1961, 1967, 1969, 1970), and Thorpe (1972a), which argue effectively that features of human language are also found in the animal kingdom, and that the major distinction is that so many features are found in one organism—man.

Gardner and Gardner (1969, 1971), Premack (1970, 1971), Rumbaugh *et al.* (1973), have been trying to resolve the continuity question empirically. Chimpanzees are the subjects entrusted with demonstrating such continuity and, because they have not shown themselves partial to vocalization as a mode of communication, they have been provided with other methods. The Gardners have been exploring the usefulness of American sign language; Premack has tried a code that associates auditory dimensions with motor dimensions, and Rumbaugh *et al.* (1973), have been investigating the use of computer-controlled training. The Gardners (1971) reported that the chimpanzee Washoe had acquired a substantial vocabulary of hand-produced words, chained them, and at times applied them appropriately to novel situations. Premack (1971) demonstrated that the chimpanzee Sarah can use plastic objects as words and can attend to their serial arrangement in ways suggesting some mastery of rudimentary syntax. Rumbaugh *et al.* (1973) report that their chimpanzee, after six months of computer-controlled language training, reads proficiently and can finish incomplete sentences.

At best, these findings argue for a great deal of agnosticism on the issue. Premack (1970) concedes that not only human phonology, but quite possible human syntax may be unique to man. Lenneberg (1969) further argues that at least five different conditions must be met in order to show empirically that Washoe is acquiring even a primitive language. One must: (a) compare the capacity of the communicational system employed in the experiment to that used by man; (b) test its efficiency as a communication system between man and chimpanzee; (c) evaluate Washoe's knowledge, understanding or awareness of the language and its ability to deal with the meaning of sentences in that language; (d) demonstrate simple language operations; and (e) meet the test requirements of semantic productivity and understanding. Moreover, Premack (1971) suggested that regardless how the results pertaining to the empirical analysis of the language continuity hypothesis are interpreted, it should be remembered that man is required to teach the chimpanzee behavioral constituents of language rather than chimpanzee teaching man or other chimpanzees. Viewed in such context, a claim to man's uniqueness, if that in itself is one of our concerns, cannot easily be challenged.

Classificatory Systems of Verbal and Nonverbal Communication[2]

While there are a number of useful classificatory systems that describe animal communication (Sebeok & Ramsey, 1969), we will limit ourselves to two models, one proposed by Sebeok (1965, 1972) and the other by Lyons (1972) based on earlier formulations of Crystal (1969).

Sebeok, a linguist-ethologist (our labeling) concerned with semiotics (defined as the general theory of signs), finds it useful and convenient to distinguish between human and infrahuman systems. There are two kinds of human semiotic systems: *anthroposemiotic,* that is, species-specific systems unique to man, and *zoosemiotic* subsystem components of human communication that are found in other infrahuman species. Ahthroposemiotics are partitioned into three categores: (a) language, (b) macrostructures pertaining to language (e.g., verbal arts, sonnet composition), and (c) those semiotic structures independent to a large degree of any natural language (e.g., music, visual arts). Zoosemiotic processes found in humans include paralinguistics, kinesics, proximics, as well as the common characteristics of animal communication proper: (a) source, (b) channel, (c) destination, (d) code, (e) message, and (f) context. Sebeok's model attempts to synthesize animal communication into the framework of semiotics, and in many respects it has been successful in providing an umbrella for analytical contributions that have been generated by such diverse areas of inquiry as anthropology, linguistics, sociology, psychology, and ethology. Some aspects of Sebeok's conceptualizations need to be continuously reevaluated. The distinction between anthroposemiotic and zoosemiotic systems, even though heuristically useful, evokes reservations stemming, in part, from our appreciation of the unproductive history of other models based on the human–animal dichotomy. At present, it is difficult to decide at what point to draw a line between human systems and those employed by the "speechless creatures." Upon observing "kinds and degrees" of animal communication, one is struck by the dimensions and wealth of "verboseness." It is left up to the individual taxonomist (linguist, psychologist, ethologist) to determine the point at which, on a hypothetical continuum of "verboseness," a distinction can be made between verbal and nonverbal communication. Lyons (1972, p. 53) concedes that there is room for much disagreement about how to partition the territories between language and nonlanguage. When it comes to human social interaction, according to Lyons, there are degrees of "linguisticness," with the verbal component at the top of the taxonomic scale of communication.

---

[2] The reader is referred to Dittmann's chapter in this book (p. 69) dealing with related taxonomic concerns.

TABLE 1
A Tentative Classification of Verbal and Nonverbal Communication

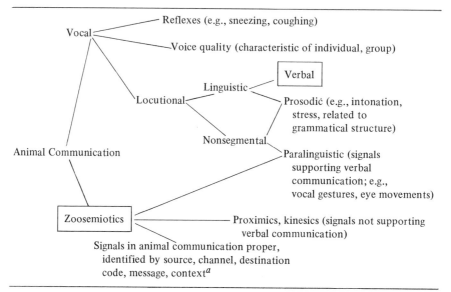

[a]Chemical (e.g., pheromones, olfactory cues), visual (e.g., expressions, gestures, displays), acoustic (e.g., cricket song), tactile (e.g., touching), thermal (e.g., infrared radiation).

Based on Lyons' (1972) model as outlined in Hinde (1972, p. 91), we are proposing a tentative classificatory scheme to illustrate the relations between verbal and nonverbal communication. Consistent with the proposed scheme (Table 1), the chapters in this text deal with various aspects of nonverbal communication and paralinguistics. Our pages in this chapter cover some comparative aspects of infrahuman communication, mainly chemical and acoustic.

COMPARATIVE APPROACH TO SOME MECHANISMS
OF ANIMAL COMMUNICATION

Sensory Channels Used by Animals

In a description of topology of sign systems in animal communication. Sebeok (1967) and Scott (1968) suggested a way of classifying types of communication by utilizing the sense modalities involved: chemical, visual, acoustic and tactile. This method of classification is quite arbitrary and artificial. An animal responds to a combination of stimuli across available modalities, in some cases across all four. The message received is rarely identical with the message that was forwarded; contextual aspects of a sender's message often differ from those at the receiving end, and the ambiguities facing the recipient are often unequivocal for the sender. Other senses such as thermal or infrared are not included. Nevertheless, the convenience of this form of taxonomy, as well as the recognition that many animals utilize one modality of communication more than others, justifies comparative application of this classificatory scheme.

Our review of the literature limits itself to an evaluation of aspects of chemical and acoustic systems in the context of their contribution to animal communication. Several considerations guided the choice of topical coverage. The inclusion of literature on all four of the modalities (chemical, acoustic, visual, and tactile) was not only beyond the scope of this chapter, but could only have been done at the cost of having the content overlap to some degree with other chapters. Moreover, chemical and acoustic modalities offer a useful tool for the evaluation of communicational analogies and homologies. Chemical communication has received little recognition to date, partly because of an excessive parochialism and preoccupation with other modes of communication thought to be more pertinent to advanced species (man in particular). In addition the various aspects of vocal–auditory channel analysis allow for some comparisons of human and infrahuman communicational systems.

Nevertheless, a few comments about visual and tactile modes of communication are in order. Sensitivity to light, colors, and patterns varies greatly throughout the animal world. In general, some insects, crustaceans, and most vertebrates have well-developed visual systems that allow for the discrimination of dark–light, color, contour, shape, and movement. There are many publications concerned with the importance of the visual system (Andrew, 1972; Crook, 1964; Eibl-Eibesfeldt, 1972; Evans, 1968; Frings & Frings, 1964; Hooff, 1967; Marler, 1965, 1968; Peters & Ploog, 1973; Wasserman, 1973, Wickler, 1967, 1968), and almost half of the chapters in this volume deal directly or indirectly with various dimensions of the visual channel and its role in nonverbal behavior.

Communication in a tactile channel is restricted to a short distance with rapid fluctuations in intensity of signals that can be readily turned on and off. The emission of tactile signals by the sender is brought about by behavior patterns that often involve specialized structures (grasping by claws, claspers, fingers). The signals are received by tactile receptors.

Tactile communication is found in insects, coelenterates, fishes, amphibians, reptiles, and all mammals, and appears to play a major role in the development of all primates (Alloway, Krames, & Pliner, 1972; Evans, 1968; Frank, 1957; Frings & Frings, 1964; Gibson, 1962; Howard, 1970; Montagu, 1971; Morris, 1971; Peters & Ploog, 1973; Sparks, 1967).

Chemical Systems in Communication

Chemical communication is ubiquitous in the animal world. It is surprising, therefore, to find that only relatively recently has it become the subject of a large and rapidly growing literature (Beroza, 1970; Bossert & Wilson, 1963; Butler, 1967; Eisenberg & Kleiman, 1972; Gleason & Reynierse, 1969; Johnston,

Moulton, & Turk, 1970; Moncrieff, 1967; Ralls, 1971; Shorey, 1973; Wilson, 1965, 1968; Wilson & Bossert, 1963). Chemical communication can be intracellular, cellular, organismic, intraspecific, or interspecific, and among various kinds of chemical "messengers" we find neurotransmitters, neurohormones, hormones, and pheromones. Chemicals were probably the first messengers in the evolution of animal communication. A similarity in chemical composition and function between pheromones and hormones (Whitten, 1966) indicates that pheromones might have been functional precursors to other kinds of chemical messengers. Haldane (1955) proposed that chemical communication among protozoan cells must have existed before the formation of metazoans. Cells in the metazoan body communicate with each other by neurotransmitters, hormones . . . thus offering mute, built-in evidence of their evolution. It is not surprising to find that even in mammals there is often a close interaction between neuroendocrine systems and intraspecific communication that is mediated by chemicals through organs of smell and taste (Whitten and Bruce Effects). For example, if a female mouse is mated to a male, she will normally become pregnant. However, if a mated female is removed from her partner and exposed to a strange male, in many cases under the influence of a "pheromone," pregnancy will be blocked and she will return to estrus within 3—4 days (the Bruce Effect). To illustrate the complexity of the interaction, it should be added that a pregnancy block is strongly influenced by the quality of olfactory stimulation, strain differences between two males, and by the presence or absence of the initial mating partner when the second one is introduced (Bruce, 1965). It seems that odors of strange males inhibit the release of pituitary prolactin which is necessary for the ovary to secrete the progesterone that maintains the pregnancy. Peters and Ploog (1973), in summarizing some of the primate literature, conclude that olfactory cues may function in territorial demarcation, sex, state of sexual receptivity, individual identity, and dominance status.

Karlson and Butenandt (1959) coined the term "pheromone" to describe substances that are secreted by one organism and modify the behavior or development of a conspecific. Limiting the definition of a pheromone to intraspectific exchange only, while useful, probably has its exceptions (Watkins, Gehlbach, & Balbridge, 1967; Wilson, 1965). The pheromones are grouped into primer and releaser substances existing in liquid or gaseous state. The releaser pheromones have a relatively immediate but reversible effect on the behavior of the recipient via receptor—conductor—effector pathways, while the effect of primer pheromones is to trigger a chain of physiological events (e.g., hormonal) in the recipient (Wilson, 1965, 1968). In insects, for example, sex pheromones would be those chemical substances that either "release" or "prime" sexual behavior, and it is now evident that these sex pheromones play a central role in the mating behavior of most insects studied. In Lepidoptera alone, 140 species have been listed in which the female releases a sex pheromone. In 55 of these species, the males also have been found to possess sex pheromones (Beroza, 1970). These sex pheromones can serve multiple functions. The female producing a releaser pheromone can attract and perhaps sexually excite the male, as in many moths (Beroza, 1970; Wilson & Bossert, 1963) and in some butterflies (Beroza, 1970; Brower, Brower, & Cranston, 1965). Usually such pheromones fade slowly and permit communication over large distances, and their emission and transmission is affected by certain environmental conditions such as weather, photoperiod, or diet (Brower *et al.*, 1965; Reddiford & Williams, 1971; Wilson & Bossert, 1963). The male sex pheromone, utilized at short distances, acts as an aphrodisiac and induces the female to become both acquiescent and sexually responsive (Beroza, 1970; Reddiford & Williams, 1971).

Responses to odoriferous stimulation have been studied in a threefold manner: behavioral evaluation, neural analysis, and the comparative measures between neural and behavioral responses (Stürckow, 1970). Even though an understanding of the precise mechanisms of the pheromone action is unclear, it is known that male moths, for example, can detect minute quantities. Through the use of electroantenograms (EAG), the responses of a single sensor to pheromones have been recorded. Schneider (1969) and Schneider and Seibt (1969) have calculated that relatively few molecules are needed to elicit a response and that only one molecule of pheromone per sensor was needed to trigger the sensor reaction. The work of Reddiford (1970) revealed that in three species of saturnid moths, a specific antennal protein is responsible for binding of the pheromone molecule and that this protein, if destroyed, is rapidly replaced. The possibility that pheromones will prove to be species-specific biological control agents (a welcome substitute to insecticides) has spurred much research on isolation and artificial synthesis of these "chemical messengers" (Beroza, 1970). Carlson, Mayer, Silhacek, James, Beroza, and Bierl (1971) have isolated from the cuticle and feces of the female house fly a sex pheromone that attracts a male fly, identified it as (Z)-9-tricosene and proved that chemical and biological comparison of the natural and synthesized compound show them to be identical. In a similar fashion, male sex attractants have been isolated from primate females (Michael, Keverne, & Bosnell, 1971).

Since the number of pheromones with known chemical identity is small and the classification based on chemical properties of pheromones is nonexistent, a wide spectrum of functional classifications is in use: sex attractants; simple assembly; territory and home range; nonterritorial dispersal; recognition of an individual, rank, or group identity; recruitment, alarm, and trail pheromones (Gleason & Reynierse, 1969; Wilson, 1968). The presentation of some of the literature dealing with sex, territorial, and recognition pheromones will suffice to indicate that chemical signals play an important, if not the key role, in the life cycles of all organisms.

Sex Pheromones

As the name suggests, sex pheromones may produce sex recognition, simple attraction, sexual behavior, or variations of attraction and behavior. While best known in insects (Jacobson, 1972), sex pheromones have been recorded and studied in fish (Tavolga, 1956, 1968), amphibians (Marler, 1959; Noble & Bradley, 1933) as well as mammals (Eisenberg & Kleiman, 1972; Sharman, Calaby, & Poole, 1966; Whitten & Bronson, 1970). In many species of butterflies, moths, true bugs, roaches, beetles, and flies, the aphrodisiac quality of the male pheromone renders the female susceptible to sexual advances, while the female pheromones help attract the male. In mammals, pheromones are important in sex attraction and sex recognition, where chemical cues produced from various sources such as apocrine glands, sebaceous skin glands, urine, and the estrous female, serve as communicational mediators (Gleason & Reynierse, 1969; Peters & Ploog, 1973; Tembrock, 1968; Whitten & Bronson, 1970).

Olfactory communication may be less important for primates than for many other mammals. In general, primates appear to rely more on the visual and vocal signals. Nevertheless, both prosimians and New World monkeys have permanent scent glands and various forms of olfactory communication exist among primate species (Jolly, 1972; Peters & Ploog, 1973). The male rhesus recognizes estrus in the female mainly by the vaginal scent (Michael & Keverne, 1968) and male sex attractant pheromones have been isolated (Michael et al., 1971).

It is debatable whether we, like the prosimians, possess specialized scent structures, but it is interesting to note that our axillary hair may have had the function of scent dispersal, as well as physical lubrication. In our culture, females are expected to shave their underarms, and not only sexual odor but any body odors fall into a category of unpleasant stimuli. While human sexual odors are taboo, paradoxically, various preparations of sexual organs of plants and animals (rose, civet, musk) seem to provide socially acceptable substitutes and are liberally applied at frequent intervals much to the gratification of a profitable industry (Knapp, 1972, p. 76).

Territorial Pheromones

A variety of manifestations of territoriality in different animals have presented many difficulties for attempts to provide a single, clear, embracing and valid definition. In general, the consensus seems to be that territory is an area occupied relatively exclusively by an animal or a group by means of repulsion through defense of an overt nature—territorial aggression—or through communication with territorial markings, which may be acoustic (e.g., bird song), visual (e.g., various displays), as well as chemical (e.g., territorial pheromones). While the existence of territoriality has been observed for over a half a century, it is relatively recently that it has received long overdue identification and recognition (Ardrey, 1966; Barker, 1968; Esser, 1971; Hall, 1966; Klopfer, 1969; Sommer, 1969; Watson, 1970). From an interdisciplinary point of view, the volume edited by Esser is a particularly useful compilation of observations on the use of space of all animals—men included.

The marking of territories with a chemical scent, in contrast to visual and acoustic displays, has the advantage of communicating the ownership even when the resident is absent. Territorial, chemical messengers are placed on prominent and salient features of the environment reflecting the *Umvelt* of the species. The odors are passed in excrement or urine, or they are produced by glands which, depending on taxon, have varied anatomical locations: pedal, carpal, tarsal, metatarsal, preorbital, occipital, anal, preputial. For example, deer and antelope utilize a gland above the eye, antorbital, to chemically ward off conspecific intruders (Hediger, 1955), while a Europian rabbit utilizes "chinning," which leaves scents from the submandibular glands (Mykytowycz, 1965). Adults of the flour beetle, *Tribolium confusum,* do not appear to mark their territory, but they aggregate at low population densities, distribute themselves in a random fashion at intermediate density, and distribute themselves uniformly apparently due to secretion of quinones, at high density (Naylor, 1959).

Territorial demarcation is often accomplished by urination and/or defecation. For example, the dwarf hippopotamus marks its territory with urine and dung (Hediger, 1950). The Indian rhinoceros utilizes dung markings (Wynne-Edwards, 1962) while lemurs (Ilse, 1955) and cats utilize mainly urine (Hediger, 1950; Leyhausen & Wolff, 1959). In light of our emphasis on a close evolutionary relationship between various kinds of chemical messengers (pheromones, hormones), it is interesting to note that current evidence suggests that, at least in mammals, territorial marking is under androgen control. In rabbits (Mykytowycz, 1965) and in gerbils (Thiessen, Friend, & Lindzey, 1968) males mark much more than females. Marking is reduced in castrated males, and in gerbils it can be returned to an original level with a testosterone replacement therapy.

In many species territorial aggression is predominantly a male characteristic, and androgens have been implicated in the analysis of the neuroendocrine substrate of aggression. Thus a chemical messenger—androgen—while responsible for the reproductive competence of males, indirectly appears to affect the establishment, defense, and maintenance of a territory and through such behavior the reproductive competence of a species.

Recognition Pheromones

The literature on recognition pheromones provides good examples of some of the methodological and empirical difficulties encountered in the study of chemical communication. In contrast to sex, trail, territorial, or alarm pheromones, the evidence supporting the utility of the recognition messengers is sketchy.

Odor recognition of group members appears to be universal in the social insects. Nixon and Ribbands (1952) demonstrated that recognition scents in the honeybee are, in part, due to peculiarities of a diet and Lange (1960) has proved that in the ant, *Formica polyctena,* both diet and the nest wall contribute to odor recognition of a colony. In termites the origin of the colony odor (pheromonal, metabolic, environmental, or a mixture) is not known, but on a behavioral level it has been recorded for many years that when two colonies of the same species are placed together, the individuals of one group will jointly repel those from the other colony (Stuart, 1970). In two species of bumble bees, Free (1958) found that the odor of an alien colony can be used to contaminate an intruder, which would then be attacked upon returning to its own colony.

Even though recognition signals of various kinds are widespread across many taxa, the existence of chemicals involved in recognition of an individual seems to be limited to vertebrates. Wilson (Johnston *et al.*, 1970, p. 200) suggests that recognition of an individual appears to be one aspect of the complexity of social evolution observed in the vertebrates (e.g., dominance hierarchy, pair-bond formation, social stratification). Consequently some of these vertebrate species have evolved and acquired very complex chemical signals pertaining to individual recognition. By contrast, insects, having neither the complexity of the neuro-endocrine system nor the requirement for this degree of interindividual relations, employ single chemical messengers.

Better examples of individual recognition based on olfactory cues have been demonstrated in mother-young recognition in Alaskan fur seals (Bartholomew, 1959), goats (Blauvelt, 1954; Klopfer, Adams, & Klopfer, 1964) and possibly rats (Leon & Moltz, 1971). Prairie dogs identify each other by "kissing" (King, 1955) which, beside being tactile, has an important chemical–olfactory component, and prairie dogs can discriminate an individual on the basis of a trail consisting of specific body odors.

Acoustic Systems in Communication

Many factors have contributed to making the investigation of acoustic systems the most advanced area of study in animal communication. Contributions from many disciplines—anatomy, physiology, neurophysiology, psychophysiology, psychophysics, physical acoustics, ethology—have been brought to bear on the task of analyzing and understanding the sources, channels, destinations, codes, messages, and contexts of acoustic signals. The sound spectrograph has provided a means of analyzing vocal communication that is unparalleled by anything presently available for visual, tactile, and chemical signals. Technical and scientific progress has led to thousands of publications. An encyclopedic volume edited by Busnel (1963) presents an excellent review of the literature through the late 1950s, while a sample of subsequent surveys (Alexander, 1967; Beer, 1970; Busnel, 1968; Hinde, 1969; Marler, 1970; Marler & Hamilton, 1966; McNeill, 1970; Nottebohm, 1970; Tavolga, 1964, 1967) provides an indication of the excitement and productivity still generated by the issues involved in acoustic systems of communication.

Source of a Signal

Acoustic signals either have a mechanical origin generated by specialized or unspecialized emission organs, or are produced by vibrations conveyed to the medium by a part of the animal body acting as an amplifier. Examples of the latter would include ground-tapping by rabbits or woodpecking by birds. Utilization of unspecialized emission organs from diverse anatomical locations is found throughout the animal kingdom. In Orthoptera and Crustacea, the friction of vibrating body parts such as wings, antennae, thorax, legs, abdomen produces, a variety of sound signals. Some examples in vertebrates would include vomerine teeth (in certain fish), osseus, rattletype apparatuses as in rattlesnakes, wing-beating (wood pigeon), drumrolling (hazel grouse), or breast-beating of the gorilla.

Many vertebrates, however, possess specialized organs such as: vocal cords, muscular glottal lips, the larynx of odontocetes, and the larynx and syrinx of birds. Evolved in a close relationship with these organs are related structures serving as air reservoirs and resonators (e.g., clavicular and cervical air sacs in the ostrich crane and morse, vocal sacs in the gibbon, and the hyoid bone resonating chamber of the New World howler monkey).

Channel

Each organism functions in its own perceptual world, its *Umwelt,* which reflects the ecological niche of the species. Many species possess sensory capabilities that allow them to have a *Disney World* of their own, a world to which other organisms are denied admission. Thus, on the basis of high-frequency echos, bats may be capable of constructing pictures of their own environment (Griffin, 1958), a feat matched perhaps in a different ecological setting by dolphins and porpoises (Lilly, 1967; Norris, 1966). Since many forms of physical energy propagation can be exploited in communication, one of the tasks of bioacoustics is to specify the characteristics of the various channels that are used to transmit energy for the purposes of communication. The constraints of the transmission channel determine both the structure and perception of the signal. An illustrative description of some of the characteristics of the vocal–auditory channel, based on presentations of Hockett and Altmann (1968) and Thorpe (1972a), is offered in our discussion (see also Table 3, page 38).

Destination

When we discuss various levels of analysis involved in the study of the vocal–auditory channel and its contribution to verbal and nonverbal communication, we are assuming that a specialized structure produces a signal (in terms of specific units and characteristics of energy) to be carried through a medium to a receiving auditory system. The receiving system is the first physiological step in message reception, and it is circumscribed by the whole series of functionally, anatomically, and physiologically complex processes (Table 2) that characterize its receiving organs: mechanoreceptors; hair sensillae; statoacoustic structures; external, middle, and inner ear structures. Sounds, depending on their nature, can be quite directional. Generally, sounds of higher frequency can be received at a distance with better directionality.

Code, Message, and Meaning

A *code* consists of a set of transformation rules by which the physical characteristics of a message are converted to functional properties that constitute a communicative signal. A *message* consists of the physical characteristics of a stimulus (signal) emmitted by the signal-producing mechanisms of a sender, while *meaning* represents the functional properties of the signal as it is perceived by the recipient. In most species, a particular signal is emitted in a specific environmental setting and under conditions that permit the examination of its origin, code, message, and potential adaptive value. Functionally, signals are grouped according to the behavior that they elicit in a receiver: sexual (calling, courtship, rivalry), filial (parent–young, family acoustic exchange), and social (e.g., acoustic communication pertaining to hierarchy, territorial behavior, group activity, alarm). In many species the male signals, particularly sexual, differ from that of the female, but when both sexes emit sounds, the transmitter's identity appears to be accomplished by small variations in the physical constitution of a signal.

Context

Evaluation of the contribution that context makes to the emission of a signal and the meaning of a message is one of the most important and most difficult problems in the comparative study of communication. Under the rubric of signal context, we have to consider the immediate endogenous and exogenous state of sender and recipient, as well as the ontogenic history of the individual and species. The dynamics of the relationship are schematically illustrated in Table 2.

Crickets and Birds: Examples Illustrating the Importance of Acoustic Signals in Animal Communication

Crickets

In a southeastern region of the United States, during summer, there are as many as 20 different species of tree crickets producing discrete sounds, mostly the calling song of the male, whose function is to attract the female for the purpose of mating. How does a female distinguish the sounds of a conspecific? Studies have demonstrated that males of each species have a particular pulse rate in their song and it is this pulse rate that provides a female with discriminative cues. It is also interesting to note that the metabolic and physiological processes in a cricket are functionally affected by outside temperatures, so that a pulse rate in the song changes with temperature, earning some species the appropriate label of "thermometer crickets." The refinement of the evolved system is remarkable when one considers that physiological mechanisms that determine females' responsiveness to a signal change at the same time in a parallel fashion as the changes in males' pulse rate take place.

TABLE 2
Schematic Illustration of Contextual Aspects
Involved in Signal Production and Reception

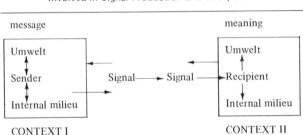

The sound-producing repertoire of the male cricket serves a number of functions: (a) facilitating and establishing sexual contact (the calling song); (b) mediating sexual attraction at a relatively short distance (the courtship song); (c) signaling a departure of a courting female (the courtship interruption song); (d) repelling or dominating other males (the aggressive sound); (e) maintaining contact between a mated pair (the postcopulatory song); (f) a wide range of what appear to be recognition sounds (Alexander, 1962, 1967, 1968).

There are approximately 3000 species of crickets of which field crickets make up a special group of about 400 species. We are most familiar with field crickets. They are relatively large, yellowish brown insects known for their rather loud, musical chirping. Crickets produce sounds by rubbing together stridulating areas located on the forewings of the male and utilize a rapid fluttering motion to produce a typical vibrato chirp. The receiving auditory organs are tympana located within slits on the forelegs. Most cricket species chirp at night. However, some chirp during the day and others chirp both day and night. In general, our understanding of neurophysiological mechanisms involved in cricket bioacoustics has few parallels, if any, in the animal literature (Alexander, 1968; Bentley & Kutsch, 1966; Bentley & Hoy, 1974; Ewing & Hoyle, 1965; Huber, 1962; Suga, 1963).

How does this brief commentary about cricket bioacoustics illustrate the importance of acoustic communication in cricket speciation and evolution, and what are some of the factors that maintain the species-specific integrity of a gene pool of some 20 different species of tree crickets that are not geographically isolated? The species-specific characteristics of the calling song of the male and the recognition of that song by a conspecific female were identified as one of the important isolating mechanisms (Alexander, 1962, 1968; Walker, 1957, 1962). Isolating mechanisms are numerous and varied. The principal ones are divided into two basic groups, prezygotic (those that prevent fertilization and zygote formation) and postzygotic (fertilization takes place and hybrids are formed but these are inviable, weak, or sterile). Among prezygotic isolating mechanisms we find:

a. geography and habitat, such that populations occupy different habitats and, even though reproductively compatible, do not come in contact with each other;

b. seasonal or temporal, referring to the fact populations are reproductively mature at different times;

c. ethological, in that there is a difference and incompatibility in behavior of reproductively isolate populations;

d. mechanical, where anatomical differences prevent reproduction.

Viewed in the context of our understanding of some of the evolutionary processes, crickets tell an interesting story. Among the 3000 species, many are isolated by their geography and habitat. When a number of species occupy the same habitat, then temporal, ethological, or mechanical isolating mechanisms maintain species integrity. Thus, one species will chirp at night and another during the day (temporal isolation). If more than one species occupy the same habitat and "sing" at the same time, then the differences in the pulse rate (ethological isolation) maintain species identity. Therefore, acoustic communication serves in prezygotic isolation of closely related species.

Postzygotic isolating mechanisms generally manifest themselves in three ways:

1. F_1 hybrid progeny may be weak, inviable, or developmentally deficient.

2. If by any chance F_1 hybrids are vigorous, then there is complete or partial sterility of these hybrids.

3. Any F_2 progeny that is produced by any vigorous F_1 hybrids is weak and sterile.

Therefore, the action of postzygotic isolating mechanisms may be characterized as the inability of the parental genes to function in a biologically appropriate way toward propagation of a hybrid or its progeny.

The literature on the ontogeny of acoustic communication in crickets also deserves more attention from behavioral scientists than it has received to date. It should be kept in mind that many insects mature with no chance to hear the signals of their own species, and they are exposed to many sounds that absolutely have no resemblance to any signals that they as mature adults must eventually produce. As Alexander (1968) has pointed out, there must have been intensive selection pressure for resistance to any kind of acoustic influence and in the direction of a fixed relationship between acoustic genotype and phenotype. Experiments investigating the genetic correlates of communicative signals in several species of crickets offer further support for this thesis (Alexander, 1966, 1968; Bentley, 1971; Bentley & Hoy, 1974; Bigelow, 1960; Fulton, 1933; Hörmann-Heck, 1957). For example, Fulton as early as 1933 hybridized *Nemobius allardi* and *Nemobius tinnulus*. These are two sibling species of ground crickets that are mature at the same time, overlap geographically and ecologically, but sing different songs. Fulton was able to develop F_1 and F_2 hybrids, carry out F_1 backcrosses with both parental species, and analyze the songs of various crosses. Fulton's results were generally clear-cut and straight-forward. Pulses in the song of F_1 hybrids were delivered at a rate intermediate between the two parental generations. The songs of backcross progeny were more like the parent utilized in the backcross. Generally, in all species investi-gated, wingstroke rate differences between species seem to depend on a number of genes, whereas differences in chirp patterns may depend on a different gene or genes located on another chromosome (Bigelow, 1960; Alexander, 1968).

This brief introduction to cricket bioacoustics is but one example chosen to illustrate a number of points (for example, ontogeny, physiology or immediate causation, survival value, and evolution of behavior) that are important to an ethologist trying to investigate communication in animals. As can be seen from Table 3, p. 38, cricket signals possess some important basic characteristics (that is, design features) of language (Hockett & Altmann, 1968; Thorpe, 1972a) such as specialization and discreteness. Many other design features are lacking and about some (for example, tradition) there is doubt.

Birds

The importance of acoustic signaling has been nicely demonstrated by experi-ments on hens by Baeumer (1955, 1959) and Brückner (1933), and on turkeys by Schleidt, Schleidt, and Magg (1960). In turkeys, for example, Schleidt and his co-workers found that the female, surgically deafened, would lay and sit on her eggs normally, but, after hatching, that same female could not distinguish her own brood, so the hatchlings would be killed as if they were predators approach-ing the nest, in spite of the information in a visual channel. Thus, it appears that the important functions of the acoustic signal provided by the hatchlings are to inhibit maternal aggressiveness and enable maternal recognition of the young.

Our own research (Hess, 1972a, b; Hess & Petrovich, 1973a, b; Ramsay & Hess, 1954), as well as that of others (Gottlieb, 1968, 1971, 1973) have demonstrated extensive parent–young interaction among ducks even prior to hatching. While investigating the effects of prenatal and postnatal auditory experiences on postnatal auditory discrimination and imprinting, we have found (Hess, 1972a, b; Hess & Petrovich, 1973a, b) that prenatal exposure (an expo-sure prior to hatching) to a natural maternal call facilitated its recognition. Mallard ducklings lacking any experience with a maternal call imprinted as well to a duck decoy that uttered artificial sounds as to a decoy that emitted a specific mallard cluck. Ducklings that had been exposed to a maternal call prior to hatching imprinted better to a decoy that emitted the mallard cluck. We found, however, that the immediate posthatching experience with a female mallard on the nest could strongly determine the degree of filial attachment and make imprinting to artificial sounds impossible. Therefore, while acoustic signals in mallards do not have a determinative effect on the survival of the offspring as

TABLE 3
A Comparison of the Communication Systems of Animals and Men[a]

Design features (all of which are found in verbal human language)	1 Human paralinguistics	2 Crickets, grasshoppers	3 Honey bee dancing	4 Doves	5 Buntings, finches, thrushes	6 Mynah	7 Colony nesting sea birds	8 Primates (vocal)	9 Canidae nonvocal communication	10 Primates—chimps e.g., Washoe
1. Vocal–auditory channel	Yes (in part)	Auditory but nonvocal	No	Yes	Yes	Yes	Yes	Yes	No	No
2. Broadcast transmission and directional reception	Yes	Yes	Yes	Yes	Yes	Yes	Yes	Yes	Partly yes	Partly yes
3. Rapid fading	Yes	Yes	?	Yes	Yes	Yes	Yes	Yes	No	No
4. Interchangeability (adults can be both transmitters and receivers)	Largely yes	Yes partial	Partial	Yes	Partial (yes if same sex)	Yes	Partial	Yes	Yes	Yes
5. Complete feedback ('speaker' able to perceive everything relevant to his signal production)	Partial	Yes	No?	Yes	Yes	Yes	Yes	Yes	No	Yes
6. Specialization (energy unimportant, trigger effect important)	Yes?	Yes?	?	Yes	Yes	Yes	Yes	Yes	Yes	Yes

No.	Feature									
7.	Semanticity (association ties between signals and features in the world)	Yes?	No?	Yes	Yes (in part)	Yes	Yes	Yes	Yes	Yes
8.	Arbitrariness (symbols abstract)	In part	?	No	Yes	Yes	Yes	Yes	No	Yes
9.	Discreteness (repertoire discrete not continuous)	Largely no	Yes	No	Yes	Yes	Yes	Partial	Partial	Partial
10.	Displacement (can refer to things remote in time and space)	In part	—	No	Time no, space yes	Time no, space yes	No	Yes	No	Yes
11.	Openness (new messages easily coined)	Yes	No	No	Yes	Yes	No?	Partial	No?	Yes?
12.	Tradition (conventions passed on by teaching and learning)	Yes	Yes?	No?	Yes	Yes	In part?	No?	?	Yes
13.	Duality of patterning (signal elements meaningless, pattern combinations meaningful)	No	?	No	Yes	Yes	No?	Yes	Yes	Yes
14.	Prevarication (ability to lie or talk nonsense)	Yes	No	No	No	No(?)	No	No	Yes	Yes
15.	Reflectiveness (ability to communicate about the system itself)	No	No	No	No	No	No	No	No	No
16.	Learnability (speaker of one language learns another	Yes	No(?)	No	Yes (in part)	Yes	No?	No?	No	Yes

[a]Based on the design features of Hockett and Altmann (1968) and taken from Thorpe (1972a).

is the case in turkeys, they play an important role in the development of filial attachment. In addition, individual idiosyncracies in the vocalization patterns of female mallards may play some part in enabling the young to identify their parent as well as in enabling an adult to recognize another individual (Hess, 1972a; Hess & Petrovich, 1973b).

Birds utilize sound as a medium of communication more extensively than any other animal group, and they possess a rich repertoire of signals that serve such varied functions as sexual (for example, calling, courthip songs), filial (for example, begging call of the young), and social (for example, territorial, aggressive, alarm calls) (Marler & Hamilton, 1966; Thorpe, 1961). The function of a song may be an important feature involved in the analysis of its ontogenic and phyletic history. For example, the alarm calls utilized by woodland species in Britain are very similar, and they serve as interspecific signals communicating danger (Marler, 1957). By contrast, male songs in many species carry a major burden as an important feature of prezygotic reproductive isolation, so that even species that are closely related from a phylogenetic standpoint, generally have highly divergent song patterns (Marler, 1957; Marler & Hamilton, 1966; Marler & Mundinger, 1971). It is not surprising therefore, to discover that three species of the European warbler that look extraordinarily alike were first distinguished taxonomically on the basis of the variations in their songs.

In addition, it is reasonable to postulate that the importance of learning in the development of the songs of some species is a function of selection pressures exerted by their ecological niches. Songs of many species can be heard in a given area and since the effectiveness of prezygotic isolation depends on the uniqueness of the song, the ability for change leading to that uniqueness must have been initially selected for in the course of evolution. Today we find that bird vocalizations distinguish not only species, but also among subpopulations within species (Marler, 1963, 1970; Marler & Mundinger, 1971: Marler & Tamura, 1962, 1964), groups (Marler, 1967; Thorpe, 1958, 1961) and individuals (Beer, 1969, 1970; Thorpe, 1972b). As the literature reviewed by Thorpe (1972b) indicates, there is no room to doubt that there are species of birds that can acoustically distinguish their mates, territorial neighbors, and offspring, as well as subtle individual idiosyncracies.

From an ontogenic and evolutionary perspective, we find ourselves in agreement with Thorpe's (1972b) conclusions:

> ... the variability of the 'songs' of birds is adapted, primarily by genetic programming and secondarily by imitative adjustment, to distinguish the species from every other species, and to distinguish one individual more or less certainly from all others in a population.
> These ends may be accomplished in different species by differences in the degree of competence of the innate neural template for song structure [p. 172].

Some of the more systematic and consistently superior research in ethology, deals with problems of ontogeny of bird songs (Immelmann, 1969; Konishi,

1963, 1965a, b; Konishi & Nottebohm, 1969; Marler, 1963, 1970; Marler & Mundinger, 1971; Nelson, 1973; Nicolai, 1964; Nottebohm, 1970, 1972; Thorpe, 1958, 1961, 1972b). Marler (1969, 1970) and Nottebohm (1970) have recently underscored the many parallels that are to be found between song ontogeny and the development of language. Acoustical stimulation allows sounds to be heard and remembered; it allows the organism to hear itself and match that against what has been acquired and learned previously or against the template. Auditory feedback is critical for development but does not appear to be as important subsequently. Learning is involved in the transition from a subsong or babbling to the adult type of vocalization. Vocal learning is to some extent "stimulus free" and independent of extrinsic reinforcement. Learning is most likely to occur during specific maturational periods—critical periods. There are specific predispositions to learning of certain sounds over others, and in both cases—bird song and language ontogeny—there is lateralization of control in the central nervous system.

Marler stresses that these observations do not imply the existence of discovery of language in birds, but they do suggest that there may be a set of rules that would evolve in nature in organisms engaging in vocal learning.

One of the more complete systems that has been developed to facilitate a comparison between the communicative abilities of animals and men is that of Hockett (1959, 1960) and Hockett and Ascher (1964). Thorpe (1972a), in turn, has adapted Hockett's model of design features to compare what he calls "animal 'languages' with those of men [pp. 38–39]" (Table 3) and the product of his efforts reflects the magnitude of the task facing an ethologist interested in the comparative aspects of communication.

COMMENTS FROM AN ETHOLOGICAL PERSPECTIVE
ON SOME OF THE ISSUES IN ANIMAL COMMUNICATION

The concept of evolution has become the great unifying principle in the biobehavioral sciences. Since animal communication (e.g., verbal, chemical, tactile) is a product of the evolutionary process, a brief introduction to some of the issues is in order.

Evolution may be defined as any change in the gene frequency of a population that consists of a number of interbreeding organisms. Ideally genes are distributed at random from generation to generation. However, factors such as mutations, selection, breeding, structure of the population, size of the population, and migration affect the composition of the gene pool (Stebbins 1966; Wilson & Bossert, 1971).

Species-typic behavior (for example, communication) is an important component and product of the dynamics of the evolutionary process. The two interrelated issues—the influence of evolution on behavior and behavior on evolution—comprise a field of inquiry about which our knowledge is increasing and about which ethology should have much to say, particularly since the ethological method is defined as the study of ontogeny, causation, survival value, and evolution of behavior (Tinbergen, 1963).

One of the strong points of the ethological approach to behavioral analysis is that it allows us to see the issues of behavioral ontogeny (nature–nurture, instinct–learning) in perspective. For example, all animals, at least above the Annelid level, show both ends of the behavioral continuum from "innate to acquired." But the development of these ends varies widely as a result of the animals' adaptations to specific and different ecological requirements, for all animals must respond to their environment with a well-adapted behavioral repetoire if they are to survive. In smaller animals, particularly invertebrates with relatively short life spans, the selection has favored the evolution of inherited behavior patterns that are adapted to the normal environmental requirements, one example being a cricket song (Alexander, 1962, 1968; Huber, 1962). In many birds, the ontogeny of species-specific song often provides a classic example of the genotype-dependent process involving the coaction of inherited predispositions and learning (Marler & Mundinger, 1971). Toward the other end of the continuum are those vertebrates (particularly primates) whose lifespans are relatively long and start with a period of infancy that often involves an extensive social interaction between parents, offspring, and siblings. In such circumstances, the opportunities for modification of behavioral responses are abundant and the advantages of preset inherited behavior patterns are reduced. Therefore, selection has favored specialization toward a plasticity which, in its extreme form, is represented by the evolution of a behavioral capacity often called *"animal tradition"* (Lorenz, 1969, pp. 61–69; see also Table 3, Design Feature 12).

Animal tradition is illustrated by any act of passing a specific bit of information or knowledge, through mechanisms of learning, from one individual to the other or from one generation to the next generation. In Japanese macaques, for example, initial observations by Itani (1958) which demonstrated the cultural acquisition and propagation of a new food habit in a particular troop of monkeys have been often corroborated, and offer evidence for "cultural transmission" of traits that produce a primate subculture.

Tradition represents cultural inheritance. On the molar level of analysis, tradition is Lamarckian in nature, leading Lorenz (1969) to observe:

> What comes into existence with the human form of tradition is neither more nor less than the famous inheritance of acquired characters. Instant information, a flash of insight or an unforseen success of exploratory behavior is retained with tenacity almost equal to that of the genome Lorenz, 1969, [p. 63].

The "ethnic gesture" is but one component of man's tradition. The stored variability of tradition is not genetic in nature but consists of ideas, inventions, laws, customs, folklore, manufacturing of tools, and many other acquired behaviors by which a social unit may be regulated, maintained, and sustained. We think that the evolution of tradition in animals has played an important role in the evolution of animal communication, language in particular. The diversity of communications in animals must exist in order to maintain species specificity, allow for elicitation of different yet specific responses from another animal, and also in order for an organism to have the ability to select among the various kinds of signals that are available. The evolution of complex forms of social interaction requiring not only the recognition of various "social niches," but also the recognition of an individual, has contributed to selection pressures in the direction of environmental control of communication and away from the preset genetically programmed modes of exchange. Once established biologically and culturally, the increased flexibility paved the way for the more remarkable forms of communication.

At this point, in light of some of our remarks and observations, let us return to certain aspects of the discontinuity theory of language evolution as proposed by Chomsky and Lenneberg. Chomsky (1968) finds in human language "no striking similarity to animal communication systems [p. 62]." He is convinced that human language is an entirely different type of communication and suggests that it is pointless ". . . to speculate about the evolution of human language from simpler systems—perhaps as absurd as it would be to speculate about the 'evolution' of atoms from clouds of elementary particles;" and he concludes on the same page, "There seems to be no substance to the view that human language is simply a more complex instance of something to be found elsewhere in the animal world [p. 62]."

Clearly, no definitive statement can be made pertaining to the ontogeny and evolution of language. We leave it to the reader to evaluate the substance and implications of Chomsky's remarks with the evidence and the interpretation of that evidence as it is presented in this chapter. In addition, it needs to be emphasized that while we concur with the nativistic orientation characteristic of the biological approach to language ontogeny, our reading of the evolution of learning and of the behavioral capacity referred to as "tradition in animals" leads us to recognize, weigh, and appreciate the contribution of psycholinguists who underscore the importance of learning in language acquisition. At the same time, an evolutionary perspective puts us on guard against excessive, fixed, nativistic interpretations of language development.

The discontinuity hypothesis can stand on its own biological merits, as the writings of Lenneberg indicate. It needs to be underscored, however, that animal communications of all kinds (for example, verbal, chemical, tactile) are a result of the evolutionary process. Indeed, we agree that the uniqueness of one form of communication, characteristic of a particular species, is explicable in biological terms and in the same way as the uniqueness of any other species. Speciation itself may be viewed as a continuous process of being and becoming unique. If the process of uniqueness is accepted as a biological fact of animal communication, then from an evolutionary standpoint a discontinuity theory of language, if carried to its logical conclusion, reduces the issue to one of relative distinction: Are not signals involved in communication among social bees (Lindauer, 1967; von Frishch, 1967) components of a bee language as far as bees are concerned? To accept and argue for the discontinuity theory of the evolution of language is to argue for a continuity theory of biological evolution of communication.

Often in the absence of empirical evidence there is tendency to reduce discussion on important issues to "science by advocacy." We must guard against such efforts and conclude that there is plenty of room for agnosticism on any of these issues relating to the evolution of language. As ethologists, (paraphrasing Lorenz, 1969) we wish to add a reminder that life itself is a knowledge process and communication is an important manifestation of life.

ACKNOWLEDGMENTS

Research supported by Grant 776 from the National Institute of Mental Health, United States Public Health Service.

REFERENCES

Ainsworth, M. D. S. Object relation, dependency and attachment: A theoretical review of the infant–mother relationship. *Child Development,* 1969, **40,** 969–1025.

Alexander, R. D. Evolutionary changes in cricket communication. *Evolution,* 1962, **16,** 443–467.

Alexander, R. D. The evolution of cricket chirp. *Natural History,* 1966, **75,** 26–31.

Alexander, R. D. Acoustical communication in arthropods. *Annual Review of Entomology,* 1967, **12,** 495–526.

Alexander, R. D. Arthropods. In T. A. Sebeck (Ed.), *Animal communication.* Bloomington: Indiana University Press, 1968.

Alloway, T., Krames, L., & Pliner, P. (Eds.) *Communication and affect: A comparative approach.* New York: Academic Press, 1972.

Altmann, S. A. (Ed.) *Social communication among primates.* Chicago: University of Chicago Press, 1967.

Andrew, R. J. The origin and evolution of the calls and facial expressions of the primates. *Behavior,* 1963, **20,** 1–109. (a)

Andrew, R. J. Evolution of facial expressions. *Science,* 1963, **142,** 1034–1041. (b)

Andrew, R. J. The information potentially available in mammal displays. In R. A. Hinde (Ed.), *Non-verbal communication.* Cambridge, England: Cambridge University Press, 1972.

Ardrey, R. *The territorial imperative.* New York: Atheneum, 1966.

Ardrey R. *The social contract.* New York: Atheneum, 1970.

Armstrong, E. A. *A study of bird song.* London: Oxford University Press, 1963.

Baeumer, E. von. Lebensart des Haushuhns. *Zeitschrift für Tierpsychologie,* 1955, **12,** 387–401.

Baeumer, E. von. Verhaltensstudie über das Haushuhn,–dessen Lebensart, 2. Teil. *Zeitschrift für Tierpsychologie,* 1959, **16,** 284–296.

Barker, R. G. *Ecological psychology*. Stanford, California: Stanford University Press, 1968.

Bartholomew, G. A. Mother–young relations and the maturation of pup behavior in the Alaskan fur seal. *Animal Behavior,* 1959, **7**, 163–171.

Beer, C. G. Laughing gull chicks: recognition of their parents' voices. *Science,* 1969, **166**, 1030–32.

Beer, C. G. Individual recognition of voice in the social behavior of birds. In Lehrman, D. S., Hinde, R. A., & Shaw, E. (Eds.), *Advances in the study of behavior*, Vol. 3. New York: Academic Press, 1970.

Bentley, D. R. Genetic control of an insect neuronal network. *Science,* 1971, **174**, 1139–1141.

Bentley, D. R., & Hoy, R. R. The neurobiology of cricket song. *Scientific American,* 1974, **231**, 34–44.

Bentley, D. R., & Kutsch, W. The neuromuscular mechanism of stridulation in crickets (Orthoptera: Gryllidae). *Journal of Experimental Biology,* 1966, **45**, 151–164.

Beroza, M. *Chemicals controlling insect behavior*. New York: Academic Press, 1970.

Bigelow, R. S. Interspecific hybrids and speciation in genus *Acheta* (Orthoptera: Gryllidae). *Canadian Journal of Zoology,* 1960, **38**, 509–524.

Birdwhistell, R. L. *Kinesics and context*. Philadelphia: University of Pennsylvania Press, 1970.

Blauvelt, H. Dynamics of the mother–newborn relationship in goats. In B. Schaffner (Ed.), *Group processes*. New York: Josiah Macy, Jr., Foundation, 1954.

Bossert, W. H., & Wilson, E. O. The analysis of olfactory communication among animals. *Journal of Theoretical Biology,* 1963, **5**, 443–469.

Bowlby, J. *Attachment and loss*. Vol. 1: *Attachment*. New York: Basic Books, 1969.

Bowlby, J. *Attachment and loss*. Vol. 2. *Separation, anxiety and anger*. New York: Basic Books, 1973.

Brower, L. P., Brower, J. V. Z., & Cranston, F. P. Courtship behavior of the queen butterfly. *Zoologica,* 1965, **1**, 1–39.

Bruce, M. Effect of castration on the reproductive pheromones of male mice. *Journal of Reproduction and Fertility,* 1965, **10**, 141–143.

Brückner, J. H. Untersuchungen zur Tiersoziologie, insbesondere zur Auflösung der Familie. *Zeitschrift für Tierpsychologie,* 1933, **128**, 1–105.

Burghardt, G. M. Defining communication. In J. W. Johnston, Jr., P. G. Moulton, & A. Turk (Eds.), *Communication by chemical signals*. New York: Appleton-Century-Crofts, 1970.

Burghardt, G. M. Instinct and innate behavior: Toward an ethological psychology. In J. A. Nevin & G. S. Reynolds (Eds.), *The study of Behavior*. Glenview, Illinois: Scott, Foresman, 1973.

Burkhardt, D. Schleidt, W., & Altner, H. (Eds.) *Signals in the animal world*. New York: McGraw-Hill, 1967.

Burton, R. *Animal senses*. New York: Taplinger, 1970.

Busnel, R. G. *Acoustic behavior of animals*. Amsterdam: Elsevier, 1963.

Busnel, R. G. Acoustic communication. In T. A. Sebeok (Ed.), *Animal communication*. Bloomington: Indiana University Press, 1968.

Butler, C. G. Insect pheromones. *Biological Review,* 1967, **42**, 42–87.

Callan, H. *Ethology and society*. Oxford: Clarendon, 1970.

Carlson, D. A., Mayer, M. S., Silhacek, D. L., James, J. D., Beroza, M., & Bierl, B. A. Sex attractant pheromone of the house fly: Isolation, identification and synthesis. *Science,* 1971, **174**, 76–78.

Chapple, E. D. *Culture and biological man,* New York: Holt, Rinehart & Winston, 1970.

Chauvin, R. *Animal societies: from bee to gorilla*. London: Gollancz, 1968.

Chauvin, R. *The world of ants: a science-fiction universe*. New York: Mill and Wang, 1970.

Cherry, C. *On human communication*. New York: Wiley 1957.

Chomsky, N. *Language and mind.* New York: Harcourt, Brace & World, 1968.

Count, E. W. *Being and becoming human: Essays on the biogram.* New York: Van Nostrand-Rheinhold, 1973.

Crook, J. H. The evolution of social organization and visual communication in the weaver birds (Ploceinae). *Behavior Supplement,* 1964, **10,** 1–178.

Crook, J. H. (Ed.) *Social behavior in birds and mammals: Essays on the social ethology of animal and man.* London: Academic Press, 1970.

Crystal, D. *Prosodic systems and intonation in English.* London Cambridge, England: Cambridge University Press, 1969.

Dart, R. A. On the evolution of language and articulate speech. *Homo,* 1959, **10,**154–65.

Darwin, C. R. *The descent of man.* London: John Murray, 1871. (Reference from Random House editions, The Modern Library Series, New York, 1966.)

Darwin, C. R. *The expression of the emotions in man and animals.* London: John Murray, 1872. (Reference from The University of Chicago Press editions, Chicago, 1965.)

Davitz, J. R. *The communication of emotional meaning.* New York: McGraw-Hill, 1964.

DeVore, I. (Ed.) *Primate behavior: Field studies of monkeys and apes.* New York: Holt, Rinehart & Winston, 1965.

Dröschler, V. B. *The magic of the senses: New discoveries in animal perception.* New York: Dutton, 1969.

DuBrul, E. L. *Evolution of the speech apparatus.* New York: St. Martin's Press, 1958.

Duncan, S., Jr. Nonverbal communication. *Psychological Bulletin,* 1969, **72,** 118–137.

Ebling, J., & Highnam, K. C. *Chemical communication.* New York: St. Martin's Press, 1970.

Eibl-Eibesfeldt, I. *Ethology: The biology of behavior.* New York: Holt, Rinehart and Winston, 1970.

Eibl-Eibesfeldt, I. Similarities and differences between cultures in expressive movements. In R. A. Hinde (Ed.), *Non-verbal communication.* Cambridge, England: Cambridge University Press, 1972.

Eisenberg, J. F., & Dillon, W. S. (Eds.) *Man and beast: Comparative social behavior.* Washington, D.C.: Smithsonian Institution Press, 1971.

Eisenberg, J. F., & Kleiman, D. Olfactory communication in mammals. *Annual Review of Ecology and Systematics,* 1972, **3,** 1–32.

Esser, A. H. (Ed.) *Behavior and environment: The use of space by animals and men.* New York: Plenum Press, 1971.

Etkin, W. (Ed.) *Social behavior and organization among vertebrates.* Chicago: The University of Chicago Press, 1964.

Evans, W. E. *Communication in the animal world.* New York: Crowell, 1968.

Ewer, R. F. *Ethology of mammals.* New York: Plenum Press, 1968.

Ewing, A., & Hoyle, G. Neuronal mechanism underlying control of sound production in a cricket: *Acheta domesticus: Journal of Experimental Biology,* 1965, **43,** 139–153.

Fox, R. In the beginning: Aspects of hominid behavioral evolution. *Man,* 1967, **2,** 415–433.

Frank, L. K. Tactile communication. *Genetic Psychology Monographs,* 1957, **56,** 209–55.

Free, J. B. The defence of bumble bee colonies. *Behavior,* 1958, **12,** 233–242.

Freedman, D. G. *Human infancy: An evolutionary perspective.* Hillsdale, New Jersey Erlbaum Associates, 1974.

Frings, M., & Frings, H. *Sound production and sound reception by insects: A bibliography.* University Park: Pennsylvania State University Press, 1960.

Frings, H., & Frings, M. *Animal communication.* New York: Blaisdell, 1964.

Frisch, K. von. *The dance language and orientation of bees.* Cambridge, Massachusetts: Harvard University Press, 1967.

Fulton, B. B. Inheritance of song in hybrids of two subspecies of *Nemobius fasciatus* (Orthoptera). *Annals of the Entomological Society of America,* 1933, **26,** 368–376.

Gardner, B. T., & Gardner, R. A. Two-way communication with an infant chimpanzee. In A. M. Schrier & F. Stollnitz (Eds.), *Behavior of nonhuman primates,* Vol. 4, New York: Academic Press, 1971.

Gardner, R. A., & Gardner, B. T. Teaching sign language to a chimpanzee. *Science,* 1969, **165,** 664–72.

Gewirtz, J. L. Mechanisms of social learning: Some roles of stimulation and behavior in early human development. In D. A. Goslin (Ed.), *Handbook of socialization theory and research.* Chicago: Rand McNally, 1969.

Gibson, J. J. Observations on active touch. *Psychological Review,* 1962, **69,** 477–491.

Gilbert, B. *How animals communicate.* New York: Pantheon Books, 1966.

Gleason, K. K., & Reynierse, J. H. The behavioral significance of pheromones in vertebrates. *Psychological Bulletin,* 1969, **71,** 58–73.

Goffman, E. *Behavior in public places.* London: Collier-Macmillan, 1963.

Goffman, E. *Interaction ritual.* Garden City, New York: Doubleday Anchor, 1967.

Gottlieb, G. Prenatal behavior of birds. *Quarterly Review of Biology,* 1968, **43,** 148–174.

Gottlieb, G. *Development of species identification in birds. An inquiry into prenatal determinants of perception.* Chicago: University of Chicago Press, 1971.

Gottlieb, G. Neglected developmental variables in the study of species identification in birds. *Psychological Bulletin,* 1973, **79,** 362–372.

Graham, C. H. (Ed.) *Vision and visual perception.* New York: Wiley, 1965.

Greenewalt, C. H. *Bird song: Acoustics and physiology.* Washington, D.C.: Smithsonian Institution Press, 1968.

Griffin, D. R. *Listening in the dark.* New Haven: Yale University Press, 1958.

Hafez, E. S. E. *The behaviour of domestic animals.* Baltimore: Williams and Wilkins, 1969.

Haldane, J. B. S. Animal communication and the origin of human language. *Science Progress,* 1955, **43,** 385–401.

Hall, E. T. *The hidden dimension.* New York: Doubleday, 1966.

Haskell, P. T. *Insect sounds.* Chicago: Quadrangle Books, 1961.

Hebb, D. O. What psychology is about. *American Psychologist,* 1974, **29,** 71–79.

Hediger, H. *Wild animals in captivity.* London: Butterworths, 1950.

Hediger, H. *Studies of the psychology and behavior of captive animals in zoos and circuses.* New York: Criterion Books, 1955.

Hediger, H. *Man and animal in the zoo: Zoobiology.* New York: Delacorte Press, 1969.

Hess, E. H. "Imprinting" in a natural laboratory. *Scientific American,* 1972, **227,** 24–31. (a)

Hess, E. H. The natural history of imprinting. *Annals of the New York Academy of Sciences,* 1972, **193,** 124–136. (b)

Hess, E. H. *Imprinting: Early experience and the developmental psychobiology of attachment.* New York: Van Nostrand-Rheinhold, 1973.

Hess, E. H., & Petrovich, S. B. The early development of parent–young interaction in nature. In H. W. Reese & J. R. Nesselroade (Eds.), *Life-span developmental psychology: Methodological issues.* New York: Academic Press, 1973. (a)

Hess, E. H., & Petrovich, S. B. Effects of prenatal and postnatal auditory stimulation on postnatal auditory discrimination and imprinting. *Proceedings 13th International Ethological Conference,* Washington, D.C., 1973. (Abstract) (b)

Hinde, R. A. (Ed.) *Bird vocalizations: Their relation to current problems in biology and psychology.* Cambridge: Cambridge University Press, 1969.

Hinde, R. A. *Animal behaviour: A synthesis of ethology and comparative psychology.* New York: McGraw-Hill, 1970.

Hinde, R. A. (Ed.) *Non-verbal communication.* Cambridge: Cambridge University Press, 1972.

Hockett, C. F. Animal "languages" and human language. In J. N. Spuhler (Ed.), *The Evolution of man's capacity for culture.* Detroit: Wayne State University Press, 1959.

Hockett, C. F. The origin of speech. *Scientific American,* 1960, **203,** 88–96.

Hockett, C. F., & Altmann, S. A. A note on design features. In T. A. Sebeok (Ed.), *Animal communication.* Bloomington: Indiana University Press, 1968.

Hockett, C. F., & Ascher, R. The human revolution. *Current Anthropology,* 1964, **5,** 135–168.

Hooff, J. A. R. A. M. van. The facial displays of the catarrhine monkeys and apes. In D. Morris (Ed.), *Primate ethology.* London: Weidenfeld and Nicolson, 1967.

Hörmann-Heck, S. von. Untersuchungen über den Erbgang einiger Verhaltensweisen bei grillenbastarden. *Zeitschrift für Tierpsychologie,* 1957, **14,** 137–183.

Howard, J. *Please touch: A guided tour of the human potential movement.* New York: McGraw-Hill, 1970.

Huber, F. Central nervous control of sound production in crickets and some speculations on its evolution. *Evolution,* 1962, **16,** 429–442.

Huxley, J., & Koch, L. *Animal language.* New York: Grosset and Dunlap, 1964.

Ilse, D. R. Olfactory marking of territory in two young male loris, *Loris tardigradus lydekkerianus,* kept in captivity in Poona. *British Journal of Animal Behaviour,* 1955, **3,** 118–120.

Immelmann, K. Sound development in the zebra finch and other Estrildid finches. In R. A. Hinde (Ed.), *Bird vocalizations: Their relation to current problems in biology and psychology.* Cambridge, England: Cambridge University Press, 1969.

Itani, J. On the acquisition and propagation of a new food habit in the troop of Japanese monkeys at Takasakiyama. *Primates,* 1958, **1,** 131–148.

Jacobson, M. *Insect sex pheromones.* New York: Academic Press, 1972.

Jarrard, L. E. (Ed.) *Cognitive processes in nonhuman primates.* New York: Academic Press, 1971.

Jay, P. C. (Ed.) *Primates: Studies in adaptation and variability.* New York: Holt, Rinehart & Winston, 1968.

Jaynes, J. The historical origins of "ethology" and "comparative psychology." *Animal Behavior,* 1969, **17,** 601–606.

Johnston, J. W., Jr., Moulton, D. G., & Turk, A. (Eds.) *Communication by chemical signals.* New York: Appleton-Century-Crofts, 1970.

Jolly, A. *The evolution of primate behavior.* New York: Macmillan, 1972.

Karlson, P., & Butenandt, A. Pheromones (ectohormones) in insects. *Annual Review of Entomology,* 1959, **4,** 39–58.

King, J. A. Social behavior, social organization, and population dynamics in a black-tailed prairie dog town in the Black Hills of South Dakota. *Contributions of the Laboratory of Vertebrate Biology,* No. 67, Ann Arbor, Michigan: University of Michigan Press, 1955.

Klopfer, P. H. *Habitats and territories.* New York: Basic Books, 1969.

Klopfer, P. H., Adams, D. K., & Klopfer, M. S. Maternal "Imprinting" in goats. *Proceedings of the National Academy of Science,* 1964, **52,** 911–914.

Klopfer, P. H. & Hailman, J. P. *An introduction to animal behavior: Ethology's first century.* Englewood Cliffs, New Jersey: Prentice-Hall, 1967.

Knapp, M. L. *Nonverbal communication in human interaction.* New York: Holt, Rinehart & Winston, 1972.

Konishi, M. The role of auditory feedback in the vocal behavior of the domestic fowl. *Zeitschrift für Tierpsychologie,* 1963, **20,** 349–367.

Konishi, M. Effects of deafening on song development in American robins and black-headed grosbeaks. *Zeitschrift für Tierpsychologie,* 1965, **22,** 584–599. (a)

Konishi, M. The role of auditory feedback in the control of vocalization in the white-crowned sparrow. *Zeitschrift für Tierpsychologie,* 1965, **22,** 770–783. (b)

Konishi, M., & Nottebohm, F. Experimental studies in the ontogeny of avian vocalizations. In R. A. Hinde (Ed.), *Bird vocalizations: Their relation to current problems in biology and psychology.* Cambridge: Cambridge University Press, 1969.

Krames, L., Pliner, P., & Alloway, T. (Eds.), *Nonverbal communication.* New York: Plenum Press, 1974.

Kummer, H. *Primate societies.* Chicago: Aldine-Atherton, 1971.

Lancaster, J. B. Primate communication systems and the emergence of human language. In P. C. Jay (Ed.), *Primates: Studies in adaptation and variability.* New York: Holt, Rinehart and Winston, 1968.

Lange, R. Über die Futterweitergabe zwischen Agehörigen verscheidener Waldameisen. *Zeitschrift für Tierpsychologie,* 1960, **17,** 389–401.

Lanyon, W. E., & Tavolga, W. N. (Eds.) *Animal sounds and communication.* Washington, D.C.: American Institute of Biological Sciences, 1960.

Lenneberg, E. H. (Ed.) *New directions in the study of language.* Cambridge, Massachusetts: M.I.T. Press, 1964.

Lenneberg, E. H. *Biological foundations of language.* New York: Wiley, 1967.

Lenneberg, E. H. A word between us. In J. D. Roslansky (Ed.), *Communication: A discussion of the Nobel conference.* New York: Fleet Academic Editions, 1969.

Lenneberg, E. H. Of language knowledge, apes, and brains. *Journal of Psycholinguistic Research,* 1971, **1,** 1–29.

Leon, M., & Moltz, H. The development of the pheromonal bond in the albino rat. *Physiology and Behavior,* 1971, **8,** 683–686.

Leyhausen, P., & Wolff, R. Das Revier einer Hauskatze. *Zeitschrift für Tierpsychologie,* 1959, **16,** 666–670.

Lilly, J. C. *The mind of the dolphin: A nonhuman intelligence.* Garden City, New York: Doubleday, 1967.

Lindauer, M. Recent advances in bee communication and orientation. *Annual Review of Entomology,* 1967, **12,** 249–270.

Lockard, R. B. Reflections on the fall of comparative psychology: Is there a message for us all? *American Psychologist,* 1971, **26,** 168–179.

Lorenz, K. *Evolution and modification of behavior.* Chicago: The University of Chicago Press, 1965.

Lorenz, K. Innate bases of learning. In K. Pribram (Ed.), *On the biology of learning.* New York: Harcourt, Brace, Jovanovich, 1969.

Lorenz, K. *Studies in animal and human behavior,* (Vol. 1). Cambridge, Massachusetts: Harvard University Press, 1970.

Lorenz, K. *Studies in animal and human behavior,* (Vol. 2). Cambridge, Massachusetts: Harvard University Press, 1971.

Lorenz, K. Z., & Leyhausen, P. *Motivation of human and animal behavior: An ethological view.* New York: Van Nostrand-Rheinhold, 1973.

Lyons, F. Human language. In R. A. Hinde (Ed.), *Non-verbal communication.* Cambridge, England: Cambridge University Press, 1972.

Manning, A. *An introduction to animal behavior.* Reading, Massachusetts: Addison-Wesley, 1972.

Marler, P. Specific distinctiveness in the communication signals of birds. *Behavior,* 1957, **11,** 13–39.

Marler, P. Developments in the study of animal communication. In P. R. Bell (Ed.), *Darwin's biological work.* Cambridge: Cambridge University Press, 1959.

Marler, P. The logical analysis of animal communication. *Journal of Theoretical Biology,* 1961, **1,** 295–317.

Marler, P. Inheritance and learning in the development of animal vocalizations. In R. G. Busnel (Ed.), *Acoustic behavior in animals.* Amsterdam: Elsevier, 1963.

Marler, P. Communication in monkeys and apes. In I. De Vore (Ed.), *Primate behavior: Field studies of monkeys and apes.* New York: Holt, Rinehart and Winston, 1965.

Marler, P. Animal communication signals. *Science,* 1967, **157,** 769–774.

Marler, P. Visual systems. In T. A. Sebeok (Ed.), *Animal communication.* Bloomington: Indiana University Press, 1968.

Marler, P. Animals and man: Communication and its development. In J. D. Roslansky (Ed.), *Communication: A discussion at the Nobel Conference.* New York: Fleet Academic Editions, 1969.

Marler, P. A comparative approach to vocal development: Song learning in the white-crowned sparrow. *Journal of Comparative and Physiological Psychology,* 1970, **71,** (2), Part 2, 1–25.

Marler, P., & Hamilton, W. J., III. *Mechanisms of animal behavior.* New York: Wiley, 1966.

Marler, P., & Mundinger, P. Vocal learning in birds. In H. Moltz (Ed.), *The ontogeny of vertebrate behavior.* New York: Academic Press. 1971.

Marler, P., & Tamura, M. Song dialects in three populations of white-crowned sparrows. *Condor,* 1962, **64,** 368–377.

Marler, P., & Tamura, M. Culturally transmitted patterns of vocal behavior in sparrows. *Science,* 1964, **146,** 1483–1486.

Masters, R. D. Genes, language, and evolution. *Semiotica,* 1970, **2,** 295–320.

Matthews, L. H., & Knight, M. *The senses of animals.* New York: Philosophical Library, 1963.

McNeill, D. *The acquisition of language: The study of developmental psycholinguistics.* New York: Harper and Row, 1970.

Mead, M. Anthropology among the sciences. *American Anthropologist,* 1961, **63,** 475–482.

Mehrabian, A. Significance of posture and position in the communication of attitude and status relationships. *Psychological Bulletin,* 1969, **71,** 359–372.

Mehrabian, A. *Nonverbal communication.* Chicago: Aldine-Atherton, 1972.

Michael, R. P., & Keverne, E. B. Pheromones in the communication of sexual status in primates. *Nature,* 1968, **218,** 746–749.

Michael, R. P., Keverne, E. B., & Bosnell, R. W. Pheromones: Isolation of male sex attractants from primate females. *Science,* 1971, **172,** 964–966.

Moltz, H. (Ed.) *The ontogeny of vertebrate behavior.* New York: Academic Press, 1971.

Moncrieff, R. W. *The chemical senses.* London: Leonard Hill Books, 1967.

Montagu, M. F. A. *Touching: The human significance of the skin.* New York: Columbia University Press, 1971.

Morris, D. (Ed.) *Primate ethology.* Chicago: Aldine, 1967.

Morris, D. *Intimate behavior.* New York: Random House, 1971.

Mykytowycz, R. Further observations on the territorial function and histology of the submandibular cutaneous (skin) glands in the rabbit, *Oryctolagus cuniculus. Animal Behavior,* 1965, **13,** 400–412.

Nash, J. *Developmental psychology: A psychobiological approach.* Englewood Cliffs, New Jersey: Prentice-Hall, 1970.

Naylor, A. F. An experimental analysis of dispersal in the flour beetle, *Tribolium confusum. Ecology,* 1959, **40,** 453–465.

Nelson, K. Does the holistic study of behavior have a future? In P. P. G. Bateson & P. H. Klopfer (Eds.), *Perspectives in ethology.* New York: Plenum Press, 1973.

Nicolai, J. Der Brutparasitismus der Viduinae als ethologisches Problem Prägungsphänomene als Faktoren der Rassen und Artbildung. *Zeitschrift für Tierpsychologie,* 1964, **21,** 129–204.

Nixon, H. L., & Ribbands, C. R. Food transmission within the honeybee community. *Proceedings of the Royal Society (London), B,* 1952, **140,** 43–50.

Noble, G. K., & Bradley, H. T. The relation of the thyroid and the hypophysis to the moulting process in the lizard, *Hemidactylus helleri. Biological Bulletin*, 1933, **64**, 289–298.

Norris, K. S. (Ed.) *Whales, dolphins, and porpoises.* Berkeley and Los Angeles: University of California Press, 1966.

Nottebohm, F. Ontogeny of bird song. *Science*, 1970, **167**, 950–56.

Nottebohm, F. The origins of vocal learning. *American Naturalist*, 1972, **106**, 116–140.

Peters, M., & Ploog, D. Communication among primates. *Annual Review of Physiology*, 1973, **35**, 221–242.

Pfaffmann, C. (Ed.) *Olfaction and taste III.* New York: Rockefeller University Press, 1969.

Piaget, J. *The language and thought of the child.* New York: Merician, 1955.

Piaget, J. Quantification, conservation and nativism. *Science*, 1968, **162**, 976–979.

Piaget, J., & Inhelder, B. *The psychology of the child.* New York: Basic Books, 1969.

Premack, D. A functional analysis of language. *Journal of the Experimental Analysis of Behavior*, 1970, **14**, 107–25.

Premack, D. On the assessment of language competence in the chimpanzee. In A. M. Schrier & F. Stollnitz (Eds.), *Behavior of nonhuman primates*, Vol. 4. New York: Academic Press, 1971.

Ralls, K. Mammalian scent marking. *Science*, 1971, **171**, 443–449.

Ramsay, A. O., & Hess, E. H. A laboratory approach to the study of imprinting. *Wilson Bulletin*, 1954, **66**, 196–206.

Reddiford, L. M. Antennal proteins of saturnid moths–their possible role in olfaction. *Journal of Insect Physiology*, 1970, **16**, 653–660.

Reddiford, L. M., & Williams, C. M. Role of the corpora cardiaca in the behavior of saturnid moths. I. Release of sex pheromone. *The Biological Bulletin*, 1971, **140**, 1–7.

Révész, G. The language of animals. *Journal of Genetic Psychology*, 1944, **30**, 117–147.

Reynolds, P. C. Evolution of primate vocal–auditory communication systems. *American Anthropologist*, 1968, **70**, 300–08.

Rumbaugh, D. M., Gill, T. V., & Glasersfeld, E. C. von. *Reading and sentence* completion by a chimpanzee (Pan). *Science*, 1973, **182**, 731–733.

Sarles, H. B. The study of language and communication across species. *Current Anthropology*, 1969, **10**, 211–221.

Scheflen, A. E. The significance of posture in communication systems. *Journal of Psychiatric Research*, 1964, **27**, 316–331.

Schleidt, M. W., Schleidt, M., & Magg, M. Störung der Mutter-Kind-Beziehung bei Truthühnern durch Gehörverlust. *Behavior*, 1960, **16**, 254–260.

Schneider, D. Insect olfaction: Deciphering system for chemical messages. *Science*, 1969, **163**, 1031–1037.

Schneider, D., & Seibt, U. Sex pheromone of the queen butterfly: Electroantennogram responses. *Science*, 1969, **164**, 1173–1174.

Schneirla, T. C. The concept of levels in the study of social phenomena. In M. Sherif & C. Sherif (Eds.), *Groups in harmony and tension.* New York: Harper, 1953.

Scott, J. P. Observation. In T. A. Sebeok (Ed.), *Animal communication.* Bloomington: Indiana University Press, 1968.

Sebeok, T. A. Animal communication. *Science*, 1965, **147**, 1006–1014.

Sebeok, T. A. Discussion of communication processes. In S. A. Altman (Ed.), *Social communication among primates.* Chicago: The University of Chicago Press, 1967.

Sebeok, T. A. (Ed.) *Animal communication: Techniques of study and results of research.* Bloomington: Indiana University Press, 1968.

Sebeok, T. A. *Perspectives in Zoosemiotics.* The Hague: Mouton, 1972.

Sebeok, T. A., & Ramsay, A. (Eds.) *Approaches to animal communication.* The Hague: Mouton, 1969.

Sharman, G. B., Calaby, J. H., & Poole, W. E. Patterns of reproduction in female deprotodont marsupials. In I. W. Rowlands (Ed.), *Symposia of the Zoological Society of London,* 1966, **15**, 205–232.

Shorey, H. H. Behavioral responses to insect pheromones. *Annual Review of Entomology,* 1973, **18**, 349–380.

Simpson, M. J. A. Social displays and the recognition of individuals. In P. P. G. Bateson & P. H. Klopfer (Eds.), *Perspectives in ethology.* New York: Plenum Press, 1973.

Skinner, B. F. *Verbal behavior.* New York: Appleton, 1957.

Smith, F., & Miller, G. A. (Eds.) *The genesis of language: A psycholinguistic approach.* Cambridge, Massachusetts: M.I.T. Press, 1966.

Smith, W. J. Message, meaning and context in ethology. *American Naturalist,* 1965, **99**, 405–409.

Smith, W. J. Messages of vertebrate communication. *Science,* 1969, **165**, 145–158.

Sommer, R. *Personal space: The behavioral basis of design.* Englewood Cliffs, New Jersey: Prentice-Hall, 1969.

Sparks, J. Allogrooming in primates: A review. In D. Morris (Ed.), *Primate ethology.* London: Weidenfeld and Nicolson, 1967.

Staats, A. W. *Learning, language, and cognition.* New York: Holt, Rinehart & Winston, 1968.

Stebbins, G. L. *Processes of organic evolution.* Englewood Cliffs, New Jersey: Prentice-Hall, 1966.

Stuart, A. M. The role of chemicals in termite communication. In J. W. Johnston, Jr., D. G. Moulton, & A. Turk (Eds.), *Communication by chemical signals.* New York: Appleton-Century-Crofts, 1970.

Stürckow, B. Responses of olfactory and gustatory receptor cells in insects. In J. W. Johnston, Jr., P. G. Moulton, & A. Turk (Eds.), *Communication by chemical signals.* New York: Appleton-Century-Crofts, 1970.

Suga, N. Central mechanism of hearing and sound localization in insects. *Journal of Insect Physiology,* 1963, **9**, 867–873.

Tavolga, W. N. Visual, chemical and sound stimuli as cues in the sex discriminatory behavior of the Gobiid fish, *Bathygobius soporator. Zoologica,* 1956, **41**, 49–64.

Tavolga, W. N. (Ed.) *Marine bio-acoustics.* New York: Macmillan, 1964.

Tavolga, W. N. (Ed.) *Marine bio-acoustics.* Oxford: Pergamon Press, 1967.

Tavolga, W. N. Fishes. In T. A. Sebeok (Ed.), *Animal communication.* Bloomington: Indiana University Press, 1968.

Tavolga, W. N. Levels of interaction in animal communication. In L. R. Aronson, E. Tobach, D. S. Lehrman, & J. S. Rosenblatt (Eds.), *Development and evolution of behavior: essays in memory of T. C. Schneirla.* San Francisco: W. H. Freeman, 1970.

Tembrock, G. Land mammals. In T. A. Sebeok (Ed.), *Animal communication.* Bloomington: Indiana University Press, 1968.

Teuber, H.-L. Lacunae and research approaches to them. In C. H. Millikan & F. L. Darley (Eds.), *Brain mechanisms underlying speech and language.* New York: Grune and Stratton, 1967.

Thiessen, D. D., Friend, H. C., & Lindzey, G. Androgen control of territorial marking in the *Mongolian gerbil. Science,* 1968, **160**, 432–433.

Thorpe, W. H. The learning of song patterns by birds, with especial reference to the song of the chaffinch, *Fringilla coelebs. Ibis,* 1958, **100**, 535–570.

Thorpe, W. H. *Bird song: The biology of vocal communication and expression in birds.* New York: Cambridge University Press, 1961.

Thorpe, W. H. Animal vocalization and communication. In C. H. Millikan & F. L. Darley (Eds.), *Brain mechanisms underlying speech and language.* New York: Grune and Stratton, 1967.

Thorpe, W. H. The comparison of vocal communication in animals and man. In R. A. Hinde (Ed.), *Non-verbal communication*. Cambridge: Cambridge University Press, 1972. (a)

Thorpe, W. H. Vocal communication in birds. In R. A. Hinde (Ed.), *Non-verbal communication*. Cambridge: Cambridge University Press, 1972. (b)

Tiger, L. *Men in groups*. New York: Random House, 1969.

Tiger, L., & Fox, R. The zoological perspective in social science. *Man*, 1966, **1**, 76–81.

Tiger, L. & Fox, R. *The imperial animal*. New York: Holt, Rinehart & Winston, 1971.

Tinbergen, N. *The study of instinct*. Oxford: Clarendon, 1951.

Tinbergen, N. *Social behaviour in animals: With special reference to vertebrates*. London: Methuen, 1953.

Tinbergen, N. Comparative studies of the behavior of gulls (Laridae): A progress report. *Behavior*, 1959, **15**, 1–70.

Tinbergen, N. *The herring gull's world: Study of the social behaviour of birds*. New York: Basic Books, 1960.

Tinbergen, N. On aims and methods of ethology. *Zeitschrift für Tierpsychologie*, 1963, **20**, 410–433.

Walker, T. J. Specificity in the response of female tree crickets to calling songs of the males. *Annals of the Entomological Society of America*, 1957, **50**, 626–636.

Walker, T. J. Factors responsible for introspecific variation in the calling songs of crickets. *Evolution*, 1962, **16**, 407–428.

Wasserman, G. S. Invertebrate color vision and the tuned-receptor paradigm. *Science*, 1973, **180**, 268–275.

Watkins, J. F., II, Gehlbach, F. R., & Balbridge, R. S. Ability of the blind snake, *Leptotyphlops dulcis*, to follow pheromone trails of army ants, *Neivamyrmex nigrescens* and *N. opacithorax*. *Southwestern Naturalist*, 1967, **12**, 455–462.

Watson, M. O. *Proxemic behavior: A cross-cultural study*. The Hague: Mouton, 1970.

White, N. F. (Ed.) *Ethology and psychiatry*. Toronto: University of Toronto Press, 1974.

Whitten, W. K. Pheromones and mammalian reproduction. In A. McLearn (Ed.), *Advances in reproductive physiology*. New York: Academic Press, 1966.

Whitten, W. K., & Bronson, F. H. The role of pheromones in mammalian reproduction. In J. W. Johnston, Jr., P. G. Moulton, & A. Turk (Eds.), *Communication by chemical signals*. New York: Appleton-Century-Crofts, 1970.

Wickler, W. Socio-sexual signals and their intra-specific information among primates. In D. Morris (Ed.), *Primate ethology*. London: Weidenfeld and Nicolson, 1967.

Wickler, W. *Mimicry in plants and animals*. New York: McGraw-Hill, 1968.

Wilson, E. O. Chemical communication in the social insects. *Science*, 1965, **149**, 1064–1071.

Wilson, E. O. Chemical systems. In T. A. Sebeok (Ed.), *Animal communication*. Bloomington: Indiana University Press, 1968.

Wilson, E. O. *The insect societies*. Cambridge, Massachusetts: Harvard University Press, 1971.

Wilson, E. O. *Sociobiology: The new synthesis*. Cambridge, Massachusetts: Harvard University Press, 1975.

Wilson, E. O., & Bossert, W. H. Chemical communication among animals. In G. Pincus (Ed.), *Recent progress in hormone research,* Vol. 19. New York: Academic Press, 1963.

Wilson, E. O., & Bossert, W. H. A primer of population biology. Stamford, Connecticut: Sinauer Associates, 1971.

Wood-Gush, D. G. M. *The insect societies*. Cambridge, Massachusetts: Harvard University Press, 1971.

Wynne-Edwards, V. C. *Animal dispersion in relation to social behavior*. New York: Hafner, 1962.

2

Parliamentary Procedure
and the Brain

Joseph Jaffe

College of Physicians and Surgeons of Columbia University
and
New York State Psychiatric Institute

Parliamentary procedure, codified in *Robert's Rules of Order,* assures the efficient and equitable conduct of business by an assembly. It requires that only one person hold the floor at a time. Yet people who have something to tell one another could conceivably do so simultaneously. The fact that they don't suggested the following experiment.

While listening to a news broadcast on the radio, I began to tell an interesting story aloud. This "split attention" task yielded an eerie experience. When I tried to speak fluently, the broadcast was reduced to gibberish, like the babble of peripheral conversation at a large cocktail party. It was unquestionably speech but was as meaningless as a poorly understood foreign language. Conversely, if I made a concerted effort to follow the gist of the newscast, my own speech became halting and repetitious and I lost the thread of my story. Performance on this task did not improve with practice. Apparently, a listener cannot simultaneously be a speaker and vice versa; the brain cannot generate and decipher novel sentences concurrently.

"Novel" is a key word here, for there was indeed one way out of the bind. The newscast remained comprehensible provided my own speech was highly automatic and overlearned. Examples of such speech are simple counting and familiar nursery rhymes, both of which can be produced at a low level of attention. Receptive capacity is not "jammed" by these automatic sequences.

Another apparent counterexample to speaking–listening incompatibility is the phenomenon of simultaneous translation, in which the two activities indeed appear to proceed concurrently. Yet even this unusual skill is partly illusory. Henri Barik (1970) showed that the simultaneous translator attempts to make good use of the speaker's pauses to deliver his own version, so as to have more time to listen without having to speak concurrently. These findings were similar for all translators studied regardless of their proficiency level or the nature of the translation task. Such contrived experiments illuminate one of our most commonplace experiences; speaking–listening incompatibility is the biological foundation of politeness, which apportions the speaking time in conversations.

Two people in informal conversation share the available speaking time; when one takes a turn as the speaker the other synchronously becomes the listener. The sending and receiving roles remain neatly reciprocal, as if an invisible parliamentarian were presiding over the interchange, signalling switches of "possession of the floor." This interaction pattern is established early in childhood and is maintained by a complex and as yet poorly understood set of coupling rules. Like most dependable prescriptions for human conduct, they are noticed more in the breach than in the observance. The participants in verbal exchange dovetail their sending–receiving states so automatically that the switching mechanism is largely unconscious until the rules are inadvertently or experimentally violated.

One breach of the reciprocity rule occurs when both partners listen simultaneously, each waiting for the other to speak. If the ensuing silence is not broken within a reasonable length of time, the verbal conversation dies. Another breach occurs when both partners speak simultaneously. If the resultant interruption was inadvertent, one of the concurrent speakers falls silent within about .5 sec, leaving the other in possession of the floor. On the other hand, a purposeful interruption by an erstwhile listener may lead to a prolonged contest for the floor with a determined speaker. These common sense illustrations suggest the following principle. There are four possible configurations of a linguistic system composed of two persons (A and B): B listens while A speaks; A listens while B speaks; both listen; both speak. *Only the first two of these configurations are compatible with stable verbal conversation.*

The case of mutual listening is trivial, but why is joint speaking so intolerable? The simplest explanation of the speaking–listening incompatibility is that a common neural substrate is employed for both the production and comprehension of speech. Linguistic machinery functions as a unit. It can be biased toward speaking or listening, but it can't do both at once.

I became intrigued by the force of conversational expectancies 30 years ago, as a young psychiatrist trying his wings in Freudian psychoanalysis (Fig. 1). The technique of this therapy required the patient to recline on a couch and to verbalize, continuously and without censorship, all thoughts "that came to mind." To facilitate this state of "free association" the doctor sat behind the patient and adopted an attitude of passive listening, that is, refraining from all vocal response for periods of up to 50 minutes. The violation of social expectancies in the name of this technique included (1) the requirement for continuous monologue by the patient who was unable to see the doctor's facial

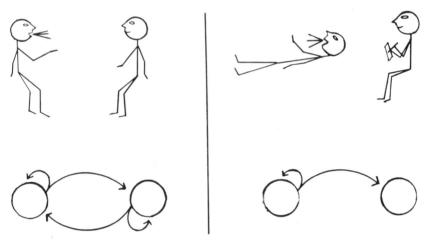

Fig. 1. On the left, a social conversation (above) and a flow diagram (below) showing the source and destination of *overt* vocal and gestural messages. Each participant can monitor himself and can send and receive messages. The system is "closed loop" in both senses. On the right, a psychoanalytic "conversation" (above) and its flow diagram (below). The patient can send and monitor himself but cannot receive; the doctor can receive but not send. The system is "open loop" (Jaffe, 1958).

expression or gestures and (2) an enforced inhibition of the doctor's customary verbal responsiveness. Thus, awkward silences in the patient's monologue were allowed to continue to the point of discomfort and questions were not answered. One purpose of these arbitrary maneuvers was to discourage conventional social discourse. This abrogation of the ordinary rules of conversational interchange made me poignantly aware of the precise social expectancies that were being frustrated. For example, the participants are not face-to-face, a situation we accept in telephone conversations but rarely in the physical presence of the other person. Another violation occurs when the patient demands a response, for example, by asking a question. While waiting for the answer, which may not be forthcoming, a mutual listening state may persist for many minutes before the patient's monologue resumes or the doctor encouragingly asks what thoughts "come to mind." Perhaps of greatest present interest is the speaker's deprivation of "listener feedback," both gestural and vocal.

Gestural feedback must be seen and includes all the body language now treated by the discipline known as kinesics. Such visual signals are highly redundant, as attested to by ordinary telephone communication and by the conversations of blind persons. In both, the information burden of the visual channel is completely assumed by the acoustic channel. Yet though redundant, some type of feedback is necessary. Purposeful omission of all vocal interjections by the listener in a telephone call is profoundly upsetting to the speaker, as anyone can verify in a few minutes.

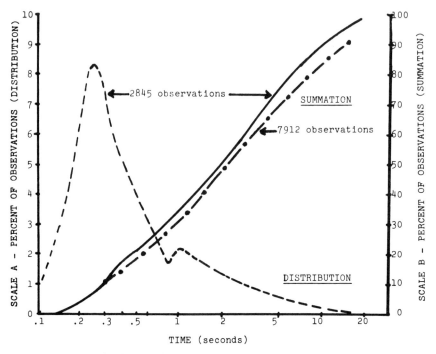

Fig. 2. Frequency distribution of the length of time between speaker switches (dashed line) and its summation (solid line). Redrawn from a pioneering study conducted almost 40 years ago at the Bell Telephone Laboratories by Norwine and Murphy (1938), who tabulated the durations of holding the floor. They defined the event as "speech by one party, inclu ling his pauses, which is preceded and followed, with or without intervening pauses, by speech from the other party." On the basis of 2845 such events they concluded, "Since most telephonic speech syllables are shorter than 0.3 second the modal value of .25-sec makes it clear that monosyllabic replies are by far the most numerous." It may be seen that these, in conjunction with terse replies or questions under one second duration, constitute about one-third of the events. More extensive data from our own laboratory on face-to-face conversations confirm this (7912 observations, shown as summation only, in a dot–dash line). The telephonic data from Bell Labs suggest that speakers who can't see their listeners should expect to hear a brief vocal interjection every 14 seconds on the average. In the face-to-face situation in our laboratory the rate drops to one every 18 sec since silent gestures probably substitute for some of the vocal ones. (Adapted with permission from *The Bell System Technical Journal.* Copyright 1938, The American Telephone and Telegraph Company.)

The gestural and vocal components of interjections are synchronized. For example, when the speaker pauses at the end of a phrase, the listener may nod and say, "I see." Vocal feedback includes all the snorts, chuckles, grunts, murmurs, and brief remarks that let us know that somebody exists at the other end of a telephone call while we are speaking. These interjections account for about one-third of the speaker switches in informal social conversation (Fig. 2).

Monosyllabic interjections by the listener are variously transcribed as "Hmmm.," "Hmmm!," "Hmmm?," "Yes.," "Yes!," "Yes?" and so forth. They possess a melodic, emotional quality, an average duration longer than that of syllables in polysyllabic speech and a time course matching the nonverbal gestures such as head nods with which they are synchronized. It is not generally realized that monosyllabic utterances are always stressed and that stressed syllables are always longer than unstressed syllables, even in polysyllabic speech (for example, MAry HAD a LITtle LAMB). Even when interjections take the form of stereotyped, polysyllabic, semisentences such as "I see," "Go on," "Too bad," "Indeed," "Really," "How's ABOUT that?" and so forth, the melodic contour alone virtually conveys the complete message in the absence of the articulated words (Fig. 3). Such mavericks of spoken messages, midway between speech and music, are generally banished by linguists to a wastebasket named *paralanguage, that is, nonlinguistic noises made with the vocal tract, which occur in a code situation between speaker and listener.* Research on paralanguage, as on kinesics, is in a rudimentary stage. Most attention to date has been directed to the utterances of the speaker rather than of the listener, for example, to the intonation contours of whole sentences, rendered orthographically as comma, period, and question mark at phrase endings. These features modify, quantify, or qualify the meaning of the sentence and partake more of the steady-state, melodic quality of vowels than of the transient, articulated quality of consonants. We now examine the

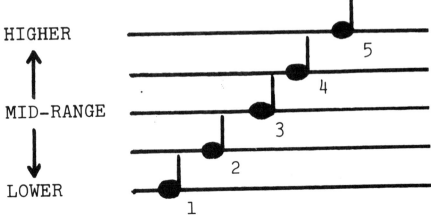

HIGHER

↑

MID—RANGE

↓

LOWER

Fig. 3. These are significant noises, occurring independently of language, that differ from one another only by the parameter of tone. In relative musical notation, they are labeled by numbers 1–5 as shown. Level 3 is variously written as ah, er, uh, hm, and is called a "hesitation vowel," signalling *Wait, I'm not finished* if produced by the speaker, or *Go on!* if interjected by the listener. A 3–4 sequence indicates assent and contrasts with a 3–5 sequence (*I thought so! I told you so.*). The 3–2 pattern signifies negation and contrasts with the 3–5 pattern (*Too bad! Sorry you hurt yourself.*). Adapted from an original analysis of the interjections called "vocal segregates" (Austin, 1972).

nature of the information conveyed by this qualitative dichotomy between "language" and "paralanguage."

For many years, degradation of speech signals by means of bandpass filtering has been a standard research technique. The effective range of the speech signal from about 30 to 12,000 Hz has been electronically dissected. When the *low* frequency range of the voice spectrum is rejected, intelligiblity of speech is preserved, but *biological* parameters such as the sex, age, and emotional state of the speaker are indeterminate. On hearing such filtered speech one is struck by the preservation of the crisp, high-frequency consonant information and the relative loss of low frequency vowel information. The impression gained is that of a sort of acoustic speedwriting, as would be produced if one could pronounce a text from which all vowel sounds were deleted. In contrast, when the signal is filtered to reject the *higher* frequency range of the voice spectrum, speech becomes unintelligible. Yet the emotional state of the speaker and the distinction of male from female and child from adult speakers is retained. Now the effect is that of hearing a murmured conversation, as through a thick door, perhaps the way a text from which all consonants had been deleted might sound if read aloud. Thus, the latter technique of low bandpass filtering has become an established method for studying the biological parameters of speakers such as maturity, sex, mood, state of alertness, and so forth, irrespective of *what* is being said but preserving information as to *who* is speaking and *how* they feel. Recalling our previous characterization of paralanguage in general, and listener's interjections in particular, as biased toward a vowel-like, steady-state, musical, emotional quality, one can characterize the results of these filtering experiments as a rough separation between the linguistic and paralinguistic aspects of spoken messages. The plight of a speaker who cannot see or hear his listener now becomes clearer. He is deprived of both paralinguistic and gestural feedback regarding the impact of his message. Is the listener drowsy, excited, bored, delighted, angry, confused, incredulous, depressed? Feedback of such information from receiver to sender "closes the loop" and permits ongoing modification of transmitted messages. Deprived of all feedback, a speaker is in an "open-loop" situation and can only guess at the quality of the human relationship in which he is engaged.

The placement of vocal interjections is never random. A fluent speaker has the option to pause briefly at phrase endings without sounding hesitant. Such "juncture pauses" mark syntactic boundaries in the speech stream and aid the listener in the decoding task. Investigators agree that listeners' interjections occur preferentially during such permissible pauses, hence the literal meaning of "interject" or the paralinguist's term "vocal segregate." Several years ago, Louis Gerstman, Stanley Feldstein, and I showed that a syntactic boundary with its characteristic intonation, especially in conjunction with a somewhat longer than average pause, is a powerful signal of a switching opportunity that virtually triggers the listener's response (Jaffe & Feldstein, 1970). About one-third of the latter are simple interjections of less than one second which "throw the conversational ball" right back to the previous speaker. To pursue the metaphor of parliamentary procedure, the listener has been briefly recognized by the chairman but the longer term sending–receiving configuration is preserved. An apt analogy might be a procedural "point of order" which when recognized by the chairman takes momentary precedence over the motion on the floor. The quality of an interjection signals the cognitive-emotional state of the interjector and also conveys the message that, having briefly said his piece, he relinquishes the floor. In the interchange some metacommunicative bookkeeping has been transacted, that is, an embedded message which calibrates the existential and/or biological state of the conversational system. This is familiar to users of one-way communication channels such as walkie-talkies. When a message ends with the question, "Do you read me? Over!", the listener replies, "Loud and clear, over!," whereupon the sender continues his substantive message.

What is the special quality of such procedural speaker switches? They have been characterized as primarily paralinguistic but their real explication requires us to delve more deeply into the neurophysiology of conversation. I shall argue that *cerebral hemispheric specialization in man has evolved under the selective pressure of efficient face-to-face conversation.* The proposed mechanism is a compulsory linguistic coupling of the left and somewhat more optional paralinguistic–kinesic coupling of the right "brains" (hemispheres) of speaker and listener, respectively. The net effect is the preservation of sending–receiving roles in the face of brief metacommunicative speaker switches.

Consider two brains confronting each other as in Fig. 4, and assume that both reside in right-handed persons, who comprise roughly 90% of the population. In general, the brain relates to the environment in bisymmetric crossed fashion. Each half of the brain can see, listen to, feel and act upon, primarily, the contralateral half of the environment. But when "the environment" consists of another person in face-to-face conversation a set of abilities come into play that are asymmetrically organized. Thus, when brain A is speaking and brain B is listening the *left half* of each is preoccupied with the same message. Brain A is encoding and transmitting; brain B is receiving and decoding.

Recent investigation has shown the two halves of the brain to be differentially specialized for the biologically significant sounds produced by the human voice. The left-brain, right-ear system is maximally sensitive to the rapid rhythm of spoken syllables, particularly those composed of the stop consonants b, d, g, p, t, and k. The right-brain, left-ear system is maximally sensitive to the slower rhythms of melodies and nonlinguistic vocal sounds such as coughing, laughing, and crying. Spoken vowels, intermediate between consonants and melody, are not preferentially lateralized. In addition, the system composed of the right-brain and left half of visual space (see Fig. 4) seems to be specially sensitive to movement, depth perception, facial recognition and emotional qualities. Most of these asymmetrical discriminations are present at birth or soon thereafter.

The realization by nineteenth century neurologists that the brain was asymmetrically specialized for speech was at first a static concept, that is, speech capacity was simply "located" in the left cerebral hemisphere. The crowning achievement of that fertile period was the dynamic approach of John Hughlings Jackson (1932). He proposed that speech is a continuum of activity ranging from stereotyped "automatic" forms at one end, carrying primarily emotional information, to more creative sentences that are original in their juxtaposition of ideas. The latter were characterized as "propositional" speech. His facetious illustration, "Thank God, I am an atheist!" was an attempt to illustrate both extremes of the continuum, the emotionally expressive expletive and the propositional assertion, which are not logically contradictory in this example in that they are not commensurate levels of discourse. He suggested different neural levels of speech organization, some under continuous cognitive control and others that are fired off "ballistically," that is, without detailed monitoring (closed-loop control) of their time course. The latter comprise stereotyped expressions, clichés, curses, expletives, swearing, and exclamations, all of which have the emotional quality of nonverbal, paralinguistic interjections. Such "automatic" speech was often preserved following left-sided brain lesions which interfered with more purposeful sentence production. These patients might say things spontaneously, in an emotional state of mind, that they could not repeat voluntarily out of the original context. Jackson's clinical insights have been amply vindicated by contemporary research.

Evidence for the continuum from emotional to propositional speech derives from studies of the control mechanisms of speech production. Continuous, or "closed-loop" control requires that the output be monitored and fed back to the generating mechanism. The extent to which this feedback is actually utilized for ongoing control varies. An alternative mode of control might be ballistic, or "open-loop," in which a complete sequence of instructions is issued to the speech musculature and runs its course without correction. One way to assess the degree of closed-loop control is to tamper with the feedback signal. A speaker literally listens to himself via air- and bone-conducted feedback, and it is technically simple to introduce a vocal–aural time lag. To the extent that control is closed-loop, the artificial delay will interfere with articulation. James Abbs and Karl Smith (1970) have shown that the right-ear, left-brain system is more affected by delayed auditory feedback than is the left-ear, right-brain system, an effect which they attribute to the susceptibility of consonants rather than vowels. Thus the right ear is engaged in monitoring the left hemisphere speech output, at least during the propositional speech which was tested. Richard Chase and his co-workers (1967) have shown that delayed auditory feedback has less of an effect upon the automatic speech that occurs, without awareness, during epileptic attacks than upon consciously produced speech. Still another index of the degree of self-monitoring is pausing during speech. Using this index, Donald Boomer and Alan Dittmann (1964) have shown that filled pauses decrease when speech is produced spontaneously without excessive deliberation whereas they increase when the speech task is rendered highly self-conscious and therefore less automatic. It is additionally significant that about 60% of all possessions of the floor in social conversation contain no pauses whatsoever. These include all the replies under one second in duration, which we have characterized as metacommunicative or procedural speaker switches, attesting to their automatic, stereotyped quality.

If the left brains of both speaker and listener are saturated by the linguistic processing of the conversation, do their right brains remain available for the kinesic and paralinguistic phenomena that calibrate the emotional quality of the conversation? Intriguing support for such speculation has recently been provided by Doreen Kimura (1973). She found that right-handers actually use their right hands more *during speaking,* but not during listening. These gestures are listener-directed and tend to synchronize with the primary stress of phrases, which occur about one per second. In effect, the right hand acts as a conductor, beating the phrase rhythm on which the 3 per second syllable rhythm is superimposed. Such gestures are often seen by the listener and it is instructive to ask, "Where are they seen?"

The gaze fixations of listeners are fortunately more constrained than the roving gaze of speakers. Most investigators agree that a listener's eyes are usually fixated on the speaker's face (Fig. 4). This finding establishes the listener's fixation point and permits the conclusion that the speaker's right-hand gestures are confined to the listener's left-visual-field, right-brain system. The same

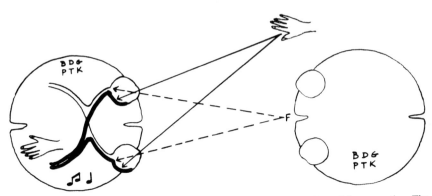

Fig. 4. Confrontation between speaker (right) and listener (left) in aerial perspective. The listener's fixation on the speaker's face (point F and dotted lines), establishes a stable optical geometry such that the images of the speaker's gesturing right hand and right half-face both project to the listener's right cerebral hemisphere. This results from the fact that the right half of each retina connects to the right half-brain (heavy lines). It is of interest that a stroke that interferes specifically with the "speaking role" also paralyzes the right hand and right half of the face in 80% of the cases. In contrast, this paralysis pattern occurs in only 20% of the strokes that specifically interfere with the "listening role."

system is known to be specialized for facial recognition, and Brenda Milner (1962) has implicated the right hemisphere in the perceptual discrimination of tonal patterns.

What biologically significant purpose could be served by such arrangements? The *speaker's* right ear is primarily engaged in monitoring his own ongoing speech; it would seem an efficient scheme to have his left ear tuned to the procedural, paralinguistic interjections of the listener. The *listener's* right ear is engaged in selecting the properly linguistic syllables of the speaker for decoding; it would seem an efficient scheme to have *his* left ear tuned to the intonational aspects of the message (Blumstein & Cooper, 1974). The time course of intonation contour is that of the phrase structure, which is also the rhythm of the speaker's right-hand gestures in the listener's left-visual field. That these paralinguistic and kinesic patterns should both arrive in the listener's right brain seems only fitting. The net effect of such hypothetical mechanisms would be the linkage of right brains for kinesic and paralinguistic rhythms just as left brains are coupled for linguistic temporal sequences. The hypothesis has testable consequences.

This mutual illumination of physiology and ordinary conversation is curiously applicable to the communication disturbances resulting from brain disease. Here we focus upon the left hemisphere exclusively. Discrete brain damage is produced when a clot forms in an artery, cutting off the blood supply to part of a hemisphere ("stroke"). The resultant communication disturbance, known as *aphasia,* occurs in two extreme forms depending on the location of the damage in the left brain (Geschwind, 1972). They can be characterized as *disorders of the speaking role and of the listening role,* respectively. Documented cases in the neurological literature reveal the coexistence of both disorders in the same individual (Brain, 1965; Lhermitte *et al.,* 1973).

We have seen that the speaker's role in a conversation imposes an output bias on the linguistic system such that speech input is jammed. Phrases are fluently generated by the motor apparatus of the left brain under continuous control of the receptive apparatus of that same hemisphere. Occasional pauses between phrases anticipate paralinguistic interjections by the listener, the quality of which may be processed by the speaker's idling right brain. Finally, the left hemisphere activation during speaking entails a rhythmic gesture of the right hand which is synchronized with the phrase rhythm. When left-brain damage produces a disorder of the speaking role, the patient seems to be *locked in the listening role of conversation.* He comprehends rather well. Although there is minimal paralysis of the muscles of articulation, speech is slow, labored, and is produced in short phrases. In the severest forms, the phrase may consist of a stressed monosyllable with prolonged vowel, such as "Yes" or "Damn," formally reminiscent of a listener's paralinguistic interjections. In less severe forms, initial unstressed syllables of words such as "untie" or "define" may be dropped. When normally unstressed grammatical parts of speech, such as articles and prepositions, are omitted the output may read like a telegram. That these patients monitor themselves accurately is attested to by their overt frustration and suffering with their dysfluent articulation and by their emotional depression. Finally, the frequent paralysis of the right hand and right half of the face in these patients renders the normal gestural accompaniment of the speaking role, beamed to the listener's right hemisphere, inoperative.

In contrast, the normal listener's role biases the linguistic system toward reception, with output confined to brief vocal interjections accompanied by head nods. The motor apparatus is subordinate to the perceptual process and its output is suppressed. When left-brain damage produces a disorder of the listening role, the patient seems to be *locked in the speaking role of conversation.* That is, he has difficulty comprehending speech although there is no deafness in the acoustic sense. He seems to have lost the ability to monitor his own speech as well, since word and/or syllable sequences exhibit destructive permutations which render them incomprehensible. We infer defective self-monitoring from the fact that these patients may be charming conversationalists, cheerfully unaware that their spoken messages don't make complete sense. They make little attempt to correct their obvious errors and, if frustrated by the communication breakdown, the frustration is not with themselves but with the listener for not comprehending. The rhythm, melody, and grammatical phrasing of speech is preserved, as is the fluency of articulation in spite of the disorganized sequencing. Inasmuch as paralysis of the opposite half of the body is infrequent in these cases, right hand and facial gestures are normally synchronized with the primary stress of the spoken phrases.

The analogy should not be pushed too far; these polar forms of aphasia are admittedly caricatures of normal speaking and listening roles. However, they do underscore the necessary interplay of these states which temporarily lock two brains into complementary configurations during normal conversation.

There has been much speculation as to why man is left-brained for handedness and speech, a specialization which must have evolved, at least within the primates, because of some selective advantage. The thrust of current theory is to invoke social and emotional determination as preferable to geographic and technological explanations. From this viewpoint, it is apparent that the sensorimotor systems that maximally dispense with symmetry in the available neural layout are precisely those that subserve face-to-face conversations. Most serious speculation postulates some sort of protoconversation which long preceded the presently evolved form. If not completely gestural, such predecessors were conceivably highly ritual, co-actional, paralinguistic, and musical; perhaps involving cheers, prayer, work songs, incantations and the like. Such displays are usually highly redundant and the matching of rhythms therein is often functionally more important than the content of speech. If only information processing efficiency were at issue as the biological utility behind speech lateralization, that asymmetry would be equiprobable, half left and half right. The same argument applies to right hemispheric specialization for slower rhythmic and spatial processing, etc. However, a congruence of left speech dominance and right spatial dominance would confer an additional advantage upon certain matched individuals as a consequence of the interpersonal geometry presented in Figure 4.

In summary the sheer fact of hemispheric specialization is explained by division of labor in the service of efficient processing of information, linguistic by the left; paralinguistic and kinesic by the right. Interpersonal geometry further suggests why such specialization should optimally be the same for conversing individuals. Perhaps the evolutionary question is better rephrased, "Why is the pattern of specialization the same for most people?" One might imagine that some random "initial kick" toward our own asymmetric pattern conferred a selective advantage upon such individuals when engaged in face-to-face conversation.

ACKNOWLEDGMENTS

Supported in part by a general research support grant from Research Foundation for Mental Hygiene, Inc.

REFERENCES

Abbs, J. H., & Smith, K. U. Laterality differences in the auditory feedback control of speech. *Journal of Speech and Hearing Research,* 1970, **13**, 298–303.

Austin, W. M. Nonverbal communication. In A. L. Davis (Ed.), *Culture, class and language variety.* Urbana, Illinois: National Council of Teachers of English, 1972, 140–169.

Barik, H. C. Some findings on simultaneous interpretation. *Proceedings of 78th Annual Convention of American Psychological Association,* Miami Beach, Fla., 1970.

Blumstein, S. & Cooper, W. E. Hemispheric processing of intonation contours. *Cortex,* 1974, **10**, 146–158.

Boomer, D. S. & Dittmann, A. T. Speech rate, filled pause and body movement in interviews. *Journal of Nervous and Mental Disease,* 1964, **139**, 324–327.

Brain, W. R. *Speech disorders.* Washington, D.C.: Butterworths, 1965.

Chase, R. A., Cullen, J. K., Jr., Niedermeyer, E. F. L., Stark, R. E., & Blumer, D. P. Ictal speech automatisms and swearing: Studies on the auditory feedback control of speech. *Journal of Nervous and Mental Disease,* 1967, **144**, 406–420.

Geschwind, N. Language and the Brain. *Scientific American,* 1972, **226,** 76–83.

Jackson, J. H. *Selected writings.* London: Hodder and Stoughton, 1932.

Jaffe, J. Communication networks in Freud's interview technique. *Psychiatric Quarterly,* 1958, **32,** 456–473.

Jaffe, J., & Feldstein, S. *Rhythms of dialogue.* New York: Academic Press, 1970.

Kimura, D. The asymmetry of the human brain. *Scientific American,* 1973, **228,** 70–78.

Lhermitte, F., Lecours, A. R., Ducarne, B., & Escourolle, R. Unexpected anatomical findings in a case of fluent jargon aphasia. *Cortex,* 1973, **9,** 436–449.

Milner, B. Laterality effects in audition. In: V. B. Mountcastle (Ed.), *Interhemispheric relations and cerebral dominance.* Baltimore: Johns Hopkins University Press, 1962.

Norwine, A. C. & Murphy, O. J. Characteristic time intervals in telephonic conversation. *Bell System Technical Journal,* 1938, **17,** 281–291.

Part II

COVERBAL BEHAVIOR:
Gestural, Facial, and Visual

3
The Role of Body Movement in Communication

Allen T. Dittmann

National Institute of Mental Health[1]

When we think of body movements as communicative events, most of us are likely to get rather dramatic in our fantasies. A phrase that comes readily to mind is "body language," and there has even been a book from the popular press with that phrase as its title (Fast, 1970). The topic has everything: the hope of reading the romantic intentions of one's girl- or boyfriend, the adventure of outsmarting a shrewd salesman, the sure thing of predicting the next move of a poker-faced gambler, the surprise of "reading through" the white lies of one's friends, the advantage of knowing what a prospective employer wants to hear.

Everybody knows, of course, that these fantasies are fantasies, that nobody can make himself invisible and listen in on forbidden conversations. And yet there is a lot of truth in the notion that people communicate in many different ways, by words, by tone of voice, by facial expressions, by body movements, by the use of the physical space between one person and another, even by certain psychophysiological responses like blushing and speed or depth of breathing. We are constantly reading each other, or trying to, using all the information we can get, and we can get it from a lot more sources than just the words that pass between us. The question for this chapter is whether all these sources of information can properly be called language, and what difference it might make if they could or could not be. The particular behaviors the chapter will concentrate on are body movements. There are many other communication media, such as facial expressions, and the principles by which this analysis is organized are general ones and could be applied to those behaviors as well.

The first thing to do in deciding whether any given set of behaviors is a language is to agree on what a language is. That will be the first task of the

[1] Now at United States Office of Education.

69

chapter, spelling out some useful criteria for categorizing body movements as either language or not language. It turns out that there is no handy sharp dividing line for this dichotomy, but there are still some good guidelines, and there won't be much difficulty in applying them.

Next, two genuine languages that use body movements will be described in terms of these guidelines. One is in common use today: the sign language of the deaf. There are many remaining unknowns about this language, but the version of it used in the United States, American Sign Language, is currently under study by a number of linguists, and there are many "native speakers" of it available when examples are needed. The other body language included in this chapter is the sign language used by American Indians to communicate with people from other tribes who had different spoken languages. This language is not common today, and what we know about it comes from historical documents and from the memories of quite old men.

With the principles and examples of body languages at hand, the chapter can then take up what we ordinarily mean by body language among the hearing, to learn to what extent we use these behaviors as a medium of communication, and to what extent they can serve as dependable sources of information about people.

THE NATURE OF LANGUAGE

Dependability is the hallmark of language. This may seem like a strange statement. When we think of dependability in language the first things that come to mind are the exceptions: words can mean more than one thing; sentences are often unclear as to referent; speech is sometimes so garbled with false starts and "ahs" that it's hard to tell what the person is talking about. But for the most part we get along fine with our language as a means of communicating. We use the context of the conversation to figure out which meaning of the word is intended and what the sentence is referring to, and we are very forgiving of the difficulties people have casting their thoughts into words—after all, we are all up against the same problems when it is our turn to speak, so we virtually don't hear most of the hesitations and tongue-slips and other fumblings that mess up the King's English (or whatever language we are speaking) as people talk in day-to-day conversations.

Language is as reliable as it is because there is an agreement, for the most part an unwritten one, about what words mean and how they are to be fitted together. In short, language is a code used by speakers and listeners to communicate whatever it is they need to get across to each other: "pure" information, orders and requests, feelings, instructions, and on down the line. The term "code" as it is used here refers to the final result of three parallel processes, simplifying the original material, organizing it so that the relationships among its elements can be clear, and restructuring the whole for easy transmission.

Simplification. The original material in the case of language consists of thoughts and ideas and all the rest of the things we need to communicate. Just what thoughts and ideas really are is beyond our present knowledge, but we know that they must be some neurophysiological processes or configurations of such processes in the central nervous system. The first step of coding, simplifying, means concentrating on the topic to be conveyed, casting aside irrelevancies, or eliminating noise so as not to confuse the listener. This is done by classifying what one is thinking about into categories so that we will be talking in terms of concepts rather than raw impressions. Our words refer to these general concepts, not to particular experiences the concepts might describe. As a result, words we use lack many of the nuances of our original thought and impressions. The great linguist, Edward Sapir (1921), wrote eloquently of this process, using the category "house" as his example:

> The elements of language, the symbols that ticket off experience, [are] associated with whole groups, delimited classes of experience rather than with the single experiences themselves. Only so is communication possible, for the single experience lodges in an individual consciousness and is, strictly speaking, incommunicable. To be communicated, it needs to be referred to a class which is tacitly accepted by the community as an identity. Thus, the single impression which I have had of a particular house must be identified with all my other impressions of it. Further, my generalized memory or my "notion" of this house must be merged with the notions that all other individuals who have seen the house have formed of it. The particular experience that we started with has now been widened so as to embrace all possible impressions or images that sentient beings have formed of the house in question. This first simplification of experience is at the bottom of a large number of elements of speech [pp. 12–13].

So collapsing all those individual experiences of "house" into one category is the essence of simplifying our thoughts.

The idea of categorizing in language is applied not only to words but to the sounds that make up words, and here the procedure is even more clear because the number of categories is so small. The words and sentences of all languages are made up of sequences of a few sounds, or phonemes (see Brown, 1958, pp. 27–50). Needless to say, there are exceptions and complications to this rule, but speakers and listeners believe that it is true, and act on it all the time. To analogize from written language, we can spell any word in our language with the few letters in our alphabet. English speech uses about 35 phoneme categories, plus or minus a few depending on dialect, and we can say anything in English using only the sounds that fall into those categories. And the categories are not only finite in number, but also sharply delineated so that there is no overlap between them in our "mind's ear," even though the differences between some of the pairs may be quite small from the standpoint of the physics of sound.

Simplifying and categorizing is one characteristic of all codes. In the case of language, very complicated material is handled by the system, and often we must be able to express the nuances and the individualized impressions that the simplification has eliminated. How do we mange to do that? We do it by adding as modifiers other categories that refer to those nuances, like "Victorian" or "white-chimneyed" to "house." Using another concept or two helps recover some of what was lost, and has an added advantage: since the modifying categories have also been tacitly agreed upon and are used commonly by all speakers and listeners, we end up being able to express ourselves very precisely. It is thus a characteristic of coded material that the information density in the final result is very high. True, each category is a simplification of many impressions, but a number of categories can be used in a short time period, and a speaker can depend heavily on his listener's sharing the meaning of what he wants to communicate.

Organization. If a number of categories are to be used to explain and modify and include all the nuances, however, there must be some way of keeping track of everything, of making clear what the relationships are among all of the categories. Every language has a set of rules and regulations for this purpose, namely the syntax or grammar of that language. The information about organization is conveyed in many ways in each language, and in an even wider variety of ways from one language to another—special words, suffixes and prefixes, word order, pitch changes, and so on. No language could possibly do without this sort of information. It tells us which are the main categories and which the modifiers, how smaller elements are combined into larger units, and those in turn into still larger ones, how these units are to be related to each other, when one sequence ends and the next one begins, and a host of other things.

Restructuring. The final characteristic of a code to be considered here is that of restructuring, and that consists of assigning some communicable labels to the categories and structural elements. The original categories and the ways they are related to each other, remember, are patterns of neurophysiological events in the speaker's central nervous system, and those are invisible and inaudible to others. They must be recast into some form or symbol that can be communicated, one symbol per configuration so as to avoid confusion. In language as we ordinarily think of it, the symbols are groupings of sounds, and the restructuring is carried out by unbelievably complex instructions to the vocal articulators to produce those sounds.

Throughout this description of what a language code is, there has been repeated reference to agreement among the members of the language community about the various aspects of the process. A bit more explanation of that agreement is due now that the elements of the process have been outlined. It would make no sense for a person to develop a coding system all for himself except for personal record-keeping. The result would certainly serve no function in communicating anything to anyone else. Every step of a coding system must be shared, be agreed upon by at least two people, and language systems are used in common by many more people than that. Where language communities number into the millions, some aspects of the agreement become fuzzy, so that there may be pockets of misunderstandings based on regional differences, social class differences, occupational differences, differences in degree of formality, and the like. Within each of these subcommunities, however, agreement will be high. Even across the subcommunities, there will be enough agreement for useful communication—especially if there is a sort of additional agreement to avoid the areas of disagreement, to stick to basics. No communication is possible without community.

Summary: Some aspects of the nature of language as a code. Codes, in the sense that language is a code, are agreed-upon systems in which:

1. The thoughts and ideas we wish to convey are simplified and grouped into categories.
2. These categories are organized so that the relationships among the categories can be clear.
3. The results of these processes are restructured into symbols of a form that can be communicated from one person to another.

To the extent that any communication system is a code in this sense, a great deal of information can be transmitted from sender to receiver in a short period of time with great dependability. In short, codes make for very efficient communication.

TWO BODY LANGUAGES

So far in this chapter, spoken language has been the prime example of a coded communication system. It is certainly the most common one, since most people have all the apparatus to produce and receive it, as well as the social surroundings to learn it. There are a few, however, who lack either the apparatus or a common speech community, and cannot use speech as their medium of exchange. This does not mean that they are without any means of communicating or that the means they use is not language. This section of the chapter will use two such languages as examples, one the sign language of the deaf, and the other the system by American Indians to communicate across tribal (and therefore language community) barriers. The former is a more complete linguistic system than the latter, for reasons that should become clear as the two are described.

American sign language. The fact that deaf people do not use speech to communicate with each other is not news. The obvious reason is that the receiver cannot hear what is spoken to him, but the more subtle reason is that hearing people learn to adjust their vocal apparatus to produce the sounds and combinations of sounds they hear other people producing, and lacking the sense of hearing, deaf people do not know either what sounds to imitate or how successful they are in their imitations. Many deaf people have been taught to speak and to read lips, but the process is laborious, and the resulting speech usually doesn't sound quite right, even though in many cases it is very usable in communicating with hearing people.

But the need to communicate is as great among the deaf as among the hearing, and many systems have been devised for this purpose over many centuries in all parts of the world, using the hands as the source mechanisms and the eyes as the receiving apparatus. Since there are comparatively few people who use these methods of communicating (profound deafness is relatively rare), few hearing people have learned them, the chief exceptions being those who have deaf family members and professionals who work with the deaf. So deaf people and their communication system are set apart and have often been viewed with suspicion, even persecuted. And those prejudices do not simply belong to the unenlightened past, but persist today: since they have difficulty speaking and reading (because writing is based on speech), deaf people do not do well on academic and ability tests designed for the hearing, and are often labeled as intellectually retarded. In addition, the dominant language community, English speakers in this country, assumes that its language is the only true one, and that different ones are not simply different, but inferior. Thus, American Sign Language (ASL) is looked down upon by those who do not understand its structure, and some version of English using a few signs and fingerspelling (a one-to-one hand configuration-to-alphabet letter set) is ordinarily insisted upon in schools, both for the deaf and for hearing people who wish to learn to communicate with the deaf. The result is that most deaf people are taught to deprecate ASL, to deny that it is a "true language," to claim that it "has no grammar," and to say that it is "incorrect." Those same people, however, use the true ASL in casual conversation with each other, and to communicate with their children.

There is a frightening parallel between this situation and that of Black English: the same attitudes prevail toward both and are held both by the dominant language community and also by the users of the special language themselves. In actual fact, both ASL and Black English have different origins than standard English: ASL is more closely related to French because it was imported from France, but it developed in this country quite rapidly so that it is now quite different structurally from both French and English; Black English came from Africa through European traders of slaves and other "merchandise," and has features of both African and European languages in addition to English. Thus the deaf comprise a true minority group so far as their language is concerned and everything that follows from it. As a group they are unfairly discriminated against. It is not an accident that many deaf people are able to understand the problems that Blacks have in the United States from having lived through very similar experiences.

Of all the manual communication systems throughout the world today, we know most about the one used by the deaf in the United States, ASL.[2] The reasons for this greater knowledge are many: the rapid growth of interest in linguistics in this country over the past 15 years, in which a wide range of language and other cognitive processes have been examined; the increased breadth of educational efforts geared for people with all sorts of handicaps; the fortunate positions of certain specialized institutions such as Gallaudet College, a Federally sponsored college for the deaf. Consequently, ASL is coming to be regarded by more and more people as a language in its own right, not as an incomplete communication system that limits the intellectual accomplishments of its users.

American Sign Language starts where every language starts: its users simplify their thoughts and ideas, boiling them down to a set of commonly used categories to be communicated from person to person. The form of the communication is peculiar to ASL: it consists of hand positions, configurations, and movements, each a set of agreed-upon categories in the same sense that the phonemes that make up the syllables of speech are for any given language; these are put together into symbolic representations of concepts parallel to words, and arranged in sequences according to syntactic rules. The result is that ASL, like all languages, can serve to express anything that a user of the language wishes to express or that any user of any other language can express.

The easiest part of the language for a nonuser to understand is the way signs are made and what they "mean" in another language. There have been identified 12 hand positions (such as at the forehead, mid-face, or some position related to the other hand), 19 configurations (mostly identified by their similarities to letters of the alphabet or to numbers in fingerspelling), and 24 movements (such as vertical, sideways, interactional), and one of each of these is used in combination to form any given sign. The numbers of positions, configurations, and movements should not be considered precise at this stage in our knowledge, because detailed study of ASL is not yet complete. Furthermore, the very list is itself more complicated than mere numbers might lead one to expect, because of the possibility of combining elements of the three factors. For example, the left hand in one configuration may serve as the position for the right hand in another configuration to relate to. In short, the number of concepts that ASL may refer to is very large, many times that of the vocabulary in common use today. In addition, facial expressions, gaze direction, and other elements of "body English" can specify, add nuances, and even contribute to the content of being

---

[2] Stokoe's work, applying the methods of structural linguistics to ASL, has formed the basis for this section (*see* Stokoe, Casterline, and Croneberg [1965] and Stokoe [1972]). Harry W. Hoemann read this section very carefully and kindly sent thoughtful notes which have helped make a more realistic description of ASL.

signed. The face can be more a part of sign language than of spoken language for an obvious and important reason: in speech many facial muscles are in movement simply in the course of articulating the speech sounds, so that many expressive facial movements are interrupted by the very act of speaking. In signing, on the other hand, all of the facial muscles are continuously available to the signer in contributing to his communication. Many people claim, in fact, that they "watch the face" of the signer and see the manual elements out of the corner of their eyes.

A given sign, then, is a combination of position, configuration, and movement. A hand is formed into one of the configurations at a particular location with respect to the signer's body (or other hand), and moved in a certain way. In the sign for *good*, the right hand is flat with fingers together, palm in; this hand first touches the fingertips to the lips, and then moves forward and down ending with its back placed in the palm of the left hand. In *college* the two hands are flat and in front of the body, right hand palm to palm over left. The sign begins with a hand clap, then the right hand circles counterclockwise just above the left.

Many signs have histories that make them seem like pantomines, such as the sign for *girl*: the right hand is folded except for the thumb, which is left extended; the thumb is brushed across the right cheek, beginning almost at the ear and moving toward the chin. This originally referred to the ribbon under the chin for an old-fashioned girl's bonnet, so in this sense it is pantomimic, but by now that movement is so abbreviated that all pictorial representation has been lost—and anyway, why should one indicate a chin ribbon with one's thumb? A number of other signs originated with the fingerspelled initial letter of the English word as the sign was invented, rather like abbreviations, for example the "V" hand used to sign "vinegar." But V also begins the English words "vacation," "valuable," and so on, so initial letters cannot be distinguishing marks for many signs. In short, signs in ASL, whatever their origins, become arbitrary inventions to refer to concepts, just like words in speech. It may be that there are more pantomimic signs in ASL than there are onomotopeic words in spoken English, because many signs were invented quite recently and the picturelike quality of some of them has not yet disappeared in the regularization process, but those would probably amount to only a small proportion of the total vocabulary. Only a handful of ASL signs could be guessed correctly by a nonsigner.

The structure of ASL is difficult to understand, because the terms of grammar we are accustomed to using in analyzing spoken languages often do not apply in the same way to ASL. One fundamental reason for this situation lies in the basic difference in dimensionality of the two types of language: in speech the smallest elements of the code are strung together one after the other, whereas in signs they are superimposed upon each other simultaneously. It is as though speech had one dimension, that of the line, whereas signs had four, those of the three dimensions of space plus time. In addition, the signer can add to the elements of his code a good deal of other information: he can indicate comparatives and superlatives by emphasis either of the speed or amount of space devoted to the movement elements; he can add personal pronouns and demonstratives by head and eye movements (so can the speaker, as discussed further, below, but these elements are more regular parts of signing), and so on. Thus what is called a single sign, with all this additional material, is often more than the equivalent for a word in English speech, and may be more comparable to the stem plus endings that make up the words of a language like Latin. In some cases a sign is even equivalent to an English phrase or brief sentence.

Thus, ASL operates differently from spoken language, and specifically from English, the dominant language of the country where it is used. The nature of those differences makes it appear to English speakers that ASL is deficient, since it lacks a number of features that are regularly used in English: it has no endings to indicate tense, number, or grammatical class—indeed the same sign can be used for the "noun" form and the "verb" form of the same concept, like "a dance" and "he danced;" ASL has no articles, nor does it have a copula (*is, are,* and other forms of *be*); it does not use the auxilliary verb *do* to form negatives and past constructions or to emphasize, and so on. The functions contributed by these various forms are not absent, but the forms themselves are not needed in ASL for a sentence to be a proper sentence in that language. If we look at spoken languages from a larger perspective than English, we find that ASL is not so unusual in any of these respects. Many languages do not use endings to words for grammatical structure. Many others have no articles or copula. Those that lack one or another of these features are not deficient as compared with those that have them; they are only different.

In spite of the very different structure of ASL, there are broad similarities to English in the way its larger units are arranged. Where subjects and predicates call for separate signs, they generally follow the same order in ASL and English. Indirect and direct objects also follow English order, and so on. There are also similarities to the original French: adjectives often follow the nouns they modify. So structure is expressed in different ways than it is in English, but it is still true structure. It provides the organization for individual signs in the same way that all coding systems take care of organizing their elements. Thus, the first two processes in coding are present in ASL: the original thoughts and ideas are simplified by classifying them into agreed-upon categories, and a system of organization helps keep track of the relationships among the categories. The third process, restructuring the resulting categories into communicable form, is achieved in ASL by casting them into combinations of specified visible forms of body movements rather than the audible forms used in speech. The specified forms comprise in their turn a set of agreed-upon categories of hand positions, configurations, and movements similar to the set of phonemes that each spoken language specifies for its community of users. In short, ASL is a body language that really is a language.

Indian Sign Language.[3] The American Indians had a very different motivation for developing a sign language than deaf people have: they needed to
communicate with people who did not share their spoken language, so as to be
able to trade with them and carry on other intertribal business, and later on to
deal as a large group with the encroaching white man. As individuals growing up
in families they were not dependent on some visible method of communication,
for they could hear and therefore speak—or like us, the vast majority of them
could. So these were people with fully developed spoken languages who set
about inventing an auxilliary language to be used across the language barriers
that existed between tribes.

We know very little about the origins of Indian Sign Language (ISL) for the
same reasons we know so little about the distant background of any language.
By the time missionaries and soldiers began making notes about it, the language
had already been in use for some time. The claim that ISL's history is not very
long, that it came into being only when the whites began invading Indian lands,
seems on the face of it unlikely, since the language would have had to develop too
rapidly to be believed. In addition, the development of sign languages for
communication among neighboring tribes is not unknown elsewhere in the
world. One such language on which research is now beginning is the system used
among the widely diverse peoples of Australia.

We might expect that ISL, being used as an auxilliary means of communicating
for rather limited purposes, would be quite primitive and capable of expressing
only a few ideas. To some extent that expectation is indeed borne out: its
vocabulary is not very large, and some aspects of its structure are quite simple.
The surprising thing about ISL, however, is that it appears to be a complete
language in the same sense that spoken language and ASL are: one can express
virtually anything in it, although one would have to take some roundabout
means in some cases.

The signs that make up ISL are combinations of 40 referents (these include
positions plus pointing to people and directions), 18 hand configurations, and 24
movements. Not all of these elements are used very often, especially not all the
referents, but they are all possible. So the total of the frequently used elements of
signing in ISL is not much different from that of ASL. Some of the referents,
configurations, and types of movement are the same as those of ASL, or at least
very similar, and some are quite different. This should not be surprising for the

---

[3] Mallery's monograph (1881) is perhaps the most important historical document on ISL,
and it has recently been reprinted. Tomkins (1926) made up a manual of ISL for Boy
Scouts that is very valuable. West's dissertation (1960), available in photocopy from
University Microfilms of Ann Arbor, Michigan, analyzed ISL using structural linguistics and
drawing data from living informants. ISL is used in specialized circumstances today, since
English serves as the *lingua franca* in intertribal business. Certain ceremonies and demonstra-
tions are about all that remain as occasions for using ISL, and in most of them the signers
give running translations in English.

same situation obtains in the case of any two spoken languages. In English and French, for example, the "n" sounds are for all practical purposes identical, but English has no sound similar to the French "u," nor French to the English "r." The point is that both languages, English and French in the case of spoken languages, and ASL and ISL in signed languages, have their own set of agreed-upon categories of elements with which their users make up the larger units of the languages.

The ideas that are expressed in ISL are the same as those expressed in any other language: thoughts, feelings, or whatever, that are basically neurophysiological processes in the central nervous system. These are simplified and regularized, as they must be with any language, into an agreed-upon set of categories to be expressed. The number of categories appears to be somewhat smaller in ISL than in ASL, although no complete inventory of them has yet been developed. And the simplification does not seem to have gone as far for most concepts in ISL as it has for those in ASL, for the signs that express them are a good deal closer to pantomine, as if the users still had some doubts about whether their intentions might be mistaken. Some 98% of ISL signs are of this form, according to one estimate (West, 1960, Vol. I, p. 29). Such elaborate pantomiming means that each concept needs more time to be cast into ISL, with the result that it is more cumbersome and slow than ASL for the same material. Finally ISL wastes time by failing to utilize one whole communication channel: the ideal signer is quite stolid as to facial expression while signing. Although signers are probably not as poker-faced as this ideal would dictate, many nuances that ASL routinely conveys in facial behavior are either lost to ISL or must be expressed in some other way.

Being pantomimic might lead to the expectation that almost anyone could understand the signs. But the regularization has gone too far for that. "Non-speakers" of the language can guess correctly only somewhat fewer than half of the signs when they are given out of context with plenty of time for guessing, and fewer than that when a conversation is under way and the next signs keep coming along. The fact is that there was a good deal of boiling down of concepts and agreement on how the signs for them were to be formed, agreement on what were the "essential" aspects of each idea that should be made the basis for its sign. Since the language was used with neighboring tribes only, some slight differences developed as to what those essential features were when communicating with different neighbors. Under these conditions, dialects had a good chance to develop. Indeed, there was one area where differences were slight, namely that of the Great Plains, and a dropping off of mutual intelligibility to the East, West, and South.

So the concepts themselves were agreed upon along with their signs, at least within a broad geographical area, but how about the way they were organized? Was that also subject to agreement so that anyone would know how a signer was relating one concept to another in connected discourse?

The structure or grammer of ISL, like that of ASL, is difficult to study in the same terms that apply to spoken language, so we do not know as much about it. Apparently the internal structure of the signs was a lot more tightly knit than the external: the way each sign was to be formed was strictly dictated, while the order in which any sequence of signs was to be presented was not. Within broad limits and with only four exceptions, the order of signs within an utterance was determined more by the style of the signer, by convenience, and by the broader line of the narrative than by anything we might consider grammatical or syntactical relationships. ISL, like ASL, is a multidimensional language, so that each sign may contain structural information, unlike individual "words" in English speech. It is in the formation of each individual sign that the grammatical rules lie, and these were apparently very strict. Thus the order of signs in an extended string was not a necessary contributor to information about how the concepts were organized. The four exceptions were the signs for beginning and ending a long utterance or narrative, the sign for questions, and the sign for negation. The first two are self-explanatory. The question sign came before the group of signs, indicating that a question was to follow. The negative, on the other hand, came at the end of the group that was to be negated.

The two processes of regularizing ideas and organizing them, the first two necessities of a coding system, are thus present in ISL, although to a lesser extent than we are used to in other languages, including ASL. It is lesser in the regularizing in that the process does not go so far as it does in other languages, most of the signs being pantomimic in character. And it is lesser in organizing in that the rules of relating one sign to another, by order or any other method, appear looser in ISL than in other languages. The third process, that of presenting the categories in some form communicable to others who are in the language community, has been worked out quite precisely in ISL, partly by the strict internal rules of organizing the elements of form and movement within the signs as they are portrayed, and partly by the pantomimic character of the signs themselves.

Summary: Coding as applied to bodily expression. The two languages, ASL and ISL, are really codes in the same sense that spoken languages are codes. They are different in the extent to which the information they convey has been subjected to the total process of coding, but they are still codes. In both cases, ideas have been boiled down, organized, and presented in ways that both the signer and the viewer have come to a tacit agreement about, so that when a string of signs comes along the two people can both know what the original idea was. The viewer does not have to guess, and the signer can be confident that he has really communicated. This description is an ideal, of course, for we all know that there are slips—the boiling-down leaves out nuances, the organization does not eliminate all ambiguities, and the means of presentation is not absolutely exact—but the system still admits of considerable precision. The users of both languages can depend on that precision quite securely as they do their daily business communicating with each other.

BODY LANGUAGE: IS IT A CODE?

From languages using body movements as their medium to "body language" as that term is used so often today, is a long step. When we talk about body language, we do not mean that we really carry on conversations through our bodies about any and all topics, but rather that there is more to conversation than an audio tape or a typescript of the words could tell us. We mean that people express themselves in all sorts of ways, sometimes adding to, sometimes—and this is the interesting part—altering or negating what they are saying in words. When we say we are "really reading" someone, we mean that we are tuned in on all of these wavelengths. Sometimes that is good, when we are feeling really at home with a friend, and sometimes it makes us uncomfortable, when the messages we feel we are getting do not add up to a very friendly total atmosphere.

But how dependable are these messages, in the sense that language is a dependable method of communicating? That is the question for this section of this chapter. To answer it, the best set of concepts is that of coding: to the extent that the source information for any system of communication is coded and the elements that make up the messages are also coded, the result is precise communication. Conversely, to the extent that the material has not been subjected to the coding processes, we are left guessing about what the messages really are. To anticipate briefly, there are a few body movements that behave like coded material in that they are easily understood by all or most members of the community. By far the greater majority of movements, however, serve more as cues from which we make inferences. If all the cues add up right, our guesses from these messages can be very good ones, but usually we don't have time for much inferring if we are to keep up with the conversation, and besides, because of the way our perceptual apparatus works, our attention in conversations is drawn to decoding the speech.

First a word about a couple of other interlocking issues. Usually when we talk about "communication" we are referring to situations where one person is deliberately sending messages to one another. He *intends* to do so, and his intentions are fully conscious. Those two characteristics, in fact, are part and parcel of many writers' definitions of communication. But the very idea of body language as it is usually thought of, especially when it refers to cues from which we infer something about a person, precludes both awareness and intention as necessary features of the process. Indeed, some of the stuff that these messages are made of, such as fidgetiness or generalized muscular tension, could not be controlled even if we intended to do so. Others, like posture and how often we look at our conversational partner, are so automatic as to be out of our usual range of consciously thought-out activities. Therefore, the term "communication" will have to take on a more general sort of meaning for the rest of this chapter. It should not be dropped as a term, however, because the messages in question are still messages whether they are deliberate ones or not: they still consist of information of some sort that is transmitted from one person to another. Both the deliberate messages and not-so-deliberate ones should obey the same laws and be accounted for by the same concepts and theories. So communication is still a good word to cover *all* messages that pass between us.

In order to examine the various movements that comprise body language from the standpoint of coding, one of the basic concepts introduced earlier needs to be spelled out more precisely: the one of categorical information. It came up first in connection with the simplifying and regularizing process we use in boiling our thought down into concepts. Information that has been treated this way is called discrete information. It comes in separate, distinct packages that do not overlap each other, and these are usually of a finite, countable number. This sort of information has another characteristic, too: the packages recur again and again, and are made up of roughly the same elements in the same configuration each time they reappear. In short, they become categories to which some community of people may assign labels or meanings. In the case of simplifying thought processes for use in language, we form our thoughts, ideas, and impressions into categories to be used over and over again, and the language community agrees to stick to those categories or concepts as their medium of exchange, and name them with words or signs.

The opposite of discrete information is the continuous, in which there may be an infinite number of values distributed along a continuum, each one shading into the next one imperceptibly. One of the features of continuous information is that it can be made artifically discrete by dividing the continuum into step intervals as we do every day in stating our age. No adult ever gives his age in steps any finer than the year unless he is specially asked to, and we have much broader age categories where we do not require the precision that years can give: baby, child, teenager, young adult, and so on. Everyone knows, of course, that these categories are artificially imposed on what is really a continuum, that not all eight-year-olds are the same age. We know, too, that the apparent nonoverlapping character of the age categories is illusory, that some pairs of eight-year-olds are more different in age than some pairs made up of an eight-year-old and a nine-year-old. But for most practical purposes a finer distinction is not needed: we know roughly what is meant by "an eight-year-old child."

In dealing with body movements there is another use of the two terms, discrete and continuous, and that is how movements appear in time. Some are performed discretely—the head nod is a good example—that is, they are brief movements that begin and end suddenly and are sharply separated from the

movements that precede them and also from those that follow. Other movements are continuous over time—like one hand stroking the other—and are not
seen as different events in time but rather as an activity that spans some period
of time.

This difference between discretely performed and continuous movements has
two features that are important to understand in the discussion that follows:
First, continuous movements cannot sensibly be made into discrete categories
simply by dividing them into step intervals. We might divide them, all right, at
the changes in direction of continuous stroking, for example, but there would be
no meaningful way of naming the resulting categories. On the contrary, we may
more easily transform discretely performed movements into continuous information, both as we notice them in social situations and also as we study them in the
laboratory, by counting their frequency of occurrence over some period of time.
We may then use the results of our counting to make such statements as, "John
nods more frequently when talking to Mary than he does when talking to Tom."

The second thing to note about the use of continuous and discrete in talking
about movements is that not all discrete movements are necessarily categories of
movement. The head nod is both: it is performed discretely, and it is recognized
as a category of movement whose meaning is agreed upon by members of the
language community. In answer to a question that calls for a "Yes" or a "No," a
nod means "Yes." In conversations, listeners insert nods from time to time, and
while their meaning is not quite so specific, they are still very wordlike,
interchangeable with "M-hm," "I see," and so on. Thus the head nod is both
discrete and categorical. Many other discretely performed movements, however,
do not make up categories that any group might agree has any meaning. Some of
the gesticulations that accompany talking, such as those that seem to punctuate
the rhythm of speech, are a good case in point. They are usually performed
discretely in time, have distinct beginnings and endings, but most of them do not
fall into nameable categories. They can be counted, as nods can, and their
frequency used as continuous information, and this is the most common way
these movements have been dealt with in research studies.

With all the necessary concepts finally at hand, the discussion may now
proceed with an examination of body language as a code.[4] It follows the same
general outline as the last section, but differs from it in one major respect. The
two sign languages, ASL and ISL, are true language systems, both coded,
although one is somewhat more completely coded than the other. The task for
this chapter was simply to describe them as examples of coded systems. In the
case of body language, on the other hand, it is not so clear that there is a code,
or if so, what aspects of it the code applies to, and to what extent. We must

---

[4] The consistency and accuracy of many points in this section have benefitted greatly from
discussions with Daphne Bugental, Paul Ekman, Wallace Friesen, Karl Heider, Maureen
O'Sullivan, and others during a workshop held at Ekman's laboratory in June, 1973.

therefore be more cautious in our approach to describing body language, examining each feature carefully to see if it could be a part of a coded system.

The elements of body language. In describing ASL and ISL, it was possible to enumerate all the elemental movements, positions, and configurations of the hands that make up the larger groupings called signs. The elements, and the larger groupings as well, are discrete and categorical in nature, agreed upon by the language community. In body language it is not clear that there exists any set number of elements of this sort: perhaps some movements or postures could be thought of as proper elements, while others could not. This discussion will leave the question open at the outset by listing those behaviors that have been studied by various researchers, and treating them as candidates for elemental categories. No claim for completeness is made, because of the practical considerations researchers must weigh in deciding what to study: they want to study what they think is important according to the theoretical ideas they hold, but they also want some assurance of success, and they may be tempted to stick to things that will be easier to handle with the techniques they already have available. Most investigators also include items that others have studied, partly because there may be alternative theories that may thus be put to the test, and partly as a check on their methods. The most likely candidates for elements in a body language system will be listed here first, the discrete, categorical behaviors, then some that are less likely, and so on down the line.

Discrete Behaviors

Categorical Behaviors

Emblems[5] are the most eligible of the discrete, categorical behaviors. They are *the* movements that have meaning and may be translated directly into words. In some parts of the world, such as Mediterranean countries, a quite complete system of emblems has been worked out and has been used for centuries by people who can hear perfectly well. Some of the stories of these gesture languages may have been exaggerated by the astonished (and artistically gifted) visitors who have described them, but clearly those people's gesture vocabulary enables them to carry on conversations far beyond the bounds that American speakers of English can do with anything but words. Mallery (1881, pp. 295–296) quotes Alexandre Dumas recounting two narratives he observed in Sicily and southern Italy, where he had an opportunity to check independently on

---

[5] The term "emblem" was used by Ekman and Friesen (1969), who used it to refer to "those nonverbal acts which have a direct verbal translation, or dictionary definition, usually consisting of a word or two, or perhaps a phrase. This verbal definition or translation of the emblem is well known by all members of a group, class, or culture [p. 63]." Ekman and Friesen credit Efron (1941) with proposing the term, although he used it in a more restrictive sense as those symbolic acts that had no relationship between their form and meaning, that is, that were not at all pantomimic.

what the Italian translation was. Efron (1941) describes emblems used by southern Italian immigrants to New York City, and the republication of his work includes a short dictionary of these gestures.

We are not entirely lacking in emblems but their number is probably not large. Many are highly pantomimic so that it would be difficult to decide if they are truly symbolic emblems—if indeed anyone had already decided that only the symbolic could qualify as emblems. The hitch-hiker's movement for thumbing a ride, for example, when it is used in its usual context, does not require an interpreter of some strange language to translate. Circling the ear with the index finger to say, "He's crazy!" on the other hand, has no obvious movement-to-words connection. Just how many emblems we have is not known precisely, although a survey is currently being made,[6] nor is there any information on how frequently they are used in comparison to other movements day by day. A number of facial expressions other than those of emotion are emblems, and the emotional expressions themselves, may be used as emblems—the surprise expression, for example, to refer to an experience of surprise. Whether the actual facial expressions of emotion are emblems is a moot point since they seem to be biologically determined (Ekman, Friesen, & Ellsworth, 1972). Certainly they function as emblems in daily life.

A related sort of movement, probably used more commonly, is referred to by Birdwhistell (1967) as the *kinesic marker*. These movements mark some aspect of the speech that is going on at the same time, such as head movements to indicate the person in a group to whom the speaker is referring in some part of his utterance (similar to ASL but not so precisely defined). Other such markers may serve as place holders in presenting contrasting ideas, to accompany "On the one hand . . . while on the other . . . ," and the like.

Eye contact (for an extensive review, see Ellsworth & Ludwig, 1972) may seem an odd behavior to include in a chapter on body movement, but one of the best ways of identifying it in a research situation is by observing the accompanying head movements: one usually turns his head to look at another person (if the two are not squared off to begin with, and people in our culture seldom place themselves that way), and if one is looking at another, he is usually looking in his eyes. Since people do not maintain eye contact for long periods at a time, the beginning and end of each contact can easily be told, and the behavior qualifies as discrete. Since it is repeated the same way each time, it is a categorical behavior.

The *smile* is an unmistakable facial behavior that has a sudden onset and usually a slow fade, and is usually of short enough duration to be called a discrete event. Smiles are not all the same, and there may be some subcategories that could be identified, although this work has only begun. One possible subtype is the listener smile (Dittmann & Llewellyn, 1968, p. 83), which has

[6] John Johnson, working with Ekman and Friesen (personal communication, 1973).

both sudden onset and sudden fade and appears to be another equivalent to the head nod and brief vocalization ("m-hm," etc.).

The *nod* is a discrete, categorical behavior whose dual meanings ("yes" and "m-hm") were mentioned earlier in this section. There may be other categories of nod, based perhaps on number of movements, but these, along with other smiles, have not been studied sufficiently for any definite statements at this time.

These three discrete, categorical behaviors, eye contact, smiles, and nods, lend themselves to forming continuous variables by counting their frequencies over longer periods of time. Most research studies concentrate on these frequencies, and people in social situations probably do, too: one notices that a friend is smiling a lot more today than last week, or a lot less, and so on. In addition, eye contact can be treated as a continuous variable by measuring the duration of each contact, or by totalling the duration of contact in a larger time period.

The *head shake,* meaning "no," usually occurs only in answer to questions that demand either a "yes" or a "no," and since those questions are rather rare, so is the head shake. The movement may also be seen in an almost continuous form in some people under some circumstances, such as during the expression (in words) of a strongly positive attitude: a person may say, "There was really beautiful photography in that movie," while shaking his head continuously.

Two postures that are discrete and categorical round out this part of the list: *arms akimbo* (or hands on hips) and the *open–closed positions of arms or legs* (hands and arms apart and knees separated for open, and arms crossed or folded and legs crossed for closed). There is some question about whether these should be called elements in the same sense as those listed above, since there are many ways of striking these poses, but the variations are not great, and they do fall into definite categories. The akimbo posture is probably rare except in the standing position.

Noncategorical Behaviors

The *gesticulations accompanying speech* are perhaps the best examples of this kind of movement, as mentioned earlier. They are hand movements, usually of small extent (although in some cultures they are quite extensive), brief, and appear to follow the rhythmic structure of the speech they accompany. They are thus discretely performed, with definite beginnings and endings. Whether they are categorical is another matter. The pattern of the movements may be quite repetitive for a given individual, or there may be a limited number of patterns a person uses, but no research results show that these patterns fall into categories that any community of people agree upon as elements for assignment of meanings. Rather, most of them appear to be formed almost randomly.

The location of these movements in the stream of speech has been the subject of two research efforts. The results show that many of the speech-accompanying gesticulations are tied to the location of hesitation forms in speech that Boomer describes in Chapter 8 (Dittmann, 1972a). And many of them begin and end with the onset and completion of units of utterance (Kendon, 1967)–Kendon discusses many more details of these issues in his chapter.

In social situations we probably notice gesticulations mostly by their frequency, and researchers have followed that lead. Number of movements per minute, per experimental condition or whatever, can be determined many ways such as by counting them in actual experimental sessions or from movies or video tapes of those sessions, by measuring muscle potentials, by attaching miniature accelerometers, and so on. The resulting numbers are distributed continuously, even though they are made up of discrete events.

Posture shifts, such as changing position in the chair, crossing and recrossing the legs, and the like are discrete movements, again made up of many possible elements and notable chiefly by their frequency over some longer period of time.

Possibly Discrete and Categorical Behaviors

These are all variations of posture and position, and the variables on which they are measured are certainly continuous. Yet it appears that the continua are divided into step intervals just as age was seen to be, in the explanation of discrete and continuous information at the beginning of this section. The result is a set of categories within each of the behaviors.

Forward and backward lean may be measured in degrees of the trunk from the vertical, a measurement that is obviously on a continuum. But as we interact with people, we cannot discriminate between slight differences in number of degrees, and we do not need to for the most practical purposes. We need only to be able to say that a person is sitting upright, is leaning forward or leaning backward. We may go further than that in some cases, saying that he is leaning slightly forward, way forward, and so on, but these are still discrete steps made of an underlying continuum. The fact that they are so easy to name indicates that they are treated as categories.

Distance between persons is also clearly a continuum, but it, too, is commonly divided into discrete step intervals, again perhaps only three: too close, comfortable distance, and too far. Just where the dividing lines are between these intervals depends on the sex and age composition of the group of people involved, and on the culture they come from (see Watson, 1970).

Body orientation means the angle formed by imaginary lines drawn through the shoulders of two people interacting. If they are facing each other squarely the angle is 0°. The usual conversational angle is a little less than 90°. It is not so clear for this variable, as for the two listed above, that discrete steps are made by people in ordinary, day-to-day situations, but it may work something like distance in that very low angles are too close and at some point beyond the right angle it becomes too distant.

Continuous Behaviors

These are intrinsically continuous over time, not discrete movements made into continuous variables by counting how often they occur. *Adaptors*[7] are often intrinsically continuous movements, such as stroking an arm or a leg, playing with a pencil, rubbing one hand with the other, squeezing the fingers of one hand in the other, moving the hands back and forth over the arm of a chair. While these movements, like all others, have beginnings and endings, we tend not to notice those features, and in research many such movements seem most meaningfully measured in terms of their duration. Some take on the appearance of fidgetiness, but just now people in social situations notice them—or if they do at all—is not known.

Rhythmical movements of various parts of the body are also performed continuously. They include foot swinging (usually with legs crossed), foot tapping, finger drumming, and a number of others.

There are a number of other continuous movements that have not been studied specifically, but which may be noticeable in social situations. Certain movements of the feet comprise one group, flexing, turning, and the like; sometimes these movements are almost invisible because the person is moving his toes inside his shoes. Turning back and forth in a swivel chair or rocking in a rocker, when those chairs are present, make up another group.

The organization of body language.   In the description of languages so far in this chapter, organization has been an easy topic, because the elements of those languages are arranged very systematically into the groupings that make up their words and signs, with relatively little variation permitted in the total configuration for each. Emblems probably behave in about the same way, although they have not been studied enough for anyone to say for sure. Neither do we know whether they occur frequently enough to be considered an important part of body language in the usual sense of that term. Other than emblems, there appear to be only a few groupings to talk about. Chief among these are postures: in the arms akimbo and the open—closed positions, a total of elements adds up to what the viewer interprets as one of those positions. But the way the elements are arranged is quite variable. In arms akimbo position, the hands may be open or made into a fist, the hands may be rotated forward or backward, and they may be placed toward the front or the back just so long as they are vaguely on the hips, and so on. For any of these variations, a number of viewers would agree that the person is standing "with arms akimbo." The open—closed positions can be made up of even more variable elements.

---

[7]These movements have been studied by several investigators who began their work on them independently and called them by different names: body-focused movements (Freedman & Hoffman, 1967); self-manipulations (Rosenfeld, 1966); and adaptors (Ekman & Friesen, 1969).

Some of the acts listed above under discrete, categorical behaviors might be considered groupings, since they contain more than one movement—the head nod, for example—but those constituents are so few that to talk about organization into a larger grouping seems like over-formalizing things. This is not to say that there may not be more than one kind of nod, depending on the details of the constituent movements, but we need a good deal more research on these details before we can differentiate among such acts in a useful way.

Most of the organization of body movements we ordinarily think of as making up body language is determined by the organization of the concurrent speech. As we talk, we divide up our stream of talk into packages of a few words, and these are marked by rhythmical features like recurring stresses toward the end of each unit and a characteristic slowing down as the unit is finished. The organization of these units is made up of the syntactic rules, or grammar, of the language (see Boomer's chapter "The Phonemic Clause: A Speech Unit in Human Communication," in this volume). Many body movements follow this unit formation, as if the fact of speaking were a powerful determiner of much of what the speaker does at the same time. When the speaker looks at his listener, and how he changes his line of regard (and also the direction his head is facing); when he inserts the kinesic markers to indicate who is being referred to, to emphasize one topic or another, or whatever; when he initiates the more random-appearing gesticulations—all these are tied to the rhythm structure of the speech that the movements are accompanying. Even larger movements such as posture shifts appear to be related to larger speech units like change of topic, beginning or ending of longer utterances, and so forth. These units of speech in turn are related to the way the speaker sorts out his thoughts, organizes them, and forms them into words. Thinking on one's feet while talking in conversational situations lays the groundwork for all sorts of "nonverbal behavior." It is nonverbal in that it does not consist of words, but it is directly influenced by the very act of talking (see Kendon, 1972).

A different organization related to speech concerns the mechanics of changing speaker turns from one person to another (see Duncan, 1972). A large number of behaviors is involved in this system, from the rhythmical packaging of the speech itself and the concomitant grammatical structure to changes in eye contact (or head orientation), to certain gesticulatory behaviors and a number of others.

In the descriptions of other languages in this chapter, one of the easily recognizable features of words and signs was that they referred to concepts that members of the language community had agreed were to be used to represent their various thoughts, ideas, feelings, and impressions. In the case of body language, some of the acts and postures have similar referents, and it will be instructive to go over the list again to see what the nature of those referents may be. Again, research findings will be the basis for the interpretations.

Among the discrete, categorical behaviors, emblems clearly have the most specific referents. Some of them are truly arbitrary, just as words are, and their referents may vary from culture to culture. The airman's sign for "A-OK," for example, used by United States astronauts and seen worldwide on television, is interpreted in some quarters as an obscene gesture. There are probably not more than a dozen or two of these arbitrary emblems in common use in the United States today. Many more of obvious pantomimic origin, the hitchhiker's thumb, for example, or the index finger to the lips for "shhh!" have referents that are just as specific as the arbitrary emblems. The movements that Birdwhistell (1967) has termed "kinesic markers," referred to above, should probably also be included among the emblems as having quite specific reference. Whether all of these should be considered parts of body language as that term is popularly intended is an open question.

The two main functions of nodding, the signal that the listener is keeping up and the specific "Yes" substitute, have already been mentioned. Frequent nodding, when this movement is thus made into a continuous variable, would seem to be a sign of friendliness (Fretz, 1966), but it has not always turned out that simply in research studies: it seems also to be the *result* of a friendly atmosphere (Rosenfeld, 1967). Frequent smiling definitely indicates a wish to be friendly and to be accepted by the other person (Fretz, 1966; Rosenfeld, 1966), a finding quite in line with anyone's expectations. Eye contacts are timed in conversation to help regulate whose turn it is to talk: a person who is about to begin talking will look away from his conversational partner, and he looks back toward the end of rhythmical units of speech as if to seek the feedback that an "m-hm" or a nod would provide (Kendon, 1967). The total length of time that a person looks at another during a conversation is associated with several variables: women look more than men, people attracted to each other look longer, extraverts look more than introverts, and so on (see Ellsworth & Ludwig, 1972, for these and related findings). Staring at another is an upsetting stimulus, possibly an aggressive one (it is definitely aggressive in other mammals), from which the recipient will usually wish to escape (Ellsworth, Carlsmith, & Henson, 1972).

The two postures, arms akimbo and the open position of arms and legs, are used by people interacting with others of lower status. In addition, the akimbo position is more likely when one is with someone whom one dislikes.[8] Forward lean, as might be expected, occurs more among people who like each other. A more complicated pattern has been found with both distance and body orientation in ordinary conversational situations: one feels more comfortable at a

---

[8] These interpretations are based on an experiment (Mehrabian, 1968) where subjects were asked to imagine how they would act under different circumstances and may thus have encouraged responses that subjects felt were expected of them in addition to natural behaviors.

greater distance and greater angle of orientation when dealing with a disliked person; he can be closest and oriented at the most direct angle with a neutral person, and somewhere in between with someone he likes.

Discretely performed hand movements (the gesticulations accompanying speech) are organized according to their relationships to speech rhythms. As mentioned above, they occur more frequently at times when the flow of speech is interrupted by hesitations, "ahs," retraces, and other fumblings (Dittmann, 1972a; Dittmann & Llewellyn, 1969). These nonfluencies are far more frequent than we realize, since the listener very kindly edits them out as he tries to follow what the speaker is saying. So nonfluent passages have more gesticulating associated with them than the fluent. When these movements are treated as continuous information by counting them over longer periods of time, they take on another, less specific meaning. A person who gesticulates a great deal may be seen as having Mediterranean background, where people are known to gesticulate a lot, for example, or if his family is obviously not from one of those countries, as being nervous and high strung. He may also be under some strain at this time of his life or in this particular social situation or at this specific moment Dittmann, 1962; Sainsbury, 1955.

Among the behaviors called possibly discrete, organization does not play much of a role since the behaviors are not made up of constituent parts in the same way as arms akimbo. The meaning is fairly clear and similar for all of these behaviors: people who lean forward toward their conversational partners, who stand close (but not too close for comfort), and who face squarely (but not completely so) are seen as friendly and warm.

The truly continuous behaviors are even less specific as to meaning. One does not know for sure, for example, if a person engaged in adaptor movements, such as stroking one hand with the other, is upset right now in this immediate situation or if he is inclined to move this way all the time. The same applies to rhythmical movements like swinging the feet and drumming the fingers. They provide information that must be interpreted in some way, not information that carries its own interpretation as discrete categories of behaviors like words and signs do.

As a matter of fact, this differentiation of the sort of information given by continuous and discrete behaviors may be applied to the whole list of movements given in this exposition of body language. The discrete, categorical movements, those that were listed as the most likely candidates for elements in a body language system, were also the most specific as to "meaning," in that the members of the community agree on what they refer to. They are thus the items with the highest information density. As the list progressed toward continuous behaviors, or as discrete behaviors were treated as continua by counting their frequencies over longer periods of time, more broadly probabilistic statements had to be made and phrases like "is associated with" began to crop up. The information density of these types of movement is lower. And these behaviors turn out to constitute most of the movements we see in social situations such as conversations.

With a few exceptions, then, we cannot look at a person's movements and know definitely what they mean in body language, the way we can see a series of signs in ASL and know the concepts they refer to. We must rather make probabilistic statements about them. If there are enough movements to yield enough probabilistic statements, we can feel more satisfied with our accuracy. In short, we can observe movement cues and make inferences from them about what is going on in the person we are observing, about what he is feeling, what his intentions are, and so on. These inferences cannot be couched in very specific terms, the way one might paraphrase what someone has said—that is, the precision of the conclusions we can draw from our inferences is not very high—but they can still serve us quite well in dealing with others day by day.

The conclusion in the last paragraph implies that the probabilistic statements were made up from individual, isolated events, like unconnected lists of words rather than sentences. But the topic for this section of the chapter is organization in body language—is there no organization into larger chunks of meaning here, comparable to the sentences of spoken language or ASL? From what is available in current thinking and research, the answer to that question would have to be "No." People "say" things about themselves in body language, but not in the form of statements that could be part of any discourse. What they say, or what is available to others to "read," has a certain unity to it, to be sure, in that it does not consist of isolated events, but the interrelationships come from the basic state a person finds himself in at any given time, from which all his behaviors derive, not from the connectedness of any syntax such as that which relates words together in sentences.

By stretching a point one could find a few systematic relationships: for example, eye contact and distance are inversely related, probably because of the implications both have for intimacy (for a review of several experiments, see Argyle & Ingham, 1972). A sort of balance is struck, apparently such that if two people are standing or sitting very close to each other, they look at each other less than they would from a greater distance. In the case of emblems, usually more than one is needed to get a point across: letting someone know of a mock astonishment at hearing a piece of gossip might entail producing the "surprise" facial expression followed by a wry smile. But longer discourse could take place only under the most artificial circumstances even with emblems and probably not at all with other sorts of movement. Finally, the relationships among all of the behaviors that are involved in changing speaker turns (Duncan, 1972) include messages in body language. These messages do not make up any discourse in and of themselves, but rather contribute to a larger system of social interaction.

Summary: Body language as a limited system of communication. In this section I have examined body language from the standpoint of its membership in the family of coded communication systems, and found it to qualify in only a few of its features. Discrete behaviors, performed in much the same way each time they appear, like emblems and a few postures, have meanings that everyone in the language community can agree upon. Most movements are not of that type, however, and they take as their organizing principles either the rhythmical structure of the concurrent speech, or their association with the state of being of the person, either long-term or situationally influenced. We use these less specific behaviors as cues to make inferences about those states in the person, and the success of those inferences varies with a number of factors. Extended discourse in body language, parallel to that possible in spoken language or ASL, does not seem to occur.

THE PAYOFF:
HOW MUCH DO WE USE MOVEMENTS TO "READ" PEOPLE?

The conclusion that body language is only a limited method of communicating may be a disappointment, but it should not come as news, to return to the first paragraphs of this chapter. It should also not be construed as a death-knell for body language, for we do take in movements as we interact with other people, and we do make inferences from them. The question of how much we use them cannot be answered fully at this stage in the development of the field of social interaction because virtually no research has been done on that aspect of the problem. Still, some quite well-informed speculations can be made even now, and as long as they are recognized for what they are, as speculations, they can serve very well until more facts come in—even guide research efforts to find those facts.

The speculations derive from another field of psychology, that of perception, and more specifically from the thinking and work of D. E. Broadbent.[9] He found that what gets through our perceptual apparatus, or what we attend to, depends on a number of features of the stimuli before us, as these relate to a specific characteristic of the perceptual apparatus itself. This characteristic is its limited capacity to handle information. It can deal with so much and no more. When we say that we cannot attend to two things at once, that is only partly true: what we cannot do is exceed the capacity of the system. Given two stimuli, the apparatus gives preference to (1) the one whose information density is the higher, and (2) the one with the greater intensity.

The application to conversations is clear: the speech we hear, being of high information density, plus any of the more highly coded body language events, are likely to get through at the expense of any other less completely coded activities that may be going on at the same time. The intensity feature becomes a

---

[9] Broadbent's original research had as its focus the problem of the interference of signals coming in from various planes in an aircraft control tower. For an explanation of the application of his thinking to human communication, see Dittmann (1972b, pp. 156–161).

leavener that allows body language material to pass the perceptual apparatus. Noncoded body language events that are intense enough will override the attention demandingness of the coded. Or a long succession of them can add up suddenly and make an impression, when for some reason attention becomes available.

The reasons attention might become available are many. There are fairly frequent lulls in conversations during which we do not need to concentrate on decoding the speech of the other person or on encoding into speech what we are trying to say. In addition, the conversation is not always about something we are eager to hear about, so we find our minds wandering. Likely, the wanderings take us to preoccupations from earlier times or to plans for what we are going to do next, but attention could turn at those times to the less densely packed information in body movements. And we need not simply become bored to have attention available for lower information messages: some topics of conversation are inherently more difficult to grasp, and demand a good deal of brain power of all sorts, while others are much simpler, and some parts of most people's talk about them are highly predictable. The amount of attention paid to body language, then, varies from moment to moment, and we get intermittent chances to glimpse at the lower information movements from which we might make inferences about the people with whom we are dealing.

These are fairly solid lines of speculation about how body language can serve as communication, even those aspects of it that have relatively low information density. Very little of it can be read as specifically as the words and signs of the more completely coded languages, but often we do not need that degree of specificity: if we keep observing, hard as that may be when we are trying to keep up with a conversation, we will find more such messages and be able to get more out of the total communication situation. We may even be able to train ourselves to be increasingly alert to body language, though there are no research results yet available that would tell us how successfully we could do so. Perhaps that should be the next step for researchers to take.

ACKNOWLEDGMENTS

Derek C. Hybels gave considerable assistance during the preparation of this chapter, both in searching the literature and in finding meaningful trends in the many results.

REFERENCES

Argyle, M., & Ingham, R. Gaze, mutual gaze, and proximity. *Semiotica,* 1972, **6**, 32–49.
Birdwhistell, R. L. Some body motion elements accompanying spoken American English. In L. O. Thayer (Ed.), *Communication: concepts and perspectives.* Washington, D. C.: Spartan, 1967.
Brown, R. *Words and things.* Glencoe, Illinois: Free Press, 1958.
Dittmann, A. T. The relationship between body movements and moods in interviews. *Journal of Consulting Psychology,* 1962, **26**, 480.

Dittmann, A. T. The body movement–speech rhythm relationship as a cue to speech encoding. In A. W. Siegman & B. Pope (Eds.), *Studies in dyadic communication.* New York: Pergamon Press, 1972. (a)

Dittmann, A. T. *Interpersonal messages of emotion.* New York: Springer, 1972. (b)

Dittmann, A. T., & Llewellyn, L. G. Relationship between vocalizations and head nods as listener responses. *Journal of Personality and Social Psychology,* 1968, 9, 79–84.

Dittmann, A. T., & Llewellyn, L. G. Body movement and speech rhythm in social conversation. *Journal of Personality and Social Psychology,* 1969, 11, 98–106.

Duncan, S., Jr. Some signals and rules for taking speaking turns in conversations. *Journal of Personality and Social Psychology,* 1972, 23, 283–292.

Efron, D. *Gesture and environment.* New York: King's Crown, 1941.

Ekman, P., & Friesen, W. V. The repertoire of nonverbal behavior: categories, origins, usage, and coding. *Semiotica,* 1969, 1, 49–98.

Ekman, P., Friesen, W. V., & Ellsworth, P. C. *Emotion in the human face: Guidelines for research and an integration of findings.* New York: Pergamon Press, 1972.

Ellsworth, P. C., Carlsmith, J. M., & Henson, A. The stare as a stimulus to flight in human subjects: a series of field experiments. *Journal of Personality and Social Psychology,* 1972, 21, 302–311.

Ellsworth, P. C., & Ludwig, L. M. Visual behavior in social interaction. *Journal of Communication,* 1972, 22, 375–403.

Fast, J. *Body language,* New York: Evans, 1970.

Freedman, N., & Hoffman, S. P. Kinetic behavior in altered clinical states: approach to objective analysis of motor behavior during clinical interviews. *Perceptual and Motor Skills,* 1967, 24, 527–539.

Fretz, B. R. Postural movements in a counseling dyad. *Journal of Counseling Psychology,* 1966, 13, 335–343.

Kendon, A. Some functions of gaze direction in social interaction. *Acta Psychologica,* 1967, 26, 22–63.

Kendon, A. Some relationships between body motion and speech, an analysis of an example. In A. W. Siegman & B. Pope (Eds.), *Studies in dyadic communication,* New York: Pergamon Press, 1972.

Mallery, G. Sign language among North American Indians. *First Annual Report of the Bureau of American Ethnology,* pp. 263–552. Washington, D.C.: U.S. Government Printing Office, 1881. Republished, The Hague: Mouton, 1972.

Mehrabian, A. Inference of attitudes from the posture, orientation, and distance of a communicator. *Journal of Consulting and Clinical Psychology,* 1968, 32, 296–308.

Rosenfeld, H. M. Approval-seeking and approval-reducing functions of verbal and nonverbal responses in the dyad. *Journal of Personality and Social Psychology,* 1966, 4, 597–605.

Rosenfeld, H. M. Nonverbal reciprocation of approval: an experimental analysis. *Journal of Experimental Social Psychology,* 1967, 3, 102–111.

Sainsbury, P. Gestural movement during psychiatric interview. *Psychosomatic Medicine,* 1955, 17, 458–469.

Sapir, E. *Language: An introduction to the study of speech.* New York: Harcourt, Brace, 1921.

Stokoe, W. C., Jr. *Semiotics and human sign languages.* The Hague: Mouton, 1972.

Stokoe, W. C., Casterline, D. C., & Croneberg, C. G. *A dictionary of American sign language on linguistic principles,* Washington, D.C.: Gallaudet College Press, 1965.

Tomkins, W. *Universal American Indian sign language.* San Diego, California: Tomkins, 1926.

Watson, M. O. *Proxemic behavior, a cross-cultural study.* The Hague: Morton, 1970.

West, L., Jr. The sign language, an analysis. Vols. I and II. Unpublished doctoral dissertation, Indiana University, 1960. (*Dissertation Abstracts,* No. 60-2854.)

4
Facial Expression[1]

Paul Ekman

University of California, San Francisco

In just a moment or two expression flashes on and off the face. Wrinkles appear where the skin was smooth, or permanent wrinkles momentarily deepen. The eyebrows, eyelids, and mouth temporarily change their shape. Are these quick changes in the face expressions of emotion? How many emotions are shown on the face? Are these expressions true indications of how a person feels, or can they be falsified? Are most people able to read accurately facial expressions? What are the clues to emotion in the face; how is each feeling registered in the wrinkles and features of the face? Are the facial expressions of emotion the same for all people, or do they vary with culture, language, age, sex, and personality?

Literally hundreds of experiments have attempted to answer these questions, dating back to 1914. The type of research that has been conducted and the answers obtained to each question are described in this chapter. The conclusion describes a new set of questions about facial expression that are just now becoming the focus of research.

WHICH EMOTIONS DOES THE FACE SHOW?

Does the face tell us only whether someone feels pleasant or unpleasant, or does it provide more precise information, conveying which unpleasant emotion is experienced? If the latter, how many of these specific emotions does the face show—6, 8, 12, or what number? The typical method used to determine just

[1] This material is based in large part on a chapter from *Unmasking the Face* by Ekman and Friesen (1975). The research was supported by a grant from NIMH MH 11976 and from ARPA AF-AFOSR-1229. A more thorough discussion of most of the material presented here can be found in *Emotion in the Human Face*, by Ekman, Friesen, and Ellsworth (1972).

97

which emotions can be read from the face has been to show photographs of facial expressions to observers, who are asked to say what emotion they see in each face. The observers may be given a predetermined list of emotion words to choose from, or left to their own resources to reply with whatever emotion word comes to mind. The investigator analyzes the answers of the different observers to determine what emotions they agree about in describing particular faces. He might find, for example, that 80% of the observers agree in describing a particular face with the word "afraid." They might not agree about a word to describe some other face; for example, a face called "disinterest" by some observers might be called other emotions by other observers. On the basis of such results, the investigator reaches a conclusion about which emotions the face can convey.

The six emotions that are the subject of this chapter—happiness, sadness, surprise, fear, anger, and disgust—were found by every investigator in the last 30 years who sought to determine what emotions can be shown by facial expressions. These studies are reviewed in Ekman, Friesen, and Ellsworth (1972, Chapter 13). There are probably other emotions conveyed by the face—shame, interest, and excitement, for example, but these have not yet been as firmly established.

ARE JUDGMENTS OF EMOTION ACCURATE?

It is not enough to determine what emotions are read from facial expressions. It is also crucial to discover whether the interpretations of the observers are correct or not. When people look at someone's face and think that person is afraid, are they right or wrong? Are facial expressions an accurate reflection of emotional experience? Or, are the impressions gained from facial expression merely stereotypes—all agree about it, but they are wrong? To study this question the investigator must find some people whom he knows to be having a particular emotional experience. He must take some photographs, films or videotapes of these people, and then show them to observers. If the observers' judgments of the facial expression fit with the investigator's knowledge of the emotional experience of the persons being judged, then accuracy is established.

In our analysis of all the experiments conducted over the last 50 years, we found consistent and conclusive evidence that accurate judgments of facial expression can be made. Some of these studies were conducted in our own laboratory. In one experiment (Ekman & Bressler, 1964) photographs were taken of psychiatric patients when they were admitted to a mental hospital and again when they were less upset and ready for discharge. Untrained observers were shown these photographs and asked whether each facial expression was shown at time of admission or at time of discharge. The judgments were accurate. These same photographs were shown to another group of observers who were not told they were seeing photographs of psychiatric patients but

instead were asked to judge whether the emotion shown was pleasant or unpleasant. Again accuracy was proven (Ekman & Rose, 1965) since the facial expressions shown at admission were judged as more unpleasant than those shown at
discharge from the hospital. In another study (Ekman, 1965) other observers
were asked to judge how pleasant or unpleasant the facial expressions were, but
the faces shown to them were of psychiatric trainees undergoing a stress
interview. Without knowing which was which, the observers judged the facial
expressions during stress as more unpleasant than the facial expressions drawn
from a nonstressful part of the interview. In still another experiment (Ekman,
1972) observers were shown films of college students, taken when they had been
watching a very unpleasant film of surgery and when they had been watching a
pleasant travelogue film. The observers accurately judged which film the college
students were watching from their facial expressions.

All of these studies were concerned with spontaneous facial expressions that
naturally occur when a person does not deliberately try to show an emotion in
his face. But what of those situations in which a person deliberately tries to
show an emotion, to look happy or angry, and so forth? Many studies have
found that observers can accurately judge which emotion is intended when a
person deliberately tries to convey an emotion through facial expression (Drag &
Shaw, 1967; Dusenbury & Knower, 1938; Kanner, 1931; Kozel & Gitter, 1968;
Levitt, 1964; Osgood, 1966; Thompson & Meltzer, 1964).

ARE THERE UNIVERSAL FACIAL EXPRESSIONS OF EMOTION?

Are facial expressions of emotion the same for people everywhere, no matter
what their background? When someone is angry, will we see the same expression
on his face regardless of his race, culture, or language? Or, are facial expressions
a language, the meaning of which we must learn anew for each culture, just as we
need to learn verbal language? A little more than 100 years ago, Charles Darwin
(1872) wrote that facial expressions of emotion are universal, not learned
differently in each culture. They are biologically determined, Darwin said, the
product of man's evolution. Since Darwin's time many writers have emphatically
disagreed. Klineberg (1940) wrote that the evidence was in favor of the "hypothesis of cultural or social determination of emotional expression [p. 180]."
LaBarre (1947) reviewed many anthropological reports and concluded, "there is
no 'natural' language of emotional gesture [p. 55]." Most recently, Birdwhistell
(1963) has said, ". . . this search for universals was culture bound. . . . There are
probably no universal symbols of emotional state. . . . We can expect them to be
learned and patterned according to the particular structures of particular societies [p. 126]."

Neither Darwin nor those who opposed him had much definitive evidence.
Their arguments were based on logic, buttressed by bits and pieces of evidence,
usually collected incidentally by investigators who were not primarily studying

facial expression. It is only recently that a number of scientists from different disciplines have focused their attention on the question of whether there are some facial expressions which are universal.

Many studies have examined facial expressions of young infants who have had little opportunity to learn facial expression, and of blind children who could not learn by imitating others (cf. review of these studies by Charlesworth & Kreutzer, 1973). Many studies have examined the facial expressions of other primates evaluating Darwin's claim that human facial expression had evolved from other species (cf. review of this research by Chevalier-Skolnikoff, 1973). Both psychologists and ethologists have studied facial expression in more than a dozen cultures, some literate and some preliterate (cf. review of this work by Ekman, 1973). The evidence is now remarkably broad in scope, consistent in findings, and conclusive in showing that there are at least some emotions for which the facial expression is universal. As we will explain later, there are also cultural differences in regard to when these universal facial expressions are shown.

Research conducted in our laboratory played a role in settling the dispute over whether facial expressions are universal or specific to each culture. In one experiment (Ekman, 1972), stress-inducing films were shown to college students in the United States and to college students in Japan. Part of the time each person watched the film alone and part of the time the person watched while talking about the experience with a research assistant from the person's own culture. Measurements of the actual facial muscle movements, captured on videotapes, showed that, when they were alone, the Japanese and Americans had virtually identical facial expressions (see Fig. 1). When in the presence of another person, however, where cultural rules about the management of facial appearance (*display rules*) would be applied, there was little correspondence between Japanese and American facial expressions. The Japanese masked their facial expressions of unpleasant feelings more than did the Americans. This study was particularly important in demonstrating what about facial expression is universal and what differs for each culture. The universal feature is the distinctive appearance of the face for each of the primary emotions. But people in various cultures differ in what they have been taught about managing or controlling their facial expressions of emotion.

In another experiment (Ekman, 1972; Ekman, Sorenson, & Friesen, 1969) we showed photographs of the different emotion expressions to observers in the United States, Japan, Chile, Argentina, and Brazil. The observers in these different cultures had to choose one of the six emotion words for each photograph they saw. If facial expressions were a language that differs from culture to culture, then a facial expression said to be *angry* by Americans might be called *disgust* or *fear* by people in Brazil, or might not mean anything to them. Just the opposite was found. The same facial expressions were judged as showing the same emotions in all these countries, regardless of language or culture (see Fig.

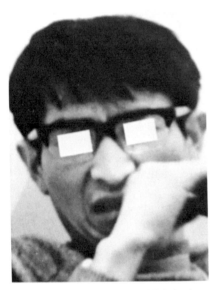

FIG. 1. Video frames of facial behavior scored as showing disgust; a Japanese subject on the left and an American subject on the right. (Copyright © 1972 by Paul Ekman.)

2). Essentially the same experiment was carried out independently at the same time by Carroll Izard (1971) with observers in eight different cultures, and the same evidence of universality was found.

While we wished to interpret our findings as evidence that some facial expressions are universal, one loophole remained. All of the people studied had some shared visual contact, usually not directly but through the mass media. It was still possible that facial expressions might really differ in all the cultures studied, but the people might have learned, through movies, television, and picture magazines, what each other's facial expressions of emotion looked like. Or, facial expressions of emotion might be similar in all the cultures we studied precisely because the people have all learned how to show emotion on their face by watching the same actors in the movies or television and imitating their facial expressions. We had not eliminated the possibility that among people who did not have the opportunity to view mass media portrayals of facial expressions of emotion, emotions would be shown by entirely different facial muscular movements. The only way to settle this question was to study visually isolated people who had no contact with the mass media and little if any contact with the outside world.

We conducted a series of experiments (Ekman, 1972; Ekman & Friesen, 1971) in the Southeast highlands of New Guinea where we were able to find people who met these criteria. Because these people were in no way accustomed to taking psychological tests or participating in experiments, and because we did

FIG. 2. Examples of judgments of emotion in five literate cultures. Many more photographs were shown and similar results were found.

	Percentage of agreement in how photograph was judged across cultures				
	United States (N=99)	Brazil (N=40)	Chile (N=119)	Argentina (N=168)	Japan (N=29)
	97 Happiness	95 Happiness	95 Happiness	98 Happiness	100 Happiness
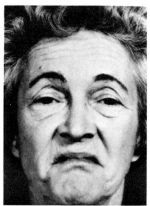	92 Disgust	97 Disgust	92 Disgust	92 Disgust	90 Disgust
	95 Surprise	87 Surprise	93 Surprise	95 Surprise	100 Surprise

FIGURE 2 *(continued)*

Percentage of agreement in how photograph was judged across cultures

	United States (*N*=99)	Brazil (*N*=40)	Chile (*N*=119)	Argentina (*N*=168)	Japan (*N*=29)
	84 Sadness	59 Sadness	88 Sadness	78 Sadness	62 Sadness
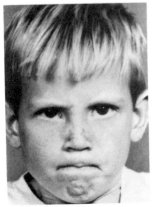	67 Anger	90 Anger	94 Anger	90 Anger	90 Anger
	85 Fear	67 Fear	68 Fear	54 Fear	66 Fear

not know their language but had to work through translators, we had to modify our experimental procedure. In other countries we had shown a single photograph of one or another of the facial expressions and given the observer a choice among a list of emotion words. In New Guinea, we showed the person three photographs at once, had a translator read an emotion story, such as "A person's mother died," and asked the observer to point to the photograph that fit the story. Table 1 shows that these people selected the same face for the same emotion as did people in all the other cultures we had studied. There was but one exception: the New Guineans failed to distinguish between the *fear* and *surprise* facial expressions.

In a related experiment, other New Guineans were told an emotion story and each was asked to show the emotion on his own face. Videotapes were taken of these intended emotion expressions, some examples of which are shown in Fig. 3. Analysis of these New Guineans' facial expressions showed again that the same facial expressions were produced for the same emotions as had been found in other cultures with the exception of fear and surprise, which were confused with each other. Further confirmation of the universality of facial expressions

TABLE 1
Judgments of Emotion by Observers in a
Preliterate Culture, the Fore of New Guinea[a]

Emotion described in the story	Percent choice of the emotion expected that would agree with judgments by members of literate cultures	
	Adults	Children[b]
Happiness	92	92
Sadness	79	81
Anger	84	90
Disgust	81	85
Surprise	68	98
Fear from anger, disgust, or sadness	80	93
Fear from surprise	43	—[c]
Number of observers	189	130

[a]From Ekman and Friesen (1971).
[b]The higher figures for the children probably reflect the fact that they were asked to choose from a pair of photographs rather than sets of three.
[c]Through an oversight, this discrimination was not tried with the children.

FIG. 3. Video frames of attempts to pose emotion by subjects from the Fore of New Guinea. The instruction for the top left photograph was "your friend has come and you are happy"; for the top right "your child has died"; for the bottom left "you are angry and about to fight"; and for the bottom right "you see a dead pig that has been lying there for a long time." Copyright © 1972 by Paul Ekman.

was obtained by a study of another culture in Western Iranian, the western portion of the island of New Guinea. Karl Heider and Eleanor Rosch, who were skeptical of our evidence of universality, conducted the same experiments with people even more visually isolated than those we had studied, and they also obtained evidence of universality.

Taken together, our studies, those of Izard, the Heider-Rosch study and evidence from Eibl-Eibesfeldt (1970) (an ethologist using very different methods), the evidence quite conclusively shows that Darwin was correct in claiming that there are universal facial expressions of emotion.

While the appearance of the face for each of the primary emotions is common to all peoples, facial expressions do vary across cultures in at least two respects. What elicits or calls forth an emotion usually differs; people may become disgusted or afraid in response to different things in different cultures. Also, cultures differ in the conventions people follow about attempting to control or manage the appearance of their face in given social situations. People in two different cultures may feel sadness at the death of a loved one, but one culture may prescribe that the chief mourners must mask their facial expression with a mildly happy countenance.

HOW DOES EACH EMOTION APPEAR ON THE FACE?

As we began to find evidence that there are some facial expressions of emotion that are universal, and before all of the studies were completed, we began to investigate just what these universal facial expressions of emotion look like. We sought to construct a tool for measuring the face, which would depict photographically each of the universal facial expressions of emotion. Our first step was to study what others had said about the appearance of the face for each of the primary emotions. Some writers had described which muscles were contracted in particular emotions, while others concerned themselves only with the appearance of the surface of the face. None had systematically considered all of the muscles nor all of the consequent changes in the surface appearance of the face for the six primary emotions.

Putting together what was written by Darwin, Duchenne (1862), a French anatomist whom Darwin had quoted extensively, Huber (1931), an American anatomist writing over 40 years ago, and Plutchik (1962), an American psychologist concerned with emotion, we saw part of the picture emerge. We constructed a table that listed all of the facial muscles and the six emotions, entering into the table what these men had written about which muscles were involved in what way for each emotion. There were, however, many gaps, where no one had said anything about the involvement of a particular muscle in a particular emotion. Working with Silvan Tomkins (1962), we filled in those gaps with information from our cross-cultural studies, and our shared impressions.

The next step was to photograph models who were instructed to move particular facial muscles listed in the table. We separately photographed the three areas of the face that are capable of independent movement: the brow/forehead; the eyes/lids and root of the nose; and the lower face, including the cheeks, mouth, most of the nose, and chin. The Facial Affect Scoring Technique (FAST) (Ekman, Friesen, & Tomkins, 1971) consists of a series of photographs of these three different areas of the face, each photograph keyed to one of the six emotions. As might well be expected, for each of the emotions there is more than one FAST photograph for at least one facial area. For example, for surprise there is one brow/forehead, one eyes/lids/root of nose, but four different FAST photographs of the lower face.

The next obvious question was whether FAST is correct. Are the six emotions—happiness, sadness, anger, fear, disgust, and surprise—in actuality composed of the facial appearances listed in FAST? Or, does the FAST appearance of disgust actually occur with anger, and so forth? We have conducted four experiments on the validity of FAST. Two of the experiments attempted to prove the validity of FAST by showing that measurements of the face with FAST corresponded with other evidence of the subjective emotional experience of the persons whose faces were measured. These experiments investigated the experiential validity of FAST.

The other two experiments investigated the social validity of FAST. Rather than attempting to prove that FAST measurements correspond to the person's experience, these studies investigated whether FAST measurements can predict what observers think a person is feeling when they look at his face. Although experiential and social validity should be related, they need not necessarily be so. We may not look to others how we actually feel, at least all of the time. Thus, it was necessary to study both experiential and social validity.

The studies of experiential validity drew from materials gathered in one of the cross-cultural studies of facial expressions described earlier (Ekman, 1972). College students in Japan and in the United States had individually watched pleasant and unpleasant movies while we videotaped their facial expressions. From their answers to questionnaires after the experiment, it was clear that they experienced very different emotions while watching the two types of films. In describing their reactions to the travelogue, the subjects had said it was interesting and pleasant, and caused them to feel moderate happiness. In describing their reactions to the surgical film, the subjects said they had unpleasant, disgusted, pained, fearful, sad, and surprised feelings. If FAST is valid, then measurements based on it should be able to distinguish between the facial expressions shown when these two different sets of emotions were experienced.

All of the facial muscular movements visible on the videotapes were isolated, their duration was measured, and they were classified in terms of FAST. This measurement procedure was done in slow motion, with the measurements made separately for the three areas of the face, by three separate technicians. Such precise measurement required about five hours for each minute of videotaped facial behavior. The results were very clear-cut. Measurements with FAST clearly distinguished the two emotional conditions, whether subjects had been watching a stressful film or a travelogue. And, FAST was equally successful with the facial expressions of Japanese subjects and with Americans, as it should be, since it was built to show the universal facial expressions of emotion. One limitation of this experiment, however, is that it didn't determine whether FAST correctly depicts the facial appearances for each of the six emotions. It only shows that FAST is correct in distinguishing between unpleasant and pleasant experiences.

The second experiential validity study (Ekman, Malmstrom & Friesen, 1971) provided a partial remedy to this limitation. Recent research on the physiology of emotions suggests that there are markedly different patterns of heart rate acceleration and deceleration with the emotions of surprise and disgust. Measures of heart rate and skin conductance had been gathered on the Japanese and

American subjects when they were watching the pleasant and stressful films. If FAST is correct in what it says a surprise face and a disgust face look like, then when FAST says such facial expressions occurred, there should be a different pattern of heart rate for each. When we examined the changes in heart rate which coincided with facial expressions FAST had designated as either surprise or disgust, the results showed the predicted difference.

Although this second study does provide evidence of the validity of FAST for surprise and disgust, it doesn't show that FAST is necessarily valid in what it says about the other emotions—anger, happiness, sadness, fear. Since FAST was derived by the same method for all six emotions, this evidence on surprise and disgust is encouraging about the likelihood that similar evidence could be obtained for the other emotions.

The third study examined FAST in terms of social validity. Could FAST predict how observers will interpret facial expressions? In this experiment (Ekman, Friesen, & Tomkins, 1971) photographs that had been taken by many different investigators of facial expression were obtained. These pictures were shown to observers who were asked to judge which of the six emotions was shown in each picture. Only those on which the observers had agreed about the emotion expressed in the face were further considered. If FAST correctly depicts the appearance of each of the six emotions, then measurements based on FAST ought to be able to predict the emotion seen by the observers in each of these photographs. The measurements were made separately for the three areas of the face by three separate technicians. Predictions were then made on the basis of the scoring of each area of the face. Table 2 shows that FAST measurements of each facial area did accurately predict how the total face had

TABLE 2
Comparison of Percent Correct Predictions from Each Separate
Facial Area

Emotion category	Facial area measurements			
	Brows–forehead	Eyes	Lower face	All three facial areas combined
Happiness	70	90	100	100
Sadness	70	90	0	90
Surprise	70	90	90	100
Anger	80	50	100	100
Disgust	25	0	75	75
Fear	29	71	29	43
Correct predictions across all emotion categories	49	73	67	88

been judged by observers. The best predictions were made when the measurements from all three facial areas were combined.

The fourth study (Ekman & Friesen, in prep.) was much like the one just described, except that here the facial expressions examined were those produced by dental and nursing students who had been instructed to attempt to show each of the six emotions by their facial expression. The question asked of FAST was to predict for each photograph what emotion the student had been intending to show. The measurements made with FAST succeeded.

While no one of our four experiments alone would validate FAST, taken together the evidence for the validity of FAST is much more than tentative. Of course, much research remains to be done to further validate this facial measurement procedure. Our work of the past few years has been to refine the measurement procedure, based upon a study of the anatomical basis of facial expression. FAST has been replaced by another acronym, FACS, which stands for the Facial Action Coding System (Ekman & Friesen, 1976, 1977). FACS was developed to provide a tool not just for measuring facial behavior relevant to emotion, but to distinguish all visible facial behavior. We were interested in a tool which would allow study of facial movement in research unrelated to emotion; e.g., facial punctuators in conversation, facial deficits indicative of brain lesions, etc. The Facial Action Coding System is much more comprehensive than FAST, free of any theoretical bias about the possible meaning of facial behavior. It is based upon an analysis of how each muscle of the face acts to change visible appearance. The Facial Action Coding System provides the basis for scoring any observed facial movement into anatomically based minimal action units.

The Facial Action Coding System has utility in research and in a variety of practical situations. In research it can be used to measure changes in momentary emotions, measuring these changes from videotapes taken unobtrusively. To give a few examples of the range of such research applications, work is in progress using FACS to: study clinical changes in the course of a psychotic–depressive episode; evaluate childrens' response to viewing television violence; detect differences between honest and deceitful conversations. The information contained in FACS could also be useful to practitioners—doctors, nurses, lawyers, salesmen, diplomats, and so forth—who want to be more aware of how another person is feeling.

We have recently (Ekman & Friesen, 1975) written a book aimed at such practitioners. Figure 4 shows an example of how we have tried to explain facial expression. Examine each of the four pictures. Note that the top left picture looks questioning in its surprise, the top right looks dumbfounded in surprise, the bottom left, dazed in its surprise, and the bottom right is just surprised. These variations in meaning are due to how surprise is registered on the face. All of the pictures show surprise in just two areas of the face except the one on the bottom right. Each was made by combining, in the darkroom, part of the picture on the bottom right with a neutral picture of the same person. The top left

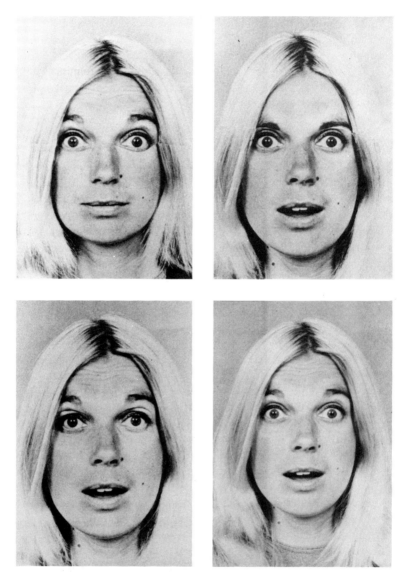

FIG. 4. Four variations on Surprise: top left, questioning surprise; top right, dumbfounded surprise; bottom left, dazed surprise; bottom right, surprise.

picture shows just the brows and eyes in surprise, with the mouth neutral; the top right shows the eyes and mouth in surprise, with the brows neutral; and the bottom left shows the brow and mouth in surprise with the eyes neutral. These are just some of the variations in how this one emotion, surprise, is registered in facial expression.

HOW ARE FACIAL EXPRESSIONS CONTROLLED?

How can we tell a real facial expression of emotion from a simulated one? When a person doesn't feel the way he looks but is attempting to mislead us about his feelings is there any way to detect his real feelings in his facial expression? In short, does the face "leak?"

We have been studying this problem for a number of years. We started with films of the facial expressions of psychiatric patients during interviews. In certain interviews we knew from subsequent events that the patients had been misleading the interviewer about their feelings. Study of these films provided the basis for a theory of nonverbal *leakage* (Ekman & Friesen, 1969), ways to tell from facial expression or body movement, feelings the person was attempting to conceal. We have been testing this theory during the last five years by studying interviews in which one person purposefully conceals from another the negative emotions experienced as a result of watching very unpleasant stressful movies. The subjects in this experiment try to convince the interviewer that the film they have seen was actually pleasant and that they enjoyed it.

Our studies of these interviews are far from complete. We do know (Ekman & Friesen, 1974) that untrained observers who look at the face are fooled, they cannot tell the honest from the deceptive interactions. We have also found that people who have been trained with the Facial Action Coding System can detect deception, but the number of people who have done this is too small to place much confidence in this result. We have developed a theory (Ekman & Friesen, 1975, Chapter 12) on exactly how to detect deception in facial expression, but it will take another few years to test by measuring expression with the Facial Action Coding System.

INDIVIDUAL DIFFERENCES IN FACIAL EXPRESSION

In the last few years we have been developing theory and conducting experiments on how personality may be manifest in facial behavior. It would be premature to attempt here more than a brief description of our approach to this phenomenon. We believe that some of the individual differences in facial behavior result from idiosyncracies in the learning of display rules. Display rules are social norms regarding facial appearance, probably learned early in life and functioning on a habitual basis. They specify which one of four management techniques is to be applied by whom to which emotion in a given circumstance. The four management techniques are 1) to intensify, 2) to deintensify, 3) to neutralize the appearance of a felt emotion, or 4) to mask it with the facial configuration of another emotion. For example, at a United States white middle-class wedding display rules specify that the groom must mask any appearance of distress or fear with a happy countenance, while the bride is not similarly constrained. Another example of a display rule is that, in a patient–physician encounter the patient, no matter what the illness, must in the initial greeting reciprocate the physician's (also required) smile, before facially displaying negative affect relevant to the illness. We believe that psychotic–depressives fail to follow this display rule and, unlike neurotic–depressives, will not as often show the initial greeting smile. We also believe that the later appearance of the greeting smile is correlated with a sign of improvement in mental state. More generally, the psychotic–depressive patient fails to follow the usual display rules regarding the management of negative affect. It is not that psychotic–depressed patients are unique in the facial appearance they show with negative affects but in their consistently maintained negative affect across situations and their seeming inability to modulate it. Put in other terms, in the depressed patient certain negative affects are *flooded.*

We believe that, as a result of particular display rules learned within the family, individuals may in their adult life show *blocks* in facial affect expression. In the extreme, the person may be *poker-faced,* never revealing in his face how he feels. A less extreme deviation is the block in expressing a particular emotion; for example, a person may never facially show anger. A lesser deviation is the block in the expression of a particular emotion toward a particular class of people. For example, the person may never show anger toward female authority figures. From a pilot study, it appears that blocks in expression may be manifest in two rather different ways. One is that the person simply does not show the facial expression of a felt emotion. In a more complex manifestation, the expression is not blocked but the feedback is, such that the person is remarkably unaware of having shown the particular expression.

We believe it may also be possible to characterize people in terms of an extraordinary facility for showing emotional expressions in their faces. For some, this may be characteristic of all the emotions, and they may get into trouble or at least be known for showing everything in their face. The facility may, however, be more specific to a particular emotion, so that the person often looks afraid or angry, and so forth. A neighboring concept, first described by Silvan Tomkins, is that of the *frozen* affect. The frozen affect is an enduring muscular set of the face; after a particular expression, the face, instead of returning to a neutral countenance, may return to a slight version of one or another affect. Thus, the person always looks just slightly disgusted or amused or melancholy, etc.

Another manifestation of personality may be in affect blends and affect sequences. In an affect *blend,* the face shows the distinctive characteristics of two emotions simultaneously. While it is possible for any given event to elicit two emotions simultaneously, resulting in a blend expression, individuals may show a blend when only one emotion has been elicited by an external event, if they have an established habit of associating a second feeling with the elicited one. For example, when disgust is aroused, some people may characteristically feel also afraid of being disgusted; others may feel angry; others may feel happy and so forth. This affect-about-the-affect will repetitively be manifest in either a blend or a rapid sequence of the two emotions in the face.

It should be clear that what has been said so far about individual differences in facial expressions of emotion is based on either pilot studies or hunch and still enjoys more the status of conjecture than formalized hypothesis. Yet these kinds of phenomena are now amenable to systematic investigation. Research on personality differences and facial behavior has been stymied by the lack of any systematic, quantitative procedure for measuring the spontaneous facial expressions of emotion. However, the Facial Action Coding System described earlier provides the investigator with one necessary tool for quantifying the moment-to-moment changes that may occur in facial behavior.

The approach to the study of individual differences discussed so far has entailed the investigation of the encoding of emotion. It is also possible to study how individuals differ in their decoding of the facial expressions of others. Personality and psychopathology may be manifest, for example, not just in a patient's blocks in the facial expression of certain emotions, but in blocks in his sensitivity to or understanding of the facial expressions of others.

We have begun a series of experiments on individual differences in the decoding of facial expression of emotion. We have developed a test which we call the Brief Affect Recognition Test (BART), which measures a person's accuracy in decoding six emotions—happiness, sadness, anger, fear, disgust, and surprise. The test employs still photographs of facial expressions that, when seen for five seconds, elicit very high agreement about the presence of one or another of these emotions. In the test we present these faces in a tachistoscope, with an exposure ranging from .01 to .04 sec. Our rationale for such a brief presentation is that it approximates usual interpersonal conditions, in which a single facial expression can easily be missed. The usual facial expression lasts only 1 or 2 sec, is embedded in preceding and subsequent facial behavior, and competes for attention with body movement, voice quality, and verbal content.

Our hypothesis is not that people will differ in their total performance, that is, in their accurate recognition of all six emotions, but that they will differ in their patterns of accuracy, recognizing three or four emotions and not the others. Two studies have been completed.

One experiment (Shannon, 1970; Shannon & Ekman, 1976) compared medical patients, schizophrenics, and depressives. No difference was found in total accuracy; as predicted, depressives were less accurate on fear, whereas schizophrenics were less accurate on disgust. In the second experiment (Ekman, Jones, Friesen, & Malmstrom, 1970), we found that subjects who had ingested marijuana performed differently from those who had ingested alcohol; moreover, there was a relationship between self-reported mood and accuracy in recognizing particular emotions. We are currently attempting to replicate these findings and standardize the BART.

Other investigators have also been interested in individual differences in facial expression, relating the ability to understand emotion in others to whether or not the person typically shows emotion in his own face. The tasks used to measure understanding of emotion and expressiveness have varied across investigators, and so have the results. As yet the contradictions have not been resolved (cf. Buck, Savin, Miller, & Caul, 1972; Lanzetta & Kleck, 1970).

CONCLUSION

Progress has been made in the study of facial expressions. Some of the emotions that can be shown in the face have been identified. Evidence has been accumulated to show that it is possible to read facial expression accurately. The universality of certain aspects of facial expression has been shown. Some of the precise muscular configurations that signify particular emotions have been isolated. Also, it has been shown that facial expression can fool at least some people when deception is occurring.

Despite this progress, knowledge about facial expression is still quite limited. Little is known about the differences between felt and phony expressions. While it is clear that individuals differ in facial expressiveness and in how well they understand the facial expressions of others, little is known about how this operates and how it is related to personality.

There are a number of other aspects of facial expression not touched upon in this chapter. Little is known about the early development of facial expression in the infant. Equally sparse is the information about how facial expression is related to other physiological measures that change with emotional arousal. What of the relationship between the facial muscles and the skeletal muscles; what is the relationship between what people do with their face and body? There is no reason to leave out the voice and words, and we can ask how facial expressions of emotion relate on a moment-to-moment basis with speech. This leads directly into study of the role and function of facial expression in interaction, examining how the facial expressions of one person interrelate with the facial expressions of another. There is much work for the next decade of research on facial expression.

REFERENCES

Birdwhistell, R. L. The kinesic level in the investigation of emotions. In P. H. Knapp (Ed.), *Expression of the emotions in man.* New York: International Universities Press, 1963.

Buck, R. W., Savin, V. J., Miller, R. E., & Caul, W. F. Communication of affect through facial expressions in humans. *Journal of Personality and Social Psychology,* 1972, **23,** 362–371.

Charlesworth, W. R., & Kreutzer, M. A. Facial expressions of infants and children. In P. Ekman (Ed.), *Darwin and facial expression: A century of research in review.* New York: Academic Press, 1973.

Chevalier-Skolnikoff, S. Facial expression of emotion in nonhuman primates. In P. Ekman (Ed.), *Darwin and facial expression: A century of research in review.* New York: Academic Press, 1973.

Darwin, C. *The Expression of the emotions in man and animals.* London: Murray, 1872.

Drag, R. M., & Shaw, M. E. Factors influencing the communication of emotional intent by facial expressions. *Psychometric Science,* 1967, **8,** 137–138.

Duchenne, B. *Mecanisme de la physionomie humaine; ou analyse electro-physiologique de l'expression des passions.* Paris: Bailliere, 1862.

Dusenbury, D., & Knower, F. H. Experimental studies on the symbolism of action and voice: I. A study of the specificity of meaning in facial expression. *Quarterly Journal of Speech,* 1938, **24,** 424–435.

Eibl-Eibesfeldt, I. *Ethology, the biology of behavior.* New York: Holt, Rinehart & Winston, 1970.

Ekman, P. Communication through nonverbal behavior: A source of information about an interpersonal relationship. In S. S. Tomkins & C. Izard (Eds.), *Affect, cognition, and personality.* New York: Springer, 1965.

Ekman, P. Universals and cultural differences in facial expression of emotion. *Nebraska Symposium on Motivation, 1971.* Lincoln: University of Nebraska Press, 1972.

Ekman, P. Cross-cultural studies of facial expression. In P. Ekman (Ed.), *Darwin and facial expression: A century of research in review.* New York: Academic Press, 1973.

Ekman, P., & Bressler, J. In P. Ekman, Progress report to National Institute of Mental Health, Bethesda, Maryland, 1964.

Ekman, P., & Friesen, W. V. Nonverbal leakage and clues to deception. *Psychiatry,* 1969, **32**(1), 88–105.

Ekman, P., & Freisen, W. V. Constants across cultures in the face and emotion. *Journal of Personality and Social Psychology,* 1971, **17**(2), 124–129.

Ekman, P., & Friesen, W. V. Detecting deception from the body or face. *Journal of Personality and Social Psychology,* 1974, **29**(3), 288–298.

Ekman, P., & Friesen, W. V. *Unmasking the face.* Englewood Cliffs, New Jersey: Spectrum–Prentice Hall, 1975.

Ekman, P., & Friesen, W. V., Measuring facial movement. *Journal of Environmental Psychology and Nonverbal Behavior,* Vol. **1,**(1), 1976.

Ekman, P., & Friesen, W. V. *Manual for the facial action coding system.* Palo Alto: Consulting Psychologists Press, 1977.

Ekman, P., Friesen, W. V., & Ellsworth, P. *Emotion in the human face: Guidelines for research and an integration of findings.* New York: Pergamon Press, 1972.

Ekman, P., Friesen, W. V., & Tomkins, S. S. Facial affect scoring technique (FAST): A first validity study. *Semiotica,* 1971, 3(1), 37–58.

Ekman, P., Jones, R. T., Friesen, W. V., & Malmstrom, E. J. Psychoactive drugs and the recognition of facial expressions of emotion. Unpublished manuscript, Langley Porter Neuropsychiatric Institute, San Francisco, 1970.

Ekman, P., Malmstrom, E. J., & Friesen, W. V. Heart rate changes with facial displays of surprise and disgust. Unpublished manuscript, University of California, San Francisco, 1971.

Ekman, P., & Rose, D. In P. Ekman, Progress report to National Institute of Mental Health, Bethesda, Maryland, 1965.

Ekman, P., Sorenson, E. R., & Friesen, W. V. Pan-cultural elements in facial displays of emotion. *Science,* 1969, **164,**(3875), 86–88.

Huber, E. *Evolution of facial musculature and facial expression.* Baltimore: Johns Hopkins Press, 1931.

Izard, C. E. *The face of emotion.* New York: Appleton, 1971.

Kanner, L. Judging emotions from facial expressions. *Psychology Monograph,* 1931, **41** (3, Whole No. 186).

Klineberg, O. *Social Psychology.* New York: Henry Holt, 1940.

Kozel, N. J., & Gitter, A. G. Perception of emotion: Differences in mode of presentation, sex perceiver, and role of expressor. Technical Report No. 18, Boston University, 1968.

LaBarre, W. The cultural basis of emotions and gestures. *Journal of Personality,* 1947, **16,** 49–68.

Lanzetta, J. T., & Kleck, R. Encoding and decoding of facial affect in humans. *Journal of Personality and Social Psychology,* 1970, **16,** 12–19.

Levitt, E. A. The relationship between abilities to express emotional meaning vocally and facially. In J. R. Davitz (Ed.), *The communication of emotional meaning.* New York: McGraw-Hill, 1964.

Osgood, C. E. Dimensionality of the semantic space for communication via facial expressions. *Scandinavian Journal of Psychology,* 1966, **7,** 1–30.

Plutchik, R. *The emotions: Facts, theories, and a new model.* New York: Random House, 1962.

Shannon, A. M. Differences between depressives and schizophrenics in the recognition of facial expression of emotion. Unpublished doctoral dissertation. University of California, San Francisco, 1970.

Shannon, A. M., & Ekman, P. Psychopathology and the recognition of facial expressions of emotion. Unpublished manuscript, 1976.

Tomkins, S. S. *Affect, imagery, consciousness.* Vol. 1. *The positive affects.* New York: Springer, 1962.

Thompson, D. F., & Meltzer, L. Communication of emotion intent by facial expression. *Journal of Abnormal and Social Psychology,* 1964, **68,** 129–135.

5
Applications of Semiosis to the Study of Visual Interaction

Ralph V. Exline
B. J. Fehr

University of Delaware

The focus of this chapter is upon the deceptively simple action of looking at one another. More particularly it is concerned with people looking at and away from each other as they find themselves engaged in face-to-face interaction. Have you found yourself catching the eye of a stranger in a subway car, a restaurant, on the sidewalk? What did it mean to you? How did you interpret it? How did it affect you compared to when you turn to find a friend looking at you? What if, instead of a friend, it were your employer? What if the stranger in the subway car was a person of the same rather than the opposite sex?

A few years ago the senior author found himself in just such a situation as was first suggested. He was seated directly opposite and almost knee-to-knee with a young Frenchman in a Parisian Metro carriage. Looking up, the author noticed the Frenchman looking steadily at him. Perhaps made self-conscious by his own research, he checked his immediate impulse to look away and tried to stare back at the Frenchman, in silence, immobile, determined to outlast him. But he couldn't. As the brief seconds ticked away he felt a rising tide of emotion akin to panic. He wanted to look away; he had to; he did. Feeling sheepish, he looked back to find the Frenchman still looking, but just at that precise moment he noticed a slight convergence of the other's eyeballs. The Frenchman seemed to be aware that he was being looked at and on the instant he looked away! The author realized that, caught up in his own definition of the situation, he had not realized that the other's eyes—level with and looking in the same plane as his own—had not been focused on his face. Lost in his own thoughts, the Frenchman was probably oblivious to the assumed battle of the eyes. But the author was not, and he still remembers the strength of the feeling that gripped him.

This anecdote is an example of why we are interested in studying eye engagements and their avoidance. We believe they have powerful effects upon our impressions of others, our feelings about the relationship, and certainly our behaviors as we interact with other persons. The phenomena are always with us when we are with others, and we look and avoid looking at different people, in different ways, in different circumstances. We are interested to learn more about why we look or do not look, at whom, when.[1]

Thus far we have made concrete references only to mutual visual interaction in conditions of silence. But our studies as well as those of others have indicated that by far the greater proportion of the time we share looks with others, we do so while talking. Eye engagements then, are one aspect of the communication process in face-to-face interaction, and we think that the study of them may help us to better understand that process and perhaps even increase the effectiveness of our communication.

We realize that visual interaction is only one of a number of nonverbal elements in the process of communication and will be most adequately decoded only when studied in coordination with other nonverbal behaviors and with speech. It can be measured independently of other phenomena, however, and it has provided us with a starting point in the study of nonverbal communication processes.

Others have shared this interest, for there exist a number of interesting general treatments of communicational interaction that contain insightful discussions of looking behavior, for example, Simmel (1921), Goffman (1959), Hall (1966), and especially Nielsen (1962), whose book on self-confrontation contains a chapter describing the long history of our species' fascination with eye engagements. In recent years, moreover, empirical studies of eye engagements, and avoidances, have appeared in increasing numbers in the professional journals. While we do not claim that our search of the literature has identified all published studies, we have noticed an accelerating trend.

The first experimental study we were able to find was published by Moore and Gilliland in 1921. It was a study in which the authors reported that the ability to maintain eye contact while performing a series of mental additions was more characteristic of "aggressive" than of "nonaggressive" persons. A second such study by Gilliland appeared in 1926, after which we know of no further visual interaction studies until around 1950 (Riemer, 1949; Steinzor, 1950). We found one in the 1950s (Riemer, 1955) and a scattering in the early 1960s (Sommer, 1962; Reece & Whitman, 1962), all of the foregoing being studies in which eye engagements were treated as phenomena of interest but were subsidiary to the

---

[1] The anecdote also points to an important problem, namely, that of valid measurement of gaze behavior. The author was directly in front of and less than 4 ft from the other, yet for several seconds he misperceived the focus of the Frenchman's gaze. We will explore this question in a later section of this paper.

main focus of investigation. It was not until the early 1960s that studies concerned with the investigation of visual interaction per se began to appear.

In the 1960 and 1961 annual meetings of the American Psychological Association, Exline reported results of two investigations of factors that affected the degree to which social interactants shared mutual glances.[2] In 1963, Gibson and Pick reported data from which they concluded that one could tell with some accuracy when he was being looked at directly. Exline (1963) published experimental results indicating that interrelationships among such variables as sex, the need for affiliation, and the competitiveness of the interaction context significantly affected the incidence of mutual glances. The publication of two additional experimental studies in 1965 (Exline, Gray, & Scheutte, 1965; Argyle & Dean, 1965) signaled the beginning of a rising curve of interest, for 29 more studies were published in the latter half of 1960s while at least 50 have so far been found for the first three years of this decade.

Reviews of research on visual interaction behavior began to appear in the late 1960s. The first, by Robson (1967), was not restricted to reviews of research on visual behavior alone. Rather, he pulled together a number of scattered references to the use of the visual channel by neonates to support the suggestion that eye-to-eye contact be considered as a primary "releaser" of maternal caretaking responses, as the basis for the establishment of the child's earliest and continuing human relationships, and as a determiner of the extent to which older children and adults will rely upon and utilize nonverbal forms of communication.[3] Other early reviews tended to subsume eye engagements in the broader context of communicational phenomena, (Diebold, 1968) especially nonverbal communication (Duncan, 1969; Mehrabian, 1969; Vine, 1970). By 1971, however, visual interaction as a research area had achieved sufficient salience to merit a review of investigations devoted solely to the study of visual behavior among human social interactants (von Cranach, 1971; Ellsworth & Ludwig, 1972), the latter specifying that they omitted studies of "... nonhuman primates and lower species, nonexperimental studies, developmental studies, and experiments involving human beings 'interacting' with photographs or thin air [p. 378]."

The first of these reviews (by von Cranach) is more a statement of a position than a comprehensive review of the published literature. He refers to Argyle and Kendon's (1967) suggestion that the gaze serves several functions in social interaction, then restricts himself to a consideration of visual interaction in terms of a postulated communicative signal function served by the movement of the eyes. Though he states that his goal is to show the relationship of eye movements to the orienting movements of the body in general, the empirical

---

[2] These papers were later published (Exline, 1963; Exline, Thibaut, Hickey, & Gumpert, 1970).

[3] In 1973, Vine published an excellent review of the ontological importance of visual interaction, a review that updated and extended the material first covered by Robson.

work which he discusses is concerned mainly with the position, and occasionally the movement, of the head. Von Cranach suggests relationships between eye movements and body postures, body movements and positions in space vis-à-vis another, which could be pursued in future empirical research.

Von Cranach's article (1971) is a valuable contribution to the literature concerning studies of visual interaction. He calls our attention to the variety of ways in which gaze behavior has been conceptualized by previous investigators, for example, eye contact, gaze direction, mutual glances. In addition, he points to the need to demonstrate that someone must respond to another's gaze behavior before it can be termed a "signal". Von Cranach discusses functions served by gaze behavior for both sender and receiver, and he demonstrates that care must be used when claiming that "eye contact" can be accurately assessed and treated as if it were a social signal. We will discuss his empirical work more thoroughly when we consider methodological problems in measuring gaze behavior. We agree with his conclusion that ". . . looking behavior is a part of a total system of orienting reactions [p. 233]." though we believe that study of the phenomena of visual interaction promises insight into much more than orienting behavior alone.

Ellsworth and Ludwig (1972) unable to find a common theme into which to fit the many and diverse studies of visual behavior, developed a series of categories that pointed to the interrelations among visual behavior, personality attributes, interaction phenomena, and other social variables. Of the nine subtopics under which empirical research was discussed, they were especially interested in attribution theory and interpersonal attraction. They perceived these categories as providing a fruitful means of integrating studies of visual behavior with more usual formulations of social psychological problems, to the subsequent enrichment of all three research areas.

In both of the abovementioned reviews the authors not only described previous research on visual behavior and interaction, but were concerned with placing it within a broader theoretical context—von Cranach treating it as part of the orientation toward a partner in social interaction, Ellsworth and Ludwig as a means of integrating nonverbal communication processes into the study of attribution theory.

Our interest is in viewing the function of the eyes as part of the total communication process between and among interactants in a social setting. Thus, both verbal and nonverbal phenomena can be conceptualized as forming a system of signs or symbols[4] that potentially link people together in a communication process. Because of the varied meanings given the term communication, it

[4] The terms sign and symbol have been defined and discussed in detail by many authors in the context of determining how humans become aware of and organize their understanding of the environment (e.g., Cassiter, 1923; Carnap, 1935; Langer, 1942). We will be using the term "sign" as Charles Morris developed it and do not mean to imply commitment to any particular model of cognitive behavior.

is necessary to clarify our use of it. It is not our purpose to explicate all the conceptions of communication but rather only to deal with a few points relevant to our position.

One way in which definitions of communication differ is in the degree to which the intention of the sender is considered to be important. Some authors (MacKay, 1972) consider communication to have occurred only when the sender consciously intends a given message to be received by another. This would include speech that is meant to communicate and some nonverbal behaviors such as pointing or standing at attention in military reviews. Other subsidiary behaviors the person may engage in are described variously as "informative," "expressive," or "indicative" (Ekman & Friesen, 1969). This particular position typically excludes most (but not all) nonverbal behavior from the category of communication because nonverbal behavior is generally not considered to be intentional. People are typically not aware of what they do with their hands, feet, or other parts of their body when they talk with others.

It is our contention, however, that these subsidiary behaviors are more than secondarily informative; they are a fully integrated part of the total message one transmits to another. The message itself would be different were they not present. For example, an employer may unintentionally, by an informal relaxed posture, let an employee know that the employee is not to be intimidated by the status difference between them. Barring phony games, this "way to take my status" information from the employer helps the employee to pinpoint the one of many meanings that could be attributed to the employer's words alone. Without the information carried by posture, the total message would be different. Given the above conceptualization of the role of nonverbal behavior, we support a somewhat different definition of communication.

Our position is that *all* behavior is potentially communicative. Any given behavior becomes communicative when it produces a change in a receiver. This change may range from the level of the neuron to the level of more overt behavior. In essence, the change is the reaction of the receiver to the communicative event. From this point of view, all aspects of a person's behavior may be part of the message one sends. It would be useful to determine the relationships between a person's behavior (verbal and nonverbal), that which the behavior designates within a given cultural group, and the corresponding response of a receiver to the behavior. Charles Morris' discussion of the semiotic in "Foundations of the Theory of Signs" (1938) provides a conceptual framework and terminology for organizing the data concerned with visual interaction.

Semiotic is the science of signs; after Morris (1938) ". . . it is both a science among the sciences and an instrument of the sciences [p. 2]." We will be using semiotic as an instrument with which to discuss a special case of sign functioning: human visual behavior. "The process in which something functions as a sign may be called *semiosis* [p. 3]." This process involves three factors: the *sign vehicle,* "that which acts as a sign;" the *designatum,* "that which the sign refers to;" and the *interpretant*, the "effect on some interpreter [p. 3]." The interpreter is sometimes considered a fourth factor in the process. In Morris' (1938) own words:

> These terms make explicit the factors left undesignated in the common statement that a sign refers to something for someone [p. 3].

> It should be clear that the terms 'sign,' 'designatum,' 'interpretant,' and 'interpreter' involve one another, since they are simply ways of referring to aspects of the process of semiosis. Objects need not be referred to by signs, but there are no designata unless there is such reference; something is a sign only because it is interpreted as a sign of something by some interpreter; a taking-account-of-something is an interpretant only in so far as it is evoked by something functioning as a sign; and object is an interpreter only as it mediately takes account of something [p. 4].

> In terms of the three correlates (sign vehicle, designatum, interpreter) of the triadic relation of semiosis, a number of other dyadic relations may be abstracted for study [p. 6].

These relations are: *syntactics*, the study of the relations of signs to signs; *semantics*,[5] the study of the relations of signs to designata; and *pragmatics*, the study of the relations of signs to interpreters or interpretants.

We propose to employ Morris' analysis of the semiotic (1) to suggest that visual behavior acts as a communicative sign, and (2) to provide a framework within which to understand and organize the research literature. Unfortunately, the study of visual behavior has not proceeded in an orderly fashion. For example, in some experiments, visual behavior is assumed to be a sign and its occurrence is then correlated with personality or behavioral measures. The score on the personality or behavioral measure is then employed to designate meaning to the look. However, if it has not been determined that the look is consistently responded to in some way, there is no certainty that it is a sign. It may be that some current findings will be less meaningful if it is determined that they are based on stimulus patterns that are not reliably detected. We hope that discussing the literature within the framework of semiosis will identify such gaps in our knowledge and stimulate research to fill these gaps.

MEASUREMENT ISSUES: VALIDITY AND RELIABILITY

Before it is possible to say that something acts as a sign in Morris' system, it is necessary to demonstrate that it is perceived by the organism in question. The aspects of visual behavior that have been studied thus far, and which, therefore,

---

[5] Semantics is generally understood to be the study of the "meanings" of signs and we will use the term in this sense. However, it should be noted that Morris believes, "Meanings are not to be located as existences at any place in the process of semiosis but are to be characterized in terms of the process as a whole [p. 45]." However, we do not feel our discussion greatly violates his definition in that we contend that a sign is only fully understood in the context of semiosis as a whole.

must be shown to be capable of being perceived, are: (1) the direction of gaze, whether it be into the eyes of someone or anywhere else in the environment; (2) the frequency of gazes; and (3) the duration of gazes. There is much subjective evidence to suggest that people are aware of where another is looking. Authors describe the strong impact of the mutual glance and feelings aroused when someone will not look at you (Chekhov, 1888; Mailer, 1968; Sartre, 1957). There are many words used to describe looking behavior which suggest considerable sensitivity to the dimension (for example, glare, stare, peek, or look askance.). Sylvan Tomkins (1963) surveys historical commentaries that discuss the importance of the eyes, especially the "evil eye." Recent work on eye spots (geometric figures of eyelike shapes) has demonstrated that the eye stimulus pattern is very compelling to humans as well as many other animals (Coss, 1970).

Prior to a discussion of the semiotic classification scheme, however, it is necessary to demonstrate that the aspects of visual behavior thought to be meaningful in social interaction may be validly and reliably measured. This particular issue has been the subject of some debate among investigators interested in the field of eye gaze. (See Vine, 1971, and von Cranach & Ellgring, 1973, for reviews of the issues.) Typically, the gazes of one person (*Sender*) at the eyes of another (*Receiver*) are recorded by a human observer (*Observer*), often from behind a one-way mirror. Disagreement exists as to whether it is possible for human observers to make valid and reliable measurements. Fairly high reliabilities have been reported though they have little meaning if the measure is invalid. The crux of the problem, therefore, is that of obtaining a valid measure. Some investigators feel that humans can tell when they are being looked at and others feel that the ability is very limited.

Gibson and Pick (1963) had six Receivers make judgments about whether they were being looked at directly or not by a female Sender seated across from them at a distance of 2 m. The Sender assumed three head positions (30° left, straight on, 30° right) and looked at seven focus points 10 cm apart on a horizontal line at the eye level of the Receiver. The center point was the bridge of the nose. For each trial, the Sender would gaze at one of the points from one of the head positions and wait until the Receiver announced his judgment (about 5–6 sec).

Though not mentioned by Gibson and Pick, Receivers directly facing the Sender reported being looked at approximately 85% of the time when, in fact, the Sender looked only at the bridge of the Receiver's nose (see Figure 4, Gibson & Pick, 1963, p. 392). Nevertheless Gibson and Pick concluded the acuity for being looked at was similar to Snellen acuity (1 min of arc). Cline (1967) and Antis, Mayhew, and Morley (1969), conducting similar experiments, reached a similar conclusion: humans have good acuity for judging gaze direction, particularly for determining when they are being gazed at directly.

On the other hand, a series of experiments carried out by M. von Cranach and his colleagues at the Max-Planck Institüt für Psychiatrie, have led to conclusions at variance with those of Gibson and Pick (see von Cranach, 1971; von Cranach & Ellgring, 1973).

Krüger and Hückstedt (1969) attempted to determine whether it was possible to discriminate gazes at different points within the face. If there is a special phenomenon of "eye contact" occurring when two people look directly into each others' eyes, then a subject (Receiver) should be able to distinguish between glances at his mouth from glances at his eye. The Sender gazed at seven points within the face of the Receiver from two distances: 80 cm and 200 cm. A greater percentage of correct responses was recorded at 80 cm (35%) than at 200 cm (10%). A replication by Ellgring (1970) gave substantially the same results— 41–49% correct responses at 80 cm compared to 21–29% correct responses at 200 cm. While the percentages obtained were generally better than chance (which was 14%), von Cranach feels that they are too low to warrant belief in the ability to distinguish being looked in the eye from being looked at in the face in general.

Emphasis then shifted to a consideration of the variables that affect one's ability to know when one is being looked at in the face in general versus the eyes specifically. Krüger and Hückstedt (1969) instructed Senders to focus on points in and around the Receiver's face using different head positions, from different distances, for varying durations. Receivers exhibited ability to discriminate gazes at the face from gazes at other parts of their body and/or the area around their head. However, there were still errors in judgment. The frequency of errors increased as the distance increased, as gaze duration decreased, and as the head deviates from a straight-on position. To create a stimulus configuration more similar to "real life," von Cranach, Schmid, and Vogel (1969) added gaze movement and head movement to the presentation. Both of these variables led to a decrease in correct responses when compared to previous conditions where they were not included.

In sum, the Max-Planck group found: Gaze direction contributes most to the judgments of the Receiver at close distances (1.5 m). As distance increases (3 m), head position comes to contribute more to the perceived gaze direction. The accuracy of the Observer is less on all dimensions than that of the Receiver. The Sender's head position has an even greater affect on the Observer's judgments than the Receiver's judgment. As the Observer moves angularly away from the Sender–Receiver axis, his judgments are almost solely based on head position. In general, this series of experiments leads von Cranach to the conclusion that humans are unable to tell with much accuracy when gazes are directed at them.

The diverging conclusions of Gibson and Pick and the von Cranach group have been interpreted in a number of different ways:

1. Argyle (1970) believes that in natural situations people either look at each other in the region of the eyes or well away. If this were true, the failure to discriminate between gazes at the face and gazes close to the head would be

unimportant. It may be the case, however, that Argyle bases his belief on behavior that occurred primarily in those situations in which the Receiver was looked at 100% of the time. Thus, when a Sender looks directly at the eye region of a Receiver, it may be socially inappropriate for the Receiver to look anywhere else on the body surface of the Sender but his eyes. Once the Sender looks away, though, the Receiver may want to look over him to investigate other aspects of his demeanor.

2. Exline (1972) suggests that it is more important where the Receiver *thinks* the Sender is looking than where the Sender is actually looking. The Receiver will respond to the social stimuli as he interprets it regardless of the actual fixation point of the other's eyes. Therefore, gazes close to the eyes, which are erroneously recorded as eye gazes, will be accurately represented as the perceived social stimuli for the Receiver. Given the high interrater reliabilities reported by Exline (.90, .94, .92) and others (Aiello, 1972; Daniell & Lewis, 1972), it would be possible for an Observer to record the perceptions of the Receiver, thus freeing the Receiver from this added chore during the course of an experiment. These considerations would appear to be most important when the investigator is interested in measuring a subject's response to social stimuli from another. This is the nature of much of the research in the area. If one is interested in the Sender's behavior, however, it becomes important to know precisely where he looks. A Sender may feel differently about someone he looked in the eye compared to someone whose mouth he scrutinized.

3. In preparation for conducting an experiment in which the behavioral data would be recorded from 16-mm film, Vine (1971) prepared a mock-up film in which two stooges interacted in a preprogrammed manner, thus providing a way to obtain information on the validity of measurements of behavior that were recorded from film instead of live observations. Vine himself recorded correctly 75.6% of the gazes to the eye. On the other hand, 18.5% of gazes away from the eyes were incorrectly recorded as eye glances. Vine's inter- and intrarater reliabilities were 73.8% and 76.4%, respectively. When measurements were made on films of naive, freely interacting subjects, the interrater reliability increased markedly to 93.8% and the intrarater reliability rose to 96.2%. Since there is no reason to believe that the Observers' ability to discriminate changed any between these two sessions, Vine suggests that the spontaneous situation is more easily discriminable than the programmed interaction because people tend either to look or to look well away. While it is not possible to judge validity from measures of reliability, the results are compelling.

4. Lastly, von Cranach and Ellgring (1973) analyze the situation in a somewhat more conservative manner. Their reevaluation of the Gibson and Pick data points out the large number of errors in judgment made by the subjects in that experiment. For example, in the head straight-on condition, 40% of the time that the Sender was actually looking at the area of the Receiver's ear, the Receiver, in error, reported being looked at directly. This suggests that the difference between the two bodies of research lies more in the conclusions than the actual

data. The usual, uncritical acceptance of Gibson and Pick's conclusions should, therefore, be questioned. In general, given the number of errors in judging when one is being looked in the eye or in the face, von Cranach and Ellgring conclude that: "It might be useful to redefine the variable, namely from 'one-sided or mutual gaze' towards a less specific term like 'orientation' [p. 411]."

The main difficulty in resolving the measurement issues raised thus far is the lack of an independent assessment of gaze direction or focus: (a) against which to compare the data coded by humans, and (b) with which to determine whether the assumptions about how people tend to distribute their visual attention are correct. The instruments developed to determine focus have been extremely obtrusive. The subjects have been required, for example, to wear cumbersome helmets, to wear contact lenses, or to have their heads clamped into position. Recently, however, a technique has been developed that allows unobtrusive moment-to-moment tracking of eye movement. This is achieved with a TV camera, directed by a tracking mechanism, connected to a computer. Also, the subject's head may move up to 6 inches in any direction before tracking is lost and then it may be manually realigned. This system (E G and G, Hel Oculometer System) will be able to provide a resolution to the validity of measurement dilemma. However, the work is not likely to be available for several years.

Let us next briefly consider the question of the reliability of visual behavior measures. Although the question of validity must be decided before the reliabilities have any meaning, one point should be noted. Some of the early investigators of social visual behavior fail to determine the reliability of their own Observers' measurements, but merely cited Exline (1963) as demonstrating that eye glances can be reliably coded. This policy is not recommended because there is no guarantee that all Observers will make reliable measurements. In fact, it is our experience that certain persons cannot accurately code the behavior because of their tendency to focus on the mouth of another rather than on the eyes.

In conclusion, given the perceived subjective importance of visual behavior, as well as the growing body of research that seems to indicate its importance in human and other primate interaction, it seems likely that humans will be found capable of accurately determining the direction of the look. However, until we can clearly specify the degree to which humans are accurate coders we suggest that the following procedures be used to create an experimental situation that, given the information presently available, will be conducive to collecting valid and reliable measurements:

1. Have the Sender and Receiver face each other directly.
2. Place the Observer directly behind the Receiver.
3. Keep the distance between Sender and Receiver in the range 1.5–2.0 m.
4. Test the visual acuity of any Observers used. Von Cranach has reported that acuity accounted for 50% of the variance in measurements.
5. Lighting should be so arranged that the eyes of the person being observed

are easily visible. This is best accomplished by placing lights at or below eye level.

6. Train Observers. Give them feedback concerning the actual fixation point of the sender. Ellgring and von Cranach (1972) have demonstrated improved discrimination ability following such training.

7. If possible, code the behavior as it actually occurs rather than from a TV screen. Antis *et al.* (1969) have found increased error due to the curvature of the screen.

8. Lastly, determine the reliability associated with the measurements of all observers under conditions identical to those of the experiment.

EXPERIMENTAL STUDIES OF VISUAL SEMIOSIS

For visual behavior to be considered a sign it must be shown to be so within Morris' system. This means that it must be shown to refer to something for someone. An experiment by Exline, Fairweather, Hine, and Argyle (1972) demonstrates the abovementioned properties of visual behavior. In this experiment an instructed confederate either gazed steadily into the region of a speaker's eyes, or, whenever the subject commenced to speak, averted his gaze to sweep the air above the speaker's head. Subjects, depending upon their orientation toward controlling others, rated the confederate who looked up and away as more or less powerful than when he looked steadily at them. In addition, the nature of the listening look systematically affected the amount of time that the speaking subject looked at his listener. In this study, the subject describes the designatum of the look for him, namely, the rating of the confederate's potency. Therefore, we argue that the visual behavior in this study does indeed represent a sign within Morris' system.

The remainder of this paper represents our attempt to use previously published studies of visual behavior to develop our position. Studies are discussed in terms of their contribution to an understanding of the rules, or at least consistencies, of: (a) relationships of gaze direction signs to other signs (syntactics), (b) consistencies in meanings attributed to eye behavior (semantics), and (c) consistencies in the impact of such signs upon the behavior of recipients (pragmatics). Such an approach may well call attention to certain research possibilities that, as yet, have not received sufficient attention. Thus, for example, to consider visual behavior in terms of syntactic relations to other signs may well point to interesting and hitherto neglected lines of research.

SYNTACTICS OF EYE ENGAGEMENT

While no act of communication is purely syntactic, certain sign-to-sign relationships involving eye engagements might well be consistently uncovered. Visual signs can be systematically related to speech signs, other visual signs and gestures. Though very few of the published studies concerning eye behavior can be said to be directed to the uncovering of syntactic relations per se, indications of such relations are often discussed in the context of studies designed to explore the meaning of eye behavior (semantics) or the effect on a participant, bystander, or co-interactant (pragmatics). Thus, while Kendon's (1967) paper entitled "Some Functions of Gaze Direction in Social Interaction" seems at first glance to be focused on the pragmatics of eye engagement, the fact that his investigation showed a consistent patterned arrangement of eye engagements to occur when one speaker turned over the floor to another can be taken as an example of an eye engagement sign that is systematically related to a speech sign.

Kendon's data showed that milliseconds before a speaker finished his verbalization he looked at and away from his listener, looking back at the other—and holding the look—just as he, the speaker, ceased talking. In this case the coordinate visual and verbal behaviors, namely, look at (while speaking)—look away (while still speaking)—look back at and hold (while falling silent), constitute a syntactic pattern.

Another example of a syntactic relationship involving eye engagement is the finding reported by several authors (Kendon, 1967; Exline, 1963; Exline, et al., 1965) that visual attention is more likely to be directed toward the eye region of another when listening to him than when speaking to him. Such differences in visual attention occur both with respect to frequency and with the average duration of the glance. A recent report (Exline, Ellyson, & Long, 1975) suggests that the pattern is more marked and consistent across members of a dyad when the interactants are peers than when they are of different status. In the case of a hierarchial dyad, the subordinate manifests significantly more visual attention while listening relative to speaking than the participant of higher status. Put another way, the subordinate looks more while listening to the superior than the superior does while listening to the subordinate, although subordinates and superiors each look at the other about the same proportion of time while speaking.

In all of the studies mentioned above, subjects were college students free from obvious psychiatric or character disorders. There is evidence that the pattern of differences in the ratios of visual attention recorded while looking and speaking described above is repeated in samples of older persons suffering from psychiatric disorders and from alcoholism. Williams (1974) recorded eye engagements during speaking and listening manifested by schizophrenic patients and by normal controls, while Hersen, Miller, and Eisler (1973) reported on visual patterns observed in discussions between alcoholic males and their wives. Williams' subjects averaged 42.6 years of age, and although Hersen et al. (1973) did not report subjects' ages, it is very likely that the married alcoholic subjects, who composed their sample, were considerably beyond college age.

Both investigators reported that their subjects looked considerably more while listening than while speaking. Williams reported that the proportions of time spent looking while speaking was 51.4 and 35.4% for normal controls and psychiatric patients, respectively. Compare the above percentages to the proportions of time spent looking while listening, which were 76.7 and 56%, respectively, for the above categories of subjects. While it is of interest that normals and schizophrenics differed significantly in the overall amount of looking behavior recorded for speaking and listening modes, more relevant to a consideration of syntactics is the finding that the *pattern* did not deviate from that earlier found for college students. Both schizophrenic and normal subjects looked more when listening than when speaking to another (Williams, 1974). Hersen *et al.* (1973) did not report their data in terms of listening and speaking specifically. Nevertheless, their finding that the amount of looking is inversely related to the amount of speaking suggests a comparable pattern. It is also of interest that Hersen's data showed that husbands looked less at wives when the conversation was concerned with drinking than with other topics, a finding that will be discussed further when we consider semantics.

The difficulty a speaker has in producing words may also be related to eye engagement. Exline and Winters (1965a) have shown that as the difficulty of the discussion topic increases, the speaker looks less at his listener. The differential ratios of looking while speaking and looking while listening may well be a consequence of the way in which our information-processing system is neurologically structured. We may be unable to take in complex sensory stimuli while simultaneously processing cognitive material for the purpose of formulating speech. Sartre (1957) states this point more eloquently when he writes: "We cannot . . . perceive and imagine simultaneously; it must be either one or the other [p. 258]."

We speculate that the lower ratio of look–speak to look–listen is a consequence of the speakers' inability to process incoming stimuli (perceive) while simultaneously formulating the cognitions (imagine) immediately to be spoken. Such a formulation suggests that when the speaker is groping or struggling to integrate his thoughts he will look away from the gaze of his listener, returning when, following a successful integration, he produces his thoughts in words. It is to be expected, as Kendon's (1967) data suggest, that during this latter period of relatively nonthinking speech, the rate of words produced per unit of time would increase and visual attention is more likely to be directed toward the listener.

Hand gestures may well be syntactically related to eye engagement signs and verbal signs. For purposes of simplification let us, borrowing from Ekman and Friesen (1969), focus only on two categories of hand gestures—"illustrators" and "adaptors." An illustrative gesture is one in which the hands move in space away from the body to emphasize or illustrate the ideas presented in words. An adaptive gesture is one in which the hands actively touch the body, either stroking, fingering, pressing, rubbing, or twisting portions of one's body or clothing in a manner likely to produce kinesthetic sensations. It seems obvious that the illustrators are unlikely to occur when one is in the listener's role, but that adaptors can and will occur both when a person speaks and when he listens. Less obvious is the suggestion that the ratio of illustrative to adaptive gestures made by a speaker will be greater when he looks than when he does not look at his listener.

To look while illustrating would seem to serve two functions; first, it is more efficient to illustrate when one knows that he has the visual attention of the other (Friedman, 1972); second, my look as I gesture enables me to assess your reaction to my total presentation. In the first instance, the look may both draw the desired attention and provide the speaker with the information that the illustrative gestures will be apprehended. In the second instance, I illustrate my speech with gestures, confident, as I see you watching me, that my gestures are functional. If I see you withdraw and deny me your visual attention as I illustrate, my once-functional gestures now impress me as mere hand waving, a useless and faintly ridiculous display.

If, during speech, one's thoughts become difficult to integrate, one may act to reduce increasing tension by adaptive, self-comforting gestures. This can occur as one looks while speaking, but would seem to be even more likely to occur when the difficulty in expressing one's thoughts in words drives the eyes of the speaker away from the face of the listener. Thus, both the avoidance glance and the adaptive gesture could be said to occur as concomitants of the tension assumed to develop as a result of momentary blockage.

The final study discussed in this section may serve as a bridge between the syntactics and semantics of eye engagements. Exline, Gottheil, Paredes, and Winkelmayer (1968) report data which suggest that one direction of gaze can be shown to be systematically and differentially related to another direction of gaze according to the affective theme that a speaker intends to communicate to another. Take the two themes of joy and sorrow. We found that the more intensely happy is the personal experience that one person tells another, the greater is the ratio of direct to downcast gazes that the speaker directs at the listener. The reverse is true when the theme of the experience is one of sadness. In the above study, the intensity of happy and sad personal experiences were coded from verbal protocols provided by ten normal women. Independent observers then coded the percent of time in which the storyteller looked directly at or directly down from the face of the listener. The difference between the percent of direct to down gazes was 42.6% for the five happiest stories to 25.5% for the five least happy stories. In the case of sad stories the comparable differences were 2.3% for the saddest and 36.5% for the least sad.

Clearly the speaker gave her visual attention to her listener as she told her happy experience, withdrawing it as she recounted her tale of sorrow. What is of special interest here is that the sign-to-sign relationship (direct gaze to down gaze) was affected by the *meaning* to the sign producer of the concomitant ideation (joy or sorrow).[6] The last point calls to mind a position first expressed

---

[6] The generality of these findings may, of course, be limited by considerations of sex and/or cultural learning. While systematic research is needed to verify and extend the above

by Theodore Piderit, a contemporary of Darwin. In *Mimik und Physiognomik*, published almost a century ago, Piderit suggested that to think of an object or event brings about similar facial responses as would occur in the presence of said object or event (Piderit, 1886). Though concerned with the total facial display, Piderit specifically suggested that a pleasant thought opens the eyes and pleasant emotions are accompanied by receptive movements. Unpleasant emotions, on the other hand, were thought to be accompanied by movements designed to impede the reception of stimuli.

The visual behaviors which characterized the affective themes of stories told by subjects in the Exline *et al.* (1968) investigation can be considered in the light of Piderit's argument. Ideation relevant to a happy experience can certainly be assumed to be generally pleasant and thus should be accompanied by receptive gaze behavior; that is, one should be more prone to look at and return the gaze of the other. Conversely, sorrow, an assumed unpleasant ideation, could be expected to be accompanied by eye movements that impede reception of stimuli provided by the other. In the latter case to look down would be consistent with the argument.

This is not to argue that the visual behavior accompanying the ideation is a conscious act. The actor thinks neither "I am unhappy; therefore, I will look down," nor (with due respect to James and Lange) "I am looking down; therefore, I am unhappy." Rather, he knows he is unhappy and, aware of it or not, tends to look down, whereas when he knows he is happy, he finds himself looking more directly at another.

From the viewpoint of an observer, however, apprehension of the nonverbal sign stimuli may well lead to inferences concerning the designatum, that is, the nature of the ideation occurring immediately prior to, or concomitantly with, the emission of signs. This brings us to a consideration of semantics.

SEMANTICS OF EYE ENGAGEMENTS

Semantics is concerned with the relations of signs to designata, or more simply, with the meaning of signs. From Morris's perspective, signs do not have meaning in and of themselves but rather refer to designata for interactors; that is,

---

findings, Paul Ekman's videotapes of members of the Fore culture in New Guinea provide evidence that suggests that the pattern is pancultural (1972). In Ekman's films, males in a near neolithic culture were asked to show how they would feel if happy ("watching children play") or sad ("death of a child"). The senior author has viewed those films and can attest to the similarity of the visual pattern (direct-down) recorded for the Fore to that observed when the women from the United States, in the study described above, recounted their happy and sad personal experience. Still photographs taken from Ekman's tapes are reproduced in Chapter 2 of this book.

"meaning" refers to the entire process of semiosis. Thus, in the experiments reported, "meaning" is determined by relating the presence of a sign or signs to characteristics or responses of the interactant. Thus, while meanings can be either idiosyncratic or commonly shared we are interested only in the latter; for without commonly shared meanings effective communication is impossible. While shared meanings can be limited to as few as two people, we are in this paper primarily interested in more generally shared meanings, that is, those held by, at the very least, a subcultural group within a cultural or societal unit.

In verbal communication the commonly shared understandings concerning the relations between verbal signs and designata are, within a language group, extensive, and the designata themselves vary widely with respect to variety and degree of abstractness. Verbal signs thus can refer to objects, processes, events, states, emotions, time periods, and so on. This is not so in the case of nonverbal signs. Common understandings of relations of hand, arm, leg, head, and/or trunk movements to designata are far less extensive, rich, and varied. When we further limit ourselves to a consideration of eye movements or fixations, we find even fewer shared agreements concerning relations between sign and designatum. Indeed, as was previously indicated, the very concept of eye behavior as a sign vehicle is complex. In most cases a time dimension is involved, and, in addition, to speak of a "mutual" look implies the activity of two sets of eyes.

In our consideration of the semantics of the look we use "meaning" in the sense of a theory of reference; that is, is our statement of the relation between sign and designatum true in fact and experience? We suggest that the basic designatum of the look as a sign is that of attention or orientation to the focal point of the look. When humans are in one another's presence we argue that each potential interactant will refer the look of the other to himself and draw inferences concerning the others' orientation (or attention), or lack of it, to himself and/or to other potential interactants. There is evidence to show that both United States and English college-age men and women, when asked to describe the meaning of a steady (100%) look from a hypothetical other, will give as a modal response the statement that the hypothetical looker is interested in or attentive to the respondent whether the respondant is speaking or listening to the hypothetical other. Conversely, a query as to the meaning of a zero look from the hypothetical other, either when one or the other is speaking or when both respondent and other are described as mutually silent, elicits as the modal response the description of the other as being uninterested or inattentive to the subject (Exline & Snadowski, 1971).

When asked to rate one's comfort with a hypothetical other who looks 100, 50, or 0% of the time while speaking, listening, or in mutual silence, respondents rate the anticipated no-look (0% look) as significantly less comfortable ($\bar{X} = 3.81$ on an 8-point scale) than the anticipated 100% look ($\bar{X} = 4.56$) or the 50% look ($\bar{X} = 5.93$).[7] Both the descriptive statements and the ratings of comfort support

---

[7] Comfort scale ranges from 1 = extremely uncomfortable to 8 = extremely comfortable.

our belief that the look of the other is most basically interpreted as a sign of attentiveness to, and/or interest in, the target of the look. The comfort data, though more relevant to the pragmatics than to the semantics of eye engagement, nevertheless strengthen our confidence in the validity of the proposed semantic relationship. It is certainly logical to expect respondents, over all conditions, to anticipate feeling more comfortable with one whose look can be taken to signify attention to oneself. Thus, we reaffirm our belief that orientation or "attention to" is the designatum of the focussed look.

A number of investigators explicitly recognize the linkage between eye behavior and attention. Hore (1970) compared Ss with respect to "visual attention," Hersen *et al.* (1973) spoke of spouses "attending to" one another, and Williams (1974) compared schizophrenic patients, nonschizophrenic patients, and normals as to their "selective attention." Finally von Cranach (1971) refers to looking behavior as part of a "total system of orienting reactions" (see page 120, this chapter). In each of the abovecited studies the investigators equated eye contact with attention. Others imply the relationship—Modigliani (1971) in a study of embarrassment, Kleck and Nuessle (1968) in studying the congruency between indicative and communicative functions of eye contact, Rutter and Stephenson (1972a) when comparing schizophrenics, depressives, and normals, and Hobson, Strongman, Bull, and Craig (1973) in examining gaze aversion in relation to anxiety.

A high degree of attention given to another implies a comparable degree of involvement, or willingness to become involved with the other. The precise nature of the involvement is not specified by the attentive look alone, additional information about context or supplementary information derived from other verbal or nonverbal activities is generally required to establish the conditions sufficient to label accurately the affective tenor of the involvement. Nevertheless, the absence of a high degree of visual attention often is taken as evidence of a disinterest in or unwillingness to become involved with another.

One method of empirically establishing the validity of the assumed relationship between visual attentiveness and involvement is to study the visual attentiveness to another or others exhibited by an individual, or individuals whose known characteristics imply that they should or should not be involved, or interested in becoming involved with actual or potential co-interactants. Thus, involvement-relevant prior information about a subject's situation, personality type, or role relationships should point to predictable amounts of relative eye engagement. A number of such studies have been reported. Subjects have been embarrassed and subsequently observed to decrease their eye engagements with others (Exline *et al.* 1965). Subjects diagnosed as schizophrenics (and thus assumed to be fearful of significant involvement with others), have been shown to be less visually attentive than are other categories of psychiatric patients and of normal controls (Rutter & Stephenson, 1972a, b; Williams, 1974). Extroverts have been shown to be more visually active than introverts (Mobbs, 1968), but perhaps only with respect to frequency of looks (Rutter, Morley, & Graham,

1972), and depressed psychiatric patients are less active than nondepressed surgical patients (Hinchliffe, Lancashire, & Roberts, 1971). Hobson *et al.* (1973) categorized their subjects as to relative degrees of trait and state anxiety but found no significant relationships between anxiety and visual behavior.

The anxiety induction used by Hobson is reminiscent of procedures used by Exline and Winters (1965b) to create aversion to a confederate. Following an initial discussion the confederate left the room. He returned to report that he had forgotten to complete the interview but that he could give the subject preliminary feedback, namely, that he and observers had decided on the basis of the immediately proceeding discussion that the subject was either very immature or quite mature for his age. In a subsequent discussion all subjects given the aversive treatment showed increased gaze aversion, all those praised showed an increase in eye contact, while uninstructed controls showed random increments and decrements of visual attention. Postexperimental questionnaires showed that subjects given the negative induction like the interviewer less, while those given the positive induction liked him more than did uninstructed controls. The aversion induction may have also increased the subjects' anxiety, though Hobson *et al.*'s (1973) failure to obtain anxiety-linked results suggests that anxiety is less influential than dislike in driving the eyes away from the other. In another study, Exline and Winters (1965b) gave both males and females an opportunity to interact with two like-sex confederates. After asking the subjects to decide which of the two they liked better, subjects were given another opportunity to speak to both together. Results showed that both males and females showed a significant increment in mutual glances shared with liked confederates at the expense of mutual glances exchanged with the less liked confederate.

Rubin (1970) carried Exline and Winter's findings to their logical conclusion when he measured the visual interaction of lovers. In a well-designed series of studies he recorded the eye engagements of dating couples classified as "strong" and "weak" lovers on the basis of an especially constructed questionnaire. His results showed that whereas "strong" and "weak" lovers did not differ in the amount of unreciprocated glances they directed at their beloved, the "strong" lovers showed a significantly greater amount of mutual eye contact. A second experiment showed that this was a function of love for a specific other, for when members of "love" dyads were matched with an opposite-sex stranger from another love dyad, mutual glances lessened and "strong" and "weak" lovers did not differ with respect to the amount of measured eye contact.

Another type of interpersonal relationship that should imply different orientations toward personal involvement with the other is a relationship in which one person possesses a greater degree of social power than does the other. In such a relationship we argue that it is to the advantage of the occupant of a low-power position to become more involved with the occupant of the higher power position than vice versa (Brown, 1965, p. 97). Furthermore, we assume that shared understandings about how people of different power should behave in their high- or low-power role would imply that both high- and low-power persons expect the person of lower power to be more attentive to high-power than vice versa.

On the basis of the above arguments, the findings reported by Exline, Ellyson, & Long (1975), which were previously discussed in the context of syntactic relations (see page 128), provide additional evidence that a basic meaning of eye engagement is one of orientation and involvement. Their data showed that when two persons of differential power were engaged in conversation, the occupant of the lower power position directed significantly more visual attention to a higher powered other when the other was speaking than when the other was listening. Such a pattern was not observed for the visual attention manifested by the occupant of the high-power position. There was, in fact, a trend in the opposite direction, namely, that the person with more power tended to look more when speaking than when listening. The observed difference in the latter case did not reach statistical significance, however.

An additional finding of the Exline *et al.* study strongly suggests that dominance as a personality attribute affects eye engagement behavior in a fashion very similar to that of power as a role related characteristic of interaction. Men who describe themselves as wanting to control others, when compared to those who do not wish to exert such control, manifest look–speak, look–listen patterns that are identical with those shown by the occupant of a high-power social role. In other words, high-control-oriented persons look less when listening than when speaking to others—it is as if, perhaps unconsciously, they act to establish themselves in a dominant posture vis-à-vis the other.

The above approach to the establishment of the "meaning" of the gaze suggests that visual attention to a co-interactant can be said to characterize the behavior of extroverts but not introverts, normals, and hospitalized patients but neither schizophrenic nor depressed patients, and submissive rather than dominant males. All of the preceding personality attributes would seem to be relevant to motivation to become actively involved with others.

In addition, such high-involvement relationships as liking and being in love with another, as well as the hypothetically low-involvement situation implied by embarrassment and high power have been shown to provide data that are consistent with the assumption that the amount and kind of eye engagements mean involvement with or attention to the other.

The meaning of an eye engagement sign can also be investigated by assessing the interpretations that observers exposed to different amounts or patterns of eye engagement apply to the behavior. There are several variations of this general technique. Subjects can be actual participants in the interaction (Exline and Eldridge, 1967; Exline *et al.* 1971; Word, Zanna, & Cooper, 1974), they can observe interactants from behind a one-way mirror (Holstein, Goldstein, & Bem, 1971) or view a videotape or film of the programmed interaction (Kleck & Nuessle, 1968; Exline *et al,* 1968).

Both interactant and observer variations were employed by Holstein *et al.* (1971), whose subjects either interviewed confederates or observed a subject interviewing a confederate. This technique permits investigation of the effect of degrees of immediacy of involvement upon assessment of the identical confederate behaviors.

In the investigations cited above, the relationship between eye contact and involvement (attention) must be inferred from the interpretations made by the subjects. Subjects in the study by Exline and Eldridge (1967), for example, were not asked to rate the degree to which the confederate attended to or became involved with them. Rather, they were asked to rate the "believability" of the confederate, as well as the confidence he had in the validity of the information provided in his statement. The data showed that ratings of the confederate's confidence were significantly higher (and tended to be so for his believability) when, in the second half of a long statement, he looked steadily at, as compared to steadily away from, his listener.

In this case we suggest that when in the questionnaire the subject's attention was directed to the confederate's "believability" or "confidence," the subject's attribution of different degrees of credibility and confidence to the confederate was based on that difference in the behavior of the confederate which implied the degree of his involvement with the judge—namely, the direction of his gaze. It is as if the judges were unconsciously thinking, "He can't be very sure of what he is saying if he is not able or willing to attend to me (become involved with me) as he says it."

Kleck and Nuessle (1968) found that high amounts of eye contact were interpreted as indicating attraction between members of a dyad, whereas low amounts were interpreted as indicative of tension.[8] It seems reasonable to infer degrees of involvement and/or attention from such relationships.

Finally, Exline *et al.* (1968), using normal and schizophrenic women as stimulus persons, not only found that the ratio of direct to down glances was greater when stimulus persons told happy than when they told sad stories, but also that judges' guesses concerning which of a set of silently presented filmed stories was happy, sad, or angry was highly correlated with relative differences in the gaze ratio across the three stories. In an as yet unpublished extension of the above study, a model relating gaze direction to judges' expectations of the gazer's affective state was developed. From this model an index of gaze direction was derived and used to rank-order stimulus persons as to the affect-appropriateness of their visual display. Stimulus persons then were rank-ordered with

---

[8] Kleck and Nuessle's study is also of interest in that it was designed to explore the significance of the distinction that some investigators make between indicative and communicative functions of nonverbal behavior (see page 121 this chapter). Kleck and Nuessle conclude that, for eye contact at least, the two functions are congruent with respect to the perception of attraction and tension; that is, that which indicates also communicates.

respect to the number of judges who guessed the affect of the stories *as would be predicted by the model.* The correlations, computed separately for normal and for schizophrenic stimulus persons, showed that judges' guesses correlated .940 with the index for normal women, but only .010 with the index for schizophrenic women.

We interpret the findings as providing support for the following set of interlocking assumptions:

1. Given the affects of happy, sad, and angry, we in our culture are most willing to share our happiness, least willing to share our sorrow, and moderately willing to involve relative strangers in our anger.

2. We expect that others in our culture will feel the same.

3. Willingness to share or involve the other in one's affect will be directly represented by the ratio of direct to down gaze. Thus, to some extent, attributions of happiness, sadness, or anger are affected by cues that imply the other's willingness to become involved with the attributor.

The relationships between the patterns of gaze direction and the judgment of affect reported above do not, in our opinion, imply that joy, sorrow, and rage are to be seen as the designata of the different ratios of direct to down gazes. In the first place we do not claim that retelling a personal affective experience invariably recreates the affect, though in the case of some stimulus persons it may very well lead to a degree of affective arousal that is congruent with the theme of the experience. We postulated earlier that "attention" is the basic meaning read into the eye engagement signs. Furthermore, we have suggested that when one human being's attention is directed toward another human being, both observer and interactant will interpret the attention sign as implying that at that moment in time the attender is involved with the focus of his or her attention.

The nature of the involvement is not clearly specified by the eye engagement signs alone, however. Eye engagements are only one of a variety of verbal and nonverbal signs emitted by the actor in the course of interaction. In the study just cited above, for example, it is very likely that the judgment of whether the story was happy, angry, or sad was strongly influenced by other kinds of nonverbal cues, for example, smiles; frowns; turned down lips; illustrative and adaptive gestures; postures that are open, turned away, or shut in; alert or flaccid body tonus, and more.

It is probable that meanings of a higher order of abstraction are attributed on the basis of a cluster of nonverbal cues, which are harmoniously blended into an affect-relevant package. Thus, a high direct-to-down gaze ratio together with a smiling face, relaxed illustrative gestures, and open postural arrangement vis-à-vis the other would combine to elicit the attribution of happiness. On the other hand, a downcast gaze, drooping face, adaptive gestures, and averted posture could combine to elicit the judgment or attribution of sadness. A harmonious blending may well make attribution relatively easy and accurate over a set of judges. In such a case, a judge need not be aware of all dimensions in order to make an accurate attribution, and different judges focusing on different dimensions could be equally accurate.

When the various dimensions do not fit harmoniously together, attribution not only may become more difficult—to the extent that the lack of congruence calls a judge's attention to the inconsistency of the total display—but accuracy is likely to suffer. Accuracy will suffer, for if one judge relies heavily upon facial displays whereas a second consistently utilizes postures or eye engagements, it is probable that different attributions, some of which inevitably will be inaccurate, will be made.

Since flat or inappropriate affective display is a defining characteristic of the schizophrenic (Bleuler, 1952), one would expect less congruence among the multidimensional affect displays of schizophrenics as compared to the normal storytellers. In the light of the above discussion it is not surprising that judges were significantly more accurate in guessing the affective theme of silent stories presented by normals as compared to schizophrenics (Gottheil, Paredes, Exline, & Winkelmayer, 1970), and that a higher correlation was found between the gaze—direction index and expected story in the case of normal as compared to schizophrenic stimulus persons (see page 136–137).

When we explore the psychological meaning of visual behavior by virtue of studying observers' or co-interactants' assessments of the gaze behavior of confederates or other subjects, we are defining meaning in terms of attribution. This approach, as has been nicely shown by Ellsworth and Ludwig (1972), permits the integration of research on nonverbal phenomena with research concerning attribution theory (Kelley, 1967; Jones & Nisbett, 1971). We firmly agree with Ellsworth and Ludwig's conclusion that utilization of nonverbal phenomena enables one to study attribution in a truly interactive situation, a fruitful development which should benefit research in both areas. We do not plan to develop additional evidence to document their conclusion, preferring to call the reader's attention to their interesting suggestions concerning the integration of two important areas of social psychological research.

We wish, however, to call attention to an important problem, which arises when we consider visual behavior as a source of attribution. If, as we have suggested, the basic designatum of a visual sign is the state of the actor that we can label attention (specifically, the sign producer's attention to the target of the gaze), what does attention mean? Attributions that are made on the basis of the observers' awareness of the actor's focus of attention, or lack of it, cannot be dependent only on the presence or absence of the visual sign. Additional information is necessary, for, as was pointed out earlier in the discussion of affect judgments visual behavior is but one component of a complex behavioral display. In addition, the display itself is located in a situational context; for example, the actor is being interviewed (Exline *et al.,* 1965), is reading instructions (LeCompte & Rosenfeld, 1971), is negotiating with another actor (Exline *et al.*, 1975), is involved in a group discussion (Weisbrod, 1966), each one of which creates in the attributor expectations about the actor that could differentially affect the meaning attributed to the actor's attention. If, for example, the actor gives the observer emotionally loaded feedback about himself (the observer), the attention of the speaker would have different meanings and lead to different attributions about the actor if the feedback is positive than if it is negative (Ellsworth & Carlsmith, 1968). Compare the previous situation to one in which the attention (or lack of it) of the actor accompanies a verbal production that is not an evaluation of the observer but is concerned with the explication of themes of varying associative difficulty (Exline & Winters, 1965a). The relative degree of attentiveness of the actor in the above two situations could result in very different attributions. In Ellsworth and Carlsmith's study the attributions would be likely to be concerned with the actor's feeling about the observer, whereas in Exline and Winter's attributions might well be concerned with the actor's confidence, or amount of knowledge about the topic material.

Finally, there is the question of the effect that the degree of interactive involvement of observer and actor has upon attributions related to the amount of the actor's visual attention. Attributions based on the actor's attentiveness should be quite different when the observer is part of the interaction, as compared to when he watches an actor who interacts with a third party. Drawing on results of an experiment by Argyle and Williams (1969), as well as the propositions of Jones and Nisbett (1971), Ellsworth and Ludwig suggest that an "observer" will interpret the actor's behavior as indicators of his stable dispositions or inner-directed moods, while one who feels he is "observed" will interpret the same cues in terms of the actor's reactions to himself and, understandably enough, as a stimulus to his (the observer's) subsequent action.

Thus, the second-order attributions based on the visual behavior of an actor will, for an outisde observer, be concerned with the actor's internally determined dispositions or moods, that is, his basic style whether introverted or extroverted, dominant or submissive, anxious or gay. Attributions based on the perceived attentiveness of a co-interactant made by an interactant—observer, on the other hand, will depend upon whether the structure and dynamics of the situation will cause the attributor to feel that he is the observer or the observed. If the former, his attributions should be similar to an outside observer. If the latter, they would be concerned with the other's reaction to self and the implications of such for one's own action. Thus, for one who feels "observed," the relative attentiveness of the other would be more likely to be interpreted as indications of the other's liking or disliking, approval or disapproval, and other reaction-oriented attributions.

Ellsworth and Ludwig's suggestion that co-interactants' attributions are more likely to be concerned with questions of action and reaction directs our attention to the pragmatics of visual behavior—the relations between signs and their impact upon the interpreter or receiver.

THE PRAGMATICS OF VISUAL BEHAVIOR

Much of the recent interest in the study of gaze behavior has been due to its undoubted influence on those who are its recipients. Approximately half of the studies reviewed for this chapter could be said to be primarily concerned with the impact of the gaze behavior of a sender upon a receiver. This is not surprising for, by definition, there must be a pragmatic element in every study in which visual behavior operates as a sign, for, unless there is a reaction of someone to the something we call a sign, the something cannot be discussed as a sign (Morris, 1938). In a broad sense, attributions (which we discussed under the heading of semantic relations) could have been considered in terms of pragmatic relationships, for attributions elicited by the investigator can be thought of as constituting a response to a visual sign.

In this chapter, however, we will limit ourselves to consideration of only those responses that have been elicited from subjects within the experimental situation, presumably as a consequence of their exposure to specified varieties of gaze behavior emitted by one or more persons within the experiment. We will not discuss responses to another's visual behavior that have been elicited from nonparticipating observers of another's visual behavior unless they are an integral part of a design in which the impact of a looker's visual behavior upon both participants and observers is the variable of interest.

The study of pragmatic relationships then, generally involves a design in which visual behavior is introduced as an independent variable to be manipulated for the purpose of studying its effects upon the behavior of another. Given this paradigm, a variety of dependent variable responses have been investigated. Varying amounts of another's gaze have been related to: (a) indications of physiological arousal, (b) active fight and flight responses, (c) initiation and withdrawal from interaction (including the subject's own visual behavior), (d) evaluative responses of a more or less emotional nature, and, as indicated above, (e) cognitive attributions.

Indications of physiological arousal used have been those of heart rate (Kleinke & Pohlen, 1971), GSR (Nichols & Champness, 1971) and EEG output (Gale, Lucas, Nissim, & Harpham, 1972). In each of the above studies the interaction took place in silence, showing increased amounts of mutual glances to be associated with significant positive increases in heart rate and GSR in the first two studies, and a significant decrease in transoccipital EEG output in the third. It is clear that an increase in the amount of mutual glances is associated with increased physiological arousal.

Direct behavioral evidence of increased arousal associated with the mutual glance has been reported in the primate literature. There are a number of reports from ethological field studies that indicate that a held mutual glance between male primates will initiate mutual threat displays, which end in physical combat unless one of the dyad breaks the glance and presents a species specific deference signal. This phenomena holds true across a number of primate species, for example, baboons (Hall & DeVore, 1965), rhesus and bonnet macaques (Hinde & Rowell, 1962), langurs (Jay, 1965), and the mountain gorilla (Shaller, 1963). In addition, the effect has been demonstrated across primate genera, as Exline and Yellin (1969) found that the incidence and intensity of aggressive responses of four male rhesus macaques studied in the laboratory was directly related to how long human experimenters held a mutual glance with the macaque. Additional indications of the arousing properties of the mutual glance were inferred from the observation that considerable displacement behavior was noted when the mutual glance was initiated and immediately broken off. Following several such quickly terminated engagements, the macaques would begin to tear at themselves, masturbate, and so forth, reactions that rarely or never occurred when threat displays were allowed to run their course.

Inhibiting properties of the averted glance (following a momentary mutual glance) were, in addition to the displacement behavior noted above, dramatically shown in the case of the most aggressive monkey. This monkey, when given a held mutual glance, typically leaped from a ledge at the back of the cage to smash into a wire door directly in front of the face of an experimenter some 4 ft away from the ledge. When the human experimenter momentarily established and then broke off the mutual gaze, there were several occasions when this macaque tumbled off his ledge in a half-leap, which left him far short of the front of the cage. It was as if he, apparently having committed himself to the leaping attack during the brief mutual glance, attempted to inhibit his leap upon observing the averted gaze with the result that he overbalanced himself and recovered by hopping off the ledge to the floor. This behavior occurred only in the condition in which the experimenter established the mutual gaze then quickly averted his eyes.

No direct analogy to the aggressive effects reported above exist in the literature of experiments with human beings. Humans, when brought into the laboratory, do not begin to make faces or otherwise threaten one another when caught up in a mutual glance.[9] Such human analogies as have come to the authors' attention are essentially anecdotal. There have been newspaper reports of juve-

---

[9] It is of interest, however, that the incidence of mutual glances, while low overall, is almost infinitesmial when subjects who are strangers to one another find themselves together in silence. Mutual glances between male strangers amount to 3% when one or the other was talking, dropping off to almost nothing during periods of silence (Exline, 1963). Employing confederates does little to alter this, for once we attempted to create a naturalistic visual dominance struggle by instructing a confederate and subject to wait silently for an experiment to begin. Seated across a table, 3 ft from the subject, the confederate was supposed to catch the subject's eye and stare him down. We were forced to abandon the attempt after testing 15 subjects, for no subject would permit the confederate to enter into a mutual glance in silence! College students, at least, find the mutual glance in silence a very aversive situation—avoiding it in the laboratory and reporting it most uncomfortable in anticipation (page 132).

nile gang fights, which describe the sparking incident as occurring when members of one gang passing through another's territory stare at members of the home gang. A school teacher whose duties required playground supervision once told the senior author that a consistent prelude to a fist fight between two boys is the situation where they confront one another, silently and intently staring at each other for several seconds. If one does not look away, a fight ensues.

An eloquent anecdote of the aggressive impact of the mutual glance can be found in Norman Mailer's *Armies of the Night* (1968). Arrested for his part in an antiwar demonstration, Mailer found himself opposite a member of the American Nazi Party. Mailer was not happy, he reports, for his eyes and the Nazi's bounced off each other "like two heads colliding." In the 20-sec staring match that followed, Mailer described his reaction as one of violent, hostile arousal "... not unlike holding an electric wire in the hand ..." (Mailer, 1968, p. 160–163). There is an indication that the feeling of strong arousal was mutual. Mailer reports "winning" the encounter with the following result: "... and the Nazi looked away, and was hysterical with fury on the instant. 'You Jew bastard,' he shouted. 'Dirty Jew with kinky hair!' [p. 163]"

Implicit in the preceding discussion of the relationship of eye engagement to aggressive behavior is the element of time. Though we spoke of mutual glances, the behavior in question could be more precisely described as held mutual eye engagements. Western people, and perhaps all human beings, appear to be keenly aware of time in relation to visual interaction, and have developed a number of terms to signify variations in time of visual fixation. In English we speak of glances, looks, gazes, stares, and glares. Intuitively, such an ordering would seem to represent a time continuum, with the final three terms implying a fixation time sufficiently long to signify some intent on the part of the looker to act vis-à-vis the target of the look. The aggressive behavior referred to above occurred in the context of mutual stares or glares. What is likely to be the consequence of a one-way stare or glare?

Ellsworth has reported a series of field experiments that bear on the last question (Ellsworth, Carlsmith, & Henson, 1972). She instructed experimenters to stand on a street corner to stare or to avoid looking at pedestrians and motorists who were waiting for a traffic signal to change. The speed with which the subjects crossed the intersection when the light changed was shown to be significantly greater when they were in the stare condition. Being stared at led to avoidance, which was interpreted as the consequence of forcible involvement in a situation in which avoidance is the most appropriate response. "... If it is assumed that staring is a salient stimulus which forcibly involves the subject in an interpersonal encounter and demands a response, the fact that there is no appropriate response becomes very important to the subject, arousing tension and eliciting avoidance at the earliest possible moment" (Ellsworth et al., 1972, p. 311).

In the Ellsworth studies, avoidance was manifested by moving away from a stationary starer. Kurtz (1972) measured avoidance responses in a situation in which subjects were moving toward a staring or nonstaring confederate. Male subjects were instructed to fill out a questionnaire, in a public room where they found two confederates working at a table facing the door. Both confederates looked up as the subject entered the room, one immediately dropped his gaze, the other stared at the subject's face until he touched one of the chairs. Avoidance was defined as taking the one of two available seats that was opposite the nonstaring confederate. Compared to a control condition (no confederates present in room), in which subjects randomly chose a seat, Kurtz found those subjects who made high hostility scores on the MAACL test (Zuckerman & Lubin, 1965) consistently avoided sitting opposite the staring confederate. Nonhostile subjects did not sit randomly, however, preferring a seat slightly closer to the door, regardless of the visual behavior of the confederate.

Kurtz tested the hypothesis that the stare could serve as a means of territorial defense. The following assumptions would seem to underlie the procedure he developed to test his hypothesis: (1) prior occupancy of a public work room would give the occupant greater territorial rights; (2) a stare is a threat sign used to defend such territory; (3) the confederate's gaze would be noticed and interpreted as "staring"; (4) staring is aversive. His results suggest that the underlying assumptions were satisfied only for the hostile subjects. Given the fact that the table was located a few feet from the door, it is possible that only those predisposed to be hostile interpreted the relatively brief look as a "stare." Alternatively, in view of the fact that the table could be reached so quickly, it is possible that both types of subjects interpreted the look as welcoming. In this case those predisposed to feel hostile may have chosen their seat to avoid an unwanted intimacy. Relevant to the alternative explanation (the look as "welcoming" rather than as defensive "staring") are findings from a subsequent study in which the pair of confederates consisted of a man and a woman. Given the same room and procedures, male subjects were found to avoid the "staring" female while females avoided the "staring" male (Kurtz, 1973). It is not clear whether one avoids the opposite-sex confederate who looks steadily because the look is interpreted as a hostile stare or because it is interpreted as an unwelcome invitation to intimacy. Perhaps the most reasonable explanation is that the steady look from a stranger of the opposite sex is perceived as deviant—as a violation of what Goffman has called the norm of "civil indifference." Given such a perception, the subject may wish to select a seat that will minimize the probability of involvement with such a person.

In order to eliminate the procedural ambiguities noted above, Kurtz carried out a third study in which subjects of each sex once again worked with two confederates of their own sex. In this study subjects were informed either that the others were waiting their arrival in order to complete an experimental group, or that the others were working on an important timed test and did not expect to be interrupted. Subjects were asked to pull a chair across the room and sit down at the table to fill out an inventory to describe their first impression of each confederate. In one half of the cases of each set (intruding or expected) both confederates, blind as to the set given the subject, would give the subject a brief glance before returning to their own task. In the other half of the cases one confederate would give the subject a brief glance while the other would continue to look at the face of the subject until the subject sat down in the chair. The table was placed several feet further from the door than was the case in the first two studies. This arrangement, by extending the length of time the confederate would look at the face of the subject, was judged to make it easier for the subject to perceive the look as a "stare"—particularly in the intrusion set.

Reasoning that the subject would expect to be the target of the other's hostility (or at least annoyance) in the "intrusion" set, and of greeting in the "expected" set, Kurtz assumed that the long look would be interpreted as a sign of hostility or rejection in the former and as a sign of welcome in the latter set. He predicted that these interpretations would be confirmed by subjects' rating of how accepting or rejecting the confederate appeared to be. In addition, he predicted that avoidance behavior would be at a maximum in that condition in which the subject, expecting annoyance and rejection, was instructed to intrude, and upon doing so became the target of a lengthy look. Avoidance was predicted to be at a minimum in the "expected" set, particularly in that condition in which the subject became the target of a long look.

Avoidance was operationally defined as a refusal to pull the chair up to the table. Subjects who did not move the chair would be put to the additional trouble of marking their forms by spreading them over their knees. Thus, subjects would be required to go to considerable trouble to avoid sitting at the table with the confederates. They must, that is, disobey the instructions of the experimenter, plus suffer the inconvenience of filling out forms without having a solid surface to work on.

The data indicated that subjects did indeed perceive significantly greater rejection by the long looker than by the brief looker in the intrusive condition and relatively less rejection by the long looking as compared to the short looking confederate in the nonintrusive condition. In addition, the ratings showed significantly greater rejection by the long looker in the intrusive than in the nonintrusive condition and the reverse for the short look. We suggest that the expectations created by instruction led the subject to perceive the long look as a "glare" in the intrusive condition (that is, fixed and prolonged attention implying fierceness or anger) and as a "gaze" in the nonintrusive condition (that is, fixed and prolonged attention implying admiration).

Data bearing on the predictions concerning the approach–avoidance behavior of the subjects tended to show the predicted results. Though the difference did not reach significance, 42% of the subjects in the condition where the long look could be considered a "glare" or "stare" refused to pull the chair to the table. Twenty-five percent refused to do so in the condition where subjects who intruded were given only brief glances by both confederates, and *no* avoidance responses were observed in both of the conditions where the subjects believed that the others were awaiting their arrival.

We have examined Kurtz's investigation in some detail for we feel that it represents a good demonstration of the interrelationship between the various semiotic levels of visual behavior. It clearly shows the interrelationships among syntactic, semantic, and pragmatic levels of analysis—sign patterns, attribution, and action—by virtue of demonstrating that prior sets and expectations concerning one's own role in an interaction affect one's interpretation of the identical visual signs and the actions that follow on the specific attribution derived from exposure to the signs. In the last study of the series (Kurtz, 1975), both those who expected to join others and those who expected to intrude upon them received the identical visual pattern—a short look from one person and a long look from the other. The first order of attribution, that of relatively more attention from the person who looked steadily, may be inferred from the pattern of perceived rejections (that is, greater differentiation between confederates and higher levels of perceived rejection by one member in the heterogeneous looking pair than by both members of the homogeneous looking pair). The second order of attribution, that is, the judgment that the attentive looker is more accepting or rejecting, depended on the subject's expectations concerning his own role vis-à-vis the others, namely, whether he expected to join (in which case he perceived the look as accepting) or intrude (in which case he perceived rejection). These distinctions at the semantic level were also reflected in behavior at the pragmatic level, the visually accepted joiner pulling the chair up to the table strikingly more often than the rejected intruder (100 and 58% approach behavior, respectively), whereas the visually rejected inturder tended to hang back more frequently than his ignored counterpart (42 and 25% avoidance behavior). Studies such as Kurtz's are necessary for a more precise understanding of the communicative properties of studies of eye engagements or gaze direction.

As Ellsworth and Ludwig pointed out in their review (Ellsworth & Ludwig, 1972), other studies of eye behavior at the pragmatic level ("interactive influence" in their terminology) have been concerned with evaluative responses to the looker (Jones & Cooper, 1971; Ellsworth & Carlsmith, 1968; Mehrabian, 1972; Holstein et al., 1971; Lefebvre & McNeel, 1971; to cite just a few representative examples), and with interpersonal regulatory behaviors. With respect to the latter, we have already cited Kendon's study of the looking pattern associated with cessation and initiation of speech (Kendon, 1967). Other examples of the regulatory function of gaze behavior are Exline's findings that subjects tend to event-match confederates and one another with respect to the amount of looking at one another (Exline, 1963; Exline, 1972); Ellsworth and Carlsmith's (1968) finding that consistent eye contact from a victim inhibited aggressive responses more effectively than did inconsistent looking; Argyle, Lalljee, and Cook's (1968) finding that seeing another's eyes facilitates synchronization of speech in face-to-face conversations; Argyle and Dean's (1965) intimacy-equilibrium theory, which predicts that proximity and looking behavior will interact to determine the level at which each is manifested; and Gardin, Kaplan, Firestone, and Cowan's (1973) data, which indicate that proxemic relations and amount of eye contact interact to regulate the amount of cooperation elicited in a prisoner's dilemma game.

Gardin et al's. (1973) study is of particular interest due to the light it throws on a possible confound inherent in Sommer's claim that cross-table "confrontation" is more characteristic of competitive situations than is a side-by-side seating arrangement (Sommer, 1969). Separating seating arrangements from the possibility of eye contact, they found that more cooperative strategies tended to be used in the side-by-side arrangement when a barrier prevented eye contact, but in conditions where eye contact was permitted, not only was cooperation significantly greater in the cross-table arrangement but subjects sat closer to each other in filling out postexperimental questionnaires. Gardin et al. (1973) point out that an across-the-table arrangement increases the chance of mutual eye contact, which could signal liking rather than competitive confrontation. Assuming that more eye contact did occur in the cross-table no-barrier condition, and we have no reason to think otherwise, it seems clear that the competitive element is subdued in the cross-table seating arrangement. Perhaps confrontations, with the associated possibility of increased eye contact, contain the seeds of future cooperation.

The previous studies stress the interrelationships among several dimensions of nonverbal phenomena. We believe they demonstrate an increasing awareness of the desirability of studying the meaning and the effects of eye engagements or avoidances in controlled interactive situations. A very interesting demonstration of the power of nonverbal phenomena to elicit behavior that serves to validate the attitudes causing the original behaviors has recently been provided by Word et al. (1974). These investigators, influenced by Mehrabian's thinking on "immediacy" in nonverbal behavior (Mehrabian, 1969)[10] and Kleck's work on physical stigmata (Kleck, 1968), postulate that nonverbal behaviors generally elicit reciprocal nonverbal behaviors. They then suggest that subjects, unaware of their own nonverbal display, will attribute the reciprocated nonverbal behavior from others to the other's disposition rather than to their own eliciting display. One's own nonverbal behavior thus serves as an integral part of a self-fulfilling prophecy.

Word et al. tested the above hypothesis by means of two experiments in an interracial setting. In the first experiment black as compared to white confederates elicited less "immediate" behaviors, namely, greater interpersonal distance,[11]

---

[10] Mehrabian defines immediacy behaviors in terms of interpersonal distance, amount of eye contact, forward lean, and directness of shoulder orientation.

[11] Contrary to previous investigations (Mehrabian, 1968; Exline & Winters, 1965b; Rubin, 1970) Word et al. (1974) did not find differences in gaze behavior that were in line with their "immediacy" expectations. Analyses of their procedures show that they induced a cooperative set in a situation wherein subjects knew that they would interview both black and white persons. In such a setting, subjects may have wished to avoid the appearance of bias by equating their visual attention across the races. In addition, they were provided incentives for team performance. Further research is necessary to determine whether incentives, demand characteristics, or both served to equalize crossracial eye contact.

from white subjects serving as interviewers. White interviewers also made significantly more speech errors and spent significantly less time with the black confederate.

Having established that blacks elicited less immediate (or affiliative) behavior from whites, the investigators conducted a second experiment in which white confederates interviewed white subjects. In this experiment the interviewers were trained to provide half of the subjects with those immediacy (or affiliative) nonverbal behaviors that black confederates had elicited from white subject interviewers in the previous study, while providing the other half of the subjects with the nonverbal behaviors that naive interviewers had manifested in the presence of white confederates. In other words, half of the subjects worked with an interviewer who sat four inches closer, made 1.17 speech errors per minute less, and spent 3.35 min more with them (immediacy condition) than with the other half of the subjects (nonimmediacy condition). Subjects reciprocated the immediacy behaviors of the confederate interviewers. Subjects in the immediacy condition moved their chairs to be significantly closer to the interviewer than did subjects in the nonintimacy condition (those in the latter condition moved away). In addition, "immediate" subjects tended to make fewer speech errors per minute than did subjects given less affiliative cues.

The most interesting feature of the above experiment, however, was the rating made by independent and naive observers of the fitness of the subject for the position for which they were ostensibly being interviewed. Videotapes taken during the experiment were later shown to judges who were unaware of the purposes of the study. Judges rated those subjects who received (and reciprocated) immediacy–affiliative cues as being significantly more qualified for the position than those subjects who received nonaffiliative cues (judges could not be affected by knowledge of the performance of the confederates, for the confederates were not shown on the videotapes).

Thus, the rating of the quality of the subjects' performance was affected by nonverbal immediacy cues of which the judges were unaware. The ratings were, of course, mediated by the immediacy behaviors of the subjects, which were, however—and this is the crucial point—elicited by the nonverbal behavior of the interviewers. The investigators conclude that these experiments provide inferential evidence that self-fulfilling prophesies occur in interracial situations, to the detriment of the evaluated minority group member. We submit that these investigators have made the more general point that any evaluator evaluatively predisposed toward the human subject of his evaluation can, by his nonverbal behaviors, elicit reciprocated behaviors that confirm his evaluative set. This study would appear to have far-reaching implications for the structuring and processing of evaluative interviews and oral examinations. Perhaps the most valid performance evaluation would result from the average of a positive and a negative interview; perhaps an evaluative interview should be conducted by a team composed of one hostile and one friendly interviewer. At the very least, evaluators should recognize that a trial by ordeal is inherently stacked in favor of a negative evaluation. Rather than providing an objective measure of the quality of another's performance such an ordeal may measure only his ability to inhibit a natural propensity to reciprocate the negative evaluative cues provided by the evaluator.

COMMUNICATIVE PROPERTIES OF VISUAL BEHAVIOR

We have attempted at some length to demonstrate that visual behavior between and among interactants in a social situation can be investigated in terms of a theory of signs, and that syntactic, semantic, and pragmatic relations and their interrelations can be identified. How does this approach help us to better understand and appreciate the role played by eye engagements and avoidances in the process of face-to-face communications among humans? From one point of view, (MacKay, 1972; Wiener, Devoe, Robinow, & Geller, 1972) it can be argued that few, if any, of the many studies of visual interaction are relevant to communication. None of the studies reviewed to date are concerned with a sender who intends to transmit a given message to a receiver whose interpretation of the message is, in turn, checked to determine the extent to which it matches the intention of the sender.

It is theoretically possible to design a study in which the use of visual behavior to encode intention is investigated concomitantly with the assessment of its effect upon the receiver's assumptions of the sender's intentions. We do not believe, however, that such a narrow approach will prove useful. Kurtz's study, though concerned only with the latter aspect of the above paradigm, strongly suggests that attributions of intention keyed to a given visual cue are dependent upon the total context in which the cue is set, particularly upon the receiver's set or expectations concerning his role vis-à-vis the other. Thus, the identical visual cue is, dependent upon the subject's understanding of the situation, perceived as an indicator of friendly or unfriendly intent.

We believe that a more fruitful approach is to think of eye engagements and avoidances not in terms of content, but in terms of statements about the communication process, that is, metamessages concerned with the relationship between the communicators. Watzlawick, Beavin, and Jackson (1967) have postulated "Every communication has a content and a relationship aspect such that the latter classifies the former and is therefore, a meta-communication [p. 67]." Thus, as Wiener *et al.* (1972) suggest, visual behaviors can be thought of as regulators that indicate that communication is occurring. From the point of view of the speaker, the listener's regulators suggest understanding, confusion, agreement, or disagreement. From the point of view of the listener, the speaker's regulators indicate that the speaker is continuing to encode, checking to see if the listener is decoding, and/or turning the floor over to the listener.

In our discussion of semantic relations we spoke of visual behavior in terms of orientation, involvement, attention (pages 131–139). We suggest now that orientation and attention are primary metamessages about the communication process, which are inherent in and, metaphorically speaking, carried by eye engagements, their absence, or their specific pattern.

At the syntactic level the focus and timing of the speakers' and listeners' attention determines what function visual behavior as a regulator plays in the interaction. At the semantic level we indicated the considerations involved in establishing the meaning of attention at higher levels of attribution, that is, beyond the attribution of attention. Finally, we suggest that the study of the pragmatics of visual behavior in terms of metamessages will be clarified by an understanding of the norms that societies have developed concerning the use or nonuse of the visual channel; norms concerned with attention to, and hence with implications for, the relationship between communicants or potential communicators. Thus pedestrians, motorists, and motorbike riders waiting for a traffic signal to change can be driven to walk or accelerate more rapidly across an intersection if they are the recipient of a long, deadpan look from a stranger standing on the corner. The investigators, as was indicated earlier in this chapter (page 142), conclude that the flight behavior occurred because there was no appropriate response to a forced encounter. An appropriate social response is a normative response, implying shared agreement among interactants. Goffman (1963) has postulated that a norm of "civil indifference" regulates the behavior of people in public places. To be consistent with this norm, visual interaction among strangers in a public place should, at the most, involve a brief glance at and then away from the other. To be the recipient of an overlong look from a stranger in public is to be made aware of his attention, which in this case signals the violation of the norm. The implication of the norm violation is that one is the focus of an intention of an unknown but probably uncivil nature. In such a case, an understandable response is to do just what the subjects did—get away before the assumed intention is translated into action, and potential involvement becomes actual involvement.

Ellsworth *et al.* (1972) set up a silent encounter. Such an encounter is likely to be one in which eye engagements carry the message about normative violation rather than to serve as a relationship-relevant comment on the content of a message. Let us now consider a situation wherein eye engagements may serve as a metamessage relevant to the normative aspects of the situations of two strangers in a state of talk. Exline (1972) has described a study in which one interactant, a confederate, looked intermittantly when speaking to a subject, but either looked steadily at, or steadily above and away whenever the other spoke. In this case, we postulate that a norm of "civil attention" (or "conversational attention") serves to regulate the behavior of interactants. The norm, we suggest, leads one to expect intermittant visual attention from a speaker, and somewhat more steady visual attention from a listener. In the study described above the confederate conformed to the norm while speaking but violated it while listening.

Rommetveit (1954) has shown that when a social norm is violated the usual reaction is to remind the other immediately of the norm. This reaction, which is called "norm sending," can be verbal but is equally likely to be nonverbal in nature. Subjects might, for example, send the norm "pay attention" by raising their voice, exaggerating their gestures, or otherwise try to attract the listener's attention. The norm "reduce attention" would be sent by more frequent looking away, postural adjustments that turn away from the listener, and other subtle behaviors designed to help the speaker avoid the gaze of the listener. In the specific study in question the investigators were interested in the attributions made by subjects who interacted with the violator.[12] The model, however, is one that permits the investigation of norm-sending reactions, as well as the study of attributions and other effects of the norm violation upon speech behavior.

IMPLICATIONS FOR FUTURE RESEARCH INVOLVING EYE ENGAGEMENTS

To view eye engagements in terms of normative considerations, and in terms of relationship-oriented metamessages, whether concerned or not with normative violations, has specific implications for future research. The first, of course, points to the need for cross-cultural research at all three levels of relationship. Most of the published research on visual interaction has involved white Anglo-American subjects. Whether the syntactic, semantic, and pragmatic relations herein described will hold for people of different cultures is, of course, an empirical question, though the obvious involvement of normative considerations at the pragmatic level makes it theoretically imperative to design cross-cultural studies at both the semantic and pragmatic levels.

Subcultural studies are also necessary. There already exists the suggestion that black people manifest very different behavior in social situations than do white people (Johnson, 1972). Johnson writes of "rolling the eyes" as an expression of disapproval of a person in an authority role, and also asserts that, in contrast to the visual attention we have found to characterize the listening behavior of white subordinates (Exline *et al.,* 1975), blacks will not look an authority-figure in the eye, particularly when the other is talking (Johnson, 1972).[13] We are aware of only one empirical study relevant to the above point (La France & Mayo, 1973), and while it provides data consistent with the argument that

[12] Specifically, the effect of personality variables upon attributions coordinate with the presence or absence of eye contact. Control-oriented persons (Schutz, 1958) were found to attribute more potency to the avoidant listener than to the direct looker. This was not done by the less control-oriented person, who also perceived the avoidant listener as less potent than did control-oriented subjects (Exline, 1972).

[13] Johnson also states that West Africans and Japanese cultures teach one in the subordinate role to avoid eye contact in order to communicate respect and acceptance of the subordinate role.

black–white differences do exist, the fact that the data are based on only one pair of blacks, one of whom also was observed talking with a white, strongly suggests the need for further investigations.

Research keyed to the proposition that eye engagements are metacommunications commenting on the relationships existing among communicators provides a second line of future research. We have already spoken of such messages in terms of inferences and attributions which can be derived from the orienting and attentional functions of the look. We believe that future research of this sort must integrate eye behavior into an ongoing stream of other behaviors, especially those concerned with postures, gestures, facial expressions and paralinguistic cues. Eye behavior, due to its attentional properties, plays a major role in the metacommunicative system, but its interrelations with other nonverbal indicators must be better understood.

An approach that combines gaze behavior with facial displays and postural orientations, for example, may help to clarify a pervasive phenomenological question raised by eye contact between two people. We refer to the difference between perceiving the other's eyes and perceiving his "gaze" (Heron, 1970), also, described as the difference between "seeing" and "looking" (Feldman, 1959), or as being the "observed" one or the "observer" (Argyle & Williams, 1969). To perceive, see, or observe has been characterized as connoting that one treats the other as an object, whereas to gaze, look, or be observed implies a more psychological relationship between the source and the target of the visual behavior. We suggest that the distinction is affected both by role relationships and the nature of the expressive display in which the visual behavior is set.

An interviewee, for example, is more likely to feel observed, than observing (Argyle & Williams, 1969). However, the impression of being "looked at" as opposed to merely "seen" (comparable to perceiving the other's "gaze" in distinction to his "eyes") may well turn out to be dependent upon complex combinations of factors involving the average length of fixations, the direction of gaze avoidance, whether the looker is speaking or listening, deadpan or facially mobile, posturally oriented toward or away,—in short a multivariate problem. An initial attack upon the problem might be to film a number of people listening to another talk, identify those listeners who impress speakers as "looking" rather than as "seeing", that is, as being more involved with the speaker, and analyzing film sequences including both speaker and listener to determine those nonverbal behaviors, if any, that differentiate those who are phenomenalogically involved and noninvolved.

Other interesting problems for future research concern the effect of the direction of gaze avoidance, left, right, up, down, upon attributions, and regulation of behavior (Libby & Yaklevich, 1973) and exploring the implications of physiological arousal related to the mutual gaze. Tinbergen, in his acceptance of the Nobel Prize for Physiology and Medicine (Tinbergen, 1974), called attention to the work of Corinne Hutt (Hutt & Ounsted, 1966; Hutt & Hutt, 1970) linking hyperarousal and gaze behavior in autistic children. Tinbergen suggested that a sensitive combination of the use of visual and tactile channels will succeed not only in drawing severely autistic children out of their shells, but also provide a strategy for healthy socialization of normal children:

> One can see a great deal of the behavior of the child out of the corner of one's eye . . . usually the child will start by simply looking intently at the stranger, studying him guardedly. One may . . . judge it safe to now and then look briefly at the child and assess more accurately the state the child is in. If . . . one sees the child avert its glance, eye contact must at once be broken off. Very soon the child will stop studying one. It will approach gingerly, and it will soon reveal its strong bonding tendency by touching one. . . . This is often a crucial moment: one must *not* respond by looking at the child (which may set it back considerably) but by cautiously touching the child's hand with one's own [Tinbergen & Tinbergen, 1972, pp. 29–30].

Tinbergen proceeds to describe how by a careful monitoring of the child's responses, by avoiding the use of intrusive looking, and by frequent and sensitive use of reassuring touch signals, the child will eventually be enabled to tolerate increasingly long periods of direct eye contact, and, finally, will literally clamor for intensive affiliative contact.

Tinbergen's intriguing report points to the value of intergrating visual, tactile, paralinguistic, and verbal behaviors in developing effective therapeutic strategies. More importantly, from the viewpoint of this volume, it suggests that the optimal therapeutic strategy is a communicative process in which nonverbal elements figure prominently. Research designed to identify those interactive patterns that create affiliative bonding would seem to provide a fruitful line of future inquiry. We suggest that attention to the pragmatics of visual attention will be a central component of such research.

REFERENCES

Aiello, J. R. A test of equilibrium theory: Visual interaction in relation to orientation distance and sex of interactants. *Psychonomic Science,* 1972, **27**(6), 335–336.

Antis, S. M., Mayhew, J. W., & Morley, T. The perception of where a face or television 'portrait' is looking. *American Journal of Psychology,* 1969, **82,** 474–489.

Argyle, M. Eye-contact and distance: A reply to Stephenson and Rutter. *British Journal of Psychology,* 1970, **61,** 395–396.

Argyle, M., & Dean, J. Eye contact, distance and affiliation. *Sociometry,* 1965, **28,** 289–304.

Argyle, M., & Kendon, A. The experimental analysis of social performance. In L. Berkowitz (Ed.), *Advances in experimental social psychology* (Vol. 2). New York: Academic Press, 1967.

Argyle, M., Lalljee, M., & Cook, M. The effects of visibility on interaction in a dyad. *Human relations,* 1968, 21, 3–17.

Argyle, M., & Williams, M. Observer or observed: A reversible perspective in person perception. *Sociometry,* 1969, **32,** 396–412.

Bleuler, E. *Dementia praecox, or the group of schizophrenics.* New York: International Universities Press, 1952.

Brown, R. *Social psychology*. New York: Free Press, 1965.

Carnap, R. *Philosophy and logical syntax*. London: Paul, Trench, Trubner & Company, 1935.

Cassirer, E. *The philosophy of symbolic forms*. Vol I: *Language*. New Haven: Yale University Press, 1923.

Chekhov, A. The name-day party–1888 (translated by C. Garnett). In A. Yarmolinski (Ed.), *The portable Chekhov*. New York: Viking Press, 1947.

Cline, M. G. The perception of where a person is looking. *American Journal of Psychology*, 1967, **80**, 41–50.

Coss, R. G. The perceptual aspects of eye-spot patterns and their relevance to gaze behaviour. In C. Hutt & S. J. Hutt (Eds.), *Behaviour studies in psychiatry*. Oxford: Pergamon Press, 1970.

Cranach, M. von, Schmid, R., & Vogel, M. V. Ueber einige Bedingungen des zusammenhanges von Lidschlag und Blickwendung. *Psychologische Forschung*, 1969, **33**, 68–78. Cited in: von Cranach & Ellgring, 1973.

Cranach, M. von. The role of orienting behavior in human interaction. In A. H. Esser (Ed.), *Environment and behavior: The use of space by animals and man*. New York: Plenum Press, 1971.

Cranach, M. von, & Ellgring, J. H. Problems in the recognition of gaze direction. In M. von Cranach & I. Vine (Eds.), *Social communication and movement*. New York: Academic Press, 1973.

Daniell, R. J., & Lewis, P. Stability of eye contact and physical distance across a series of structured interviews. *Journal of Consulting and Clinical Psychology*, 1972, **39**(1), 172.

Diebold, R. A., Jr. Anthropology and the comparative psychology of communicative behavior. In T. A. Sebeok (Ed.), *Animal communication: Techniques of study and results of research*. Bloomington: Indiana University Press, 1968.

Duncan, S., Jr. Nonverbal communication. *Psychological Bulletin*, 1969, **72**, 118–137.

Ekman, P., & Friesen, W. V. The repertoire of nonverbal behavior: Categories, origins, usage, and coding. *Semiotica*, 1969, **1**(1), 49–98.

Ekman, P. Universal and cultural differences in facial expression of emotion. In J. K. Cole (Ed.), *Nebraska Symposium on Motivation* (Vol. 19). Lincoln: University of Nebraska Press, 1972.

Ellgring, J. H. Die Beurteilung des Blickes auf Punkte innerhalt des Gesichtes. *Zeitschrift für Experimentalishe und Angewandte Psychologie*, 1970, **17**, 600–607. Cited in: von Cranach & Ellgring, 1973.

Ellgring, J. H., & von Cranach, M. Process of learning in the recognition of eye signals. *European Journal of Social Psychology*, 1972, **2**(1), 33–43.

Ellsworth, P. C., & Carlsmith, J. Effects of eye contact and verbal content on affective response to a dyadic interaction. *Journal of Personality and Social Psychology*, 1968, **10**, 15–20.

Ellsworth, P. C., Carlsmith, J., & Henson, A. The stare as a stimulus to flight in human subjects: A series of field experiments. *Journal of Personality and Social Psychology*, 1972, **21**, 302–311.

Ellsworth, P., & Ludwig, L. M. Visual behavior in social interaction. *Journal of Communication*, 1972, **22**, 375–403.

Exline, R. V. Explorations in the process of person perception: Visual interaction in relation to competition, sex, and need for affiliation. *Journal of Personality*, 1963, **31**, 1–20.

Exline, R. V. The glances of power and preference. In J. K. Cole (Ed.), *The Nebraska Symposium on Motivation* (Vol.19). Lincoln, Nebraska: University of Nebraska Press, 1972.

Exline, R. V., & Eldridge, C. Effects of two patterns of a speaker's visual behavior on the perception of the authenticity of his verbal message. Paper presented at the meeting of the Eastern Psychological Association, Boston, 1967.

Exline, R. V., Ellyson, S. L., & Long, B. Visual behavior as an aspect of power role relationships. In P. Pilner, L. Krames, T. Alloway (Eds.), *Advances in the study of communication and affect* (Vol. 2). New York: Plenum Press, 1975.

Exline, R. V., Fairweather, H., Hine, J., & Argyle, M. Impressions of a listener as affected by his direction of gaze during conversation. Unpublished manuscript, University of Delaware, 1971.   (a) (Cited in Exline, 1972.)

Exline, R., Gottheil, E., Paredes, A., & Winkelmayer, R. Gaze direction as a factor in the accurate judgment of nonverbal expression of affect. Paper presented at the meeting of the American Psychological Association, San Francisco, 1968.

Exline, R., Gray, D., & Schuette, D. Visual behavior in a dyad as affected by interview content and sex of respondent. *Journal of Personality and Social Psychology,* 1965, **1,** 201–209.

Exline, R. V., & Snadowski, A. Anticipations of comfort with various age and sex partners according to visual behavior during speech and silence. Unpublished manuscript, Psychology Department, University of Delaware, 1971.   (b) (Cited in Exline, 1972.)

Exline, R. V., Thibaut, J., Hickey, C. B., & Gumpert, P. Visual interaction in relation to Machiavellianism and an unethical act. In R. Christie & F. Geis (Eds.), *Studies in Machiavellianism.* New York: Academic Press, 1970.

Exline, R. V., & Winters, L. C. Effects of cognitive difficulty and cognitive style upon eye to eye contact in interviews. Paper presented at the meeting of the Eastern Psychological Association Meetings, Atlantic City, 1965.   (a)

Exline, R. V., & Winters, L. C. Affective relations and mutual glances in dyads. In S. Tomkins & C. Izard (Eds.), *Affect, cognition and personality.* New York: Springer Publ., 1965.   (b)

Exline, R. V., & Yellin, A. Eye contact as a sign between man and monkey. Symposium on nonverbal communication, 19th International Congress of Psychology, London, 1969.

Feldman, S. S. *Mannerisms of speech and gesture in everyday life.* New York: International Universities Press, 1959.

Friedman, N. The analysis of movement behavior during the clinical interview. In A. W. Siegman & B. Pope (Eds.), *Studies in dyadic communication.* New York: Pergamon Press, 1972.

Gale, A., Lucas B., Nissim, R., & Harpham, B. Some EEG correlates of face to face contact. *British Journal of Social and Clinical Psychology,* 1972, **11,** 326–332.

Gardin, H., Kaplan, K. J., Firestone, I., & Cowan, G. A. Proxemic effects on cooperation, attitude, and approach–avoidance in a Prisoner's Dilemma game. *Journal of Personality and Social Psychology,* 1973, **27**(1), 13–18.

Gibson, J. J., & Pick, A. D. Perception of another person's looking behavior. *American Journal of Psychology,* 1963, **76,** 86–94.

Gilliland, A. R. A revision and some results with the Moore–Gilliland aggressiveness test. *Journal of Applied Psychology,* 1926, **10,** 143–150.

Goffman, E. *The presentation of self in everyday life.* Garden City, New York: Doubleday, 1959.

Goffman, E. *Behavior in public places.* New York: Free Press, 1963.

Gottheil, E., Paredes, A., Exline, R. V., & Winkelmayer, R. Communication of affect in schizophrenia. *Archives of General Psychiatry,* 1970, **22,** 439–444.

Hall, E. T. *The hidden dimension.* New York: Doubleday, 1966.

Hall, K. R. L., & DeVore, I. Baboon social behavior. In I. Devore (Ed.), *Primate behavior: Field studies of monkeys and apes.* New York: Holt, Rinehart, & Winston, 1965.

Heron, J. The phenomenology of social encounter: The gaze. *Philosophical and Phenomenological Research,* 1970, **31**(2), 243–264.

Hersen, M., Miller, P. M., & Eisler, R. M. Interactions between alcoholics and their wives: A descriptive analysis of verbal and nonverbal behavior. *Quarterly Journal of Studies on Alcohol*, 1973, **34**(2), 516–520.

Hinchliffe, M. K., Lancashire, M., & Roberts, F. J. A study of eye-contact changes in depressed and recovered psychiatric patients. *British Journal of Psychiatry*, 1971, **119**(549), 213–215.

Hinde, R. A., & Rowell, T. E. Communication by posture and facial expressions in the rhesus monkey (*Macaca mulatta*). *Proceedings of the Zoological Society of London*, 1962, **138**, 1–21.

Hobson, G. N., Strongman, K. T., Bull, D., & Craig, G. Anxiety and gaze aversion in dyadic encounters. *British Journal of Social and Clinical Psychology*, 1973, **12**(2), 122–129.

Holstein, C. M., Goldstein, J. W., & Bem, D. J. The importance of expressive behavior, involvement, sex, and need-approval in inducing liking. *Journal of Personality and Social Psychology*, 1971, **7**(5), 534–544.

Hore, T. Social class differences in some aspects of the nonverbal communication between mother and preschool child. *Australian Journal of Psychology*, 1970, **22**(1), 21–27.

Hutt, C., & Ounsted, C. The biological significance of gaze aversion with particular reference to the syndrome of infantile autism. *Behavioral Science*, 1966, **11**, 346–356.

Hutt, S. J., & Hutt, C. (Eds.), *Behaviour studies in psychiatry*. Oxford: Pergamon Press, 1970.

Jay, P. Field studies. In A. Schrier, H. F. Harlow, & F. Stollnitz (Eds.) *Behavior of nonhuman primates: Research trends*. New York: Academic Press, 1965.

Johnson, K. R. Black kinesics: Some nonverbal communication patterns in the black culture. In L. A. Samovar & R. E. Porter (Eds.), *Intercultural communication: A reader*. Belmont, California: Wadsworth Publ., 1972.

Jones, E. E., & Nisbett, R. E. *The actor and the observer: Divergent perceptions of the causes of behavior*. 250 James St., Morristown, N. J.: General Learning Press, 1971.

Jones, R. A. & Cooper, J. Mediation of experimenter effects. *Journal of Personality and Social Psychology*, 1971, **20**(1), 70–74.

Kelley, H. H. Attribution theory in social psychology. In D. Levine (Ed.), *Nebraska Symposium on Motivation* (Vol. 15), Lincoln, Nebraska: University of Nebraska Press, 1967.

Kendon, A. Some functions of gaze-direction in social interaction. *Acta Psychologica*, 1967, **26**, 22–63.

Kleck, R. Physical stigmata and nonverbal cues emitted in face-to-face interaction. *Human Relations*, 1968, **21**, 19–28.

Kleck, R. E., & Nuessle, W. Congruence between the indicative and communicative functions of eye contact in interpersonal relations. *British Journal of Social and Clinical Psychology*, 1968, **7**, 241–246.

Kleinke, C. L., & Pohlen, P. D. Affective and emotional responses as a function of other person's gaze and cooperativeness in a two-person game. *Journal of Personality and Social Psychology*, 1971, **17**, 308–313.

Krüger, K., & Hückstedt, B. Die Beurteilung von Blickrichtungen. *J. Exp. Angew. Psychol.*, 1969, **16**, 452–472. Cited in von Cranach & Ellgring, 1973.

Kurtz, J. Agonistic signalling and territorial defense. (Master's Thesis) Unpublished manuscript, University of Delaware, 1972.

Kurtz, J. Male and female reactions to the stare of same and opposite sex. Unpublished manuscript. Psychology Department, University of Delaware, 1973.

Kurtz, J. Nonverbal norm sending and territorial defense. (Doctoral Dissertation, University of Delaware, 1975). Dissertation Abstracts International, 1975, **36**, 1508 B. (University Microfilms No. 75-20, 554)

La France, M., & Mayo, C. Gaze direction in interracial dyadic communication. Paper presented at the meeting of the Eastern Psychological Association, Washington, D.C., May, 1973.

Langer, S. *Philosophy in a new key.* Cambridge, Mass.: Harvard University Press, 1942.

LeCompte, W. F., & Rosenfeld, H. M. Effects of minimal eye contact in the instruction period on impressions of the experimenter. *Journal of Experimental Social Psychology,* 1971, 7, 211–220.

Lefebvre, L. M., & McNeel, S. P. Attractiveness and cost as mediating variables in the performer–judge relation: An extension of the reward–cost model. *European Journal of Social Psychology,* 1971, 1(2), 179–200.

Libby, W. L., Jr., & Yaklevich, D. Personality determinants of eye contact and direction of gaze aversion. *Journal of Personality and Social Psychology,* 1973, 27(3), 197–206.

MacKay, D. M. Formal analysis of communicative processes. In R. A. Hinde (Ed.), *Nonverbal communication.* Cambridge, England: Cambridge University Press, 1972.

Mailer, N. *The armies of the night.* New York: Signet, 1968.

Mehrabian, A. Inference of attitudes from the posture, orientation, and distance of a communicator. *Journal of Consulting and Clinical Psychology,* 1968, 32, 296–308.

Mehrabian, A. Some referents and measures of nonverbal behavior. *Behavior research methods and instrumentation,* 1969, 1, 203–207.

Mehrabian, A. *Nonverbal communication.* Chicago: Aldine–Atherton, 1972.

Mobbs, N. A. Eye-contact in relation to social introversion–extroversion. *British Journal of Social Clinical Psychology,* 1968, 7, 305–306.

Modigliani, A. Embarrassment, facework, and eye contact: Testing a theory of embarrassment. *Journal of Personality and Social Psychology,* 1971, 17(1), 15–24.

Moore, H. T., & Gilliland, A. R. The measurement of aggressiveness. *Journal of Applied Psychology,* 1921, 2, 97–118.

Morris, C. W. Foundations of the theory of signs. In *International Encyclopedia of Unified Science* (Vol 1., No. 2) Chicago: University of Chicago Press, 1938.

Nichols, K. A., & Champness, B. G. Eye gaze and the GSR. *Journal of Experimental Social Psychology,* 1971, 7, 623–626.

Nielsen, G. *Studies in self-confrontation.* Copenhagen: Munksgaard, 1962.

Piderit, T. *Mimik und Physiognomik.* Detmold: Verlag der Meyer' sehn Hofbiechhandlung, 1886.

Reece, M. M., & Whitman, R. N. Expressive movements, warmth and verbal reinforcement. *Journal of Abnormal and Social Psychology,* 1962, 64, 234–236.

Riemer, M. D. The averted gaze. *Psychiatric Quarterly,* 1949, 23, 108–115.

Riemer, M. D. Abnormalities of the gaze: A classification. *Psychiatric Quarterly,* 1955, 29, 659–672.

Robson, K. S. The role of eye-to-eye contact in maternal–infant attachment. *Journal of Child Psychology and Psychiatry,* 1967, 8, 13–25.

Rommetveit, R. *Social norms and roles.* Minneapolis: University of Minnesota Press, 1954.

Rubin, Z., Measurement of romantic love. *Journal of Personality and Social Psychology,* 1970, 16, 265–273.

Rutter, D. R., Morley, I. E., & Graham, J. C. Visual interaction in a group of introverts and extroverts. *European Journal of Social Psychology,* 1972, 2(4), 371–384.

Rutter, D. R., & Stephenson, G. M. Visual interaction in a group of schizophrenic and depressive patients. *British Journal of Social Clinical Psychology,* 1972, 11, 57–65. (a)

Rutter, D. R., & Stephenson, G. M. Visual interaction in a group of schizophrenic and depressive patients: A follow-up study. *British Journal of Social Clinical Psychology,* 1972, 11(4), 410–411. (b)

Sartre, J. P. *Being and nothingness.* London: Meuthen, 1957.

Schutz, W. C. *FIRO: A three-dimensional theory of interpersonal behavior.* New York: Holt, Rinehart & Winston, 1958.

Shaller, G. *The mountain gorilla: Ecology and behavior*. Chicago: University of Chicago Press, 1963.

Simmel, G. Sociology of the senses. In R. E. Park and E. W. Burgess (Eds.), *Introduction to the science of sociology*. Chicago: University of Chicago Press, 1921.

Sommer, R. The distance for comfortable conversation. *Sociometry*, 1962, **24**, 111–116.

Sommer, R. Personal space: *The behavioral basis of design*. Englewood Cliffs, New Jersey: Prentice-Hall, 1969.

Steinzor, B. The spatial factor in face-to-face discussion groups. *Journal of Abnormal and Social Psychology*, 1950, **45**, 552–555.

Tinbergen, E. A., & Tinbergen, N. Early childhood autism—an ethological approach. *Advances in Ethology*, 1972, **10**, 1.

Tinbergen, N. Ethology and stress diseases. *Science*, 1974, **185**, 20–27.

Tomkins, S. S. *Affect, imagery, consciousness*. Vol. 2: *The negative affects*. New York: Springer, 1963.

Vine, I. Communication by facial–visual signals. In J. H. Crook (Ed.), *Social behavior in birds and mammals: Essays on the social ethology of animals and man*. London: Academic Press, 1970.

Vine, I. Judgment of direction of gaze: An interpretation of discrepant results. *British Journal of Social Clinical Psychology*, 1971, **10**(4), 320–331.

Vine, I. The role of facial visual signalling in early social development. In M. von Cranach & I. Vine (Eds.), *Social communication and movement*. New York: Academic Press, 1973.

Watzlawick, P., Beavin, J. H., & Jackson, D. C. *Pragmatics of human communication*. New York: Norton, 1967.

Weisbrod, R. M. Looking behavior in a discussion group. Unpublished manuscript, Cornell University, 1966.

Wiener, M., Devoe, S., Robinow, S., & Geller, S. Nonverbal behavior and nonverbal communication. *Psychological Review*, 1972, **79**, 185–214.

Williams, E. An analysis of gaze in schizophrenia. *British Journal of Social and Clinical Psychology*, 1974, **13**, 1–8.

Word, C. O., Zanna, M. P., & Cooper, J. The nonverbal mediation of self-fulfilling prophecies in interracial interaction. *Journal of Experimental Social Psychology*, 1974, **10**(2), 109–120.

Zuckerman, M., & Lubin, B. *Manual for the multiple affect adjective check list*. San Diego, California: Educational and Industrial Testing Service, 1965.

6
Pupillary Behavior in Communication

Eckhard H. Hess

The University of Chicago

Slobodan B. Petrovich

University of Maryland Baltimore County

INTRODUCTION

Even a casual review of the subject matter presented in chapters making up this volume convincingly indicates that in recent years, research in the area of nonverbal communication has made important contributions to our knowledge of human behavior. Eye behavior has also attracted much attention, and the findings reflecting on the importance of visual interaction and eye contact in interpersonal communication are extensively covered in Ekman's and Exline and Fehr's chapters. In this section we will examine the behavior of a pupil, a component of what Magnus (1885) called "eye language."

Recorded history indicates man's preoccupation with the eye and its effects on human behavior. A few choice selections from popular literature suggest that our interest, if not our preoccupation, has not diminished: the cold look, the icy stare, shifty eyes, his eyes shot daggers, a gleam in his eye, to kill with a glance. Intimate, romantic, literary descriptions make frequent reference to large, beautiful eyes. The eye pupil has also received attention. It is interesting to note that it became popular during the middle ages for women to take belladonna in the belief that it made them look beautiful. The word "belladonna" does mean "beautiful woman" in Italian, but why was it believed that taking the drug resulted in greater beauty? Part of the answer might be that the drug served to dilate eye pupils. Atropine, a derivative of belladonna, is one of the drugs that can be used by opthalmologists to dilate pupils for eye examinations.

There are at least two cultures (or subcultures) in which it is consciously known that pupil enlargement indicates a person's positive interest in something. Gump (1962), in writing of experiences with Chinese jade dealers, wrote that prospective buyers found it necessary to wear dark glasses to shield their eyes from astute Chinese dealers, who knew that when a buyer saw an item that he liked, his pupils would dilate. The dilation cue thus prompted the Chinese dealers to raise their prices accordingly for the item in question. Turkish rug dealers are also said to have been aware of the pupil dilation phenomenon in their dealings with European merchants. Perhaps, also, in poker playing, it may be known by some that pupil enlargement can serve to indicate to other players the nature of the hand.

Pupil change, independent of change in illumination, was noted some two hundred years ago (Loewenfeld, 1958, p. 204). However, the recent interest in pupil behavior to a large degree stems from the research carried out in our laboratories at the University of Chicago. This work has been reviewed previously (Hess, 1968, 1972). Subsequently, many other investigators have used pupil behavior as an indice in assessing differential psychological responses to various stimuli, and pupillary behavior has been utilized as a measure of arousal, sensory stimulation, cognitive processes, muscular activity, attitudes, and preferences. A reasonably comprehensive coverage of this material is also available (Goldwater, 1972; Hess, 1972, 1975a; Hess & Goodwin, 1974; Janisse, 1973, 1974; Tryon, 1975; Woodmansee, 1970).

The literature reviewed and the findings presented in this chapter explicate the thesis that pupillary changes are not only related to paralinguistics, but may have to be elevated, at least in some contexts, to their own level of distinction reflecting the nature of "pupil to pupil communication."

EYE PUPIL CHANGES AND INTERPERSONAL NONVERBAL COMMUNICATION

When we found in our initial and subsequent research (Hess & Polt, 1960; Hess, 1973a) that heterosexual men tended to show greater pupil dilations to pictures of women than to pictures of men or of babies, whereas heterosexual women tended to show greater pupil dilations to pictures of men or babies than to pictures of women, it appeared reasonable to explore the question of whether eye pupil size changes served as a means of nonverbal communication. Since eye pupil size changes are not under direct voluntary control, it appeared that such non-verbal communication, if it existed, probably would be largely nonconscious since most people are normally unaware of their own eye pupil size changes.

Our pilot experiment (Hess, 1965) on this question was a simple one. We selected a facial photograph of a girl who had no particularly identifiable expression. We constructed two versions of this face: one in which the pupils of her eyes had been retouched so as to make them very small and another in which the pupils had been retouched so as to make them very large. We made slides of these two versions and projected them in our usual procedure (described in Hess, 1972, 1975a) on the screen of our pupil apparatus as part of a series of other pictures. The 20 men who saw these two pictures had twice as large increases in pupil size when viewing the picture with the large eye pupils. When the men subsequently saw photographic copies of these two pictures, some of them reported greater positive feelings toward the one with large pupils than toward the one with small pupils. Yet these men did not at all mention the fact that the eye pupil sizes were different in the two pictures and apparently thought the pictures were different in facial expression. Many of them were surprised to be told that only pupil sizes differed in the two pictures and had to be shown that this actually was the case.

Since our pilot experiment other researchers have investigated the responses of people to differences in eye pupil size in stimulus persons. Simms (1967), for example, showed two different facial photographs, one of a man and one of a woman, in two different versions each. In one version the photographs had small pupils and in the other they had large pupils. The subjects that were shown the pictures were both men and women, all married and therefore presumably heterosexual. Simms found that the subjects' pupil responses to the four photographs depended both upon the sex of the subject in relation to the photograph and upon the eye pupil size in the photograph. As might be predicted, the subjects exhibited larger pupil sizes upon viewing the photograph of the opposite sex individual that had large pupils than upon viewing the photograph of the same individual that had small pupils. Most interesting, however, were the responses of the subjects to different pupil sizes in the stimulus person of the same sex as themselves. While the male subjects' pupils did not dilate to either of the two pictures of the man, the women's pupils were the smallest in response to the picture of the woman with large pupils. Their pupil response to the picture of the woman with small pupils was the same as that to the picture of the man with the small pupils. This finding agrees with data collected by Hicks, Reaney, and Hill (1967), which indicated that women had more positive verbal responses toward a picture of a woman when she had small pupils than for a picture of her when she had large pupils.

More recently Jones and Moyel (1971) presented photographs of different men to male subjects. Some of the photographs exhibited large pupils and some exhibited small pupils. In addition, some of the photos had light colored irises, thus making the pupil highly visible, while other photos had dark colored irises, thus making reception of the pupil size difficult. In this experiment, congruent with the finding of Hicks, Reaney, and Hill (1967), Jones and Moyel (1971) reported that photos with small pupils were verbally preferred to those with large pupils. The photos with light irises elicited somewhat more friendly responses than did the ones with dark irises, perhaps because in the latter case the pupil size would be ambiguous. This difference in response to light versus dark irises possibly may not exist in a naturalistic setting since with real persons the actual pupil size may be more readily received.

Work by Stass and Willis (1967) further supports the notion that pupil dilation in a stimulus person can indicate sexually toned positive interest to a perceiver. They found that pharmacologically dilating a person's pupils serves to make that person more attractive to a heterosexual opposite-sex person. They asked both male and female subjects to chose an experimental partner from two persons of the opposite sex. One of the persons offered had normal pupils while the other had dilated pupils. Both male and female subjects were more likely to pick as their partner the stimulus person with dilated pupils. Furthermore, the subjects were not found to report the use of dilated eye pupils as a criterion for having chosen their experimental partner. This data is consistent with the finding of Hess (1965), described previously in this chapter.

Earlier work by Coss (1965) demonstrated that even schematic eyes can influence pupil responses in viewers. Coss made a series of concentric circles, some with large solid inner circles and some with small solid inner circles. These circles were shown to ten men and five women in sets of one, two, or three identical stimuli in a row. When the concentric eyespots were presented in pairs, the subjects had larger pupil sizes while looking at them than they did while looking at singlton or at tripled eye spots. The finding of larger eye pupils upon the viewing of paired eye spots rather than during the viewing of tripled eye spots is of interest because the larger amount of dark area in the tripled eye spots sets is a factor that should serve to increase eye pupil size. Hence, it appears that psychological factors mediate the larger pupil size upon the viewing of paired eye spots than when singleton or tripled eye spots are seen. Among the paired eye spots, furthermore, those that most resembled eyes with dilated pupils elicited larger pupil sizes from the subjects than did those that most resembled eyes with constricted pupils.

Research in our laboratory has given even more information regarding pupil responses to schematic eye spots. We made up slides that showed a single eye spot, a pair of eye spots, or three eye spots in a row. Not only did we vary the number of eye spots shown on each slide, but also used three different "pupil" diameters, small, medium, and very large. While Coss had placed his paired eye spots quite close together, we spaced them farther apart so that they would be the same distance from each other as if they were real eyes. We did this because we reasoned that if schematic eye spots constituted a configuration that was responded to innately in the same sense that a male robin will attack a mere red feather because it resembles the breast of a territorial rival, then placing them in the proper relation to each other should enhance the pupil responses to them.

We had 20 subjects, 10 men and 10 women, and they were shown the slides of the eye spots according to our usual procedure, with appropriate control slides. Table 1 depicts the mean pupil responses of the 20 subjects to single, double,

TABLE 1
Pupil Response to Single, Double, and Triple Eyespots
Regardless of Their "Pupil Size"

	○	○○	○○○
Male subjects	−.039	+.008	−.056
Female subjects	−.014	+.022	−.003
All subjects	−.027	+.015	−.030

and triple eye spots without regard to the "pupil size" that they had. Only the paired eye spots consistently elicited mean pupil dilations, while the singleton and tripled eye spots consistently elicited mean pupil constrictions.

Tables 2, 3, and 4 show the mean pupil responses made by the subjects to singleton, tripled, and paired eye spots as a function of different "pupil sizes." No consistent response tendencies according to "pupil size" were evident for the singletons or for the tripled eye spots. But, as Table 4 shows, both male and female subjects had larger mean pupil sizes for the medium sized "pupils" than for the small "pupils" and even larger mean pupil sizes for the largest "pupils."

These results suggest that people possess what ethologists call an innate schema for two eye spots, rather than for one or three eye spots. Jirari's (1970) findings offer some support for this thesis. On the basis of her observation of 36 neonates tested when they were under 24 hours of age, she was able to experimentally demonstrate that a schematic face (facial features, including eyes and pupils, were clearly defined and appropriately placed) was followed significantly more than a moderately scrambled face (some facial features misplaced), and the latter was followed significantly more than a scrambled, "Picasso" face. The three facial stimuli were equated for complexity, symmetry, and brightness, and thus there was probably no cue other than the form (pattern) to which the infants were responding. In another experiment, Jirari (1970) exposed 31 newborns, less

TABLE 2
Pupil Responses to Single Eyespots of Different "Pupil Size"

	⊙	◉	●
Male subjects	−.070	−.028	−.020
Female subjects	−.021	+.004	−.026
All subjects	−.046	−.012	−.023

TABLE 3
Pupil Responses to Triple Eyespots of Different "Pupil Size"

	⊙⊙⊙	◉◉◉	⬤⬤⬤
Male subjects	−.052	−.036	−.080
Female subjects	−.021	−.008	+.019
All subjects	−.037	−.022	−.031

than 24 hours old, to a real face and a mannequin face. The real face elicited more visual following than the mannequin. Thus, babies less than a day old can differentiate complex facial stimuli, differing principally in the degree of realism.

There are psychological and psychosexual factors in an individual's pupil responses to the reception of pupil size changes in other individuals. Other research has explored various aspects of the psychosexual pupil response and demonstrated that sexual interests are indeed correlated with pupil responsiveness to the relevant sexual objects. For example, in our laboratory a study by Hess, Seltzer, and Shlien (1965) investigated the pupil responsiveness of heterosexual and homosexual men to pictures of men and women. The pupil responses of the five heterosexual men were, of course, greater to the pictures of women than to the pictures of men. Four of the five homosexual men, however, had larger pupils to the pictures of men than to the pictures of women. The fifth homosexual showed a slightly more positive response to the female pictures than to the male ones.

Atwood and Howell (1971) have further corroborated that pupil responses are correlated with sexual object interest. They studied the pupil responses of pedophiliac and nonpedophiliac jail inmates to pictures of immature girls and mature women. The pedophiliacs were men that had been jailed for "nonviolently" molesting young girls. They had pupil dilations to pictures of young females but slight pupil constrictions to pictures of adult females. The nonpedo-

TABLE 4
Pupil Response to Double Eyespots of Different "Pupil Size"

	⊙⊙	◉◉	⬤⬤
Male subjects	−.008	+.002	+.029
Female subjects	+.005	+.020	+.042
All subjects	−.002	+.011	+.036

philiac men, however, showed the usual adult heterosexual pupil response pattern of strong dilation to pictures of adult females and very little dilation to pictures of young females.

Unpublished research by Simms (personal communication) has indicated further aspects of the psychosexual pupil response in relation to the reception of differential pupil size in stimulus persons. Simms found that male homosexuals definitely prefer a picture of a woman having constricted pupils over one of her with dilating pupils. Not only that, but men characterized as Don Juans had precisely the same pupil response patterns as the male homosexuals did. Simms thus suggested the possibility that male homosexuals and Don Juans both have an aversion to women who evidence sexual interest toward them. The homosexual apparently withdraws from women, whereas the Don Juan essentially appears to attack them through seduction and subsequent abandonment.

Still other research, reported by Sheflin (1969) indicates that psychosexual pupil response patterns may be very useful in understanding the nature of the psychosexual dynamics in behavior abnormalities. Sheflin found that male Schizophrenics and even paranoid male schizophrenics had heterosexual pupil response patterns. Hence it suggests that notions that paranoid schizophrenics have latent or overt homosexual tendencies is open to question.

In addition, the psychosexual response pattern can be studied from a developmental viewpoint. A beginning in this area was made by Niles Bernick (1966). He showed several types of pictures to children of both sexes and of different ages. The children were students in kindergarten, first, second, fourth, eighth, tenth, and twelfth grades. They were shown pictures of men and women, mothers with a girl or a boy, fathers with a girl or a boy, boys, girls, and babies, and their pupil responses during the viewing of each of these pictures were recoded. They were also asked to tell the experimenter which pictures they liked the most and which they liked the least.

The pupil responses of the subjects to the pictures were surprisingly consistent from one age to the next and did not conform to generally assumed ideas regarding the course of psychosexual development in normal children. In the first place, the pictures of babies elicited high pupil responses from children of all ages and of both sexes. In fact, the boys had stronger pupil responses to the pictures of the babies than to other types of pictures, thus raising the question of when and why their pupil responses to babies become as small as they are in the adult men. The boys showed stronger pupil dilations to pictures of mothers than to pictures of fathers, and stronger pupil dilations to pictures of girls than to pictures of boys. Likewise, the girls showed stronger pupil dilations to pictures of fathers than to pictures of mothers, and stronger pupil dilations to pictures of boys than to pictures of girls. While the children's pupil responses to pictures of men and women were small, there was still a somewhat stronger pupil dilation to the picture of the opposite-sex adult than to the picture of the same-sex adult in the case of both boys and girls.

The verbally stated preferences of the children, however, were much more in line with the generally accepted notions regarding psychosexual development. Many of the verbally stated preferences were for same-sex pictures, particularly among the boys. The verbal preferences of boys and girls for pictures of babies were relatively high, but the verbal preference of boys for pictures of mothers was extremely low. Hence while the verbal statements of the children partially conformed to the notion of the latency period in psychosexual development, their pupil responses indicated that their basic biological responses toward their own sex and toward the opposite sex remain the same from kindergarten through the twelfth grade. Thus, the hypothesis that children's verbally expressed preferences for males or females are largely determined by existent sociocultural expectations and not by actual interests must be given serious consideration. It is of considerable interest that while most boys are expected to express same-sex interests at certain ages, their pupil response patterns are actually heterosexual, so that even though homosexual preferences are essentially encouraged by the cultural milieu during the so-called latency period, most boys become overtly heterosexual in orientation rather than homosexual.

However, large pupil size in a stimulus person does not always appear to indicate sexually toned emotions in the adult sense. Several researchers have rediscovered that children have larger absolute pupil sizes than do adults and that age is inversely related to the absolute pupil size (Birren, Casperson, & Botwinick, 1950; Kumnick, 1954, 1956a, 1956b; Rubin, 1961, 1962; Silberkuhl, 1896; Wikler, Rosenberg, Hawthorne, & Cassidy, 1965). It would appear that having large pupil size would be advantageous to the child if it increases his visual appeal to caretakers. In other words, parents, parent surrogates, and other persons dealing with children would be more likely to protect, feed, and shelter children due to their visual appeal. These observations suggest to us the possibility that there has been an evolutionary, selective pressure for an innate schema that makes larger pupils in children appealing to adults. In fact, Lorenz (1943) has postulated that human adults must have built-in positive responsiveness to the characteristics of young children. Facial characteristics, including eye pupil size cues, appear to be among these appealing characteristics that promote the infant—caretaker bond. In addition, the larger pupil size in young people may explain the use of belladonna. It might simply make women look younger when their pupils are larger, in addition to providing nonverbal cues indicative of "positive affect."

An informal experiment which Hess conducted has not only indicated the positive responsiveness of adults to children but also that people actually possess nonconscious knowledge of pupil enlargement as an indicator of positive responsiveness toward whatever is being viewed. Two versions of a picture of a mother holding her baby were prepared and the mother's eye pupils were clearly visible. The one version showed her with large pupils. These pictures were presented to 16 students in a classroom who were asked the question, "Which mother loves her baby more?" Surprisingly, the students were unanimous in saying that the mother with the large pupils was the more loving, and none of them seemed to have noticed that the pupil sizes were different in the two versions until it was subsequently pointed out to them.

Experimentation currently in progress in our laboratory (Hess, 1973b) is providing further evidence of the nonconscious knowledge of eye pupil size cues. The initial study was carried out in the simplest possible way. It was an attempt to answer the question, "Do people know something about how big pupils should be under different emotional conditions?"

Two schematic outline faces that were three-quarters natural size were constructed. The eye and iris were drawn in, but not the pupil. One face, which was smiling, was called "happy," and the other face, which was frowning, was called "angry" (Figs. 1a, 1b). Several xeroxed copies of each face were made and then subjects were asked under quite informal circumstances, to draw appropriately sized pupils in the two faces. For this task they were given a #2 pencil with an eraser on its end. None of the subjects professed to know anything about pupil size change phenomena.

FIG. 1   Average pupil sizes drawn into schematic faces by ten men and women. They were given the two pictures with the pupils missing and asked to draw in the appropriate sized pupils for the expression shown. Fifteen out of 20 persons drew larger pupils into the "happy" face than into the "angry" face.

TABLE 5
Size of Actual Pupils Drawn by 20 Subjects
(millimeters)

Subjects	"Happy" face	"Angry" face
Ten men	4.0	2.9
Ten women	4.5	2.8
Ten subjects whose pupils were "hard to see"	3.6	3.4
Ten subjects whose pupils were "easy to see"	4.9	2.3

A total of 20 subjects, 10 men and 10 women, made up the subject pool. Fifteen of the 20 subjects drew larger pupils in the "happy" face than in the "angry" face. These 15 subjects drew an average size of 2.9 mm for the pupil diameter of the "angry" face and an average size of 4.3 mm for the pupil diameter of the "happy" face.

The men and the women were not different in the way they performed, as may be seen in the upper portion of Table 5. However, there was one significant result, which was related to the ease with which the subjects' own eye pupils were visible. For example, at a distance of 5 or 6 ft the pupils of many of the subjects were easy to see. They were mainly individuals with blue, grey, light hazel, or light brown eyes. Those with dark hazel, dark brown, or almost black irises had pupils that did not show up easily. When pupils were rank ordered in terms of "ease of visibility" and correlated with the way in which the subjects had performed in the "pupil drawing" task, a correlation of .77 was obtained. This correlation was between the degree of increase of pupil size drawn for the "happy" face over those drawn for the "angry" face and the visibility of the subjects' own pupils. In fact, the four subjects who drew larger pupils in the "angry" face were people whose own pupils were extremely difficult to see. This, of course, could well be an acquired cultural effect in that those individuals with very dark pupils did not have appropriate experiences in observing pupils and pupil size changes in their close relatives. This is a question that is currently being investigated. Our data indicate that the blue-eyed subjects discriminate better than the brown-eyed subjects the relationship between positive attributes of the stimulus and its large pupils as well as the gestalt involving negative stimulus attributes coupled with the small pupils. Moreover, blue-eyed subjects as compared to the brown-eyed ones are capable of manifesting a greater range of behavior as measured by their pupillary responses to picture stimuli that induce pupil dilation or constriction (Hess, 1975b).

PUPILLOMETRICS: METHODOLOGICAL CONCERNS

The review of the findings on pupillary behavior in nonverbal communication suggests that there is much to be learned about the role of the pupils in interpersonal communication. Moreover, given the limitations of the available literature, researchers interested in pupillary behavior must be in a position to resolve some methodologically important and procedurally difficult issues if the future experimental outcomes are to be consensually valid and of promise to behavioral analysis of interpersonal communication.

We have described 17 stimulus sources that potentially can contribute to pupillary variation (Hess, 1972) and the list of variables that could confound the assessment of pupillary behavior is growing at what at times appears to be a discomforting rate (Hess, 1975a; Janisse, 1974; Tryon, 1975; see Table 6). At the same time it is encouraging to note that some of the more systematic and fruitful research efforts in pupillometrics deal with methodological concerns (Hakerem, 1967, 1974; Hess, 1972, 1975a; Janisse, 1974).

As has been illustrated, (see Table 6) there are a number of procedural concerns that require scrutiny on the part of the investigator interested in pupillary behavior. A consideration of many of these issues has generated not only methodological advances but also interdisciplinary efforts on the part of the investigators representing such areas of inquiry as ophthalmology, optometry, physiology, bioengineering, electronics, computer technology, psychology, and psychiatry (Goldwater, 1972; Hess, 1972, 1975a; Janisse, 1973, 1974). When one considers the variables (see Table 6) that contribute to pupillary behavior, it quickly becomes apparent that most of them can be experimentally controlled. Among these we would include variables such as age, sex, alcoholic intake, incentive, binocular or monocular viewing, time of testing, nature of the manual response, information load, and the length of the testing session (Hess, 1972; Tryon, 1975). However some other variables have been the source of methodological concern and, at times, controversy. Among these we would include "inherent pupillary variability" and various reflex responses, stimulus parameter effects, subject's level of arousal and arousal decrement, iris color, as well as the general problem of measurment especially as it relates to the constriction response (Goldwater, 1972; Hess, 1975a; Hess & Goodwin, 1974; Janisse, 1973, 1974; Loewenfeld, 1958, 1966). We hope that brief discussion of the "problem variables" will stimulate a more stringent scrutiny of pupillometric research and lead toward attempts at solving some of the empirical ambiguities and theoretical controversies.

Pupillary Variability

Recent research has indicated that the innervation of the iris is much more complex than had been previously imagined, consisting of a secondary neuronal network in addition to a reciprocal autonomic inervation (Hess, 1972). More-

TABLE 6
Sources of Pupillometric Variation[a]

Sources	Descriptions	Selected documentation
1. Light reflex	Pupil constricts with increased intensity of illumination and dilates with decreased intensity of illumination.	Dennison (1968); Young and Biersdorf (1954)
2. Darkness reflex	Momentary dilation due to interrupting a constant adapting light. Different from the light reflex.	Lowenstein and Loewenfeld (1964)
3. Consensual reflex	Stimulation of one eye affects both eyes equally. Failure called dynamic anisocoria.	Lowenstein and Loewenfeld (1964)
4. Near reflex	Constriction due to decreasing the point of focus.	Lowenstein and Loewenfeld (1964)
5. Lid-closure reflex	Momentary contraction followed by redilation.	DeLaunay (1949)
6. Pupillary unrest (Hippus)	Continuous changes in pupil diameter.	Duke-Elder (1971)
7. Psychosensory reflex	Restoration of diminished reflexes due to external stimulation.	Lowenstein and Loewenfeld (1952a, 1952b)
8. Age	Decreased diameter and increased variability with age.	Kumnick (1954, 1956a, b); Birren, Casperson, and Botwinick (1950)
9. Habituation	Pupil diameter decreases, speed of contraction increases, magnitude of reflex decreases.	Lowenstein and Loewenfeld (1952a); Lehr and Bergum (1966)
10. Fatigue	Diameter decreases, amplitude and frequency of hippus increases. Age amplifies these effects.	Lowenstein and Loewenfeld (1951, 1964)
11. Alertness & Relaxation	Alertness suggestions decrease and relaxation suggestions increase pupil size.	Barlett, Faw, and Leibert (1967)
12. Binocular Summation	Constriction is greater when both eyes are stimulated.	Thompson (1947)
13. Wavelength (pupilomotor Purkinje phenomena)	Larger dilation to chromatic than achromatic stimuli. As intensity of illumination is increased proportionately more constriction is elicited by shorter wavelengths.	Miller (1966); Bouma (1962)
14. Alcohol	Dilates the pupil in proportion to the percentage of alcohol in the blood.	Skoglund (1943)
15. Sexual preference	Dilation to sexually stimulating material.	Hess (1965); Simms (1967)

(continued)

TABLE 6 *(continued)*

Sources	Descriptions	Selected documentation
16. Psychiatric diagnosis	Abnormal pupillary responses in schizophrenics and neurotics.	Duke-Elder (1971); Rubin (1964)
17. Pupil size	Stimuli involving larger pupils elicit more dilation.	Hess (1965)
18. Political attitude	Dilation for preferred political figures.	Hess (1965)
19. Semantic stimuli	Small pupil diameters are associated with high recognition thresholds.	Hutt and Anderson (1967)
20. Taste	Pleasant taste elicits dilation.	Hess (1965); Hess and Polt (1964)
21. Information processing load	Increasing dilation to increasingly difficult problems.	Simpson and Hale (1969) Beatty and Kahneman (1966); Kahneman and Beatty (1966)
22. Task relevant motor response	Having to make a motor response augments pupillary responses.	Simpson (1969); Kahneman, Peavler, and Onuska (1968)
23. Incentive	Increases diameter on easy problems only.	Kahneman *et al.* (1968); Kahneman and Peavler (1969)
24. Verbal response requirements	Increase from baseline response.	Bernick and Oberlander (1968); Hakerem and Sutton (1966); Simpson and Paivio (1968)
25. Anxiety	Increase from baseline response.	Simpson and Molloy (1971)
26. Arousal decrement	Decrease in baseline response between onset and termination of experimental session.	Peavler and McLaughlin (1967); Peavler (1974); Shrout, Beaver, and Hess (1975)
27. Iris color	Light irises are generally larger and appear to react with larger dilation.	Gambill, Ogle, and Kearns (1967); Beck (1967) Kahn and Clynes (1969)

[a]Modified from Hess (1972) and Tryon (1975).

over, Hess (1972) points out that autonomic system alone is not the only source of pupillary variability. Lowenstein and Loewenfeld (1970) support this notion and indicate that the various seemingly random fluctuations in pupil size make explicit the fact that the pupil size depends on more than sympathetic and parasympathetic innervation and is profoundly influenced by states of consciousness and various neurological activities such as those involving changes in cortico-diencephalic and reticular systems. To date there are no definite remedies that would enable an investigator to filter out the "noise level" generated by these "random pupil fluctuations." Nevertheless good reliability measures have been obtained by utilizing repeated measure designs (Hakerem, 1967, 1974; Janisse, 1974). Moreover, the experimentally induced effect is of such magnitude to allow for the methodological partitioning of random fluctuations from the pupil changes that are experimentally induced.

Stimulus Parameters

Visual, acoustic, tactile, and chemical stimuli have been utilized in pupillometric research. Application of the visual stimuli has been most controversial (Loewenfeld, 1966) since control over stimulus luminance, intrastimulus brightness, and the related effects of color are not achieved easily. For example, it is difficult to equate for brightness between a control slide and a stimulus slide, particularly if one considers the intrastimulus brightness of the stimulus slide. If color slides are utilized it is difficult to tease out the confounding effects of the psychological impact stemming from "color" to that stemming from the content of the stimulus slide. Since our research has employed visual stimuli, we have extensively investigated parameters associated with utilization of the picture slide stimuli. Color, luminous flux, or overall brightness as well as intrastimulus brightness can be adequately controlled (for the extensive description and procedural guideline see Hess, 1972, 1975a). Moreover, we have recently demonstrated that if one follows procedural safeguards for minimizing intrastimulus brightness contrast one can demonstrate that brightness contrast could not play a significant role in the pupil's response to picture slide stimuli (Hess, Beaver, & Shrout, 1975). Furthermore, it should be noted that the utility of acoustic, tactile, and chemical stimuli minimizes the methodological difficulties associated with color, luminance, and brightness contrast.

Subjects' arousal and arousal decrement

The subjects' level of arousal refers to subjects' neurophysiological as well as behavioral state while processing a stimulus input. Admittedly, the arousal concept is too inclusive and does generate some ambiguities. Arousal decrement refers to the alleged loss of subjects' interest in the experimental task as well as to subjects' "habituation" as a function of time. This decrement presumably leads to the suppression of the pupil response thus generating variabilities in the measuring of the baseline levels of pupil responding.

We have demonstrated that the gradual decrease in pupil size over time is related in part to the subjects' initial apprehension of the experimental situation rather than to a loss of interest in the experimental task. Furthermore, we have shown that the arousal decrement effects can be controlled by utilizing subjects familiar with pupillometric testing or by pretesting and "adapting" the naive subjects to the basic features of pupillometric testing. In addition, baseline variation can also be controlled to a degree by the avoidance of a lengthy testing procedure or by minimizing a number of test trials. For a more extensive treatment of some of these issues the reader is referred to Hess (1972) and Janisse (1974).

Iris Color

Observations on iris color and pupillary activity (e.g., Gambill, Ogle, & Kearns, 1967; Hess, 1975a, 1975b) suggest that pupils with lighter,–less pigmented irises are larger and respond with greater dilation than do pupils with dark irises. For example Beck (1967) presented acoustic clicks of varying frequencies to a sample of blue-eyed men, blue-eyed women, brown-eyed men, and brown-eyed women. Beck found that the blue-eyed individuals gave larger pupil responses to these stimuli and that men responded with greater magnitude than women. Thus the blue-eyed men exhibited the largest response and the brown-eyed women the smallest. Since in most pupillometric experiments iris color has not been measured or adequately controlled, there is an open question as to the generalizations and utility of some of these previously published findings.

Measurement of Pupil Responses

Several techniques, ranging from photographic–manual to electronic–automated have been utilized in pupillometric research (Hakerem, 1974; Hess, 1972, 1975a). Moreover, different laboratories have employed different "yardsticks" in the assessment of pupillary changes including such measures as average pupil size, peak size, latency-to-peak size, minimum size, and variance. In summarizing on the issues of pupil measurement, it is fair to conclude that there has been *no* unanimity as to what is the most appropriate method for monitoring and assessing pupillary behavior. Further research as well as the current availability of sophisticated new instrumentation promises a resolution of these difficulties.

The Issues of Psychologically Induced Pupil Constriction

Based on data obtained in our laboratory we have advanced the thesis of bidirectionality of the pupil response. Generally, other researchers have supported our initial findings that showed that in response to stimuli indicative of positive affect there occurs pupillary dilation. At the same time our findings of constriction to negative stimuli have been the source of controversy (e.g., Goldwater, 1972; Hess & Goodwin, 1974).

In addition to our findings, the support for the constriction phenomenon has come from other experimenters (Atwood & Howell, 1971; Barlow, 1969; Fredericks, 1970; Fredericks & Groves, 1971). On the other hand, as reviewed by Goldwater (1972), other investigators have failed to find a constriction response to be an index of a "negative affect." Woodmansee's carefully conducted

TABLE 7

Estimated Pupil Diameter Size Changes from Control to Racial Content
Test Stimuli in Eleven Equalitarian and Eleven Anti-black Female
Subjects during the First Presentation of Stimuli[a]

Subjects	First stimulus (%)	Second stimulus (%)	Third stimulus (%)	Fourth stimulus (%)
Equalitarian	+3.5	+2.6	+1.7	+2.5
Antiblack	+1.9	+0.5	−0.3	−2.0

[a]Data based upon measurement of points on Fig. 2 (page 525 of Woodmansee, J. J., The pupil response as a measure of social attitudes, in: G. F. Summers, ed., *Attitude Measurement*. Chicago, Illinois: Rand McNally, 1970). The percentage changes for each stimulus were computed by taking the difference in pupil size during the viewing of the test stimulus and during the viewing of the control which preceded it, and then calculating the percentage by which the pupil changed its size from that of the control period when the test stimulus was viewed.

research (Woodmansee, 1966, 1970) is often cited (e.g., Goldwater, 1972) as an example of failure to replicate a constriction response if "tight" experimental controls are utilized.

Woodmansee categorized 22 white college co-eds as "equalitarian" or "anti-Negro" according to their scores on a multifactor Racial Attitude Inventory, and then compared their pupillory responses to "racial content" picture stimuli. The interpretation that Woodmansee (1970) and others have advanced regarding his findings is different from ours. Table 7 shows data obtained by measurement of the points on Woodmansee's Fig. 2 (page 525, Woodmansee, 1970). Examination of data shows no overlap between the responses of the "equalitarian" and the "anti-Negro" treatment groups. During the viewing of the fourth picture stimulus, the "anti-Negro" subjects' pupils were "constricted" by −2.0% by comparison to the preceding control period. Since there were a total of eleven subjects in this group, some of the individuals have probably had extensive pupil constriction for a group mean constriction of −2.0% to be obtained since pooling and averaging of data across subjects tends to minimize the manifestation of the constriction response. Woodmansee concluded that pupillary constriction does not occur in response to "negative affect" induced in "anti-Negro" subjects by their exposure to racial content test stimuli. In our opinion, the "anti-Negro" subjects' pupils dilated in response to the first test stimulus because of the arousal or "the first stimulus effects" that normally occurs in a series of stimulus presentations shown in a pupillometric apparatus. These same subjects demonstrate a slight dilation to the second picture stimulus, a slight constriction to the third stimulus and a definite constriction to the last stimulus. While arousal decrement (Woodmansee, 1970) may in part be responsible for the results that were generated, the difference in responses between "equalitarian" and the "anti-Negro" subjects is strikingly bidirectional in nature.

As illustrated by the previous example, the issues of data interpretation generate a lack of consensus as well as excitement and productivity in pupil research. However, more troubling and methodologically difficult problems stem from the published record that indicates that constriction responses to psychologic stimuli have involved only the use of the visual modality. This suggests that the apparent psychopupil constriction indicative of negative affects may in fact be an experimental artifact produced by utilization of particular visual stimuli. Even though there are no definitive answers on this issue, it is encouraging to note that the methodological concerns dominate current research in pupillometrics (Hess, 1972; Janisse, 1974; Woodmansee, 1970) and in our laboratory we are intensively exploring experimental approaches toward examining the nature of the pupillory constriction phenomenon.

CONCLUDING REMARKS

As the survey of the findings presented in this chapter indicate, there is much more to be learned about the role of eye pupils in nonverbal communication. Particularly noticeable are the lacunae in the areas of cross-cultural and cross-species analysis. For example, research in our laboratory has indicated that blue-eyed individuals manifest a wider range of pupillary constriction and dilation responses than do brown-eyed individuals. In addition, blue-eyed people appear to be more sensitive to pupillary changes as indicators of a psychological state (Beck, 1967; Hess, 1975a, 1975b). It is conceivable that since the pupils of the blue-eyed individuals are more readily visable than are the pupils of brown-eyed persons, there has been an evolutionary pressure for developing and maintaining the communicative aspects of the pupil in social interactions more in blue-eyed people than in brown-eyed ones. On the other hand, brown-eyed people would probably develop other types of nonverbal signals, such as hand gestures. Thus among Europeans, eye pupil interaction in nonverbal communication should be more common among blue-eyed peoples of the north and not as prevalent or nonexistent among peoples of the south who, in turn, would have evolved other kinds of nonverbal signals. In addition, the interaction of pupillary behavior with other facial expressions in nonverbal communication requires further research.

Comparative literature dealing with the role of the pupil in interspecific communication is practically nonexistent. Our examples are limited to observations that pupillary changes can be used as a measure of interest and arousal in the house cat (Polt & Hess, 1963). In addition, Leyhausen (1967, p. 300) states that a sudden narrowing of the pupils announces imminent attack, especially in cats, while dilation indicates readiness for defense or escape, depending on the context. Furthermore, Leyhausen reports (personal communication) that this information is put to good use by wild cat trainers who claim that if animal pupils are large they know that they have things fairly well under control, but when the pupils narrow and become small it indeed is an indication of the animal's intention to attack.

On the productive side, it needs to be emphasized that even though the scientific interest in pupillometrics is of relatively recent origin, there is accumulating evidence for the sensitivity and potential applicability of the pupillary system as an index of various psychological states (Goldwater, 1972; Hess, 1972, 1973a, 1975a; Janisse, 1974).

However, as is the case with any new developing field, there is a need for systematic, definitive studies of basic parameters of pupillary behavior. This is particularly apparent as we glance at the literature dealing with the role of pupils in nonverbal communication. Evidence available to date ranges from anecdotal observations to scientific studies under controlled conditions. For example, Chinese jade dealers and wild cat trainers in their endeavors have apparently relied heavily on pupillary changes. A limited number of scientific, naturalistic studies (e.g., Hess, 1965) indicate the importance of pupil dilation in triggering a positive affect. Other laboratory investigations suggest that even "eye spots" can be studied as mimics of pupillary signals of some psychological states (Coss, 1970). Thus, even though available evidence is scattered across a wide range of phenomena, it does indicate that, at least in some contexts, pupillary behavior plays a role in nonverbal communication.

REFERENCES

Atwood, R. W., & Howell, R. J. Pupillometric and personality test score differences of female aggressing pedophiliacs and normals. *Psychonomic Science,* 1971, **22,** 115–116.

Barlow, J. D. Pupillary size as an index of preference in political candidates. *Perceptual and Motor Skills,* 1969, **28,** 587–590.

Bartlett, E. S., Faw, T. T., & Leibert, R. M. The effects of suggestions of alertness in hypnosis on pupillary response: Report on a single subject. *International Journal of Clinical and Experimental Hypnosis,* 1967, **15,** 189–192.

Beatty, J., & Kahneman, D. Pupillary changes in two memory tasks. *Psychonomic Science,* **1966, 5,** 371–372.

Beck, B. B. The effect of the rate and intensity of auditory click stimulation on pupil size. Paper presented at the APA annual convention, Washington, D.C., September, 1967.

Bernick, N. The development of children's preferences for social objects as evidenced by their pupil responses. Unpublished doctoral dissertation, University of Chicago, 1966.

Bernick, N., & Oberlander, M. Effect of verbalization and two different modes of experiencing on pupil size. *Perception and Psychophysics,* 1968, **3,** 327–330.

Birren, J. E., Casperson, R. C., & Botwinick, J. Age changes in pupil size. *Journal of Gerontology,* 1950, **5,** 216–221.

Bouma, N. Size of the static pupil as a function of wave-length and luminosity of the light incident on the human eye. *Nature*, 1962, **193**, 690–691.

Coss, R. G. *Mood provoking visual stimuli: Their origins and applications.* Los Angeles: Industrial Design Graduate Program, University of California, 1965.

Coss, R. G. The perceptual aspects of eye-spot patterns and their relevance to gaze behavior. In C. Hutt & S. J. Hutt (Eds.), *Behavior studies in psychiatry.* Oxford: Pergamon Press, 1970.

DeLaunay, J. A note on the photo-pupil reflex. *Journal of the Optical Society of America.* 1949, **39**, 364–367.

Dennison, B. L. A mathematical model for the motor activity of the cat iris. *Dissertation Abstracts*, 1968, **28**(8-B), 3258–3259.

Duke-Elder, S. *Systems of ophthalmology*, Vol. 12. St. Louis: Mosby, 1971.

Fredericks, R. S. Repression–sensitization and pupillary response to pleasant and unpleasant stimuli. *Dissertation Abstracts International* 1970, **31**, 2982B.

Fredericks, R. S., & Groves, M. H. Pupil changes and stimulus pleasantness. *Proceedings of the Annual Convention of the American Psychological Association*, 1971, **6**, 371–372.

Gambill, H. P., Ogle, K. N., & Kearns, T. D. Mydriatic effect of four drugs determined with pupillograph. *Archives of Opthalmology*, 1967, **77**, 740–746.

Goldwater, B. C. Psychological significance of pupillary movements. *Psychological Bulletin*, 1972, **77**, 340–355.

Gump, R. *Jade: Stone of heaven.* New York: Doubleday, 1962.

Hakerem, G. Pupillography. In P. Venables and I. Martin (Eds.), *A manual of psychological methods.* Amsterdam: North Holland Publ., 1967.

Hakerem, G. Conceptual stimuli, pupillary dilation and evoked cortical potentials: A review of recent advances. In M. P. Janisse (Ed.), *Pupillary dynamics and behavior.* New York: Plenum Press, 1974.

Hakerem, G. & Sutton, S. Pupillary response at visual threshold. *Nature*, 1966, **212**, 485–486.

Hess, E. H. Attitude and pupil size. *Scientific American*, 1965, **212**(4), 46–54.

Hess, E. H., Pupillometric Assessment. *Research in Psychotherapy*, 1968, **3**, 573–583.

Hess, E. H. Pupillometrics: A method of studying mental, emotional, and sensory processes. In N. S. Greenfield & R. A. Sternbach (Eds), *Handbook of psychophysiology.* New York: Holt, Rinehart & Winston, 1972.

Hess, E. H. Some new developments in pupillometrics. In: *Die normale und die gestorte Pupillenbewegung.* Syn. sium der Deutschen Opthalmologischen Gesellschaft, vom 10–12, Mäiz 1972, in Bad Nauheim. Munich: Bergman Verlag, 1973, pp. 246–262 (a).

Hess, E. H. What people know about the size of eye pupils. Paper presented at Eighth Pupil Colloquium, Detroit, May 26, 1973. (b)

Hess, E. H. *The tell-tale eye: How your eyes reveal hidden thoughts and emotions.* New York: Van Nostrand-Reinhold, 1975. (a)

Hess, E. H. The role of pupil size in communication. *Scientific American*, 1975, **233**, 110–119. (b)

Hess, E. H., Beaver, P. W., & Shrout, P. E. Brightness contrast effects in a pupillometric experiment. *Perception and Psychophysics*, 1975, **18**, 125–127.

Hess, E. H., & Goodwin, E. The present state of pupillometrics. In M. P. Janisse (Ed.), *Pupillary dynamics and behavior.* New York: Plenum Press, 1974.

Hess, E. H., & Polt, J. M. Pupil size as related to interest value of visual stimuli. *Science*, 1960, **132**, 349–350.

Hess, E. H., & Polt, J. M. Pupil size in relation to mental activity during simple problem solving. *Science*, 1964, **143**, 1190–1192.

Hess, E. H., Seltzer, A. L., & Shlien, J. M. Pupil responses of hetero and homosexual males to pictures of men and women: A pilot study. *Journal of Abnormal Psychology,* 1965, **70,** 165–168.

Hicks, R. A., Reaney, T., & Hill, L. Effects of pupil size and facial angle on preference for photographs of a young woman. *Perceptual and Motor Skills,* 1967, **24,** 388–390.

Hutt, L. E., & Anderson, J. P. The relationship between pupil size and recognition threshold. *Psychonomic Science,* 1967, **9,** 477–478.

Janisse, M. P. Pupil size and affect: a critical review of the literature since 1960. *Canadian Psychologist,* 1973, **14**(4), 311–329.

Janisse, M. P. (Ed.). *Pupillary dynamics and behavior.* New York: Plenum Press, 1974.

Jirari, C. Form perception, innate form preference and visually mediated head-turning in the human neonate. Chicago: The University of Chicago Press, 1970.

Jones, Q. R., & Moyel, I. S. The influence of iris color and pupil size on expressed affect. *Psychonomic Science,* 1971, **22,** 126–127.

Kahneman, D., & Beatty, J. Pupil diameter and load on memory. *Science,* 1966, **145,** 1583–1585.

Kahneman, D., & Peavler, W. S. Incentive effects and pupillary changes in association learning. *Journal of Experimental Psychology,* 1969, **79,** 312–318.

Kahneman, D., Peavler, W. S., & Onuska, L. Effects of verbalization and incentive on the pupil response to mental activity. *Canadian Journal of Psychology,* 1968, **22,** 186–196.

Kahn, M., & Clynes, M. Color dynamics of the pupil. *Annals of the New York Academy of Sciences,* 1969, **156,** 931–950.

Kumnick, L. S. Pupillary psychosensory restitution and aging. *Journal of the Optical Society of America,* 1954, **44,** 735–741.

Kumnick, L. S. Aging and pupillary response to light and sound stimuli. *Journal of Gerontology,* 1956, **11,** 38–45. (a)

Kumnick, L. S. Aging and the efficiency of the pupillary mechanism. *Journal of Gerontology,* 1956, **11,** 160–164. (b)

Lehr, D. J., & Bergum, B. O. Note on pupillary adaptation. *Perceptual & Motor Skills,* 1966, **23,** 917–918.

Leyhausen, P., The biology of expression and impression (1967). In K. Lorenz and P. Leyhausen (Eds.) *Motivation of human and animal behavior.* New York: Van Nostrand-Rheinhold, 1973.

Loewenfeld, I. E. Mechanisms of reflex dilation of the pupil. Historical review and experimental analysis. *Documenta Ophthalmologica,* 1958, **12,** 185–448.

Loewenfeld, I. E. Comment of Hess' findings. *Survey of Opthalmology,* 1966, **11,** 293–294.

Lowenstein, O., & Loewenfeld, I. E. Types of central autonomic innervation and fatigue. *Archives of Neurology and Psychiatry,* 1951, **66,** 580–599.

Lowenstein, O., & Loewenfeld, I. E. Disintegration of central autonomic regulation during fatigue and its reintegration by psychosensory controlling mechanisms: I. Disintegration. Pupillographic studies. *Journal of Nervous and Mental Disease,* 1952, **115,** 1–21. (a)

Lowenstein, O., & Loewenfeld, I. E. Disintegration of central autonomic regulation during fatigue and its reintegration by psychosensory controlling mechanisms: II. Reintegration. Pupillographic studies. *Journal of Nervous and Mental Disease,* 1952, **115,** 121–145. (b)

Lowenstein, O., & Loewenfeld, I. E. The sleep–waking cycle and pupillary activity. *Annals of the New York Academy of Sciences,* 1964, **117,** 142–156.

Lowenstein, O., & Loewenfeld, I. The pupil. In M. H. Davson (Ed.), *The eye,* (Vol. 3). New York: Academic Press, 1970.

Lorenz, K. Z. Die angeborenen Formen moglicher Erfahrung. *Zeitschrift für Tierpsychologie,* 1943, **5,** 235–409.

Magnus, H., *Die Sprache der Augen.* Wiesbaden, 1885.

Miller, R. L. The clinical validation of the pupillary response: The effect of chromatic and achromatic stimuli upon pupil responsivity. (Doctoral dissertation, Michigan State University, Ann Arbor, Michigan: University Microfilms, 1966, No. 66, 14, 152)

Peavler, W. S. Pupil size and performance. In M. P. Janisse (Ed.), *Pupillary dynamics and behavior*. New York: Plenum Press, 1974. (a)

Peavler, W. S. Individual differences in pupil size and performance. In M. P. Janisse (Ed.), *Pupillary dynamics and behavior*. New York: Plenum Press, 1974. (b)

Peavler, W. S., & McLaughlin, J. P. The question of stimulus content and pupil size. *Psychonomic Science*, 1967, 8, 505–506.

Polt, J. M., & Hess, E. H., The pupil response as a measure of interest in the cat. *Proceedings, Eighth International Ethology Congress*, Haag, Holland, 1963.

Rubin, L. S. Patterns of pupillary dilatation and constriction in psychotic adults and autistic children. *Journal of Nervous and Mental Disease*, 1961, **133**, 130–142.

Rubin, L. S. Autonomic dysfunction in psychoses: Adults and autistic children. *Archives of General Psychiatry*, 1962, 7, 1–14.

Rubin, L. S. Autonomic dysfunction as a concomitant of neurotic behavior. *Journal of Nervous & Mental Disease*, 1964, **138**, 558–574.

Sheflin, J. A. An application of Hess' pupillometric procedure to a psychiatric population: An approach utilizing sexual stimuli. Doctoral dissertation, Purdue University, 1969. *Dissertation Abstracts International*, 1969, **29**, 1907B.

Shrout, P. E., Beaver, P. W., & Hess, E. H. Decreased "arousal decrement" as a function of subjects' experience with pupillometric experiments. Ninth pupil colloquium, Iowa City, May 1975.

Silberkuhl, W. Untersuchungen uber die physiologische Pupillenweite. *Albrecht von Graefe's Archiv für Opthalmologie*, 1896, 42, 179–187.

Simms, T. M. Pupillary response of male and femald subjects to pupillary difference in male and female picture stimuli. *Perception and Psychophysics*, 1967, **2**, 553–555.

Simpson, H. M. Effects of a task-relevant response on pupil size. *Psychophysiology*, 1969, 6, 115–121.

Simpson, H. M., & Hale, S. M. Pupillary changes during a decision-making task. *Perceptual and Motor Skills*, 1969, 29, 495–498.

Simpson, H. M., & Molloy, F. M. Effects of audience anxiety on pupil size. *Psychophysiology*, 1971, 8, 491–496.

Simpson, H. M., & Paivio, A. Changes in pupil size during an imagery task without motor response involvement. *Psychanomic Science*, 1966, 5, 405–406.

Skoglund, C. R. On the influence of alcohol in the pupillary light reflex in man. *Acta Physiologica Scandinavica*, 1943, 6, 94–96.

Stass, W., & Willis, F. N., Jr. Eye contact, pupil dilation, and personal preference. *Psychonomic Science*, 1967, 7, 375–376.

Thompson, L. C. Binocular summation within the nervous pathways of the pupillary light reflex. *Journal of Physiology*, 1947, **106**, 59–65.

Tryon, W. W. Pupillometry: A survey of sources of variation. *Psychophysiology*, 1975, **12**, 90–93.

Wikler, A., Rosenberg, D. E., Hawthorne, J. D., & Cassidy, T. M. Age and effect of LSD-25 on pupil size and knee jerk threshold. *Psychopharmacologia*, 1965, 7, 44–56.

Woodmansee, J. J. Methodological problems in pupillographic experiments. Proceedings of the 74th Annual Convention of the American Psychological Association, Washington, D.C., 1966.

Woodmansee, J. J. The pupil response as a measure of social attitudes. In G. Summers (Ed.), *Attitude Measurment*. Chicago: Rand McNally, 1970, 514–533.

Young, F. A., & Biersdorf, W. R. Pupillary contraction and dilation in light and darkness. *Journal of Comparative and Physiological Psychology*, 1954, **47**, 264–268.

Part III

VOCAL BEHAVIOR

7
The Telltale Voice: Nonverbal Messages of Verbal Communication

Aron Wolfe Siegman

University of Maryland Baltimore County

INTRODUCTION

The organization of this chapter reflects an historical perspective. We first address ourselves to a question that preoccupied early researchers in this area: Are there personality traits or predispositions that are associated with specific voice qualities? We then turn to a contemporary derivative of the same concern: What are the vocal or extralinguistic correlates of changes in affective states, with special attention to the effects of anxiety arousal on speech. In the second half of this chapter, we discuss the effects of the social context and of cognitive planning and decision making on the encoding process—both representing recent developments in psycholinguistic research.

Before we address ourselves to these specific issues, a few general observations on what we mean by the "nonverbal" aspects of spoken messages or communications are in order. The usage of the term nonverbal to designate gestural and other "purely" nonverbal correlates of human communication requires little justification. In its broadest sense, however, the term nonverbal also includes all the vocal features of a message that remain after we subtract the words themselves. The more technical terms, *nonlexical, extralinguistic,* and *paralinguistic,* have been used to refer to limited aspects of the vocal, nonverbal domain. Unfortunately, there is no general agreement as to precisely which aspects of vocal nonverbal behavior are covered by these terms. Some authors use the terms interchangeably, while others use them to designate different but overlapping aspects of vocal, nonverbal communication. Note that all three terms imply definitions by exclusion; they refer to what is excluded rather than what is included. To a large extent, this is the case because scientific interest in this area is relatively recent, and there is no consensus as to what should be included and what should be excluded. In fact, we do not yet have a generally accepted system for classifying the nonverbal, vocal features of spoken messages, despite some recent efforts in that direction (e.g., Crystal & Quirk, 1964; Trager, 1958, 1961).

To imply that all of the vocal "residue" of a spoken message is unrelated to the meaning of the message is, of course, incorrect, because nonverbal vocal aspects of speech, such as intonation and stress, impart both meaning and structure to spoken messages.

The following examples of how vocal emphasis can modify the meaning of a message are given by Knapp (1972):

1. *He's* giving this money to Herbie.
   (*HE* is the one giving the money; nobody else.)
2. He's *giving* this money to Herbie.
   (He is GIVING, not lending, the money.)
3. He's giving this money to *Herbie*.
   (The recipient is HERBIE, not Lynn or Bill or Rod.)

Ambiguous sentences such as the one above have been cited by Chomsky (1965) as evidence of the proposition that sentences with an apparently simple "surface" structure frequently conceal several underlying "deep" structures. It can be argued, however, that such ambiguities are a characteristic of the written code, but not of spoken language. The sentence, "I like Chomsky roasting" when read with equal stress on all the words, could mean: I like the fact that Chomsky is doing the roasting, or it could mean: I like the fact that Chomsky is being roasted. Vocal stress on either the word Chomsky or on the word roasting, resolves this ambiguity. Similarly, intonations and stresses, pauses and hesitations provide structure and tell us whether a statement is intended as a positive assertion or a question, or perhaps as sarcasm. It would seem fairly obvious that these nonverbal features of speech are not peripheral to but very much an integral part of spoken messages, of their meaning and structure. They certainly are nonlexical, but they are not extralinguistic. Yet traditionally the science of linguistics and the various theories and models of language have typically been based on written language, and thus have failed to consider the nonverbal domain although, developmentally and historically, spoken language precedes written language; individuals and cultures speak before they write.

Not all nonverbal vocal cues are an integral part of the meaning of a message. Some may reflect the speaker's background, changes in his mood, his attitudes and feelings toward the person whom he is addressing, or even cognitive decision making. It is this category of nonverbal vocal cues, perhaps best designated as extralinguistic (or paralinguistic), that is the primary focus of interest in this chapter.

Since there does not yet exist a generally accepted system for categorizing the various vocal features that make up the extralinguisic domain, we will simply list some of the more prominent variables in the extralinguistic research literature. Some are acoustic in nature, such as pitch level and pitch range, loudness and loudness range. These can be measured in terms of their physical properties or in terms of listeners' judgments. Others involve voice qualities, such as a nasal voice or a raspy voice; still others are related to the linguistic encoding process, such as speech tempo, pausing patterns, and speech disruptions. Some of these variables will be discussed in greater detail in the context of specific studies.

In addition to the meaning- and syntax-related nonlexical aspects of speech and the expressive extralinguistic (or paralinguistic) aspects of speech, mention should be made of yet a third category. This category consists of vocal nonverbal cues, whose primary function is to regulate the flow of speech between two or more communicants. Of course, such regulatory cues need not be nonverbal; they can be, and frequently are, lexical in nature. They are messages about the message, and as such, the term metalinguistic is an appropriate designation for this category, except that one is reluctant to add to the already existing profusion and confusion of terms. This category is examined most closely by Rosenfeld (Chapter 11) and will be referred to only indirectly in the present chapter.

EXTRALINGUISTIC CORRELATES
OF DEMOGRAPHIC AND PERSONALITY VARIABLES

Two review articles, *Speech and Personality* by Sanford (1942) and *Judgment of Personal Characteristics and Emotions from Nonverbal Properties of Speech* by Kramer (1963) summarize the early research dealing with the vocal channel. Most of these early studies address themselves to the question of whether demographic variables (such as gender, age or occupation) or personality variables (such as extraversion and social dominance) can be reliably and validly inferred from the nonverbal properties of speech. In this context reliability refers to the level of listener agreement and validity to the correlation of the listeners' consensus with some independent criterion of the background or personality variable under investigation. Few of the early investigators looked at *specific* vocal correlates of demographic and personality variables. Instead, they were interested in listeners' global judgments of a speaker's background or personality characteristics, based on *all* vocal cues that remain after one removes the semantic content of the speaker's message. The limited availability of sophisticated instrumentation for the measurement and quantification of specific vocal variables was no doubt responsible, at least in part, for the methodology that characterizes the early studies. Additionally, however, the approach was justified in terms of a philosophical commitment to the superiority of "holistic" over "atomistic" studies. In order to avoid contamination of the vocal cues by the content of the message, the early investigators typically asked their speakers to read a uniform passage, frequently of a fairly innocuous nature, which, as we will see later, raises serious methodological problems.

It is clear from these early studies that many demographic background variables can be reliably and validly inferred from a speaker's nonverbal vocal characteristics. In regard to personality variables, however, the results of these early studies suggest moderate to high reliability but low validity; that is, there is agreement among the judges, but there is little evidence for its objective validity. A more detailed discussion of these findings follows below.

Demographic Background Variables

Gender and age. Of the various background variables, gender and age are the easiest to identify on the basis of nonverbal vocal cues. However, even in relation to these variables there are as yet some unresolved issues, most of which revolve around the nature–nurture question, that is, how much of the variability is due to anatomical and physiological differences, and how much of the variability is due to culture and social roles, that is, to learning.

The major difference between males and females in relation to speech is, of course, their pitch level, but there are other differences as well. There are phonetic variations (Labov, 1972), differences in intonation patterns, with more "surprise," "hesitation," and "request for confirmation" patterns among women than men (Lakoff, 1973), and variations in voice quality, with men, for example, speaking more nasally than women.

Recent studies suggest that even the gender differences in relation to pitch level are not wholly anatomical and physiological, although the lower fundamental frequencies of male speech are undoubtedly related to secondary sexual dimorphism at puberty, which produces a larger larynx and longer and thicker vocal cords in males than in females. Yet gender differences in frequency level are typically much greater than can be reasonably accounted for in terms of variation in vocal tract size (Mattingly, 1966). Also, judges can reliably identify the gender of preadolescents, although there is no anatomical basis for differences in formant frequency (Sachs, Lieberman, & Erickson, 1973).

It is fairly obvious that beginning at a very early age, boys and girls are socialized into different speaking styles. Much work remains to be done, however, in identifying the precise nature of these differences, and the conditions that tend to elicit them. In relation to eliciting conditions, a recent study by Markel, Prebor, and Brandt (1972) is of interest. They report higher intensity (loudness) levels on the part of male than female interviewees, when responding to someone of their own gender. However, both male and female interviewees increase their speech intensity level when the interviewer is of the opposite gender.

More precise information on intracultural and intercultural variations with regard to gender-related speech differences should help shed some light on the nature–nurture issue. With respect to intracultural differences, one would want to know, for example, what relationship, if any, there is between sex-role identifications in both males and females, and vocal style. Answers to this and related questions, however, must await further research.

Next to gender, age is probably the background variable that can be most readily and accurately identified solely on the basis of vocal cues. It is not quite clear yet precisely which cues are involved in this judgment, but most likely it is based on a combination of cues.

A number of investigators have looked at changes in frequency and pitch as a function of age. It is generally agreed that in males there is a lowering in pitch level from infancy to middle age, followed by an increase in pitch level from middle age to old age. It should be noted, however, that in females there apparently is no such upward shift in pitch level from middle age to old age (McGlone & Hollien, 1963). Furthermore, at least one investigator (Mysak, 1959) has suggested that this upward shift in males reflects a combination of age-related physiological changes and emotional tensions due to decreasing self-sufficiency, diminishing intellectual ability, forced retirement, and so on. It would be interesting to see whether there are specific nonverbal vocal correlates of emotional adjustment in old age.

There is reason to believe that variables other than frequency and pitch level enter into the age judgment. According to Mysak (1959), the average fundamental frequency of males in the 65–79 age range is not significantly different from that of college-age males, and yet judges do fairly well in discriminating between speakers from these two age groups. Similarly, fairly accurate age judgments are made of female speakers above the middle-age range, even though there apparently are no corresponding changes in pitch level. Some of the other vocal characteristics that have been identified as possible cues for age judgments are pitch flexibility, rate of speech, loudness, and articulatory control. Mysak (1959) did look at indices of pitch range and speech rate. The pitch range values that he obtained for his middle-age and old-age groups are comparable to those reported for college-age students. The data for the temporal indices, however, are more interesting. He obtained significant rate differences between his middle-age and old-age groups on a reading task but not on a speaking task. Furthermore, the speaking-rate values for both the middle-age and old-age groups seem to be considerably lower than those reported in the literature for young adults, but, unfortunately, it is not at all clear that these values have been obtained from comparable groups.

Very little data are available on developmental changes in the extralinguistic domain at the other end of the life-span, that is, in young children, except perhaps with regard to temporal variables. According to Goldman-Eisler (1968) pausing in speech is considered to reflect cognitive activity at that moment in time. Frequent and/or long pauses in any stretch of speech indicate that new, creative speech is being formulated; few and/or short pauses indicate that what is being uttered is a well-practiced, habitual sequence of words. Assuming that children's repertoire of habituated word sequences increases with age, simply because they practice speaking, they should evidence fewer and/or shorter pauses as they grow older. This hypothesis is supported by recent findings (Kowal, O'Connel, & Sabin, 1975) which indicate an increase in speech-rate with age, due primarily to a corresponding decrease in the frequency and duration of pauses.

We need to know much more about developmental changes in relation to other extralinguistic indices at both ends of the life span. Furthermore, we need to know more about the role of physiological, cognitive, social, and emotional factors in these age-related changes.

Socioeconomic background.   It is widely recognized that socioeconomic background influences a variety of speech dimensions such as vocabulary, syntax, and pronounciation. This influence is most pronounced in societies that are rigidly stratified along socioeconomic lines. There is some ambiguity, however, about what precisely is the major determinant of these differences. For a long time, it was assumed that differences in education account for most, if not all, of these social-background-related speech differences. Furthermore, it was assumed that to the extent that one has had an adequate education, social-background influences on speech are negligible at best. There is mounting evidence, however, that even with education held constant, pervasive speech differences related to social background do exist. It would appear, then, that these differences have their roots in an early developmental period when language is first acquired and that they are not readily overcome by education alone. Ellis (1967), for example, had a group of college students, apparently with fairly homogeneous intelligence levels, record their impromptu versions of "The Tortoise and the Hare." Judges listened to brief selections of these recordings and then estimated the students' socioeconomic backgrounds. The judges' estimates correlated .85 with the students' socioeconomic backgrounds as measured by the Hollingshead Index. In a subsequent study, a similar group of subjects was asked to role play that they were honor students selected to conduct the University President and his guests on a tour of a new dormitory. Furthermore, the speakers were told to use their very best grammar and voice quality and to try to "fake" their voices to make them sound upper class. In this group, the judges' ratings correlated .65 with the Hollingshead Index, still an impressive correlation. A further analysis of the actual speech samples revealed that, although subjects in both socioeconomic groups used proper grammar, their choice of vocabulary, sentence length, and sentence structure varied considerably. Nevertheless, there is reason to suspect that the judges' ratings were based mostly on vocal and pronounciation cues. The basis for this hunch is another study in which the judges were asked to identify the social backgrounds of students solely on the basis of a recording in which the students counted from 1 to 10. Again, the judges ratings correlated .65 with the Hollingshead Index. The results of the second of the three studies just cited suggest that even in the U.S. today, social background is a significant source of variance in a variety of speech dimensions, independently of the speakers' education and intelligence level.

On the basis of observations made in England, Basil Bernstein (1961) proposed a theory according to which there are two linguistic codes, one of which is used primarily by members of the lower class, the other by members of the middle and upper class. The elaborated code, which is used by the middle and upper class, is characterized by a verbal elaboration of meaning and the articulation of the speaker's intent in a verbally explicit form. Furthermore, in the elaborated code, the speaker selects from a variety of lexical and syntactic alternatives and therefore the probability of predicting the pattern of what the speaker is saying is fairly low. In the restricted code, which is used by the lower class, the choice of lexical and syntactic alternatives is limited, which increases the predictability of the speaker's message. Furthermore, according to Bernstein, certain child-rearing practices found mainly among lower-class families result in the child mastering only a single code—the restricted code—while the child-rearing practices characteristic of the middle class result in the child mastering both codes. For an elaboration of the precise nature of this relationship, the reader is referred to Bernstein's own discussions of this topic (Bernstein, 1961, 1964, 1972).

Most of the studies that have been undertaken to validate Bernstein's major hypothesis, namely, that members of the lower class and middle class typically use different codes, were conducted in England, and their relevance to the United States is open to debate. However, at least one major validating study was conducted in the United States with positive results (Hess & Shipman, (1965). Nevertheless, Bernstein's contention that the lower class is locked into a single code, in contrast to the middle-class, which is capable of code-switching, has been challenged (Houston, 1970), and some critics have suggested that the reverse may very well be the case (e.g., Taylor & Clement, 1974). The fact is that, although widely cited, Bernstein's hypothesis has yet to be validated.

Of special interest from the point of view of the present chapter is Bernstein's hypothesis that the two codes are associated with different extralinguistic encoding patterns. The basis for this hypothesis is Goldman-Eisler's (1968) contention that cognitive planning and decision-making is associated with pausing—an issue which will be discussed in greater detail later in this chapter. Since the elaborated code is characterized by more complex linguistic choices than the restricted code, it should also, according to Bernstein, be associated with more pausing. In a study of the extralinguistic behavior of lower-class and middle-class 16-yr olds of roughly equal intelligence, Bernstein (1962) found that the lower-class group spent less time pausing and used longer phrases than the middle-class group. The former finding is, of course, consistent with Bernstein's notions, but it is less obvious how one is to view the latter finding. Since the distinguishing characteristics of the elaborated code include: (a) the elaboration of meaning, and (b) complex syntactic forms, one can expect this code to be associated with relatively long utterances (due to *a*) and, if anything, relatively long rather than short phrases (due to both *a* and *b*). The finding, then, that the lower class rather than the middle class used relatively long phrases presents a problem for Bernstein's position. Also, of the two socioeconomic groups matched for IQ scores, the lower-class group was the more productive of the two. It must be pointed out, however, that there were only five subjects in each of these groups, hardly enough for broad generalizations about class-related speech differences. Furthermore, the fact that in this study the topic of subjects' discussions was limited to their views on capital punishment, restricts the generalizability of the study's findings—a point that will be elaborated upon shortly.

In an interview study by Siegman and Pope (1965a) with 50 female nursing students, a significant correlation ($r = .28$, $p < .05$) was obtained between subjects' socioeconomic background, as measured by the Hollingshead Index[1], and the proportion of silent pauses (2 sec and over)[2] in subjects' responses. Contrary to Bernstein's (1962) findings, in this study the lower- and lower-middle-class subjects showed more pausing than the upper-middle-class and upper-class subjects. There is, however, a major difference between the two studies. In Bernstein's study, the subjects conversed with their peers, in the Siegman and Pope study they talked with a high-status (and upper-class) interviewer. Perhaps of greater significance is that in the Siegman and Pope study, the correlation between socioeconomic background and pausing was a function of the topic under discussion. When the interviewer focused on subject's family experiences, the correlation was highly significant ($r = .37$, $p < .01$), but when he focused on their school experiences it was clearly not significant ($r = .19$, $p > .10$). Perhaps the family topic was more problematical for the lower-class interviewees than for the middle-class and upper-class interviewees, or perhaps lower-class individuals are less accustomed to discussing their family relations with strangers than are the others—and there are yet other possible explanations for this finding. The significant methodological point to be made is that in research on class-related speech differences, it is essential to control for the meaning of the topic and for social context.

---

[1] The index gives a high score to lower-class subjects, and the correlations should be interpreted accordingly.

[2] Details about this measure will be presented later in the chapter.

Personality and Vocal Style

A popular research topic during the 1920s–1940s was the ability of naive judges to correctly identify a speaker's personality traits from noncontent voice characteristics. These studies went out of style, however, at least in part, because of the disappointing results. Typically, it was found that there was a surprisingly high level of agreement among the judges as to the speaker's position on a particular personality trait, but that it was difficult to validate this consensus on the basis of external criteria of the speaker's personality. It was widely concluded that the listeners' consensus was based on theatrical conventions for portraying certain personality types, but that it had no objective validity. Additionally, the spate of studies in the post World War II period, which demonstrated the poor performance of the traditional personality measures—objective as well as projective—in predicting behavior, led to a reduced interest in the whole field of individual differences, if not to a questioning of the very concept of stable personality differences or traits.

It is a fact that the early studies on the identification of personality traits from vocal characteristics were beset by many methodological problems, some of which tended to bias the results in favor of a relationship, others against it. In light of the renewed research interest in this topic, it may be useful to review the problems that plagued the early studies in this area. One major problem is the difficulty of obtaining independent, valid criteria of the speaker's position on specific personality traits.

Many of the early studies used paper-and-pencil personality tests, which were developed on an ad hoc basis, in order to measure the specific personality dimension under investigation, without any evidence that these tests met even the most basic psychometric requirements of reliability and validity.

Finally, assuming adequate reliability and validity, it is not always clear that the judges' understanding or definition of the personality dimension that is under investigation corresponds to what is being measured by the standardized test. Such a lack of correspondence would, of course, conspire against obtaining positive results.

In order to avoid these and other problems that accompany the use of objective and projective personality tests, some investigators have turned to peer evaluations. These evaluations are typically in the form of ratings obtained from the speaker's acquaintances, and therefore may very well be based on the same cues as those used by the judges, that is, the speaker's vocal style. In other words, positive findings obtained with this method may be artifactual and spurious.

The early studies on speech and personality are beset by yet another problem, which involves the nature of the speech samples. Frequently they are not representative of natural conversation. Instead, in the typical study, a subject is asked to *read* a passage or a sentence, all too frequently of an insipid if not altogether nonsensical nature. The reason for this procedure is to eliminate content cues, but it raises a host of other problems, all of which may combine to reduce the possibility of demonstrating that personality traits or predispositions can be reliably and validly identified from a speaker's voice characteristics. First, there are systematic differences between a person's speaking voice and reading voice, and to use a sample of the latter is hardly appropriate for testing the hypothesis under scrutiny. Second, the artifical circumstances under which these speech samples are obtained may affect the speaker's voice and mask whatever vocal correlates of personality exist. Third, it is not unreasonable to argue that specific interpersonal conditions may be necessary for eliciting the vocal correlates of personality characteristics such as introversion–extraversion and social dominance. At the very least, speech samples should be obtained in a context of dyadic social interactions. Monologues or readings do not provide the appropriate conditions for testing the effects of personality variables such as social dominance on speech. Considering the variety of methodological problems that characterize the early studies, it was probably premature to conclude, on the basis of these studies, that naive judges cannot correctly identify a speaker's personality from his voice alone.

Following a period of quiescence, there are signs of a renewed interest in the whole question of personality and speech. The focus of interest, however, is no longer on the ability of naive judges to make accurate personality evaluations from voice qualities, although at least one investigator (Scherer, 1972a,b), is pursuing this question in a series of carefully designed studies. Instead, the focus of most of the recent studies is on identifying, by means of objective measurements, the vocal correlates of specific personality variables. The results, which will be summarized below, indicate that such correlates do exist, at least as far as extraversion–introversion is concerned.

Vocal correlates of extraversion–Introversion.   One of the first comprehensive studies on the ability of naive subjects to make accurate personality judgments on the basis of voice quality, was conducted by Allport and Cantril (1934). They used many subjects representing a wide range of backgrounds. In most of their samples, subjects were able to identify a speaker's extraversion–introversion level, as measured by Heidebreder's self-rating instrument, at better than a chance level. The authors state that they deliberately made no attempt to find out which specific aspect of the speaker's voice provided the basis for the listeners' judgments regarding his extraversion–introversion level. "To attempt to correlate pitch with one personal quality, speech with another and intensity with a third, would be to make the whole problem absurdly atomistic, and as is the case with all studies with such correlations between mere meaningless fragments of well structured personalities, the study would be doomed to failure" (Allport & Cantril, 1934, p. 39). They do not explain, however, why one would necessarily have to limit oneself to a single voice quality, rather than some combination thereof, which would be the proper alternative to the "atomistic" approach, if the latter indeed ended in failure.

It is ironic that recent studies, which have adopted research strategies characterized by Allport and Cantril (1934) as "atomistic" and which have been rejected by them because they are unlikely to produce positive results, have in fact produced rather encouraging results.

The results of one of the first studies to reopen the whole question of extraversion–introversion and speech, indicate that extraverts can be distinguished from introverts by their speech tempo (Siegman & Pope, 1965b). In this study, Eysenck's E-scale was used to determine the speakers' extraversion–introversion levels. Previous research (Siegman, 1962) suggests that this scale consists of a sociability factor and an impulsivity factor, the latter reflecting a preference for quick action versus deliberation. Considering both of these factors, it was hypothesized that extraverts would exhibit shorter latencies, speak more quickly and with fewer hesitations than introverts, especially in their initial contacts with stangers. It was felt that interviewees' verbal behavior in an initial interview situation could serve as an appropriate test for this hypothesis. The results showed that interviewees' E-scale scores correlated significantly with the following temporal indices: a latency measure, a measure of silent pauses (2 sec and over) and a measure of "filled" brief pauses (ahs and allied hesitation phenomena). All the correlations were in the predicted direction, that is, with extraversion associated with more quickly articulated and with more fluent speech.

Similar findings are reported by Ramsey (1966, 1968). The sound/silence ratios were significantly higher for extraverts than introverts. This difference occurred because the extraverts exhibited shorter silent pauses between utterances. The tasks included reading, responding to interview questions, and responding to TAT cards—descriptions of the cards followed by stories about them. The difference in speech tempo between extraverts and introverts was negligible on the reading task, but otherwise about the same on the different tasks, despite the different levels of interpersonal involvement associated with the interview and the TAT tasks. Perhaps it is the impulsivity factor in the extraversion–introversion dimension, rather than the sociability factor, which is the significant source of variance in relation to speech tempo.

It is clear, then, on the basis of different studies using different subject populations, that there is a correlation between extraversion–introversion and speech tempo. The above studies do not reveal whether such differences in speech tempo can be discriminated by naive listeners, and if they can be discriminated, whether the differences are attributed to the speakers' extraversion–introversion level. The results of a recent study by Addington (1968) suggest that both these questions can be answered in the affirmative. This investigator used trained speakers (two males and two females) to simulate seven voice qualities (breathy, throaty, nasal, tense, thin, flat and rotund), three levels of speech rate, and three levels of pitch variability. Only those speech samples that could be reliably identified by naive listeners as having the vocal qualities that they were intended to demonstrate, were retained for the study. These were then rated, by other subjects, on forty personality-related adjectives, including extraversion–introversion. The results show that as both male and female speakers increased their rate of speaking they were perceived as more extraverted. Increase in pitch variability also resulted in the speakers being perceived as more extraverted, but this perception occurred only for female speakers.

Also relevant in this context is a study by Markel, Phillis, Vargas, and Howard (1972). Earlier work by Markel (1965) had shown that naive listeners can make judgments regarding a speaker's pitch level, loudness level, and speech tempo with a high degree of reliability—although judgments of pitch are more difficult to make than the others. Using such judgments of loudness and tempo, Markel and his associates divided a group of speakers into four voice-quality groups: Loud-Fast, Loud-Slow, Soft-Fast and Soft-Slow, and compared their scores on the various MMPI scales. Of the two dimensions used to determine the voice profiles—loudness and tempo—the latter contributed the most to the personality differences on the MMPI, the largest of which was noted on the Social Introversion scale. As was the case in the other studies, the fast speakers were more extraverted than the slow speakers. This difference, however, was small among the loud speakers, but fairly pronounced among the soft speakers, with soft-slow speakers scoring more than one standard deviation higher than the soft-fast speakers on the Social Introversion scale. It is of interest that this difference was obtained even though the speech samples consisted of subjects reading a standard passage, rather than dyadic conversation. This fact, however, should be kept in mind when evaluating the obtained interaction between loudness and tempo.

The results of a recent study by Scherer (1972a) suggest that loudness level may in fact be a significant correlate of the extraversion dimension, and may play a significant role in judges' ratings of voice samples on this trait. In the Scherer study judges were asked to rate voice samples, obtained from simulated jury deliberations, on five personality variables: conscientiousness, emotional stability, extraversion, assertiveness, and agreeableness. As in previous studies, there was a high degree of agreement among the judges concerning the personality correlates of the various voice samples, except with regard to agreeableness. Another group of judges was asked to rate the voice qualities of the same speech samples for loudness level, pitch level, warmth, and so forth, and yet another group of subjects was asked to rate each of the voice qualities on the above five personality traits. The results of the latter procedure indicate that there are indeed culturally shared inference rules regarding the personality correlates of specific voice qualities. Moreover, Scherer could predict the judges' personality ratings, given the culturally shared inference rules and given the judges' perceptions of the speakers' voice qualities.

The validity of the judges' personality ratings was determined by correlating them with personality ratings obtained from the speakers' acquaintances. As pointed out earlier, this is a questionable procedure since the acquaintances ratings could very well be influenced by the speakers' voice qualities. Even so, only the judges' ratings of the extraversion dimension correlated significantly with those of the speakers' acquaintances. Scherer points out that personality judgments based on voice characteristics can be valid only if the personality variables are in fact associated with specific voice qualities and only if they can be accurately decoded by naive listeners. He suggests that of the personality dimensions that he investigated, perhaps only the extraversion–introversion dimension does in fact have specific vocal correlates. There are, of course, other factors which can account for the lack of validity in the judges' personality ratings, such as a lack of correspondence between the judges' inference rules and the actual vocal correlates of the personality variables. A closer inspection of the inference rules used by the judges of this study suggests one possible source of error, namely, the ubiquitous "halo effect." The socially desirable voice qualities seem to have been matched with socially desirable personality traits, resulting in a very similar voice profile for a number of personality traits.

The indication that judges matched socially desirable voices with socially desirable personality traits suggests an alternate model for the process involved in such judgments. It suggests that such judgments may be determined by the position of each (that is, the voices and the personality traits) in semantic (connotative) space. In a recent study (Brown, Strong, Rencher, & Smith, 1973), subjects were asked to rate all possible combinations of three levels of pitch, rate, and intonation on a variety of semantic differential scales, that is, polar adjectives, such as pleasant-unpleasant, strong-weak, and so forth. A factor analysis of these ratings yielded two factors that were labeled, benevolence and competence, both of which, of course, are reminiscent of Osgood's (1957) evaluative and potency factors. The rate manipulation contributed the most to the variance of both factors, accounting for 86% of the variance in the competency ratings and 48% of the variance in the benevolence ratings. According to this model, judges match voices and personality traits on the basis of their similarity in semantic space. For example, a pleasant and strong voice is likely to be matched with a personality trait that has the same connotative meaning. This model, then, does away with the assumption, inherent in Scherer's model, that judges "carry around with them" an atlas of the personality traits that are associated with different voices. It should be pointed out that the similarity in connotative meaning may itself be a result of experience with speakers in whom the personality traits and the voice qualities covary. Further in this section (page

199), we will suggest an elaboration of this model, which provides yet another basis for the validity of voice-personality judgments to the extent that such validity in fact exists.

Let us now summarize the evidence relating to voice and personality discussed thus far. It has repeatedly been shown that the extraversion–introversion dimension correlates significantly with various temporal indices. There is also evidence that "naive" listeners can discriminate between different levels of speech tempo, and that these discriminations play a significant role in the listeners' inferences regarding the speakers' extraversion–introversion level. Finally, there is evidence that such inferences can be validated against various external criteria of the introversion–extraversion dimension. Of course, extraversion–introversion may have other speech and vocal correlates besides tempo—according to Scherer (1972b) loudness is a likely candidate—and they in turn may interact with tempo (Markel, Phillis, Vargas, & Howard, 1972). Thus far, however, the evidence is only suggestive. Nevertheless, there is reason to believe (Scherer, 1972b) that listeners' attributions of extraversion–introversion, as well as other personality traits, are based on more than a single extralinguistic cue—perhaps even on a pattern of voice and speech characteristics. Scherer's findings, however, also lead one to suspect that of the extralinguistic cues that naive listeners use to make judgments regarding a speaker's extraversion–introversion level, some are unrelated to that dimension. This is one factor that is likely to attenuate the validity of naive listeners' attributions of extraversion–introversion on the basis of speech and vocal cues.

Thus far there are very little reliable data concerning the vocal correlates of personality variables other than extraversion–introversion. This author correlated a number of extralinguistic variables—primarily indices of speech tempo and verbal fluency—that were obtained in an interview study (Siegman & Pope, 1965a) with interviewees' MMPI scores. Although there were a few significant correlations, they did not exceed the number that could be expected to occur by chance. Scherer (1972b) sampled a broad spectrum of speakers' voice qualities—which were evaluated by voice experts—and none covaried with the speakers' level of conscientiousness, assertiveness, and agreeableness, which were determined on the basis of ratings obtained from the speakers' acquaintances.

Somewhat more encouraging, as far as the vocal correlates of personality are concerned, are the results of the study by Markel, Phillis, Vargas, and Howard (1972), mentioned earlier. They divided speakers into three voice quality types and looked at their performance on Cattell's 16 PF and on the MMPI. However, instead of correlating the voice quality types with individual scale scores, they tested and confirmed the hypothesis that subjects' voice quality profile was a significant source of variance in subjects' test *profiles*. This suggests the advisability of looking at subjects' relative rather than absolute standing on both the voice quality and personality dimensions.

The studies discussed thus far are all correlational in nature, as is typically the case when investigators look at the behavioral correlates of personality traits. Stable personality predispositions do not readily lend themselves to experimental manipulation. This, however, need not rule out entirely the experimental method in personality research. A recent study (Scherer, London, & Wolf, 1973) illustrates the point. The purpose of this study was to investigate the vocal correlates of confidence versus doubt. Speaker confidence was manipulated simply by asking a subject to read a text once with and once without confidence. The authors found that confidence was expressed, extralinguistically, by increased loudness of voice, rapid rate of speech, and infrequent silent pauses. It is, of course, entirely possible that subject merely acted out the conventional stereotype of a confident voice. On the other hand it is not at all difficult to conceive of experimental manipulations that would generate feelings of confidence or doubt. It is, of course, possible that the vocal correlates of such experimentally manipulated *states* of confidence or doubt will not be identical with the vocal correlates of the more chronic *trait* of the same name. Nevertheless, the information generated by such experimental personality state manipulations would be extremely valuable.

Person Perception and Extralinguistics

The fact that the extralinguistic cues of spoken messages elicit fairly clear-cut personality stereotypes or attributions about a speaker, has important implications for the psychology of person perception, even if these attributions lack empirical validity. Yet the full implications of this process escaped the early investigators because of their preoccupation with the validity issue. It can be argued, and some have (Lee, 1971; Robinson, 1972), that it is unwarranted to generalize from a highly artificial situation in which one is asked to make decisions regarding someone's personality with nothing but a disembodied voice to go on, to situations in which there are other more relevant cues as well. A number of recent studies, however, indicate that a person's voice qualities, extralinguistic style and regional accent are in fact all used to make attributions regarding his personality and/or his attitudes and/or his motivations, even in the presence of other cues, although they too, no doubt, enter into the attribution process.

Of relevance in this context are the studies on the sources of the *experimenter bias effect,* which refers to the powerful influence of an experimenter's hypotheses or expectations on his subjects' responses (Rosenthal, 1966). On the assumption that this influence is mediated via nonverbal cues, Duncan and Rosenthal (1968), looked at the coverbal[3] and extralinguistic correlates of the instructions

---

[3] The term coverbal refers to hand gestures and other nonvocal correlates of speech.

given to subjects by two sets of "experimenters" whose hypotheses regarding the outcome of the experiment were manipulated so that they would be divergent. Although the instructions to subjects, which included a description of their response alternatives, were standardized, each set of experimenters emphasized the response alternative that was consistent with their expectation. The correlation between differential experimenter emphasis and subject response was .72. In a subsequent study by Duncan, Rosenberg, and Finkelstein (1969) the investigators experimentally manipulated experimenter coverbal and extralinguistic emphasis, with similar results.

The results of another study are suggestive of the powerful influence that extralinguistic cues may exert in everyday social interactions. In this study (Milmoe, Rosenthal, Blane, Chafetz, & Wolf, 1967) the authors were able to postdict doctors' success in referring alcoholic patients for treatment from the level of anger and irritation in the doctors' voices when discussing their experiences with alcoholic patients. Of course, this being a postdictive-correlational study, one can only speculate about a possible causal relationship between the doctors' voice qualities and the patients' behavior—but it is certainly a hypothesis deserving further experimental investigation.

In a series of studies, Lambert and his associates (Lambert, 1967) have used a "matched guise" technique, in order to investigate whether different personality attributions are made as a function of a speaker's language, accent, or regional dialect. These studies are typically disguised as voice and personality investigations, in which subjects are asked to rate the personality characteristics of what they have been led to believe are different speakers reading the same message in either different languages or different dialects. In fact, however, the various speech samples are always read by the same person who is proficient in the various languages, dialects, and so on, under investigation. The major finding is that the personality traits attributed to speakers who can be identified, on the basis of their accent or dialect, as members of ethnic minority groups, or otherwise low-prestige groups, tend to be unfavorable, and reflect the popular stereotypes associated with such groups. This is true even of individuals who on the usual ethnic prejudice questionnaires deny subscribing to such ethnic stereotypes. Also of interest is the finding that some members of ethnic groups tend to make the same unfavorable personality attributions to a speaker of their own group as do majority group members—the degree to which this is the case probably being a function of the level of ethnic identification characteristic of that ethnic group (Anisfeld, Bogo, & Lambert, 1962; Anisfeld & Lambert, 1964; Lambert, Anisfeld, & Yeni-Komshian, 1965).

Giles (1970) used the "matched-guise" technique in Britain to determine the prestige levels associated with a variety of English accents. He found that speakers could be placed on a continuum, with speakers of the standard accent (Received Pronounciation, RP) accorded the highest status, regional accented speakers next, and those with accents of industrial towns, the lowest status. Not all the favorable personality traits, however, are attributed to RP speakers. Although perceived as being more competent than regional speakers, the RP speakers are also perceived as having less integrity and social attractiveness (sincerity, kind-heartedness, etc.) than the regional speakers. Furthermore, Giles and his associates have also explored the behavioral implications of such attributions. In one such study, they found that arguments presented with the prestigious RP accent are more persuasive than arguments presented in a regional accent (Giles, 1973; Powesland & Giles, (1975). Requests for information in a face-to-face situation elicited longer responses when made with the prestigious RP accent rather than a nonstandard urban accent (Giles, Baker & Fielding, 1975). On the other hand, the standard English accent can be a disadvantage in areas where the local speech style serves as a marker of ethnic or national identity. Welsh bilinguals were more responsive to a request for completing a questionnaire when the request was made in Welsh rather than standard prestige English, while monolingual English-speaking Welshmen completed as many questionnaires when the request was made in accented (Welsh) English as when the request was made in prestige, standard English (Bourhis & Giles, in press).

In a related line of research, it has been shown that subjects tend to attribute favorable personality traits to bilingual speakers who accommodate to and adopt subjects' preferred language or dialect. Moreover, subjects tend to reciprocate the accommodation, that is, they make an effort to speak the other person's preferred language or dialect. Subsequent research has shown that both responses, that is, the positive evaluation and the reciprocal accommodation, are a function of the motivations and effort attributed by subjects to the accommodating speaker. Both responses are most likely to occur if subjects believe that the speaker who accommodated himself to their preferred language or dialect had a choice in the matter, and that the accommodation required some effort on his part (Giles, Taylor, & Bourhis 1975; Simard, Taylor, & Giles, in press). This type of linguistic accommodation, while peripheral to the central concern of this chapter, is very much reminiscent of an accommodation process that takes place between speakers in relation to the extralinguistic aspects of communication, which will be taken up later in this chapter and which may shed some light on it.

By way of summary, then, it can be concluded, on the basis of the studies cited above, that a speaker's dialect, accent, and voice qualities (as well as the phenomenon of code switching) are all sources of personality, attitudinal, and motivational attributions made by a listener about a speaker, which in turn exert wide ranging effects on the listener's behavior toward the speaker. Of course, vocal and other nonverbal components of the listener's response to the speaker will in turn influence the speaker's subsequent nonverbal behavior, and so on. What we have here, then, are some basic features of a quasi-cybernetic model of communication, applied to nonverbal communication. One implication of this model is that what generally goes by the term "personality" may very well be, at least in part, a product of one's nonverbal behavior, vocal and otherwise. Thus, if a person's voice and other nonverbal cues connote lack of competence, then this may lead others to respond to him in a manner that tends to reinforce that quality. Of course, the cycle of events can be benign as well. To the extent that such a benign or a vicious cycle of events has in fact occurred in relation to a particular individual, judges' ratings of his personality based on his voice quality should show not only high reliability but also validity.

VOCAL CORRELATES OF TRANSIENT EMOTIONAL STATES

During the 1950s and 1960s studies concerned with the question of whether one can accurately identify a speaker's background and personality from his voice all but disappeared from the literature. They were replaced by an ever increasing number of studies on the vocal correlates of transient affective states, especially anxiety. In these studies the primary interest was in the actual vocal correlates of anxiety and some other mood states, and only secondarily, if at all, in listeners' ability to accurately identify emotional states from a speaker's voice.

Several factors were responsible for this change in interest from background and personality variables to anxiety and other emotional states. First, during this period—the 1950s and 1960s—evidence began accumulating which cast serious doubt on the validity of many widely used personality measures, both of the projective and objective variety. It became increasingly clear that at best these personality tests account for only a very small portion of the intersubject variability on any behavior of interest to psychologists today. In response to the rather dismal performance of these tests in predicting behavior, some psychologists began questioning the very concept of stable personality traits. Others simply decided to ignore the question of individual differences and instead turned their attention to experimentally manipulable variables and their effects on behavior. One such variable—a rather popular one during the 1950s—was situationally produced stress or anxiety. Anxiety is, of course, a significant construct in a number of psychological theories, but the ease with which it can be manipulated in the laboratory setting no doubt contributed to its popularity. Many studies were published on the effects of anxiety and stress on perception, conditioning, and serial learning, and it was inevitable that sooner or later investigators would turn their attention to its effects on speech. It is, thus, against a background of systematic theorizing about the effects of anxiety on behavior, and a considerable body of empirical findings, that investigators began to look at the effects of anxiety on speech.

There was yet another development during this period which contributed to the new interest in the nonverbal correlates of anxiety and other affective states. It is during this period that clinical psychology began coming into its own as an empirical discipline. Widely held assumptions among clinicians began to be subjected to empirical validation by research psychologists, not always with encouraging results. Some psychologists addressed themselves to the efficacy of psychotherapy, an area that is now referred to as psychotherapy *outcome* research. The same period witnessed the mass production of inexpensive, high-fidelity audio and video recording devices, which made it possible to subject therapist and patient interactions, their verbal and nonverbal exchanges, to careful empirical investigation. This type of investigation has come to be known as psychotherapy *process* research.

Since psychoanalytically based or derived psychotherapies consist essentially of verbal exchanges between patient and therapist, it is only natural that psychotherapy researchers began to conceptualize the process in terms of more general informational exchange models (e.g., Gross, 1972; Lennard & Bernstein, 1960; Siegman, 1974a; Siegman & Pope, 1972). Psychoanalytically-oriented psychotherapists, however, are less interested in the objective referents of their patients' communications than in the clues that they provide for the patients' affective states such as anxiety, anger, depression, and so forth. Because of this perspective, psychoanalytically oriented psychotherapists have become very much attuned to the nonverbal aspects of their patients' communications, including, of course, the vocal characteristics of their patients' messages. Thus, Sullivan (1954) writes:

> The beginning of my definition of the psychiatric interview states that such an inter-view is a situation of primarily vocal communication—not verbal communication alone. . . . But if consideration is given to the nonverbal but nonetheless primarily vocal aspects of the exchange, it is actually feasible to make some sort of crude formulation of many people in from an hour and a half to, let us say, six hours of serious dis-course. . . . Much attention may profitably be paid to the telltale aspects of intonation, rate of speech, difficulty in enunciation, and so on—factors which are conspicuous to student of vocal communication [p. 5].

Anxiety is of special interest to psychotherapists, because of its central role in psychopathology and because the occurrence of anxiety during psychotherapy is interpreted as evidence of emotional conflict. As is apparent from the above quotation, the assumption has been that anxiety has a disruptive effect on speech, that it is associated with difficulties in articulation, silent pauses, and other interruptions in the normal flow of speech. In the following paragraphs we will summarize the relevant empirical studies.

The Voice of Anxiety

Anxiety and disrupted speech. One of the first to investigate the effects of anxiety on speech in a programmatic fashion was George Mahl. His working hypothesis was essentially the clinically derived assumption that anxiety has a disruptive effect on the normal flow of speech. In an attempt to quantify this disruptive effect he developed the Speech Disturbance Ratio (SDR),[4] which

---

[4] The term "disturbance" suggests pathology, which is of course unwarranted. Even the term "disruption" may imply an unwarranted assumption.

comprises the following categories: *repetition* (superfluous repetition of one or more words), *sentence incompletion or reconstruction* (the speaker stops leaving a sentence unfinished or starts it again), *omission* (the omission of a whole word or part of a word), *tongue slip, stutter, intruding incoherent sounds,* and *"ahs,"* and their allied hesitation phenomena ("er," "um," etc.).

In a preliminary study, Mahl (1956) divided a series of therapeutic interviews with a single patient into high-anxiety, high-conflict phases versus low-anxiety, low-conflict phases, and found that the former were associated with a significantly higher SDR than the latter. It should be pointed out that for the purpose of categorizing the interviews into high and low conflict and anxiety phases he used a typescript from which all speech disturbances had been removed. Additional analyses indicated that anxiety had no effect on the occurrence of "ahs" and similar expressions, which led Mahl to remove this category from the SDR. The basic finding of a positive association between anxiety arousal and the SDR, was replicated by Kasl and Mahl (1965) with a group of college students, in which anxiety arousal was manipulated by means of a stress interview. Despite an early failure to replicate Mahl's finding (Boomer & Goodrich, 1961), the results of many subsequent studies provide impressive support for the claim that anxiety arousal is associated with an increase in SDR. Furthermore, Mahl's contention that although anxiety arousal increases what he has called the "Non-ah" SDR, it has no such effect on the Ah Ratio (or the Filled Pauses Ratio, as it has been referred to by others), has also been corroborated by the results of three independent investigations (Cook, 1969; Feldstein, Brenner, & Jaffe, 1963; Siegman & Pope, 1965a). All three studies experimentally manipulated their subjects' anxiety level by subjecting them to a stress and a control interview. One caveat about this procedure is that it confounds anxiety arousal with interviewer topical focus, for the interviewer's questions in the stress interview typically concern different topical areas than his questions in the control interview. Since there is evidence, as is shown later in this chapter, that the SDR increases as a function of the cognitive difficulty of the task, it is not unreasonable to argue that interviewer topical focus could be a significant source of variance in interviewee's SDR, independent of his anxiety arousal. An interviewee may very well show a relatively high SDR when responding to questions in a topical area about which he is unfamiliar, or which concerns remote events, or which, for some other reason, produces few strong associations.

There is, however, at least one study which does indicate that there is a relationship between anxiety-arousal and the SDR, independent of topical focus. In this study (Pope, Siegman, & Blass, 1970) an experimental group and a control group of student volunteers were interviewed twice. The second interview was a repeat performance of the first, and was justified to subjects on the basis that the tape recording of the first interview, which was necessary for the study, was accidentally erased. It was expected that for the control subjects, the second interview, being a repeat of the first and therefore involving practice, would show a significant decrease in the SDR, which it did. Subjects in the experimental group, however, whose anxiety level was aroused prior to the second interview by being informed that their test responses revealed serious psychological problems, showed no decrease in their SDR during the second interview. In other words, the effects of practice and anxiety canceled each other. These findings suggest that the association between anxiety arousal and the SDR is indeed independent of the particular topic under discussion.

Anxiety and speech tempo. In his analysis of a series of psychotherapeutic interviews Mahl (1956) also looked at the effects of anxiety arousal on silent pauses in the patient's responses. He assumed that the high-anxiety, high-conflict phases would be associated with longer pauses than the low-anxiety, low-conflict phases, which they were. Mahl himself apparently did not pursue this issue in his subsequent experimental studies, but others who did, frequently found that anxiety arousal and stress can have an accelerating rather than a slowing-down effect on speech.

One can approach this question, that is, the effect of anxiety arousal on speech tempo, from a theoretical perspective, which has proved useful in predicting the effects of anxiety and stress on conditioning and serial learning. Conceptualizing anxiety in terms of drive, Spence and his associates hypothesized that anxiety arousal would facilitate simple conditioning and simple serial learning and would interfere with complex serial learning (Taylor, 1951; Taylor & Spence, 1952). This hypothesis is based on the Hullian postulate that response strength is a multiplicative function of habit strength and drive. Thus, anxiety arousal should facilitate learning in situations in which the dominant response is the correct one, that is in simple learning tasks, and impede the learning process in situations involving multiple conflicting response tendencies, that is complex learning tasks. The results of a number of investigations have confirmed this hypothesis (e.g., Montague, 1953; Siegman, 1957). By the same token, anxiety arousal should accelerate speech tempo, provided the speaker is not faced with conflicting response tendencies. From this perspective, Mahl's (1956) study is of little help in clarifying the relationship between anxiety arousal per se and speech tempo, since it deliberately confounds the anxiety and conflict variables. The results of subsequent studies, which have attempted an experimental manipulation of the anxiety variable unconfounded by other variables, are generally consistent with the drive approach to the effects of anxiety arousal on speech tempo. These studies will now be discussed in some detail.

Siegman and Pope (1965a, 1972) investigated the effects of anxiety arousal and stress on speech tempo within the context of the initial interview. Differential anxiety levels were aroused in the interviewees by means of topical manipulation. Specifically, interviewees were preselected so that questions focusing on their family relations would be more anxiety provoking than questions focusing on their school experiences. A postinterview questionnaire revealed that this objective was in fact achieved, although the topical manipulation produced only mild anxiety arousal. The temporal variables looked at in this study were: reaction or response time (RT), speech or verbal rate (SR), silence quotient (SQ), and articulation rate (AR). *RT* was defined as the silent interval between the last word of the interviewer's question and the first word of the interviewee's response. The *speech rate* was obtained by dividing the total number of words in an interviewee's response by its duration. The *silence quotient* was obtained by summating all silent pauses 2 sec and over[5] and dividing that by the response duration. Finally, *AR* was obtained by dividing the number of words in a response by total response time, minus all silent pauses 2 sec and over. It should be pointed out that the term "articulation rate" is misleading. Theoretically, variations in the *AR* could be a function of variations in actual articulation tempo or of variations in brief silent pauses (i.e., under 2 sec). Goldman-Eisler (1968), however, found that actual articulation rate, that is, the variation in rate which remains after one has removed all silent pauses .25 sec and over, is a remarkably invariant personality constant, and is not significantly affected by situational manipulations. If this is in fact the case, then the *AR,* at least in this study, is best viewed as an inverse measure of short silent pauses (under 2 sec). In this connection, it is of interest to note that the correlation between long and short pauses in four separate studies were, $-.30$, $-.22$, $.00$, and $-.09$, all of which are nonsignificant, suggesting that short pauses (under 2 sec) and long pauses (over 2 sec) may measure different psychological processes. Similar findings were obtained by Levin and Silverman (1965) who compared pauses of under and over 1 sec duration. Turning now to the Siegman and Pope study on the effects of anxiety on speech tempo, the results show that the anxiety-arousing topic, in contrast to the neutral one, was associated with a higher speech rate $(.05 < p < .10)$, a lower SQ $(p. < .02)$,[6] a shorter RT $(.05 < p. < .10)$, and a higher AR (not significant). Using a similar experimental paradigm, Feldstein *et al.* (1963) found that the anxiety-arousing interview topics were associated with a higher speech rate (or

---

[5] Originally we used a 3-sec cutoff point, but a reanalysis of the data using a 2-sec cutoff yielded essentially the same results. In subsequent studies, therefore, we adopted a 2-sec cutoff point. In the present and subsequent studies, the relevant time measurements were made with a stopwatch, while listening to an audio recording and following a typescript. Interscorer reliability (r) for the various temporal measurements was .96 and better.

Although Boomer and Dittmann (1962) found that, depending on their location in a sentence, silent pauses up to 1 sec are frequently missed by human judges, there is evidence (Hargreaves & Starkweather, 1959) that this is not true of pauses exceeding 1 sec. It should be noted that in our laboratory we have obtained correlations of about .80 between manually derived Silence Quotients, based on a 2 sec cutoff point, and automated electronic measurements of all silent pauses .3 sec and over. This certainly indicates that the Silence Quotient index accounts for a good portion of the variance in pausing behavior.

[6] This probability value is at variance with the *p* value cited in Siegman and Pope (1972). The reason for this discrepancy is that the earlier *p* value is for raw SQ scores while the present *p* is for transformed (log) SQ scores.

verbal rate, as they refer to it) than the neutral interview topics. Cook (1969) obtained similar results, but only with low trait-anxiety subjects (i.e., subjects obtaining low scores on inventories measuring chronic anxiety level), while the opposite trend was obtained with high trait-anxiety subjects. Cook suggests that this interaction effect is inconsistent with a conceptualization of anxiety in terms of drive and activation. If anxiety does have an activating effect, so Cook argues, it should be most pronounced with high trait-anxiety subjects. For them, "an already high drive level is being increased still further" by the anxiety-arousing experimental manipulation. It should be pointed out, however, that if we accept the qualification that only mild or moderate anxiety levels are associated with more rapid speech, and that this effect levels off or even reverses itself at very high anxiety levels, a possibility that will be discussed shortly, his findings are not necessarily in conflict with a drive-activaction interpretation of anxiety. The high trait-anxiety group may have been so aroused by the anxiety-arousing probes that the facilitating effect—which was noted in the low trait-anxiety group—did not occur.

A more serious limitation of the above studies is that interviewees' anxiety arousal was achieved via topical manipulation. Consequently, one cannot be certain that the results reflect variations in anxiety-arousal rather than variations in topical focus. There are, however, other findings that indicate that experimentally produced anxiety arousal is in fact associated with an acceleration in verbal tempo, independent of topical focus. In a series of studies Kanfer (1958a,b) used electric shock preceded by a tone with subjects who were instructed to say separate words until asked to stop. Subjects showed an increase in posttone verbal rate and a decrease in post shock verbal rate, suggesting that anxiety arousal had an accelerating effect on subjects' verbal rate.

The findings in the Siegman and Pope interview study (1966b, 1972) that mild anxiety arousal was associated with an increase in interviewee productivity (longer responses) and vocabulary diversity provide additional support for a drive-activation-arousal conceptualization of anxiety and stress. Here again, subsequent studies indicate that the facilitative effect of anxiety on productivity (Pope, Siegman, & Blass, 1970), and vocabulary diversity (Sunshine & Horowitz, 1968)[7] is independent of topical manipulation. A positive correlation between anxiety arousal and productivity is, of course, to be expected on the basis of the Hull–Spence–Taylor position, which clearly states that anxiety arousal will make previously below-threshold responses suprathreshold. The positive correlation between anxiety arousal and vocabulary diversity suggests that the facilitative effect of anxiety arousal involves not only autonomic but also cortical arousal. This is, of course, a highly speculative hypothesis, and it should be noted that

---

[7] Sunshine and Horowitz used the Zipf rank-frequency curve as an index of vocabulary diversity, while Siegman and Pope used the Type Token Ratio.

other investigators have reported negative correlations between anxiety and vocabulary diversity.

The inverted U hypothesis.   In discussing the energizing–facilitating effects of arousal on behavior, a number of authors have argued that this effect is likely to reach an asymptote with increasing levels of arousal, and that eventually it reverses itself (Duffy, 1962; Hebb, 1955; Fiske & Maddi, 1961). If this is indeed the case, then even if mild and moderate levels of anxiety arousal tend to accelerate speech, very high levels of anxiety arousal should be associated with slower speech, more pauses, and so forth. This hypothesis, although reasonable from a common-sense and perhaps even a theoretical viewpoint, is difficult to test empirically. It is difficult to calibrate levels of anxiety arousal and to identify in advance precisely which anxiety levels will produce a facilitating effect and which will produce the reverse effect. The failure to obtain the hypothesized asymptote or reversal in any particular study can always be attributed, post hoc, to insufficient arousal.

While there are no studies which were specifically designed to test the inverted U hypothesis in relation to anxiety and speech, the results of several studies seem to be relevant. Perhaps the most clear-cut evidence in favor of the inverted U hypothesis comes from a study by Fenz and Epstein (1962) in which the authors obtained stories in response to TAT-like stimulus cards from a group of novice parachutists on their day of jumping and from a control group. In addition to the control group of nonparachutists, the parachutists served as their own controls by responding to the cards on a nonjumping day. Subjects always responded to three kinds of cards: neutral (no relevance to parachute jumping), low relevance, and high relevance. The RT data clearly suggest that anxiety arousal has an activating effect on response latency. Conditions that can be assumed to have aroused mild-to-moderate anxiety were associated with a decrease in RT. On the other hand, the one condition that probably aroused very high anxiety levels, namely, the high-relevance cards on the day of jumping, was associated with a steep increase in RT (Figure 1). Pauses in the parachutists' stories on the day of jumping also showed an activation effect, with lower SQs in the low-relevance than the neutral cards, and higher SQs in the high-relevance than the low-relevance cards. There were no significant differences in the control group. Subjects' verbal-rate data also follow a similar pattern, but these differences are not significant. By and large, the results of the Fenz and Epstein study provide fairly strong support for the inverted U hypothesis, as far as anxiety and temporal indices of speech are concerned.

There is one study, however, the results of which, at least on first glance, appear to be inconsistent with the inverted U hypothesis. In this study (Pope, Blass, Siegman & Raher, 1970) six psychiatric, hospitalized patients spoke into a tape recorder each morning for the entire period of their hospitalization, describing for about 10 min any of their experiences during the preceding day

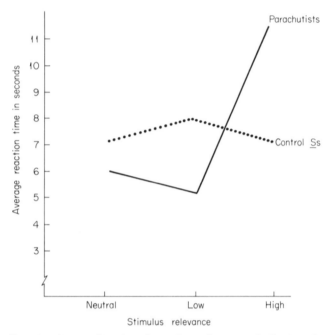

FIG. 7.1.   Reaction time as a function of experimental group and stimulus relevance. (From Fenz & Epstein, 1962. Copyright 1962 by Duke University Press.)

that they chose to discuss. The patients were also rated each day by a team of trained nurses on a number of manifest anxiety scales. The speech samples recorded during each patient's eight most anxious and eight least anxious days were compared. It should be noted that all patients had psychosomatic diagnoses and that occasionally they all manifested extreme anxiety, as well as stretches of calm and relaxed behavior. The results are based on a within-subjects' comparison (high-anxiety versus low-anxiety days) and are not confounded by subjects' psychiatric diagnoses. Speech samples recorded during subjects' high-anxious days, in contrast to speech samples recorded during subjects' low-anxious days, were associated with a faster speech rate, lower SQs and high AR (which, it will be recalled, is best viewed as an inverse index of relatively brief pauses), but only the differences for SR and SQ were significant (this study did not yield RT scores). These findings, then, suggest that even high anxiety arousal—there is little doubt that during the high-anxiety days these patients were very anxious indeed—is associated with a higher speech rate, due to a reduction in long pauses. But, as will be argued in the following paragraph, even this finding can be reconciled with the inverted U hypothesis, provided it is limited to speaking tasks involving choices between conflicting response tendencies, that is, complex tasks.

Anxiety, speech tempo, and the nature of the task. Strangely enough, most of the studies investigating the effects of anxiety arousal on speech have ignored the role of task variables such as task complexity. As was pointed out earlier, however, whether anxiety arousal is likely to have a disruptive or a facilitative effect on behavior, at least within the Hullian framework, is primarily a function of the nature of the task. The same level of anxiety arousal that facilitates simple learning tasks (tasks in which the predominant response tendency is the correct one) will interfere with complex learning tasks (tasks that elicit competing response tendencies) (Siegman, 1957; Taylor & Spence, 1952). By the same token the effects of anxiety arousal and stress tempo should also be a function of the nature of the speaking task. The same arousal level that accelerates highly habituated speech sequences or "automatic" speech, such as is involved in discussing a familiar topic, is likely to slow down speech that requires planning and decision making, such as is involved in making up stories in response to TAT cards. This would account for the fact that even fairly high anxiety levels accelerated patients' speech when they were asked to talk about anything that occurred to them, but had the opposite effect on the subjects in the Fenz and Epstein study, who were asked to make up creative sotires about ambiguous TAT-like cards.

There is yet another factor that can attenuate or even reverse the positive correlation between anxiety arousal and speech tempo, and that is the extent to which one has learned to cope with a specific anxiety-arousing situation by means of denial, repression, and so forth. Although a mildly anxiety-arousing topic—in an interview situation—is associated with an accelerated speech tempo, this is not the case if the interviewer focuses on subjects' sexual experiences. Kanfer (1959, 1960), for example, found that interviewees increase their speech rate when they talk about personal problems as opposed to a neutral topic. Yet, their speech rate decreased significantly when the interviewer focused on their sexual experiences. The same distinction is suggested by findings obtained by Cassotta, Feldstein, and Jaffe (1967), who compared interviewees' verbal behavior in a stress versus a nonstress interview. In the stress interview they were told: "Everyone has dreams and daydreams in which they see themselves doing things which would normally be embarrassing to them, perhaps because they might be illegal, immoral, or unethical. I would like you to tell me of any such dreams or daydreams that you may have had." There was a significantly higher rate of pauses in the stress interview, even though in a previous study Feldstein and his associates (1963) found that an anxiety-arousing topical focus was associated with a higher verbal rate than a neutral one. These findings suggest that the accelerating effect of anxiety arousal will not occur if the topic involves material which the speaker has learned to repress.

Trait anxiety, speech tempo and speech disturbances. The studies cited thus far dealt primarily with the effects of situational anxiety, that is, experimentally produced or naturally occurring moment-to-moment fluctuations in anxiety level, on speech variables. A related issue is the relationship between subjects' anxiety threshold or trait anxiety level, as indexed by the Taylor Manifest Anxiety Scale (MAS)[8] or some similar inventory, and speech behavior. A review article by Murray (1971) cites six studies which correlated measures of trait anxiety with response latency. All six correlations were negative, three significantly so. Siegman and Pope (1965b) obtained a significant negative correlation between the Taylor MAS (Bendig's short form) and an index of short silent pauses (less than 2 sec), and a positive correlation between the same trait anxiety index and a measure of relatively long silent pauses (more than 2 sec). Preston and Gardner (1967) obtained negative correlations between various indices of trait or predispositional anxiety and the *frequency* of pauses 1.5 sec and over, and positive correlations between the trait anxiety indices and the duration of such pauses. If we assume that trait anxiety is associated with a decrease in the frequency of short pauses and with an increase in the frequency and/or duration of long pauses, these findings are not as paradoxical as they may appear. As suggested earlier, the two types of pauses can be independent of each other, and it might be profitable to distinguish between them. In the same review article it is also reported that out of seven studies, which correlated trait anxiety measures and speech quantity or verbal productivity, six obtained positive correlations, four of which were significant (Murray, 1971). By and large, then, the studies on trait anxiety and speech tend to be consistent with a drive-activation conceptualization of anxiety. Concerning the more specific question of the relationship between trait anxiety and speech tempo, it seems that it decreases response latency and relatively short silent pauses, but may increase the frequency and/or duration of relatively long silent pauses.

Rather puzzling, at least on first glance, is the finding that although situational anxiety or stress is consistently associated with an increase in speech disturbances, as measured by Mahl's SDR, there is no evidence for a similar positive correlation between trait anxiety and SDR (Cook, 1969; Kasl & Mahl, 1965; Siegman & Pope, 1972). How is one to explain this discrepancy between situational and trait anxiety as far as their impact on the SDR is concerned? The following is one possible, although admittedly highly speculative, explanation. It was suggested earlier that the increase in the SDR associated with the experimental manipulation of subjects' anxiety level is not a direct manifestation of anxiety arousal, but rather an indirect manifestation of the increase in subjects' speech tempo. Fluent speech, in the sense of it being free of speech disruptions, requires planning, which takes place during silent pauses. The reduction of such

---

[8] A high score on this scale indicates that subject readily responds with upset or arousal to a wide variety of situations, but it does not indicate the *level* of subject's arousal in a particular situation. Whether a given level of situational stress is likely to produce a higher arousal level in high than in low MAS scorers is debatable. The concept of trait anxiety is obviously far less clear than that of state anxiety, which may account for some of the discrepant findings.

pauses, due to anxiety's activation-arousal effect, inevitably raises the SDR. High trait-anxiety scorers, that is, chronically anxious individuals, however, may have learned to speak fluently despite their generally increased speech tempo. A specific strategy that they may employ is suggested by the divergent impact of trait anxiety on brief versus relatively long pauses, noted earlier. The long pauses occurring within the context of an otherwise accelerated speech tempo may very well serve the purpose of planning fluent speech sequences.

Audience Anxiety and Speech

Public speaking is an anxiety-arousing situation for many people, and its effects on speech have been investigated in a series of studies by Levin and Paivio and their associates. Considering the effects of situational anxiety on speech summarized earlier in this chapter, one would expect public speaking, in contrast to dyadic conversation, to have several distinguishing extralinguistic features. First and foremost, one would expect public speaking, to the extent that it is in fact anxiety arousing, to be associated with speech disturbances as measured by Mahl's SDR. Second, public speaking should be associated with an accelerated speech tempo if the speaking task is a simple one, and with a reduced speech tempo if the speaking task is a complex one. Third, public speech, as opposed to private speech, should be associated with greater productivity, i.e., relatively long speeches. The actual findings will be reviewed separately for each of the three speech variables.

Speech disturbances. A number of investigators have looked at the effect of public speaking anxiety or audience anxiety, as it is referred to in the literature, on speech disturbances. In some cases the authors combined the speech disturbance categories with silent pauses and filled pauses into a single disfluency index (e.g., Levin, Baldwin, Gallwey, & Paivio, 1960), which makes an evaluation of the results difficult. Of several investigators who looked specifically at the impact of audience anxiety on Mahl's SDR or on its separate major component categories, none obtained the expected disruptive effect (Geer, 1966; Levin & Silverman, 1965; Paivio, 1965; Reynolds & Paivio, 1968). Considering the consistency with which situational anxiety has been found to be associated with an increase in the SDR, this is a puzzling finding. Before attempting to provide an explanation for this finding, we will first present the other data.

Speech tempo. In a study by Levin and Silverman (1965) on the effects of audience anxiety on speech in children, subjects were asked to complete story stems (a story completion task) either in front of an audience of four adults, or to a microphone while no one was listening. The public speaking condition was found to be associated with significantly more brief pausing (less than 1 sec) and more filled pauses (which approached significance), but had no effect on relatively long pauses.

Reynolds and Paivio (1968) looked at the effects of audience anxiety on speech in a group of college students, whose task was to define a series of abstract and concrete nouns. In the audience condition subjects sat facing 10–15 peers; in the control condition they talked to the experimenter. The experimental manipulation had no independent significant effect on either of the two temporal indices: response latency, and silence pause ratio (SPR). There was, however, a significant interaction between subjects' scores on an inventory designed to measure audience sensitivity (ASI) and the experimental manipulation on the silence ration. High ASI scorers showed an increase in silent pauses (SPR) from the control to the public-speaking condition, low ASI scorers a decrease. Moreover, in the control condition the high ASI scorers obtained lower SPR's than the low ASI scorers (see Fig. 2). A similar interaction between subjects' ASI scores and public versus private speaking is reported by Paivio (1965) in relation to speech rate. On the assumption that the public speaking situation produced mild anxiety arousal in the low ASI scorers and fairly high anxiety levels in the high ASI scorers, the results of these two studies are consistent with the inverted U hypothesis, namely, that mild anxiety arousal accelerates speech and that strong arousal has the reverse effect. In the Paivio (1965) study, subjects' task consisted of describing and interpreting a series of cartoons, with description

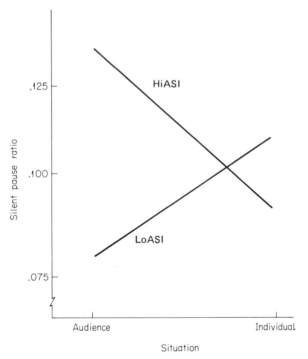

FIG. 7.2. Silent pause ratio as a function of audience sensitivity level and audience situation. (From Reynolds & Paivio, 1968.)

presumably being a simple task and interpretation a complex one. The slowing down effect of the audience condition in high ASI scorers noted above was limited to the interpretation task.

By and large, then, the evidence indicates that a high level of audience anxiety slows down speech tempo, provided the speech task is a complex one. There is also some evidence to suggest that a mild level of audience anxiety accelerates speech tempo, even if the speaking task is a complex one. Both of these findings are consistent with a drive-activation approach to anxiety. The expectation that even high anxiety levels would accelerate speech tempo, provided the speaking task is a fairly simple one, was not supported by the findings of the one study that clearly distinguished between task difficulty (Paivio, 1965).

The implications of the audience anxiety studies for the more general issue of the effects of anxiety on speech, are tempered by a number of methodological problems that characterize these studies. First, almost all the audience anxiety studies involve complex speaking tasks, such as making up stories, interpreting cartoons, providing definitions, and so on, rather than highly habituated speech sequences such as are involved in most dyadic conversations. Other methodological problems concern the proper control condition for evaluating the effects of audience anxiety. In some of the studies (e.g., Levin & Silverman, 1965; Reynolds & Paivio, 1968) the control condition required that subjects speak into a tape recorder, with no other person present. This presents at least two problems. First, speaking into a tape recorder, certainly if it is for the first time, can be a stressful experience (Sauer & Marcuse, 1957). Second, as is shown later in this chapter, the mere presence of another person or persons produces pressures on a speaker which he does not have to contend with if he is left alone. It can be argued, therefore, that the proper control condition for audience anxiety is one in which the speaker addresses one other person. A parametric study, in which audience size is systematically varied from a single listener to a large group would, of course, be ideal. Finally, there is the problem that in some studies there is a confounding between audience size and status. Thus in one study (Levin & Silverman, 1965), in which the speakers were children, the audience consisted of higher status adults, and in another study (Reynolds & Paivio, 1968) in which the audience condition consisted of peers, the control condition involved the presence of a high-status experimenter. Considering the evidence, to be presented later, that listener status influences a speaker's paralinguistic behavior, such confounding between audience size and status presents a serious problem.

Verbal productivity. In one of the early studies on the effects of audience stress on speech, the authors found a reduced productivity level in the public-speaking condition (Levin *et al.,* 1960). The magnitude of the difference between the audience and the control condition was substantial and highly significant. Moreover, the effect was obtained for both high and low scorers on the ASI inventory.

It is not at all certain, however, to what extent one can generalize from this finding, since subsequent studies on audience anxiety and speech fail to mention such an effect even though verbal productivity was included among the dependent variables (Levin & Silverman, 1965; Paivio, 1965). More importantly, even if this is a valid finding, it does not necessarily present a serious challenge to the drive-activation approach to anxiety. The reduced productivity level in the audience condition may simply reflect the fact that by terminating their speech early, subjects terminate their anxiety state. It is of interest to note that in the control condition of the Levin et al. (1960) study, the high ASI scorers were more productive than the low ASI scorers, which is, of course, consistent with a negative correlation between trait anxiety and verbal productivity, as reported earlier.

Concluding remarks on the effects of audience stress on speech.   The findings concerning the effect of audience stress on speech disturbances are clearly contrary to expectations, those concerning speech tempo and productivity may or may not present a problem to the drive-activation interpretation of anxiety. We simply do not have sufficient data. It may very well be, however, that the public-speaking situation is not the proper testing ground for the effects of anxiety per se on speech. People simply may use a more formal and careful speaking style when addressing a relatively large audience than when conversing with one other person. In other words, public speaking may be closer to written than to spoken language. If this is indeed the case, then one should expect public speaking to be associated with relatively few speech disturbances, brevity, and a relatively slow speech tempo. Whether this is indeed the case, and precisely under what circumstances, remains to be answered by further carefully controlled studies. At any rate, the relevance of the audience anxiety findings to the more general question of the effects of anxiety arousal on speech is debatable.

Anxiety and Speech: Some General Observations

In the early literature on anxiety and speech, especially in the clinical literature, it was simply assumed that the effects of anxiety on speech can only be of a disruptive and disorganizing nature. If the authors of this literature had major reservations about this generalization, they certainly were not very explicit. The experimental data indicate that the picture is much more complex than is suggested by the aforementioned literature. Suffice it to cite the finding that within the context of the initial interview, anxiety arousal is associated with relatively productive interviewee responses, as an indication that the consequences of anxiety arousal are not necessarily disruptive in nature. Also, anxiety arousal is not always associated with disruptive silent pauses but, depending on the conditions, can be associated with more fluent speech, in the sense of a somewhat accelerated speech tempo, free of silent pauses. It was suggested that a conceptualization of anxiety in terms of drive—in the Hullian sense—provides a parsimonious theoretical framework for explaining these various experimental findings. One implication of this approach is that the effects of anxiety on speech are a function of task difficulty, a variable that has all but been ignored in the literature on anxiety and speech. Clearly, we need more studies to clarify the effects of task difficulty, of anxiety level, and of the interaction between these two variables on speech. Finally, any model for the effects of anxiety on speech, should allow for individual differences, that is, for different learned response tendencies to anxiety arousal. There is evidence, for example, that the speech behavior of chronically anxious individuals (that is, high scorers on anxiety inventories such as the Taylor Manifest Anxiety Scale) parallels the speech behavior produced by situational anxiety arousal, with, however, one major exception. The exception is that chronically anxious individuals do not show more speech disturbances, as indexed by Mahl's SDR, than nonanxious individuals, despite the fact that an increase in the SDR is one of the most reliable consequences of situational anxiety arousal. Perhaps chronically anxious individuals have learned to compensate for this particular consequence of anxiety arousal.

In the literature on nonverbal communication one frequently comes across the statement that expressive nonverbal behavior is at best only minimally controllable. Presumably this is so because people have no awareness of their expressive, nonverbal behavior patterns that tend to reflect changes in the autonomic nervous system. Certainly, the assumption regarding the lack of awareness is debatable. There is evidence that trained actors do very well in mimicking or simulating the extralinguistic features of anxiety arousal and of other emotional states (Feldstein, 1964). There is also evidence that people accurately identify the emotions that the actors portrayed, and that on this task laymen do as well as trained psychiatrists (Feldstein, Jaffe, & Cassotta 1964). Clearly, then, people must be aware of the extralinguistic correlates of anxiety arousal and other emotional states, at least when they occur in others. As to the capacity for covering-up or compensating for the expressive nonverbal correlates of one's own emotional states, certainly the work of Neal Miller and many others on biofeedback, indicates that even autonomic nervous system correlates are not beyond self-control.

One final note. The emphasis in the preceding sections has been on the effects of anxiety arousal on the temporal aspects of speech encoding, with brief forays into a few other extralinguistic parameters, such as productivity and speech disruptions. It should be obvious, however, that anxiety-arousal may affect other parameters as well—such as intensity or loudness and other vocal manifestations of tension. The fact that these have not been discussed simply reflects the sparsity of empirical data regarding the impact of anxiety arousal on these other parameters.

Vocal Correlates of Anger and Depression

Although most studies on the vocal correlates of affective states or experiences have focused on anxiety, there are a few studies that have focused on other emotional experiences as well. For example, Feldstein and Jaffe (1962) investigated the relationship between anger and the SDR, and found no correlation between the two. This suggests that the widely reported increase in the SDR as a function of anxiety arousal may be specific to anxiety rather than a correlate of all states that involve emotional arousal. While one can hardly reach such a conclusion on the basis of a single study, there is additional support for this finding from another study as well. In this study (Feldstein, 1964), professional actors were asked to read a standard passage while simulating a variety of emotional states (hate, anger, depression, sadness, joy, fear, and nervousness) as well as normal conversation. The recorded simulations were analyzed for speech disruption, breath intake, vocal intensity and pause time. The speech-disruption ratio was significantly higher in the simulations of nervousness and fear than in all other simulations, while the SDRs were roughly equivalent. Mean intensity fluctuation was the only variable that clearly distinguished anger from the other simulations, with a higher mean intensity fluctuation for anger than for the others. It is surprising that despite the current interest in aggressive behavior, there have not been more studies on the vocal correlates of anger.

Next to anxiety, depression is the affective state or experience about which we have the most information in terms of its vocal correlates, even though the number of studies concerned with this issue is relatively few.

In Feldstein's (1964) study on the vocal correlates of simulated emotional experiences, depression (and sadness) could be distinguished from all others and from normal conversation by a lower respiration rate, lower intensity fluctuation, and higher percent pause time. The finding that depression is apparently associated with more frequent and/or longer silent pauses was confirmed in the study by Pope, Blass, Siegman & Raher (1970), discussed earlier, in which six hospitalized psychosomatic patients made daily recordings of their experiences during the previous day. Daily ratings were made, by a group of trained nurses, of each patient's level of depression. Recordings obtained from each patient during his eight most depressed and his eight least depressed days over a period of three months, were then analyzed in terms of their temporal and other extralinguistic characteristics. On the basis of the clinical observation that slow and retarded speech is a prominent symptom of depressed patients, it was expected that the recordings obtained during the high-depression days would be associated with a slower speech rate than those obtained during the low-depression days. This expectation was fully confirmed. Additional analyses revealed that only the index measuring relatively long pauses (2 sec and over) but not the index measuring relatively brief pauses (under 2 sec), discriminated between the high- and low-depression days. Contrary to expectation, the Filled Pauses (or "Ah") Ratio did not discriminate between the two speech conditions. It was expected that it would, because it is usually associated with hesitant and cautious speech. The slower speech rate during states or experiences of depression apparently is not an indication of cautious speech, but rather of a low energy and activation level. Finally, as in Feldstein's study, depression had no significant effect on the SDR.

That depression is associated with a slower speech rate and a higher silence ratio was also noted in a study by Aronson and Weintraub (1972) who compared depressed and other patient groups, as well as normal controls, on several extralinguistic as well as content-oriented variables. In terms of the extralinguistic measures, the depressed group could be readily distinguished from the others on the basis of reduced productivity, a slower verbal rate, and higher silence ratios. Finally, in a group of patients with various psychiatric diagnoses, Kanfer (1960) obtained a significant negative correlation between their scores on the Depression scale of the MMPI and speech rate.

The empirical data, then, consistently indicate that the experience of depression in depressed patients and in others who do not carry such a diagnostic label is associated with more and/or longer pauses, resulting in a slower speech rate. As to the cause of this finding, we can only speculate. As will be shown later in this chapter, the mere presence of another person in dyadic conversation exerts pressure on the temporal pacing of speech, which is probably the reason why dialogues contain fewer silent pauses than monologues. The social withdrawal of depressed patients could, therefore, have the effect of increasing the frequency and duration of silent pauses in dyadic conversation. It will be recalled, however, that the increase of silent pauses was also noted in monologue-type speech. Physiological factors, such as under-arousal, could, of course, account for these findings.

THE SOCIAL AND INTERPERSONAL CONTEXT

Although the early literature on the extralinguistic aspects of speech focused primarily on the role of personality differences and the effects of emotional arousal, it is becoming increasingly clear that there are other factors that are of equal if not greater significance in terms of their contribution to the total variance of the extralinguistic domain. The remainder of this chapter will be devoted to two such factors: the social—interpersonal context and cognitive processes.

There are some fairly obvious reasons for assuming that the social context is a significant contributor to the variance of the extralinguistic domain. Speech, whether directed to one individual or to a larger audience, is clearly an interpersonal activity. It can be argued that even monologues have an implicit audience. It would seem, therefore, only reasonable to assume that the demographic characteristics of one's audience, and the relationship between speaker and audience will determine not only what is being said but also how it is encoded. It is surprising, therefore, that the literature concerned with the effects of the speaker's and listener's demographic backgrounds and of their relationship to each other on extralinguistic variables is fairly sparse.

Extralinguistic Behavior in Mixed Company

At the beginning of this chapter, evidence was cited suggesting that gender is a signi-ficant source of variance in the extralinguistic domain. For example, there is evidence that men speak more loudly than women. It was also pointed out, however, that this relationship tends to vary as a function of situational variables. One such variable, in dyadic interactions, is the gender of the other speaker. There is evidence to suggest that both men and women speak differently when addressing a member of their own sex than when speaking to a member of the opposite sex. Thus, both men and women apparently speak more loudly when addressing some-one of the opposite sex as opposed to someone from their own sex (Markel, Prebor, and Brandt, 1972). In relation to some extralinguistic behaviors, however, the mixed-gender situation may have different effects on males than on females. For example, in an interview study recently conducted in our laboratory, there was a significant interaction between interviewer and interviewee gender and response latency. Females responded more quickly than males to same-gender interviewers. In mixed-gender dyads, however, the female interviewees *increased* their response latencies, while the male interviewees *decreased* their. Similar results were ob-tained in relation to silent pauses. In this study, then, the mixed-gender situation produced more than a simple exaggeration of baseline gender differences. In fact, different motivating factors may have been at work for males and females—pre-cisely which factors, however, remain an issue for further investigation.

Also relevant in this context are the results of a study (Siegman, 1975) that was designed to assess the social reinforcement value of eye contact between interviewer and interviewee, when cues other than eye contact, such as verbal signals, are used to regulate the initiation and termination of both the inter-viewer's and interviewee's comments. Interviewees, both males and females, rated their interviewer as warmer and they were more attracted to their inter-viewer when there was eye contact between them, than when it was eliminated, independent of the interviewer's gender. In relation to interviewees' productivity levels, however, there was a significant interaction between the gender composi-tion of the interviewer–interviewee dyad and eye contact. Elimination of eye contact inhibited productivity in same-gender dyads, and facilitated productivity in mixed-gender dyads. Although this finding deals with productivity, whose status as an extralinguistic variable may be somewhat marginal, it has significant methodological implications. It suggests that gender composition is, in the terminology of Kogan and Wallach (1964), a significant moderator variable. Relationships obtained in same-gender dyads may not be obtained, or may even be reversed, in mixed-gender dyads. In studies with a single experimenter, male or female, and male and female subjects, potentially significant results may simply cancel each other out, unless separate analyses are made for the male and the female subjects.

Voices of Love and Power

Factorial analyses of dyadic interactions involving such diverse relationships as parent—child, husband—wife, employer—employee and interviewer—interviewee consistently have identified two basic dimensions: power or dominance and love or warmth (Foa, 1961; Pope & Siegman, 1972). It is not unreasonable to assume that the opposite poles of these dimensions are likely to be associated with varying nonverbal behaviors. In fact, this has been shown to be the case in relation to eye contact (see Exline & Fehr, Chapter 5). Very little experimental research, however, has been done on the effects of different affective or status relationships on extralinguistic behavior, except within the context of initial interviews. In the following paragraphs, we will summarize the findings of a number of such studies conducted in our laboratory.

Warmth and the flow of communication in the initial interview. Textbooks on the initial interview, written from a clinical perspective, typically exhort the novice interviewer to be warm, friendly, and understanding rather than neutral and reserved, and certainly not outright cold, challenging, and rejecting. This advice is based on the general assumption that interviewees will be more attracted to a warm than to a cold interviewer, and on the further assumption that such attraction is likely to enhance interviewee productivity and self-disclosure. The latter assumption is frequently couched in social-reinforcement theory terms. Interviewees, it is said, should want to prolong exchanges that are pleasant and rewarding, and to terminate those which are unpleasant and painful, either of which can be achieved by the proper manipulation of productivity level. As to self-disclosure, it is argued that the risk of rejection is the most obvious reason why people tend to withhold information that is of an intimate nature and potentially self-damaging. Of course, this risk is less of a consideration if an interviewer is warm and accepting rather than reserved and neutral. It is somewhat less clear what effects warmth and attraction are likely to have on the extralinguistic domain. One possibiltiy is that people are likely to feel more relaxed with a warm than with a cold interviewer and therefore will tend to adopt a less formal style, or a less "elaborated code," to use Bernstein's (1961) terminology. If so, interviewees may be more fluent, that is, exhibit fewer and shorter silent pauses, when addressing a warm rather than a cold interviewer. What does the evidence suggest in relation to these expectations?

The expectation that interviewees would feel more attracted to a warm than to a cold interviewer was confirmed in numerous studies in our laboratory and is consistent with a conceptualization of interpersonal attraction in terms of social reinforcement theory (Byrne, 1971). The expected inverse relationship between interpersonal attraction and pausing was confirmed in three out of four studies that addressed themselves to this question. In our first experimental study of the initial interview, which was described in greater detail earlier in this chapter (pp. 203—204), an attempt was made to assess interviewees' attraction to their interviewers. To that end, each interviewee was administered an adaptation of the Libo Picture Impressions Test (Libo, 1956) pre- and postinterview, with the change in scores constituting interviewee's attraction scores. The correlation between subjects' attraction scores and a pausing index, combining latency and within-utterance pauses, was significant ($r = -.38$, $N = 50$, $p < 01$). The correlation between interviewees' attraction scores and a hesitation index, combining "ahs" and relatively brief pauses, fell short of significance ($r = -.25$, $.05 < p < .10$), but the correlation between their attraction scores and the Ah ratio alone was significant ($r = -.28$, $p < .05$). There was no significant correlation, however, between subjects' attraction scores and their SDRs (Pope & Siegman, 1966). In a recent study (Siegman, 1976c), which included a strong manipulation of the warm–cold dimension, interviewer warmth was again a significant source of variance in the combined silent pause index. A separate analysis of the interviewees' SQs and RT scores showed that the difference in relation to the former was clearly significant ($F = 4.90$; $df\ 1/52$; $p < .05$). The difference in relation to the RT scores, was significant only for the first half of the interview ($F = 4.05$; $df\ 1/52$; $p < .05$). The results of yet a third study (Siegman, 1974c), in which only the SQ index was used, showed a close correspondence between experimentally manipulated interviewee–interviewer attraction and interviewees' SQ scores.

The expectation that interviewer warmth would facilitate interviewee productivity level fared less well. In four out of five studies that addressed themselves to this issue, no evidence could be found to support the hypothesis that interviewer warmth per se facilitates interviewee productivity or that interviewer coldness per se has an inhibiting effect. Although reinforcement theory is occasionally invoked in order to explain the presumptive beneficial effect of interviewer warmth on interviewee productivity, it can be shown that this represents an unjustified application of the theory. Reinforcement, properly understood, is the rewarding of an operant response. Therefore, for an increase in interviewee productivity to occur, it is necessary that social reinforcers be dispensed on a contingent basis, that is, only after the occurrence of productive interviewee responses. The indiscriminate (noncontingent) dispensation of social reinforcers on the part of an interviewer may very well create a general ambience of friendliness and warmth, and our studies indicate that they do, but there is no basis in reinforcement theory for the assumption that such ambience is likely to enhance interviewee productivity. This conclusion is supported by the results of several studies in which interviewer "mm-hmms," the ubiquitous verbal social reinforcers, were used on a noncontingent basis (Siegman, 1976a). Although the interviewer's "mm-hmms" were perceived as the social reinforcers that they were intended to be, they were not associated with an increase in productivity. The clinical observation that interviewees tend to be more productive in response to warm than to cold interviewers may very well be a valid observation but for reasons other than interviewer warmth or coldness per se. It is not unreasonable to assume that, generally speaking, interviewees expect their interviewer to be warm and accepting. To the extent that interviewees are in fact less productive in response to cold than to warm interviewers, it may reflect their disappointment of having their expectation (that their interview will be warm and understanding) disconfirmed. Interviewees who are forewarned that their interviewer is a cold and reserved person may very well be as productive as with a warm interviewer. Precisely this was found in a number of interview studies conducted in our laboratory (Siegman, 1974a, 1976c).

To summarize, then, it would seem that the effect of interviewer warmth and interviewee–interviewer attraction on interviewee's extralinguistic behavior is primarily evident in the frequency and/or duration of silent pauses. This finding has implications for other areas in social psychology as well. For example, social psychologists today are very much concerned with the determinants of interpersonal attraction, but most of the data in this research area are derived from simple rating scales in which subjects indicate how much they liked their partner in an experimental task and whether they would like to work with him again. These measures, however, are very vulnerable to acquiescence and related response biases. Clearly, what is needed in this research area is a behavioral index of interpersonal attraction. A recent study (Siegman, 1976c) that was designed to test Aronson's (1969) gain–loss model of interpersonal attraction supplemented conventional rating scales with the SQ as an index of interpersonal attraction. As a result, it was possible to attribute some puzzling findings obtained with the scales, to experimenter demand characteristics. More importantly, the use of these extralinguistic indices of attraction made it possible to monitor changes over time, something which cannot be done very well with the usual rating scales.

Finally, in the above study, it was also noticed that interviewees showed greater readiness to disclose intimate and potentially embarrassing information to a warm than to a cold interviewer. To the extent that this is, in fact, the case, it may attenuate the positive correlation between interviewer warmth and interviewee fluency (fewer and/or briefer silent pauses). It was pointed out earlier in this chapter, and it will be pointed out again later, that potentially embarrassing topical areas are associated with a relatively high SQ score. If such topics are more likely to come up with a warm than with a cold interviewer, they may attenuate the positive correlation between interviewer warmth and interviewee fluency. In other words, it is suggested that topical focus may very well be a moderating variable in the relationship between interviewer warmth and interviewee extralinguistic behavior—a possibility that should be investigated in future research on the extralinguistic correlates of interpersonal attraction.

Power and the flow of communication in the initial interview. A major dimension of interviewees' perceptions of their interviewer involves status or competence. It is not unreasonable to expect, therefore, that an interviewer's status or perceived competence could influence an interviewee's extralinguistic behavior, although precisely in what way is not clear. It may be that people are likely to adopt a more formal style when addressing a high-status person than when conversing with a peer. If so, one can also expect people to speak more carefully, with more hesitations and perhaps with more silent pauses, when addressing high-status as opposed to a low-status person. Specifically in terms of the interview, perhaps one can expect interviewees to speak more freely about intimate matters to a high-status than to a low-status interviewer.

The results of a study (Pope & Siegman, 1972) that addressed itself to the above questions provide partial support for both hypotheses. In this study, 32 female nursing students were interviewed twice, once by someone introduced as a senior professor and experienced interviewer, and once by someone introduced as a beginning novice. Two interviewers alternated between the high-status and the low-status role. In order to protect the credibility of the status manipulation, the two interviewers—who differed in age—conducted the interviews from behind a screen. The subjects never did see their interviewers. The manipulation also provided a plausible cover story, namely, that the purpose of the study was to investigate the effects of the screen on the interviewee. The interview itself was divided into two segments, one focusing on interviewee's family relations. the other on interviewee's school experiences. Of the two syntactic variables presumably related to speech formality, that is, the subordinate clause ratio and the passive-verb ratio, only the latter was significantly affected by interviewer status. As expected, the interviewees showed a higher passive-verb ratio when responding to the high-status than to the low-status interviewer. Interviewees also responded with significantly shorter response latencies (RTs) but with higher SQ to the high-status than to the low-status interviewer, suggesting that in addressing a high-status person, one is under pressure to respond promptly, but that the response itself is associated with more pausing, perhaps because of its more formal style. A further analysis indicated that these effects did not occur across the board in the two interview segments. Rather, they were limited to the segment focusing on the interviewee's school experiences, perhaps because it was to this segment that the interviewer's status as a professor was most salient. There was one other significant finding in this study: the high-status interviewer elicited significantly fewer speech disruptions in the family relations topic than the low-status interviewer, suggesting that interviewees found it less anxiety arousing to discuss this topic with the high-status than with the low-status interviewer.

On the whole, the impact of interviewer status on interviewees' speech was fairly minimal, less than was expected. (In fact, its impact was less pronounced than the impact of the topical manipulation.) Perhaps in an interview situation, any interviewer, whether a professor or a student, is in a dominant position vis-à-vis the interviewee. In other words, perhaps the crucial factor is not one's social status but one's role in a specific dyadic interaction. Clearly, much more information is needed to clarify how status and power relationships between communicants affect the encoding process and the flow of communication.

The Role of the Other Person in Dyadic Interactions

The discussion thus far, especially the findings on the effects of interviewer warmth and interviewer status, may lead some readers to conclude that the other partner in a dyadic conversation has only a marginal impact on the speaker's extralinguistic behavior. Dramatic evidence to the contrary is provided by a phenomenon variously called synchrony or congruence. It is a common observation that we tend to adjust the loudness level of our speech to that of our conversational partner. Recent evidence indicates that such congruence or synchrony between partners occurs in relation to many other speech variables as well. In one of the early studies of synchrony, Matarazzo and Wiens (1972) found that interviewees tend to match the duration of their responses to that of the interviewer. Long interviewer remarks are followed by relatively lengthy interviewee responses, and short interviewer queries are followed by brief interviewee replies. Controlling for potentially confounding influences, such as interviewer ambiguity—specificity level and topical focus, Siegman, Pope, and Blass (1969) still obtained the synchrony phenomenon, although the effect was weaker than in the Matarazzo studies, and obtained only within the first of two interview sequences. Also, the expectation that the magnitude of the synchrony effect would be a function of the interviewer's status—that is, experienced professor versus student novice—did not materialize. This, however, could be due to the possibility that was mentioned earlier, that the interviewer is always in a dominant position vis-à-vis the interviewee, independent of the former's social status.

In a study of informal conversations, Feldstein (see Chapter 10) did not find the kind of moment-to-moment matchings found by Matarazoo and his associates within the context of structured interviews. He did find, however, that the average duration of a speaker's utterances covaried with those of his partners, when matched with different partners in a series of conversations.

Synchrony or congruence has also been found in relation to response latency (Matarazzo & Wiens, 1972), interruptions (Matarazzo & Wiens, 1972), duration of silent pauses (Feldstein, 1972), rate of speech—defined as number of syllables divided by phonation time—(Webb, 1972), loudness (Welkowitz, Feldstein, Finkelstein, & Aylesworth, 1972; Natale, 1975), and precision of articulation (Tolhurst, 1955). Finally, the language and dialect accommodation phenomenon discussed at the beginning of this chapter can also be understood in terms of a synchrony effect, analogous to that found in relation to the extralinguistic variables.

A detailed discussion of the synchrony or congruence phenomenon will be found in Feldstein and Welkowitz's chapter in this book. Whatever its explanation may be, the synchrony phenomenon certainly illustrates the profound interactional nature of dyadic speech.

Speaking Without Seeing

There is yet another way in which the "other" partner in a dyadic conversation influences the speaker's extralinguistic behavior. If conversation is to proceed in an orderly fashion, without the participants talking to each other at the same time, there must be an orderly exchange of speaker and listener roles. The speaker must provide the listener with appropriate cues indicating when he is ready to relinquish the floor, and he must also monitor the listener for indications that he wants to assume the floor. The cues that serve this regulatory function are complex and are discussed in some detail in Chapter 10. For our purposes, suffice it to say that while these cues are mostly visual in nature, they also involve some of the extralinguistic vocal variables discussed thus far. For example, according to Maclay and Osgood (1959) ahs or filled pauses, serve, at least in part, as signals to the listener that the speaker is not yet ready to give up the floor. According to Maclay and Osgood, then, filled pauses are the speaker's responses to his own silences.

What extralinguistic effects are likely to occur if the participants in a dyadic conversation cannot see each other? If it is indeed correct that in normal conversation a speaker relies primarily on visual cues, such as eye contact, to indicate whether or not he is ready to relinquish the floor, and only secondarily—during times when he needs to pause—on ahs, then it seems reasonable to assume that situations in which visual cues are unavailable to a speaker, for example, in telephone or telephonelike conversations, there will be an increase in filled pauses. One may also speculate that in such situations a speaker will exhibit fewer silences, lest he be interrupted and lose the floor. The evidence indicates that dyadic conversation without face-to-face contact is, in fact, associated with an increase in the Filled Pauses Ratio (Kasl & Mahl, 1965; Siegman & Pope, 1972). That it is indeed the possibility of being interrupted that is responsible for the increase in filled pauses when visual cues are unavailable is supported by the finding that when the speaker knows that he will not or cannot be interrupted, the same circumstance (i.e., absence of speaker–listener visual contact) produces a significant decrease in filled pauses. This finding has been reported by Feldstein et al. (1963), and has been replicated in a study in our laboratory. The latter study will now be described more fully because it contains additional data relevant to the effects of face-to-face contact on speech.

In this study, one half of the subjects were interviewed in the usual manner, that is, interviewer and interviewee confronting each other, the other half with the participants sitting in adjoining rooms. Prior to the interview, subjects in both conditions were requested to use the word "finished" to indicate when they had completed their response to the interviewer's queries. It was made clear to them that the interviewer would not interrupt them, nor proceed with the next question, until they had used the agreed upon cue to indicate that they had completed their response. Since all of the interviewer's communications were in the form of questions, it was always clear to the interviewees when he was finished with his messages. For all interviewees, one half of the interviewer questions were of a personal character, the others impersonal. Furthermore, there were three types of response conditions: speaking, dictation, and writing.

In this study, in which interviewees did not have to contend with the possibility of being interrupted, the primary effect of eliminating visual contact between the communicants was to reduce the interviewees' filled pauses to half ($F = 10.65$; df 1/16; $p < .01$). Also of interest is the finding that both the separation of interviewer and interviewee and the mode of response (speaking versus dictating versus writing) moderated the impact of topical focus on interviewees' productivity level. In the face-to-face interview condition, subjects were less productive when replying to highly personal than to impersonal interviewer questions. This is consistent with other findings and is to be expected considering that people tend to be defensive about highly personal matters. This effect, however, was attenuated, and eventually reversed, as the interview situation and response mode became more impersonal. Interviewees' reluctance to talk about intimate matters dissipated when the usual interpersonal pressures that exist in face-to-face communications were removed, either by separating the participants or by giving the interviewee the opportunity to respond in writing (see Table 1).

By way of summary, then, we find that the absence of face-to-face contact complicates the communication process, as is evidenced by the higher incidence of filled pauses, unless the speaker does not have to fear being interrupted and losing the floor. In the latter circumstance, the absence of face-to-face contact may, in fact, have a relaxing effect on the speaker, especially if the topic under discussion is of an intimate nature.

Concern over "losing" the floor and its effects on extralinguistic behavior may be involved in yet another finding. A comparison of pausing behavior in interviews as opposed to TAT responses, indicates that the latter are associated with fewer filled pauses but more silent pausing (Siegman & Pope, 1966a). The relatively high pausing ratio in the TAT responses can, of course, be attributed to task difficulty which, however, does not account for the relatively low incidence of filled pauses. A parsimonious explanation for both findings is that in the TAT situation there is less pressure on the subject to respond promptly and to go on talking lest he lose the floor than in the interview situation and, hence, the fewer ahs and increased pausing.

Feedback from one's conversational partner, interviewer, or experimenter may play a role in yet another phenomenon, which was noted in the above TAT study. As subjects progressed in their task of making up stories, there were changes on a number of extralinguistic variables, simply as a function of time. Response latencies became somewhat longer but speech increased in fluency: fewer filled and unfilled pauses. Similar results were obtained by Lalljee and

TABLE 1

Interviewee Productivity Level as a Function of Topic, Mode of Communication, and Interviewer Presence

| | Speech | | | | Dictation | | | | Writing | | | |
| | Neutral | | Personal | | Neutral | | Personal | | Neutral | | Personal | |
Conditions	M	SD	M	SD	M	SD	M	SD	M	SD	M	SD
Interviewer present	266.77	254.43	139.33	48.51	199.00	127.07	142.11	104.88	56.66	30.29	61.55	35.35
Interviewer absent	173.55	96.80	369.55	212.64	190.22	97.17	242.33	213.03	89.88	64.07	93.55	33.51

Cook (1973) within the context of the initial interview. Moreover, they found that this apparent adaptation effect takes place within the first 3 min of the interview, after which there is a leveling off in interviewee's fluency level. One possible explanation for this phenomenon is that in any encounter between strangers, the participants tend to experience a certain uncertainty, which is reduced by feedback from their partners, and which is reflected in their extralinguistic behavior. It is of interest that, in addition to an intrasession adaptation effect, there apparently is also an intersession adaptation process (Siegman, 1974b). As subjects return for a second interview or testing session, they show less hesitation—as indexed by the above extralinguistic variables—than they do at the very outset of their first session, but more than they show after having leveled off.

It must be stressed that the problem of visual contact between speakers and its impact on speech is a highly complex one. It involves not only whether or not the sender of a message can see the receiver and obtain feedback from him, but also whether or not he is seen by him. People tend to be highly uncomfortable in situations in which they can be seen by their partner but they cannot see him. Argyle, Lalljee, and Cook (1968) suggest that to be seen by one's partner but not being able to see him is to be in a relatively inferior or submissive relation to him, and hence the feelings of discomfort. How this is manifested in extralinguistic behavior remains to be investigated.

By way of summary, then, it can be said that conversation is a social activity par excellence. Perhaps the findings that illustrate this observation most dramatically are those which go by the name of synchrony or congruence, but there is other evidence as well. For conversation to proceed in an orderly fashion, the participants must let each other know whether they wish to hold on, relinquish, or take over the floor. This they usually do by means of visual and extralinguistic cues. It is not surprising, therefore, that as a rule communication proceeds more smoothly with than without visual contact between participants. There are, however, circumstances when the absence of face-to-face contact facilitates communication—for example, when the topic of discussion is potentially embarassing to the participants. Finally, it was hypothesized that the demographic characteristics of one's conversational partner affect one's extralinguistic behavior. Clearly, people speak differently when they talk to someone of like gender than to someone of the opposite gender. There is also evidence that interpersonal attraction affects a number of extralinguistic variables. It was suggested that code formality may be the intervening variable, with people adopting a less formal style when addressing someone they like and are attracted to than when talking to someone about whom they are indifferent.

COGNITION AND HESITATION

Preceding sections focused on the role of personality factors, transient affective states, and the social context in extralinguistic behavior. There is increasing evidence, however, that there is yet another major source of variance in the extralinguistic domain, especially in relation to the fluency and hesitation indices that have been the focus of this chapter. The results of recent research leave little doubt that cognitive processes play a significant role in extralinguistic behavior, and an increasing number of researchers are now attempting to clarify the precise nature of this relationship.

This "new look" in psycholinguistic research no doubt reflects the general *Zeitgeist,* with its emphasis on cognition. Nevertheless, considerable credit for the shift in emphasis from affective to cognitive factors must go to the work of Goldman-Eisler (1968), even though it has been questioned on a variety of methodological grounds (see Boomer, 1970).

In an early study Goldman-Eisler used a guessing technique in order to determine the predictability of words following hesitations (pauses) in a speaker's communication. She found that ". . . where guessers found themselves at a loss for predicting the next word as spoken originally . . . the original speaker also seemed to have been at a loss for the next word, for it was at these points that he tended to hesitate [p. 42]." On the basis of these findings Goldman-Eisler concludes that hesitation pauses reflect the speaker's lexical decision-making process, that is, his word choices.

Boomer (1970), who has questioned Goldman-Eisler's work on a variety of methodological grounds believes that such pauses involve primarily structural syntactic decisions. In part, his position is based on the finding that hesitation pauses tend to cluster immediately following the first word in a phonemic clause (see Chapter 8). Perhaps the hesitation pauses at the very beginning of a clause do involve syntactic planning, in contrast to subsequent hesitation pauses that involve lexical decisions. Goldman-Eisler, however, states (1968) that syntax is a matter of habit or skill rather than of cognitive planning.

> The examination of sentence structure in the light of the concomitant hesitation pauses showing an absence of any relationship between the two indicates that the hierarchical structuring of sentences and embedding of clauses is more a matter of linguistic skill than of planning. Syntactical operations had all the appearance of proficient behaviour as distinct from the volitional aspect of lexical and semantic operations [p. 80].

Perhaps comparing the frequency of pauses in sentences with and without subordinate clauses—which is what Goldman-Eisler did—is too crude a test of the hypothesis that syntactic complexity involves cognitive planning. Moreover, as will be shown later in this chapter, the silent pause clearly is only one of many manifestations of cognitive activity.

In another frequently cited study, Goldman-Eisler (1961a,b, 1968) compared the ratio of silent and filled pauses in speech associated with tasks of varying levels of difficulty. Specifically, she asked subjects first to describe and then to interpret a series of *New Yorker* cartoons. Each subject was given the following instructions: "You will be shown a series of cartoon stories with no verbal captions. You are asked to have a good look at them. As soon as you have got the point, say 'Got it' and proceed to describe the content of the story as depicted in the pictures before you; conclude by formulating the general point, meaning, or moral of the story in as concise a form as you can. . . ." A comparison of the descriptions and the interpretations showed that the latter were associated with a significantly higher silent pause ratio (but not filled pause ratio) than the former. This was true not only of the group as a whole, but every single subject in the study evidenced a higher silent pause ratio in the interpretations than in the descriptions. Although the RTs or initial delays for the descriptions (the period from when the subject said "Got it" to the first word of the description) were roughly the same as the initial delays for the interpretations, Goldman-Eisler argues that it took subjects proportionately more time to plan and to organize the interpretations than the descriptions, since the former contained fewer words than the latter (fewer than a third). This argument is based on the assumption that everything else being equal there should be a positive correlation between RT and subsequent productivity—an assumption which is clearly contradicted by the data obtained in our laboratory.

Be that as it may, it is Goldman-Eisler's position that since interpretation is a more complex task than description, it also requires longer planning than description and that this planning takes place during the initial delays. Furthermore, this planning during the initial delays involves primarily content and semantic decisions in contrast to within-utterance pauses, which involve primarily lexical choices. That the interpretations were associated with more hesitant speech than the descriptions is clear, but precisely what is responsible for the hesitations is less clear. The pauses could, of course, reflect lexical decision making, as Goldman—Eisler believes they do, since the words generated in the interpretations were in fact less predictable than those of the description. However, the interpretations were also syntactically more complex than the descriptions, which may account for the difference in the silent pause ratio associated with the two tasks. Goldman-Eisler considered this possibility, but dismissed it because interview responses are associated with a lower silent pause ratio than the cartoon interpretations, despite the fact that the two are of equal syntactic complexity. To this one can reply that:

1. The interview responses probably contain a higher ratio of overpracticed word sequences or automatic speech than the cartoon interpretations.

2. In the interview situation, syntactic complexity may be associated with other types of hesitation phenomena, such as filled pauses and speech disruptions.

Yet another possible explanation for the higher pause ratio of the interpretations than the descriptions may be the fact that subjects were instructed to formulate the interpretations in as *concise* a form as possible. As a matter of fact, Goldman-Eisler reports that in the interpretations (but not in the descriptions)[9]

---

[9] This, of course, may be due to the fact that only in the interpretation condition were subjects instructed to be concise.

there was a positive correlation between conciseness or brevity of expression, and silent pause ratio. Apparently the attempt to eliminate redundancy and to formulate concise responses, is associated with an increase in silent pauses.

The confounding, in Goldman-Eisler's study, between the experimental manipulation (description versus interpretation) and the requirement to be concise, plus negative results obtained by Rochester et al. (in press) prompted Siegman (1976b) to attempt to replicate Goldman-Eisler's findings. In this study 12 male and 12 female subjects were asked to *describe* four New Yorker cartoons and two TAT cards, and to *formulate* the meaning of four other cartoons as well as to *make-up a story* about two other TAT cards. The order of experimental task—description versus interpretation and story-making—and the two sets of stimuli were counterbalanced between subjects. Furthermore, for one half of the subjects, the instructions for *both* tasks included the requirement that they formulate their responses in a concise manner. The dependent variables were: response latency, average duration of pauses, pause frequency, and within response pausing time, with the latter two adjusted for response duration.

The nature of the task, that is, description versus interpretation, was a significant source of variance in relation to all the dependent variables except pause frequency, with longer pauses associated with the interpretations than the descriptions. This effect, however, was significantly stronger for the cartoons than the TATs. On the whole, then, the results of this study replicate Goldman-Eisler's findings that cognitive planning and decision-making is associated with hesitation pauses.

A question which remains to be answered is: why did the experimental manipulation have a significantly weaker effect when the stimuli involved TAT cards rather than cartoons? Perhaps formulating the meaning of cartoons, which presumably have only a single correct meaning, is a more complex task than making up stories for TAT cards, where the subject is under relatively few constraints once he has decided on a theme. This speculation is supported by the finding that the average pause duration was significantly higher for the cartoon interpretations than for the TAT stories.

It may very well be the case that in order for an increase in task difficulty to produce hesitation pauses, the subject must be operating at or near his information processing capacity. If the more difficult of the two tasks is relatively undemanding, the experimental manipulation may have no significant effect on subjects' pausing behavior. This situation probably occurred in the study by Rochester *et al.* (1977), and hence their failure to replicate Goldman-Eisler's findings.

It should be noted that although the description versus story-making manipulation had only a weak effect on subjects' within response pauses in the TAT, it did have a clear-cut impact on subjects' SDRs. Subjects showed significantly higher SDRs in the story-making task than in the description task.

That cognitive complexity can affect a rather wide range of hesitation phenomena, not just silent pauses, is indicated by the results of yet another study.

Reynolds and Paivio (1968) asked subjects to define a series of abstract and concrete nouns. The abstract definitions, in contrast to the concrete ones, were associated with longer latencies, silent pauses exceeding 1.5 sec, and filled pauses. It is fairly clear, then, that cognitive complexity or difficulty is associated with a relatively high level of pre- and within-utterance pausing, as well as other hesitation indices. The specific hesitation indices affected may, of course, be a function of the kind of decision to be made, but they may also be a function of the social context. Cognitive planning and decision making is more likely to be manifested by silent pausing in some situations, such as cartoon interpretations and story making, than in others, such as dyadic conversations. The moderating effect of the interpersonal context and the speaking task on the relationship between cognitive planning and hesitation phenomena is illustrated by several studies to which we now turn.

Cognition and hesitation in the initial interview. Siegman, Pope, and their associates (1965a, 1972) looked at the effect of cognitive planning and decision making on hesitation indices within the context of the initial interview. Specifically they investigated the effects of ambiguous versus specific interviewer questions on a broad sampling of hesitation phenomena. An ambiguous interviewer remark was defined as one that requires that the interviewee decide between many response alternatives (that is, one requiring planning and decision making). "Tell me about your family" is one example of a moderately ambiguous interviewer question. By way of contrast, a specific interviewer remark is one to which there is only one or a restricted number of response alternatives. Thus, "What kind of work do you do?" is an example of a highly specific interviewer question. In the first of a series of studies (Siegman & Pope, 1965a) ambiguous interviewer probes were found to be associated with more frequent filled and unfilled brief pausing than specific interviewer probes. Interviewer ambiguity, however, was not related to relatively long silent pauses, as indexed by the RT and SQ measures, nor was it related to the SDR.

In subsequent studies, however, ambiguous interviewer remarks, in contrast to specific ones, also elicited longer latencies and silences in interviewees' responses (Pope, Blass, Bradford, & Siegman, 1971; Siegman & Pope, 1972). The discrepancy between the first and the later studies may very well be the result of a procedural difference between them. In the first study the decision as to when an interviewee had completed his or her response to the interviewer's query was left to the subjective decision of the interviewer. In subsequent studies, however, interviewers were either instructed to wait a fixed period of time after each interviewee response before proceeding to the next question, or they were told not to begin their response until signaled by the interviewee that he had finished his. It is not unreasonable to assume, therefore, that in the first study subjects were under greater pressure than in subsequent studies to respond promptly and to refrain from long silent pauses, lest they lose the floor. This may explain why in the first study interviewer ambiguity did not affect interviewees' response latencies nor their silent pause ratios. It should be pointed out that in none of the studies, however, did we find a significant relationship between interviewer ambiguity and interviewee speech disruptions.

In another study, Siegman and Pope (1966a) investigated the effects of stimulus ambiguity in the TAT on hesitation phenomena in subjects' story completions. Stimulus ambiguity was defined in terms of the variability of themes evoked by the different cards. In this study, stimulus ambiguity was associated not only with an increase in the various hesitation indices listed earlier but also with an increase in the SDR. Perhaps speaker uncertainty is more likely to be associated with speech disruptions in tasks requiring new word combinations, as is the case in the TAT, than in the interview that, as pointed out earlier, involves a considerable amount of "automatic speech," that is, habituated or over practiced word sequences.

In a recent study, Rochester and Gill (1973) found that sentences containing noun-phrase complements (NPC) were associated with more speech disruptions than sentences containing relative clauses (Rel Cl.). The magnitude of this effect, however, was a function of the speech context, in this case, dialogues versus monologues, with the difference more pronounced in the latter than in the former. Furthermore, speech context interacted with the location of disruptions. For dialogues, disruption location was of little consequence. In monologues, however, disruption location was a critical variable. When disruptions were measured at clause boundaries, there was a 30-percentage-point spread between the proportions of disrupted NPC sentences and disrupted Rel Cl. sentences. But when disruptions were measured at other locations, the proportion of disrupted sentences were about the same regardless of type of sentence. The authors attribute the difference in speech disruption frequency in the two types of sentences to the fact that complement-type constructions are syntactically more complex than relative clause constructions. The fact that this difference was most pronounced in monologues, suggests to Rochester and Gill that the role of syntax may recede as one moves from monologues to dialogues.

An alternate possibility is that syntactic complexity is associated with different hesitation phenomena in monologues than in dialogues. The previously cited studies by Siegman and Pope argue strongly in favor of the proposition that cognitive planning and decision making can produce a variety of hesitation phenomena, depending on the nature of the task and on the interpersonal context. For example, when a speaker feels constrained not to remain silent for too long, cognitive decision making manifests itself by an increase in brief filled or unfilled pauses rather than long silent pauses. Similarly, syntactic complexity may be associated with speech disruptions in monologues, but with some other hesitation index in dialogues where fluent speech, that is, disruption-free speech, is at a greater premium. In other words, with regard to hesitation phenomena, we are proposing a form of "symptom equivalence."

In their studies on stimulus ambiguity and verbal fluency, Siegman and Pope (1965a, 1966a) also addressed themselves to the potential role of anxiety as a mediating variable. It has been suggested that cognitively complex tasks are more anxiety arousing, and that such affective arousal may account for the hesitant speech. In order to test whether the effects of interviewer ambiguity on interviewee verbal fluency, are in fact mediated by anxiety arousal, one half of the interviewer's questions were designed to be anxiety arousing, the other neutral. Moreover, subjects were divided, on the basis of their Taylor Manifest Anxiety Scale scores into an anxious and nonanxious group. Should the effects of interviewer ambiguity be mediated by anxiety arousal, these effects should be more pronounced in the anxiety-arousing than the neutral questions, and for the anxious than the nonanxious group. This was clearly not the case. In the TAT too, the effects of stimulus ambiguity on verbal fluency were independent of the anxiety-arousing characteristics of the cards. The latter were determined by a content analysis of subjects' stories, and held constant by means of an analysis of covariance. It seems fairly clear, then, that the hesitation phenomena associated with uncertainty and cognitive planning are not mediated by anxiety arousal.

One obvious methodological implication of the studies cited earlier is, that in investigating the effects of cognitive planning and decision making on speech, one needs to sample a wide range of hesitation phenomena, not just pausing, as did Goldman-Eisler (1968) or speech disruptions, as did Rochester and Gill (1973).

Intelligence Test Scores and Hesitation Phenomena

Considering the rather clear-cut evidence that cognitive planning and decision making are associated with hesitant speech, it is only reasonable to speculate about the role of intelligence in the various hesitation indices. Do individuals who obtain high vocabulary test scores speak more fluently, with fewer silent pauses, then low scorers? If Goldman-Eisler is correct in her assertion that within-utterance silent pauses reflect lexical decision making, one could argue that the answer to the above question should be in the affirmative. On the other hand, both high and low scorers may be equally involved in lexical decision making, but on different levels of difficulty. In that case there may be no significant correlation between vocabulary skill and the silent pause ratio. Similar questions can, of course, be asked in relation to the SDR, the Filled Pauses Ratio and other hesitation indices. Furthermore, to the extent that a speaker's decisions involve not only lexical choices but also structure and syntax, intelligence measures other than vocabulary scores—perhaps measures of abstraction ability—may be significant sources of variance in the various hesitation indices.

Data obtained as part of the interview study described earlier (Siegman & Pope, 1965a) provide partial answers to the above questions. In this study all

TABLE 2
Correlations (*rs*) between Shipley-Hartford Scales and Pausing

Shipley-Hartford Scales	Reaction–Time		Silence–Quotient	
	Specific Qs	Ambiguous Qs	Specific Qs	Ambiguous Qs
Vocabulary	−.355**	−.109	−.318*	−.252
Abstraction	−.072	−.228	−.146	−.136

*p < .05
**p < .01

interviewees took the Shipley–Hartford Retreat Scale, which consists of a vocabulary subtest and a subtest designed to measure the ability to find higher order commonalities among diverse visual patterns. The interview itself, it will be recalled, consisted of both ambiguous and specific interviewer remarks. To the extent that there is a relationship between vocabulary skill and the absence of hesitation phenomena, it was expected to be strongest in response to interviewer questions that involved planning and decision making. The results indicate that the expected negative relationship between vocabulary test scores and hesitation—response latency and silent pauses—was obtained, but only in the interview segment consisting of specific interviewer probes (Table 2). Significant negative correlations between vocabulary proficiency and within-utterance silent pauses have also been reported by Preston and Gardner (1967). In contrast to the findings of our interview study that vocabulary proficiency rather than abstraction ability is the significant source of variance in hesitation pauses, Bernstein (1962) reports data suggesting the very opposite to be the case. On the basis of his findings, Bernstein concludes that hesitation pauses are related to code complexity rather than simple vocabulary choice. However, considering the contradiction in the data base, his conclusion may have been a bit premature.

Finally, it would seem that neither vocabulary nor abstraction skills are significant sources of variance in speech disruptions or the frequency of filled pauses—a conclusion which is supported by the findings of other investigators (Feldstein *et al.,* 1963; Preston & Gardner, 1967).

SOME CONCLUSIONS AND SUGGESTIONS
FOR FURTHER RESEARCH

In relation to many of the issues discussed in this chapter, there is either insufficient evidence or evidence that is too contradictory for any definite conclusions to be drawn. In relation to some issues, however, the data allow for at least some tentative conclusions.

Personality as a source of variance in extralinguistic behavior. Despite the near contempt with which some contemporary experimental psychologists have approached this issue, a number of investigators have reopened the question, and are bringing to bear on it considerable methodological and conceptual sophistication. It is too soon to tell whether these efforts will bear fruit. Thus far, the most promising personality variable is extraversion–introversion, and the most promising extralinguistic variable is speech tempo—with extraverts showing a more accelerated speech tempo than introverts. An interesting question in relation to this finding concerns the mediating process or processes. Extraverts are reputed to be more socially responsive, that is, more aware of and more responsive to others with whom they interact than are introverts. This tendency could very well have the effect of reducing long silent pauses and accelerating speech tempo. On the other hand, extraverts are also reputed to be more impulsive and less reflective in their responses. This, too, as we have shown in this chapter, could reduce silent pauses and other hesitation phenomena. It remains, then, for further experimental research to clarify which of these factors—the social or the cognitive—independently or in combination, mediates the relationship between extraversion–introversion and speech tempo. One more point on this issue: speech tempo is a very broad category, which could be effected by a variety of temporal parameters (for example, an increase or decrease in long pauses, or in short pauses, or in word articulation). We need to know more about which of these are related to the extraversion–introversion dimension. There is also reason to believe that the location of pauses and other hesitation phenomena within clauses is significant. A more precise determination of which temporal parameters in which specific location are affected by the extraversion–introversion dimension may help clarify the question of the mediating processes.

There is considerable evidence that listeners tend to agree among themselves about a speaker's personality traits—other than extraversion–introversion—although researchers have yet to demonstrate the validity of these judgments. To account for the high level of interjudge reliability, it is suggested that voice types and personality traits are matched on the basis of their similarity in semantic space. Furthermore, it is suggested that personality, attitudinal, and motivational attributions that a listener makes about a speaker influence the listener's verbal and nonverbal behavior to the speaker. Consistent personality attributions can, therefore, initiate a process of self-fulfilling prophecies.

Anxiety and speech. Early investigators of the effects of anxiety on speech approached the issue from a clinical perspective. Accustomed to think of anxiety as a source of symptoms and pathology, they assumed that its effects on speech are likely to be of a disruptive nature. They expected anxiety arousal to be associated with speech disruptions, with hesitant speech, and with frequent and long silent pauses. The evidence is fairly consistent with the expectation regarding speech disruptions but not with the other expectations, where the evidence, at least on first glance, seems contradictory. The author of this chapter has suggested that the Hull–Spence conceptualization of anxiety arousal in terms of drive can provide a parsimonious theoretical framework for the available empirical findings.

On the basis of the Hull–Spence drive conceptualization of anxiety, one would expect the effects of anxiety arousal on speech to be a function of the difficulty of the speech task. Anxiety arousal is likely to facilitate speech, that is, reduce silent and filled pauses and generally accelerate the speech tempo in *simple* speaking tasks (i.e., tasks involving highly habituated word sequences), and to have the opposite effect in *complex* speaking tasks (i.e., tasks involving complex lexical and/or structural choices). In both cases, however, anxiety arousal should be associated with an increase in speech disruptions. It is this author's view that this theoretical approach provides the best "fit" for the available data. However, *systematic investigations* of the effects of anxiety arousal on speech as a function of the complexity of the speech task—a variable which strangely enough has been overlooked in past research—remain to be conducted.

We also need to know much more (1) about the effects of different *levels* of anxiety arousal and (2) about the attenuating effects of learned response tendencies to anxiety arousal (the role of "defense mechanisms" or personality factors).

Although it is fairly clear that at least mild anxiety arousal accelerates speech involving overlearned word sequences, the precise temporal parameters that are affected may very well vary as a function of the social context.

Finally, although we have argued for some sort of functional equivalence among the various hesitation phenomena, their location may make a difference. Future studies on anxiety and speech should, therefore, not only distinguish among the various hesitation indices but also determine whether they are located within utterances or at their boundaries.

Studies on the effects of *audience anxiety* on speech typically find that people speak more hesitantly when confronting an audience than when alone or when addressing a single person. On first glance, this may seem to be in conflict with the drive-activation approach to the effects of anxiety arousal on speech. It should be pointed out, however, that almost all of these studies involve complex speaking tasks. In the few studies in which the authors differentiated between simple and complex speaking tasks, the results tend to be consistent with the hypothesis that anxiety arousal has an activating effect on speech. Moreover, to the extent that an audience slows down speech, factors other than anxiety arousal may be operating. People tend to adopt a more formal style when addressing an audience than when speaking to a single individual, even if he is a stranger. A formal speech style tends to be more concise and syntactically more complex than an informal style and, for this reason alone, is likely to be associated with a variety of hesitation phenomena.

Social context. There is evidence to suggest that the mere presence of another person from whom one can expect visual and other feedback, facilitates the flow of communication in dyadic conversations, provided the topic of discussion is a nonthreatening one. If, however, the topic of conversation is potentially embarrassing, the mere presence of such a person can inhibit the flow of communication because of the speaker's expectation of negative feedback.

Gender composition is another social variable that influences extralinguistic behavior in dyadic conversation. Both males and females speak differently when addressing members of their own sex than when addressing persons of the opposite sex. Equally important, from a methodological point of view, is the finding that gender composition is a significant moderator variable. Relationships between social–psychological variables and extralinguistic behavior that are obtained in same-gender groups can be attenuated and even reversed in opposite-gender groups, and vice versa.

Finally, there is reason to assume that the degree of attraction between conversants as well as their status and role relationships are significant sources of variance in the extralinguistic domain. Strangely enough, however, there has been very little systematic research of these issues, and we can only speculate about the mediating processes. It has been suggested in this chapter that code formality is one such mediating variable—a hypothesis that needs much more study. Less speculative is the finding that the temporal patterning of speech, specifically the occurrence of silent pauses and their duration, is affected by both interpersonal attraction and status relationships in dyadic communication. These relationships, however, like many others, are affected by the topic of discussion.

Cognition and hesitation. The evidence concerning the effects of cognitive planning and decision making on speech is much more clear-cut than is the evidence in relation to anxiety and speech. Cognitive planning clearly is associated with a variety of hesitation phenomena, such as silent pauses, speech disruptions, and filled pauses. The precise indices that are affected depend upon the nature of the decision-making process, for example, choosing among several alternative responses to an ambiguous question, or choosing among syntactic alternatives, and on situational constraints. A speaker is under greater pressure, for instance, to avoid long silent pauses in dialogues than in monologues or when asked to make up stories in response to TAT cards. Therefore, in dialogues, hesitation is much less likely to take the form of long unfilled pauses than in the latter situations. This, of course, is the principle of the functional equivalence of hesitation indices referred to earlier. The methodological implication should be obvious. In trying to determine whether a speaker is engaged in cognitive planning and decision making on the basis of the presence or absence of speech hesitation, it is important to choose the appropriate hesitation index. If there is no clear-cut empirical basis for such a choice, the investigator has no alternative but to sample a broad range of hesitation indices. Many classical studies in this area are subject to the criticism that they did not sample a sufficiently wide range of hesitation indices.

One of the still unsettled issues is the basic question of how sentences are generated. There is no question that lexical decision making is associated with hesitation in speech, but whether these hesitations indicate proximal decisions, that is, decisions about the word immediately following the hesitation, or more distal decisions, is as yet unclear. Also to be settled is the question whether structural—syntactic decisions are a matter of learned habits, as is claimed by Goldman-Eisler, or of cognitive decision making, as is claimed by her critics. If the latter is the case, we need to know what type of structural—syntactic decisions are made at which point of the encoding process.

Despite all these unanswered basic questions, we have come a long way from the days when hesitation phenomena were conceptualized *exclusively* in terms of anxiety and emotional arousal. The clinical observation that emotional conflicts are associated with hesitant speech is probably an accurate one, but precisely because such conflicts also involve difficult cognitive choices and decision making. To the extent that there is an association between emotional conflict and hesitation, the relationship is probably mediated by cognitive factors, rather than by anxiety arousal. In fact, as was pointed out earlier, anxiety arousal per se is likely to accelerate rather than slow down speech, unless difficult cognitive decision making is involved.

In conclusion, it may be worth noting several recurrent themes in this chapter. One is the moderating effect of topical focus on many of the relationships that we have examined in this chapter. Another is the importance of cognition in extralinguistic behavior. Finally, there is the prominence of temporal variables. Whether we looked at personality and speech, the effects of anxiety arousal on speech, or the effects of the social context and of cognition on speech, the significant dependent variables invariably involved the temporal dimension. Perhaps this reflects nothing more than the relative ease with which the temporal dimension can be quantified, or nothing more than the role of fadism in social science research. On the other hand, it may illustrate the profound importance of temporal patterning in human speech.

REFERENCES

Addington, D. W. The relationship of selected vocal characteristics to personality perception. *Speech Monographs,* 1968, **35,** 492–503.

Allport, G., & Cantril, H. Judging personality from the voice. *Journal of Social Psychology,* 1934, **5,** 37–55.

Anisfeld, M., Bogo, N., & Lambert, W. E. Evaluational reactions to accented English speech. *Journal of Abnormal and Social Psychology,* 1962, **65,** 221–231.

Anisfeld, E., & Lambert, W. E. Evaluational reactions to bilingual and monolingual children to spoken languages. *Journal of Abnormal and Social Psychology,* 1964, **69,** 89–97.

Aronson, E. Some antecedents of interpersonal attraction. In W. J. Arnold & D. Levine (Eds.), *Nebraska Symposium on Motivation* (Vol. 17). Lincoln: University of Nebraska Press, 1969.

Aronson, E., & Weintraub, W. Personal adaptation as reflected in verbal behavior. In A. W. Siegman & B. Pope (Eds.), *Studies in dyadic communication.* New York: Pergamon Press, 1972.

Argyle, M., Lalljee, M., & Cook, M. The effects of visibility on interaction in a dyad. *Human Relations,* 1968, 21, 3–17.

Bernstein, B. Social class and linguistic development: A theory of social learning. In A. H. Halsey, J. Floud, & A. Anderson (Eds.), *Economy, Education and Society.* Glencoe, Illinois: Free Press, 1961.

Bernstein, B. Linguistic codes, hesitation phenomena and intelligence. *Language and Speech,* 1962, **5,** 31–46.

Bernstein, B. Elaborated and restricted codes: Their social origins and some consequences. *American Anthropologist,* 1964, **66,** Part II, 55–64.

Bernstein, B. Social class, language and socialization. In S. Moscovici (Ed.), *The psychology of language.* Chicago, Illinois: Markham, 1972.

Boomer, D. S. Review of F. Goldman-Eisler, Psycholinguistics: Experiments in spontaneous speech. *Lingua,* 1970, **25,** 152–164.

Boomer, D. S., & Dittmann, A. T. Hesitation pauses and juncture pauses in speech. *Language and Speech,* 1962, **5,** 215–220.

Boomer, D. S., & Goodrich, D. W. Speech disturbance and judged anxiety. *Journal of Consulting Psychology,* 1961, **25,** 160–164.

Bourhis, R. Y., & Giles, H. The language of cooperation in Wales: A field study. *Language Sciences,* in press.

Brown, B. L., Strong, W. J., Rencher, A. C., & Smith, B. L. Fifty-four voices from two: the effects of simultaneous manipulations of rate, pitch, and variance of intonation on ratings of personality from speech. *Proceedings, 81st Annual Convention, APA,* 1973, pp. 193–194.

Byrne, D. *The attraction paradigm.* New York: Academic Press, 1971.

Cassotta, L., Feldstein, S., & Jaffe, J. The stability and modifiability of individual vocal characteristics in stress and nonstress interviews. Unpublished manuscript, The William Allanson White Institute, 1967.

Chomsky, N. *Aspects of the theory of syntax.* Cambridge, Massachusetts: M.I.T. Press, 1965.

Cook, M. Anxiety, speech disturbances and speech rate. *British Journal of Social and Clinical Psychology,* 1969, 8, 13–21.

Crystal, D., & Quirk, R. *Systems of prosaic and paralinguistic features in English.* The Hague: Mouton, 1964.

Duffy, E. *Activation and behavior.* Wiley, New York, 1962.

Duncan, S., Jr., & Rosenthal, R. Vocal emphasis on experimenters' instruction reading as unintended determinant of subjects' responses. *Language and Speech,* 1968, **11,** 20–26.

Duncan, S., Jr., Rosenberg, N. J., & Finkelstein, J. The paralanguage of experimenter bias. *Sociometry,* 1969, **32,** 207–219.

Ellis, D. S. Speech and social status in America. *Social Forces,* 1967, **45,** 431–437.

Feldstein, S. Vocal patterning of emotional expression. In J. H. Masserman (Ed.), *Science and Psychoanalysis,* Vol. 7. New York: Grune & Stratton, 1964.

Feldstein, S. *Temporal patterns of dialogue: Basic research and reconsiderations.* In A. W. Siegman & B. Pope (Eds.), *Studies in dyadic communication.* New York: Pergamon Press, 1972.

Feldstein, S., Brenner, M. S., & Jaffe, J. The effect of subject sex, verbal interaction, and topical focus on speech disruption. *Language and Speech,* 1963, **6,** 229–239.

Feldstein, S., & Jaffe, J. The relationship of speech disruption to the experience of anger. *Journal of Consulting Psychology,* 1962, **26,** 505–509.

Feldstein, S., Jaffe, J., & Cassotta, L. A profile analysis of affective expression in speech. Unpublished manuscript, The William Allanson White Institute, 1964.

Fenz, W. D. J., & Epstein, S. Measurement of approach–avoidance conflict along a stimulus dimension by a thematic apperception test. *Journal of Personality,* 1962, **30,** 613–632.

Fiske, D. W., & Maddi, S. R. (Eds.) *Functions of varied experience.* Homewood, Illinois: Dorsey, 1961.

Foa, U. Convergences in the analysis of the structure of interpersonal behavior. *Psychological Review,* 1961, **5,** 341–353.

Geer, J. H. Effects of fear arousal upon task performance and verbal behavior. *Journal of Abnormal Psychology,* 1966, **71,** 119–123.

Giles, H. Evaluative reactions to accents. *Educational Review.* 1970. **22,** 211–227.

Giles, H. Communicative effectiveness as a function of accented speech. *Speech Monographs,* 1973, **40,** 330–331.

Giles, H., Baker, S., & Fielding, G. Communication length as a behavioral index of accent prejudice. *International Journal of the Sociology of Language,* 1975, **6,** 73–78.

Giles, H., Taylor, D. M., & Bourhis, R. Towards a theory of interpersonal accommodation through language: Some Canadian data. *Language in Society,* 1975, **2,** 177–192.

Goldman-Eisler, F. Hesitation and information in speech. In C. Cherry (Ed.) *Information theory.* London: Butterworths, 1961. (a)

Goldman-Eisler, F. A comparative study of two hesitation phenomena. *Language and Speech.* 1961, **4,** 18–26 (b)

Goldman-Eisler, F. *Psycholinguistics: Experiments in spontaneous speech.* New York: Academic Press, 1968.

Gross, H. S. Toward including listening in a model of the interview. In A. W. Siegman & B. Pope (Eds.) *Studies in dyadic communication.* New York: Pergamon Press, 1972.

Hargreaves, W. A., & Starkweather, J. A. Collection of temporal data with the duration tabulator. *Journal of Experimental Analysis of Behavior,* 1959, **2,** 170.

Hebb, D. O. Drives and the C.N.S. (conceptual nervous system). *Psychological Review,* 1955, **62,** 243–254.

Hess, R. D., & Shipman, V. C. Early experience and the socialization of cognitive modes in children. *Child Development,* 1965, **36,** 869–888.

Houston, S. A re-examination of some assumptions about the language of the disadvantaged child. *Child Development,* 1970, 41, 947–962.

Kanfer, F. H. Effect of a warning signal preceding a noxious stimulus on verbal rate and heart rate. *Journal of Experimental Psychology,* 1958, **55,** 78–80. (a)

Kanfer, F. H. Supplementary report: Stability of a verbal rate change in experimental anxiety. *Journal of Experimental Psychology,* 1958, **56,** 182. (b)

Kanfer, F. H. Verbal rate, content, and ajudstment ratings in experimentally structured interviews. *Journal of Abnormal and Social Psychology,* 1959, **58,** 305–311.

Kanfer, F. H. Verbal rate, eyeblink, and content in structured psychiatric interviews. *Journal of Abnormal and Social Psychology,* 1960, **61,** 341–347.

Kasl, S. V., & Mahl, G. F. The relationship of disturbances and hesitations in spontaneous speech to anxiety. *Journal of Personality and Social Psychology,* 1965, **1,** 425–433.

Knapp, M. L. *Nonverbal communication in human interaction.* New York: Holt, Rinehart & Winston, 1972.

Kogan, N., & Wallach, M. A. *Risk-taking: A study in cognition and personality.* New York: Holt, Rinehart & Winston, 1964.

Kowal, S., O'Connel, D. C., & Sabin, E. J. Development of temporal patterning and vocal hesitations in spontaneous narratives. *Journal of Psycholinguistic Research,* 1975, **4,** 195–207.

Kramer, E. Judgment of personal characteristics and emotions from nonverbal properties of speech. *Psychological Bulletin,* 1963, **60,** 408–420.

Labov, W. *Sociolinguistic patterns.* Philadelphia: University of Pennsylvania Press, 1972.

Lakoff, R. Language and woman's place. *Language in Society,* 1973, **2,** 45–79.

Lalljee, M., & Cook. M. Uncertainty in first encounters. *Journal of Personality and Social Psychology,* 1973, **26,** 137–141.

Lambert, W. E., Anisfeld, M., & Yeni-Komshian, G. Evaluational reactions of Jewish and Arab adolescents to dialect and language variations. *Journal of Personality and Social Psychology,* 1965, **2,** 84–90.

Lambert, W. E. A social psychology of bilingualism. *Journal of Social Issues,* 1967, **23,** 99–100.

Lee, R. R. Dialect perception: A critical review and re-evaluation. *Quarterly Journal of Speech,* 1971, **57,** 410–417.

Lennard, H. L., & Bernstein, A. *The anatomy of psychotherapy.* New York: Columbia University Press, 1960.

Levin, H., Baldwin, A. L., Gallwey, M., & Paivio, A. Audience stress, personality, and speech. *Journal of Abnormal and Social Psychology,* 1960, **61,** 469–473.

Levin, H., & Silverman, I. Hesitation phenomena in children's speech. *Language and Speech,* 1965, **8,** 67–85.

Libo, L. M. *Manual for the Picture Impression Test.* University of Maryland School of Medicine, Baltimore, 1956.

Maclay, H., & Osgood, C. E. Hesitation phenomena in spontaneous English speech. *Word,* 1959, **15,** 19–44.

Mahl, G. F. Disturbances and silences in the patient's speech in psychotherapy. *Journal of Abnormal and Social Psychology,* 1956, **53,** 1–15.

Markel, N. N. The reliability of coding paralanguage: Pitch, loudness, and tempo. *Journal of Verbal Learning and Verbal Behavior,* 1965, **4,** 406–408.

Markel, N. N., Phillis, J. A., Vargas, R., & Howard, K. Personality traits associated with voice types. *Journal of Psycholinguistic Research,* 1972, **1,** 249–255.

Markel, N. N., Prebor, L. D., & Brandt, J. F. Biosocial factors in dyadic communication: Sex and speaking intensity. *Journal of Personality and Social Psychology,* 1972, **23,** 11–13.

Matarazzo, J. D., & Wiens, A. N. *The interview: Research on its anatomy and structure.* Chicago: Aldine-Atherton, 1972.

Mattingly, I. G. Speaker variation and vocal tract size. *Journal of the Acoustical Society of America,* 1966, **39,** 1219.

McGlone, R. E., & Hollien, H. Vocal pitch characteristics of aged women. *Journal of Speech and Hearing Research,* 1963, **6,** 164–170.

Milmoe, S., Rosenthal, R., Blane, H. T., Chafetz, M. E. & Wolf, I. The doctor's voice: Postdictor of successful referral of alcoholic patients. *Journal of Abnormal Psychology,* 1967, **72,** 78–84.

Montague, E. K. The role of anxiety in serial learning. *Journal of Experimental Psychology,* 1953, **45,** 91–96.

Murray, D. C. Talk, silence and anxiety. *Psychological Bulletin,* 1971, **75,** 244–260.

Mysak, E. D. Pitch and duration characteristics of older males. *Journal of Speech and Hearing Research,* 1959, **2,** 46–54.

Natale, M. Convergence of mean vocal intensity in dyadic communication as a function of social desirability. *Journal of Personality and Social Psychology,* 1975, **32,** 790–804.

Osgood, C. E., Suci, G. J., & Tannenbaum, P. H. *The measurement of meaning.* Urbana: The University of Illinois Press, 1957.

Paivio, A. Personality and audience influence. In B. A. Maher (Ed.), *Progress in experimental personality research* (Vol. 2). New York: Academic Press, 1965.

Pope, B., Blass, T., Bradford, N. H., & Siegman, A. W. Interviewer specificity in seminaturalistic interviews. *Journal of Consulting and Clinical Psychology,* 1971, **36,** 152.

Pope, B., Blass, T., Siegman, A. W., & Raher, J. Anxiety and depression in speech. *Journal of Consulting and Clinical Psychology,* 1970, **35,** 128–133.

Pope, B., & Siegman, A. W. Interviewer–interviewee relationship and verbal behavior of interviewee. *Psychotherapy,* 1966, **3,** 149–152.

Pope, B., & Siegman, A. W. Relationship and verbal behavior in the initial interview. In A. W. Siegman & B. Pope (Eds.), *Studies in dyadic communication.* New York: Pergamon Press, 1972.

Pope, B., Siegman, A. W., & Blass, T. Anxiety and speech in the initial interview. *Journal of Consulting and Clinical Psychology,* 1970, **35,** 233–238.

Powesland, P. F., & Giles, H. Persuasiveness and message accent incompatability. *Human Relations,* 1975, **28,** 85–93.

Preston, J. M., & Gardner, R. C. Dimensions of oral and written language fluency. *Journal of Verbal Learning and Verbal Behavior,* 1967, **6,** 936–945.

Ramsay, R. W. Personality and speech. *Journal of Personality and Social Psychology,* 1966, **4,** 116–118.

Ramsay, R. W. Speech patterns and personality. *Language and Speech,* 1968, **11** 54–63.

Reynolds, A., & Paivio, A. Cognitive and emotional determinants of speech. *Canadian Journal of Psychology,* 1968, **22,** 164–175.

Robinson, W. P. *Language and social behavior.* London: Penguin, 1972.

Rochester, S. R., & Gill, J. Production of complex sentences in monologues and dialogues. *Journal of Verbal Learning and Verbal Behavior.* 1973, **12,** 203–210.

Rochester, S. R., Thurston, S., & Rupp, J. Hesitation as clues to failures in coherence: A study of the thought-disordered speaker. In S. Rosenberg (Ed.), *Sentence production: Developments in theory and research.* Hillsdale, N.J.: Lawrence Erlbaum Associates, 1977.

Rosenthal, R. *Experimenter effects in behavioral research.* New York: Appleton-Century-Crofts, 1966.

Sachs, J., Lieberman, P., & Erickson, D. Anatomical and cultural determinants of male and female speech. In R. Shuy & R. W. Fasold (Eds.) *Language attitudes: Current trends and prospects.* Washington, D.C.: Georgetown School of Language, 1973.

Sanford, F. H. Speech and personality. *Psychological Bulletin,* 1942, **30,** 811–845.

Sauer, R. E., & Marcuse, F. L. Overt and covert recording. *Journal of Projective Techniques,* 1957, **21,** 391–395.

Scherer, K. R. Inference rules in personality attribution from voice quality: The loud voice of extraversion. Unpublished manuscript, University of Pennsylvania, 1972.   (a)

Scherer, K. R. Judging personality from voice: A cross-cultural approach to an old issue in interpersonal perception. *Journal of Personality,* 1972, **40,** 191–210.   (b)

Scherer, K. R., London, H., & Wolf, T. J. The voice of confidence: Paralinguistic cues and audience evaluation. *Journal of Research in Personality,* 1973, **7,** 31–44.

Siegman, A. W. Some relationships of anxiety and introversion–extraversion to Serial learning. Unpublished doctoral dissertation, Columbia University, 1957.

Siegman, A. W. A cross-cultural investigation of the relationship between introversion–extraversion, social attitudes and anti-social behavior. *British Journal of Clinical and Social Psychology,* 1962, **2**, 196–208.

Siegman, A. W. Interviewer warmth and its effects on interviewee verbal behavior. Symposium paper presented at the 18th International Congress of Applied Psychology, Montreal, Canada, July, 1974. (a)

Siegman, A. W. Interview-conversations as testing ground for psychological theories. Symposium paper presented at the annual meetings of the American Psychological Association, New Orleans, Louisiana, August, 1974. (b)

Siegman, A. W. The gain–loss principle and interpersonal attraction in the interview. *Proceedings of the Division of Personality and Social Psychology,* 1974, pp. 85–88. (c)

Siegman, A. W. Some effects of eliminating eye-contact in the interview. Paper read at annual meeting of the Eastern Psychological Association, New York, April, 1975.

Siegman, A. W. Do noncontingent interviewer mm-hmm's facilitate interviewee productivity? *Journal of Consulting and Clinical Psychology,* 1976, **44**, 171–182. (a)

Siegman, A. W. The effects of cognition on hesitation phenomena in speech. Symposium paper presented at the Interdisciplinary Conference on Perspectives on Language, University of Louisville, Louisville, Kentucky, 1976. (b)

Siegman, A. W. The effects of interviewer warmth on interviewee extralinguistic behavior. Unpublished manuscript, University of Maryland Baltimore County, 1976. (c)

Siegman, A. W., & Pope, B. Effects of question specificity and anxiety producing messages on verbal fluency in the initial interview. *Journal of Personality and Social Psychology,* 1965, **4**, 188–192. (a)

Siegman, A. W., & Pope, B. Personality variables associated with productivity and verbal fluency in the initial interview. *Proceedings of the 73rd annual convention of the American Psychological Association,* 1965, pp. 273–274. (b)

Siegman, A. W., & Pope, B. Ambiguity and verbal fluency in the TAT. *Journal of Consulting Psychology,* 1966, **30**, 239–245. (a)

Siegman, A. W., & Pope, B. The effect of interviwer ambiguity–specificity and topical focus on interviewee vocabulary diversity. *Language and Speech,* 1966, **9**, 242–249. (b)

Siegman, A. W., & Pope, B. The effects of ambiguity and anxiety on interviewee verbal behavior. In A. W. Siegman and B. Pope (Eds.), *Studies in dyadic communication.* New York: Pergamon Press, 1972.

Siegman, A. W., Pope, B., & Blass, T. Effects of interviewer status and duration of interviewer messages on interviewee productivity. *Proceedings of the 77th annual convention of the APA,* 1969, pp. 541–542.

Simard, L. M., Taylor, D. M., & Giles, H. Attribution processes and interpersonal accommodation in a bilingual setting. *Language and Speech,* in press.

Sullivan, H. S. *The psychiatric interview.* New York: Norton, 1954.

Sunshine, N. J., & Horowitz, M. K. Differences in egocentricity between spoken and written expression under stress and nonstress conditions. *Language and Speech,* 1968, **11**, 160–166.

Taylor, J. A. The relationship of anxiety to the conditioned eyelid response. *Journal of Experimental Psychology,* 1951, **41**, 81–92.

Taylor, J. A., & Spence, K. W. The relationship of anxiety level to performance in serial learning. *Journal of Experimental Psychology,* 1952, **44**, 61–64.

Taylor, D. M., & Clement, R. Normative reactions to styles of Quebec French. *Anthropological Linguistics,* 1974, **16**, 202–217.

Tolhurst, G. C. *Some Effects of Changing Time Patterns and Articulation upon Intelligibility and Word Perception.* Contract N6 onw-22525, Project No. NR 145-993. NMRI Project NM 001 104 500 40. U.S. Naval School of Aviation Medicine, Naval Air Station,

Pensacola, Florida, and Ohio State University Research Foundation, Columbus, Ohio, January, 1955.

Trager, G. Paralanguage: A first approximation. *Studies in Linguistics,* 1958, **13,** 1–12.

Trager, G. The typology of paralanguage. *Anthropological Linguistics,* 1961, **3,** 17–21.

Webb, J. T. Interview synchrony: An investigation of two speech rate measures in an automated standardized interview. In A. W. Siegman & B. Pope (Eds.), *Studies in dyadic communication.* New York: Pergamon Press, 1972.

Welkowitz, J., Feldstein, S., Finkelstein, M., & Aylesworth, L. Changes in vocal intensity as a function of interspeaker influence. *Perceptual and Motor Skills, 1972,* **35,** 715–718.

8
The Phonemic Clause:
Speech Unit
in Human Communication

Donald S. Boomer

Laboratory of Psychology and Psychopathology
National Institute of Mental Health

INTRODUCTION

The scientific study of any phenomenon requires the identification and specification of manageable units that can be examined and manipulated. The size and nature of the unit employed will vary according to the kind of question that is being asked. In neurophysiology, for example, an investigator who is interested in the relative response time to visual versus auditory signals in the monkey must study whole, live monkeys that can see, hear, and respond in some fashion—pressing a lever, say.

Another investigator who wishes to determine the density of neurones in the monkey's visual projection area may require only a number of 1-mm.^{2} sections of tissue from that area of a monkey's cortex for examination under a microscope. Obviously neither investigator's unit would be of use to the other.

Let us refine the analogy a bit further before applying it to speech research. A physiologist who wishes to learn about the architecture of the circulatory system in cats can do so by dissecting embalmed dead cats. If he is interested in moment-to-moment variations in blood pressure, however, he must study live cats.

This analogy brings us closer to psycholinguistics. Many questions that interest psycholinguists involve the study of tape recordings of spontaneous speech in "live" natural or experimental situations. A high-quality tape recording is a faithful record of speech behavior in all its richness; it preserves not only the words that were said, but a great deal of additional information about emphasis, about changes in loudness, pitch, and voice quality, about the occurrence of hesitations, *ahs* and *ers*, repetitions, stammering, false starts, corrections, and tongue slips. Most importantly, the tape recording preserves information about how all of these features are patterned in real time, a matter of great importance in the understanding of speech processes.

Regrettably, a great many speech researchers never study their tape recordings. Instead, the tapes are turned over to a typist who produces a transcript that is then substituted for the tape as the object of research. Everything but the lexical content is discarded, and even that is frequently distorted by the typist's well-meaning editorial efforts to turn the speech into acceptable written English. Such a transcript is not speech in the sense that the tape recording is. To return to the physiological analogy: a transcript is the wrong unit for the study of speech; a dead cat is being used to study a living process.

An investigator who wishes to study tape recordings directly, however, still needs an appropriate unit. The sentences, paragraphs, and punctuation conventions used in written English provide a poor fit for live speech. What is needed is an indigenous unit, a unit that grows out of speech itself rather than one that is arbitrarily overlaid on it. The purpose of this chapter is to describe one such unit, the *phonemic clause,* a natural unit of spoken, as opposed to written, English, and to present some research that bears on this unit.

THE PHONEMIC CLAUSE

In spontaneous speech there are discernible "chunks," sequences of a few syllables, usually from one to seven or eight, that seem to be spoken as a unit, a single speech act. This unit is the phonemic clause, a formal linguistic unit that was named and described by Trager and Smith (1951). Sustained speech is made up of such chunks, one after another. If you listen carefully to someone talking spontaneously—thinking on his feet—you will be able to hear these repeating units.

The physical features that mark off phonemic clauses are patterns of voice pitch, rhythm, and loudness. These features are easy to demonstrate in a lecture, but very difficult on the printed page, a direct illustration of the contention in the introduction that the conventions that are applicable to writing provide a poor fit for speech. Despite this limitation it is necessary to try to convey in this section some sense of the nature of the phonemic clause.

Consider the following sentence:

The man who called me yesterday just telephoned again.

In print this is a single sentence. As spoken, however, it would probably come out in two phonemic clauses:

the man who called me yesterday/just telephoned again/[1]

If you say this aloud in a natural conversational way, or ask someone else to say it to you, you will probably hear the break where the first slash has been inserted. Let us consider how pitch, rhythm, and loudness divide this utterance into two phonemic clauses.

1. *Pitch.* The "tune" accompanying this utterance will have certain regular pitch characteristics. In the first chunk *the man who called me* will be said with only minor pitch variation. During the *yes-* in *yesterday* the speaker's voice will move abruptly to a higher pitch and will glide back down to the opening level during *-terday.* The second chunk will show a similar, though not identical, pitch pattern. The initial level pitch will extend over *just telephoned a-.* The pitch movement over *-gain* is likely to be a rapidly executed rise–fall. If the speaker does not intend to say anything further, the final pitch will drop to a point slightly lower than the opening level.

These patterns of pitch movement are called *pitch contours* or *intonation contours.* Their characteristic patterns have been studied and described by a number of linguists, including Trager and Smith (1951), Halliday (1963), Bolinger (1964), and Crystal (1969).

2. *Rhythm.* If you listen carefully to someone saying this sample utterance, you may also hear a change in the syllabic rhythm, coinciding with the pitch changes. That is, *the man who called me* and *just telephoned a-* will be said relatively evenly and rapidly. *Yesterday* and *-gain* will be heard as slightly longer, or stretched—not quite drawled, but tending in that direction. This is a subtle difference and difficult to hear, but it can be demonstrated with instruments that measure sound durations. The difference is more apparent if the same syllable occurs in different places in the same utterance, for example:

yesterday was the final day/

If you listen to this utterance being spoken, you can probably hear that the second *day* is longer than the first.

3. *Loudness.* This difference is even more difficult to hear, but the *yes-* in the first chunk and the *-gain* in the second are likely to be somewhat louder than the rest of the utterance.

Notice that *yes-* and *-gain* are the points in the two chunks where the change begins in all three features. These syllables stand out from the rest of the

[1] Capitalization and punctuation have been deliberately omitted here and hereinafter wherever sample phonemic clauses are presented. This conforms to our research practice of not forcing speech transcripts into orthographic conventions.

utterance because of the simultaneous changes in pitch, rhythm, and loudness.[2] This quality of standing out, or prominence, is called *primary stress.*

Primary stress is one of the identifying characteristics of the phonemic clause. The primary stress typically occurs at or near the end of the phonemic clause, as it does in both the clauses in our sample utterance. The patterned change in pitch, rhythm, and loudness that begins on the primary stress continues to the end of the clause. The span over which the changes occur may be a single syllable (-gain) or two, three, or more syllables (yesterday). During this period the pitch movement and the stretching continue, and the increase in loudness may also persist. The end of the phonemic clause is signaled at the point of discontinuity where the change in all of these features ends and their values level off again in the beginning of the next phonemic clause, i.e., back to relatively level pitch, more rapid enunciation, and reduced volume. This abrupt leveling off is the other identifying feature of the phonemic clause. Trager and Smith have termed this feature *terminal juncture,* the point of joining of one clause to the next. The phonemic clause, then, is marked by one, and only one, primary stress and a terminal juncture. Two additional points about the terminal juncture will complete this highly condensed exposition of the phonemic clause:

1. The pitch rise that begins on the primary stress may continue to rise until the juncture. This rise occurs, for example, in a question that calls for a yes–no answer, and is termed *rising juncture.* Alternatively, there may be a shorter rise followed by a quick return to the base level. This pattern, termed *sustained juncture,* typically occurs when the speaker intends to continue with at least one more clause. Because of the terminal fall to base level, there is no perceptible pitch discontinuity across the juncture. There is a third possible terminal pattern: the contour may fall to a level markedly lower than the baseline. This pattern is termed *falling juncture.* This is a final-sounding intonation contour, which, in a dialogue, constitutes one of the signals that the speaker is prepared to yield the floor. In our sample utterance, the pitch movement over *yesterday* corresponds to a sustained juncture; that over *again* to a falling juncture.

2. The juncture may be accompanied by a pause, an actual brief silence before the next phonemic clause begins. This is known as a *juncture pause.* Its occurrence is another cue for identifying a juncture, but like the other cues it isn't always present. In two separate studies conducted in this laboratory, involving a total of more than 3,000 phonemic clauses, the proportion of junctures followed by pause was about half.

---

[2] Also note that in the discussion of the three features, words like "may" and "probably" and "usually" were used. This caution is necessary because none of these features is *invariably* present in a stressed syllable. Instrumental research on the subject suggests that pitch is the most reliable feature, although not invariant, and the other two may or may not be present in any given instance.

Furthermore, the likelihood of a pause occurring is differentially associated with the kind of juncture. The sustained juncture is much less likely than either of the others to be followed by a pause. In an unpublished study of 1,500 phonemic clauses, Dittmann found that only 15% of sustained junctures were followed by a pause, while rising and falling junctures were followed by a pause in 60 and 80% of their occurrences, respectively.

This brief and oversimplified description of the phonemic clause necessarily omits a great deal of technical detail and glosses over a number of theoretical issues about which there is still considerable dispute among linguists. The intent of this description is simply to give the reader a general impression of the phonemic clause and to introduce some of the terms that will be used later in the chapter.

RESEARCH ON THE PHONEMIC CLAUSE

The phonemic clause is a linguistic unit; that is, it has specific linguistic properties, and it has a place in a formal linguistic system that aims to describe language. Whether it also has significant behavioral properties is the question that is addressed in this section.

For a number of years we have studied the phonemic clause from a behavioral standpoint in the effort to learn more about how people plan and execute their own speech and how they process the speech they hear. It is our view, based on our research findings, that the phonemic clause is more than a linguistic convention, that it is a functional unit in speech as well. Specifically, our evidence suggests that speech is formulated in phonemic clauses, each of which is planned and executed as an organized speech act. This view is contrasted with other prevailing views that the production units are (1) sentences, or (2) individual words, serially chained together by some associative process.

We believe that the perception of speech is also based on a chunking strategy in which incoming phonemic clauses are processed as successive coherent packages of sound, syntax, and sense. Is seems reasonable to hypothesize that speech is produced and perceived in the same units. As Lashley (1951) pointed out in a penetrating essay on the neurophysiological aspects of speech, "The processes of comprehension and production of speech have too much in common to depend on wholly different mechanisms."

Hesitation Pauses and Juncture Pauses

The first psycholinguistic study of the phonemic clause dealt with perception (Boomer & Dittmann, 1962). The underlying hypothesis ran as follows: if the phonemic clause is in fact heard and dealt with by the listener as a unitary chunk, then a pause in the middle of the clause—a break in the rhythm—will be sensed by the listener as interruption. By contrast, a juncture pause, occurring, as it does, between clauses will be less noticeable. If, on the other hand, the phonemic clause is merely a linguistic convention with no function in speech, pauses should be equally noticeable wherever they occur. Our experimental design, therefore, attempted to gauge the relative salience for listeners of these two types of pause. The method was straight psychophysical paired comparison.

The experimental materials were four tape-recorded spontaneous utterances taken from a recorded radio broadcast of a panel discussion among four men. These utterances, one from each speaker, were so chosen that each contained a subject and a predicate (a "sentence" when transcribed); each contained one terminal juncture followed by a pause (juncture pause), and one pause elsewhere in the utterance, within a phonemic clause (hesitation pause).

A number of duplicate tape recordings of each utterance were prepared. By tape cutting and splicing, artifical pauses of varying lengths were substituted for either the existing juncture pause or the hesitation pause.

Each utterance was prepared in six versions: one set of three with an artificial juncture pause of 100, 200, or 500 msec. and no pause at the hesitation location. The opposite set had the same three artificial pause durations at the hesitation location and no pause following the juncture. For experimental control purposes two additional tapes of each utterance were prepared with no pause at either location. It should be added that it was not apparent to listeners that the tapes had been tampered with; all versions of the four utterances were natural-sounding.

Each of the 32 experimental utterances thus produced was spliced to a standard version of that utterance with no pause at either point. In half the pairs the standard version preceded the experimental version; in the other half the order was reversed. In each pair a 2-sec. leader, or length of blank tape, was spliced between the two versions. These 32 pairs were then spliced together randomly with an 8-sec. leader between each pair. The following tape-recorded instructions were spliced onto the head of the reel:

> You are going to hear a number of spoken sentences. These will be played to you in pairs: first a sentence and then an immediate repetition of that sentence. You are to judge, for each pair, whether the original and the repetition sound the same to you, or different.

> In each pair the voice and the words will be precisely the same. The only difference will lie in the pauses between words. In some of the pairs the second version will strike you as different from the first in terms of the spacing of some words. If you notice a difference, mark "D" after that number. If they sound the same, mark it "S."

> Listen in a relaxed fashion, relying on your "feel" for the rhythm of speech to tell you when the two versions are different.

The subjects were 25 adult native speakers of American English, both men and women. Using earphones, they listened to the instructions and the 32 pairs of utterances, checking their protocols "same" or "different" after each pair, depending on whether or not the interpolated pause was discriminable for them.

The data clearly support our hypothesis that hesitation pauses are more noticeable than juncture pauses. Figure 1 shows the result of 800 (32 × 25) experimental judgments. Hesitation pauses are discriminated significantly better than juncture pauses at all three durations. (For 100 msec. $p < 0.05$; for 200 and 500 msec. $p < 0.001$.) (See Fig. 1)

These results support our view that the phonemic clause is a functional unit in speech production; specifically, that the phonemic clause corresponds to a unitary speech act, held together by an internal rhythm. A break of a given duration in this rhythm is noticeable, whereas the same length of break between units is much less noticeable.

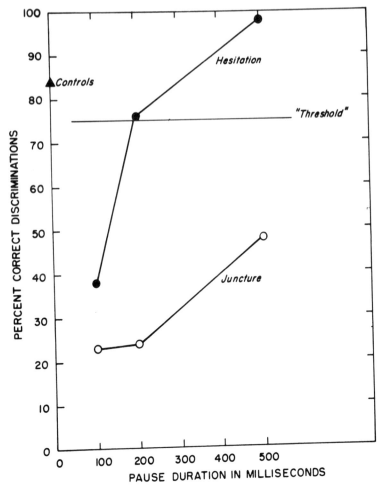

FIG. 1. Percentages of correct discriminations of juncture and hesitation pauses of three durations. (After Boomer & Dittmann, 1962.)

Tapping Rhythms

A supporting finding has been reported from outside psycholinguistics by Fraisse (1963), in connection with a broad program of research on the subject of rhythm in human behavior. Fraisse presented subjects with patterns of tapping rhythms that they were to reproduce. In one experiment he presented a familiar rhythm pattern followed, after a pause, with a repetition of the pattern, for example, the familiar shave-and-a-haircut rhythm:

BUM diddy BUMBUM—BUM BUM (*pause*)
BUM diddy BUMBUM—BUM BUM

In the course of the experiment, several versions of each stimulus pattern were presented, the only difference among them being the length of the pause before the repetition. When asked to tap out what they had heard, subjects matched the internal rhythm of the pattern with great precision, but did not notice or reproduce the experimenter's variations in the pause between repetitions. In our view this result is directly related to the results of our own experiment involving rhythmic verbal patterns and pauses between them.

Articulatory Rhythms

In the field of psycholinguistics proper, a team of Russian investigators (Kozhevnikov & Chistovich, 1965) have reported an experiment that fits well both with our results and with those of Fraisse. It is likely that these investigators were operating with a Russian equivalent of the phonemic clause, although the term they used was translated as *syntagma*. Kozhevnikov and Chistovich's (1965) very brief description can be compared to our discussion of the phonemic clause:

> . . . a syntagma is clearly connected with articulation and must definitely be pronounced at one output. Syntagmas are distinguished from each other by pauses, while words within them are run together. Its average length in free speech amounts to seven syllables [p. 74].

The rationale for their experiment was described as follows:

> [We assume] that our syntagma corresponds with one articulatory program and, for the pronunciation of a sentence consisting of several syntagmas, several consecutive articulatory programs are used correspondingly. . . . Therefore, our experiments were begun with an attempt to determine whether one articulatory program corresponds to a sentence consisting of two syntagmas or whether two programs are used for its articulation [p. 75].

The experiment they conducted was extremely simple in conception. They devised two test utterances that were not unlike the sample utterance we presented earlier to illustrate the discussion of the phonemic clause. The utterances were single grammatical sentences, each composed of two syntagmas. These two test utterances were buried in a set of eight nonexperimental "buffer" utterances to preclude self-conscious attention to these two.

Some experimental subjects (*N* not reported) repeated this entire list of utterances 40 times into a tape recorder. The subjects were instructed to maintain a standard rate of speech for the entire speech task. As expected, speakers usually introduced a spontaneous pause between the two syntagmas in each utterance.

From oscillograph tracings of the tape recordings, the durations of the syntagmas and the pauses between them were then measured for all of the repetitions of the two test utterances. The mean durations of the four syntagmas and the two pauses were calculated, as were their standard deviations. These data, presented in Table 1, show that the variability of the pauses was extremely large relative to the variability of the length of the syntagmas. The coefficients of variation for the pauses are from 15 to 20 times as large as the coefficients of variation for the syntagmas. These results support the hypothesis that the syntagma, not the sentence, has a corresponding articulatory program. If the entire sentence had one articulatory program, the length of the pause between syntagmas would also be programmed and thus no more variable than are the lengths of the syntagmas themselves.

Thus, in an independent investigation, based in a different language, the psychological reality of the articulatory unit was supported. The Russian data on production complement our own data for perception. The two studies converge to suggest the unitary nature of the speech act (phonemic clause, syntagma), which is produced as a unit and perceived as a unit. These studies also support the position taken in the introduction to this chapter that the sentence, a unit appropriate for written English, is inappropriate for the study of speech.

The Phonemic Clause and Hesitation

Our second study of the phonemic clause focused on speech production (Boomer, 1965). Specifically, we examined the location of hesitation pauses (silence and filled pause: *ah, er, um,* and the like) in spontaneous speech. As in the previous study, our interest was not in the pauses themselves, but rather in what their distribution could tell us about the functional units that speakers use.

TABLE 1
Variability of Syntagmas and Pauses (Kozhevnikov & Chistovich, 1965)

	Utterance 1		Utterance 2	
	Mean duration (msec)	Coefficient of variation ($\sigma/\bar{X}$)	Mean duration (msec)	Coefficient of variation ($\sigma/\bar{X}$)
First syntagma	630	.047	620	.052
Second syntagma	1000	.029	1470	.035
Pause between syntagmas	350	.610	160	.875

The reasoning behind the study was straightforward: We assumed that pauses in spontaneous speech reflect the speaker's uncertainty about what he is going to say next. If the speaker is planning phonemic clauses, then hesitation pauses should occur at or near the beginning of phonemic clauses, reflecting indecision about the whole chunk. If the speaker is selecting one word at a time to build utterances, there should be no such bunching up of hesitations at the beginning of phonemic clauses. Hesitations could be expected to occur at any point in the phonemic clause where the following word is problematic for the speaker.

In this study we used tape recordings of the spontaneous speech of 16 male native speakers of American English. Careful typewritten transcripts were prepared in conventional orthography, as usual, without punctuation or "sentence" capitalization. Such a transcript is not used as a substitute for the tape, but as a grid in which to locate and study speech events abstracted from the tape.

Two kinds of events were identified from the tape and entered into the transcripts: hesitations and terminal junctures. The junctures were recorded first by a colleague, Allen Dittmann, who was unaware of the purpose of the study. His task was to listen to the recording and to mark terminal junctures on an otherwise unmarked transcript. Repeat reliability of .93 has been reported by Dittmann and Wynne (1961) for the location of terminal junctures. The location of each silence of more than 200 msec. was then determined from an oscillograph record of the original tapes. The location of these silences was also entered into the transcript. Finally, each instance of a vocalized hesitation or filled pause (*ah, er, um*) was underlined in the transcript.

The object of this analysis was to establish the location of each hesitation in the phonemic clause in which it occurred. Since pauses almost always occur at word boundaries, the successive word boundaries in a given phonemic clause can be regarded as an ordered series of opportunities for hesitation. These locations can be illustrated for one of our sample phonemic clauses:

the man who called me yesterday/
 1   2   3   4   5   6

Thus, there are six possible hesitation locations in a six-word phonemic clause, one at the leading boundary of each word. This is the arrangement that was used in this study to describe hesitation locations.

The total body of speech totaled 1,593 phonemic clauses, of which 713 contained one or more hesitations. There were a total of 1,127 hesitations, 749 pauses, and 378 filled pauses. Each hesitation was tabulated by its location number in the clause where it appeared.

The hypothesis that hesitations tend to occur at the beginning of phonemic clauses was strongly supported. Figure 2 shows the proportion of hesitations that did occur at each location plotted against the proportion that would have occurred if hesitations were distributed by chance. The frequency at Location 2, the first internal word boundary in the clause, markedly exceeds chance; the frequencies at all other locations are at or below chance.

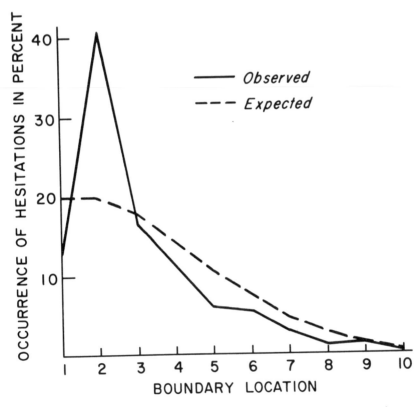

FIG. 2. Percentages of hesitations occurring at successive word boundary locations compared with those expected by chance. (After Boomer, 1965.)

This finding furnishes additional evidence for the psychological reality of the phonemic clause as a functional speech act. Decisions and planning, as evidenced by hesitation, do not apply to single words, nor to grammatical sentences, but to phonemic clauses, the chunks or packages in which people speak.

Listener Responses

A separate line of research on the phonemic clause has examined so-called listener responses—head nods and short vocalized interjections like *uh huh, oh, yes,* and *I see*—as behavioral indices of speech decoding.

The first study in this series (Dittmann & Llewellyn, 1967) set the following hypothesis:

The listener must wait until an entire phonemic clause has been uttered before he can discriminate the main lexical item from the other material in the group. Until he has made that discrimination, he has not, in effect, heard what the speaker has said during that time. A major clue that a clause has come to an end lies in the rhythmic pattern of stress and pitch in the group of words and the juncture that marks its end. Our hypothesis was that listening responses will occur predominantly following junctures at the ends of phonemic clauses and seldom at any point within a clause [p. 343].

The subjects in this experiment were paired off, placed in separate rooms, and asked to talk to one another in a simulated telephone conversation. One, the designated speaker, was asked to spend about 2-min. telling the other about something that had happened to him, a film he had seen, or any such topic. The other, the listener, was asked to respond as he ordinarily would on the telephone, letting the speaker know that he was listening in whatever ways he would ordinarily use in a telephone conversation. At the end of 2-min. they exchanged roles, the listener becoming the speaker and vice versa.

The two participants were recorded on separate channels of the tape. This provision made it possible to listen to the speaker's channel and mark terminal junctures without hearing where the listener interjected his listener responses. Pause locations were determined, as in earlier experiments, from an oscillograph tracing of the tape. The listener's channel was then added and his interjections located on the speaker's typescript. The conjunction of listener responses and junctures strongly supported the hypothesis. Of 124 listener responses, 110 immediately followed terminal junctures.

Since about half of any speaker's junctures are accompanied by juncture pauses, the possibility remained that the listener response was inserted as a response to the pause rather than the juncture. If listeners respond during pauses as such, these responses should also occur at hesitation pauses within clauses. This did not prove to be the case. In 123 hesitation pauses, only four listener responses were interjected; in 195 juncture pauses, 97 listener responses were interjected.

In a subsequent study of face-to-face dialogue (Dittmann & Llewellyn, 1968) listeners' head nods were recorded by an observer in an adjoining room who could see the participants through a window but could not hear what was being said. Subsequent analysis revealed that the ratio of head nods at junctures to head nods during clauses was more than 50:1.

Both of these kinds of listener responses, brief interjections and nods, prove to be very strongly associated with terminal junctures. In this markedly different experimental situation, the phonemic clause was again responded to behaviorally, adding to our conviction that it is indeed a functional speech unit and not simply a descriptive linguistic convention.

Tongue Slips and the Phonemic Clause

The research to be reported in this section, (Boomer & Laver, 1968) deals with another class of speech error, the tongue slip. For our purposes, tongue slip may be defined as a localized sector of an utterance in which the speaker has involuntarily deviated from his intention. The deviant sector may be a single sound or cluster of sounds, a syllable, or a word.

There are a number of identifiable categories of tongue slip, the best known of which is probably the so-called "Freudian slip," the incidence of which is attributed to some unconscious motivation of the speaker. For our own purposes, however, we elected to study tongue slips linguistically, without regard to their possible motivation. In most of the slips we examined, a plausible origin for the intrusion could be found in a nearby part of the utterance. This was not true of the examples that Freud presented; the intrusions represented in his illustrations had their presumed origins outside the utterance in words or ideas that were not meant to be spoken.

Freud (1901) explicitly recognized this distinction in *Psychopathology of Everyday Life:*

> The disturbance in speaking which is manifested in a slip of the tongue can ... be caused by the influence of another component of the same speech. .... The disturbance could however be of a second kind ... it could result from influences outside this word, sentence, or context, and arise out of elements which are not intended to be uttered and of whose excitation we only learn precisely through the actual disturbance [p. 56].

In the bulk of our examples, there may be seen a kind of scrambling or garbling of an intended utterance in which a nearby component appears to intrude and interfere with articulation. This process can best be clarified by an example:

is measured on a scowl . . . a scale of relative loudness

Here the vowel sound *ow* from *loud* appears to have interfered with the articulation of *scale* to produce *scowl*. Note that the speaker has noticed his slip, paused briefly, and corrected himself before proceeding. Most of the slips we have studied exhibit this detection–correction pattern, which is convenient since it makes it possible to compare the actual utterance with the speaker's intention, which he immediately clarifies for us in the correction. In our analysis, we laid out the interrelationship among these elements in this way:

$$\overset{\text{S}}{\text{Utterance: is measured on a scowl . . . a scale of relative loudness}}$$

$$\overset{\text{T}}{\phantom{\text{Intention: is measured on a}}}\overset{\text{O}}{\phantom{\text{scale of relative loudness}}}$$

Intention: is measured on a scale of relative loudness

The superscripts S, T, and O stand for *slip, target,* and *origin,* respectively. S, slip, identifies the aberrant syllable; T, target, the syllable the speaker was aiming at; and O, origin, the syllable in the intended utterance that intruded on the articulation of the target.

The speech material for this study was a collection of more than 100 tape-recorded tongue slips that had been assembled over a period of several years by the present author. These were short excerpts of recorded spontaneous speech, each containing a slip and some context. They were taken from recorded lectures, conference discussions, conversations, radio and television broadcasts, and psychotherapy interviews.

These excerpts were rerecorded on tape loops, to permit repeated listening, and subjected to a detailed linguistic and phonetic analysis jointly by the two authors. In the interest of simplicity, only the directly relevant aspects of this analysis will be reported here.

In each excerpt, the terminal junctures and primary stressed syllables were identified and the slip, target, and origin were labeled. For our example above, the protocol would look like this, with terminal junctures indicated by (/) and primary stress by ('):

S   T

vocal inténsity/is measured on a scowl·. . . a scale

O

of relative loúdness/and expressed in décibels/

This example illustrates the two general features of tongue slips that are relevant to the phonemic clause encoding hypothesis:

1. Target and origin are in the same phonemic clause.
2. The interaction is anticipatory; that is, the origin is later in the phonemic clause than the target.

As was pointed out earlier, perfect regularity is not found in any aspect of speech, and these features of tongue slip are not perfectly lawful either. Because of the idiosyncratic irregularity of speech and speakers, and the unavailability of an adequate mathematical model to assess probability of occurrence and non-occurrence, we were not able to apply any rigorous statistical test to our findings. These two generalizations, however, were the two most powerful of a set of six tongue slip "laws" that, when applied as a set to the 100-odd tongue slips, produced 80% "hits" and 20% exceptions. In a behavioral process as fast and complicated as speech, misarticulations can occur from a multiplicity of causes, many of which remain ambiguous or obscure. Nevertheless, the two features listed above apply with sufficient regularity as to constitute a powerful, if not exceptionless, generalization.

Let us now consider the theoretical implications of these findings for our central thesis concerning the phonemic clause. First, the fact that target and origin are typically in the same phonemic clause supports the unitary conception of the phonemic clause as an integrated speech act. If the lexical components of a phonemic clause were assembled in the central nervous system as a pattern, and partially "primed" before articulation begins, this state of affairs would maximize the likelihood of interactional performance confusion between elements in this interim assembly.

If, on the other hand, the operative behavioral units were either single words or sentences containing two or more phonemic clauses we would expect to find slip interactions between pairs of words that, though proximate, are separated by a juncture. In the complete text of the illustrative utterance presented above, for instance, a word or a sentence model of production would permit slip interactions between *intensity* and *is—istensity*, perhaps—or between *loudness* and *expressed*. There are, in point of fact, no clear-cut examples of this kind of interaction in the 100-odd slips we studied, nor in an additional 200 that have since been collected and analyzed.

The second feature, the fact that the typical slip is anticipatory, also argues for the phonemic clause as a functional unit. Consider that in about 90% of our slips the misarticulation involves interference from something that hasn't yet been said but that clearly exists somewhere in the brain as an intention, as can be seen when the slip is corrected and the phonemic clause completed as the speaker had intended.

In summary, the anticipatory nature of slips provides strong evidence for planning and preselection before articulation. Furthermore, the highly regular juxtaposition of target and origin within the same phonemic clause argues for the phonemic clause as the unit of planning, rather than any larger or smaller unit.

Some additional evidence bearing on this specific point has been presented for another language. An independent study of tongue slips in Dutch (Nooteboom, 1967) was being carried out without our knowledge while our study was in progress. Nooteboom's phonetic analysis of 787 slips yielded two generalizations of interest to us:

1. About 80% of the slips were anticipatory.
2. The syllabic span between target and origin rarely exceeded seven syllables.

The first generalization directly supports our findings for English as regards planning and preselection before articulation. The second generalization provides weaker support; it is at best consonant with our finding that target and origin are predominantly in the same phonemic clause. It does not furnish any direct support since Nooteboom's analysis did not involve any speech unit larger than the syllable. This fragmentary evidence from Dutch, however, taken together with the studies of syntagma in Russian and tapping rhythms in France, suggests that the phenomena we are studying may have a generality that transcends language boundaries.

SUMMARY AND IMPLICATIONS

Summary. The central argument of this chapter is that speech is organized, patterned, and packaged in ways that are no longer apparent once the spoken words have been transcribed and regularized according to orthographic conventions. The research summarized here demonstrates that when speech is studied in its own terms, that is, not as words on a page, but as patterns of vocal noises in real time, the characteristic rhythms, tunes, roughnesses, and errors that are thus preserved have a good deal to tell us about how speech, as opposed to language, is organized.

The phonemic clause, an indigenous speech unit, was presented, together with a number of lines of evidence in support of our contention that this unit has behavioral, as well as linguistic, reality. Pause production and perception, tongue slips, and two kinds of listener responses were shown to be lawfully ordered to this unit. Neither a sentence planning model nor a single word model would account for all of these regularities.

It is always reasonable to inquire how any research direction fits into broader scientific endeavors. For the phonemic clause, there are two potential areas of application: human communication research and neuropsychology.

Communication. As the chapter headings of this book demonstrate, people use a variety of channels of communication beyond the purely verbal. Some of these channels, such as gesture and eye contact, seem to be more closely tied to verbal communication than others, such as facial expression and proxemics. The investigation of relationships between a nonverbal channel and speech requires a functional speech unit against which to juxtapose the nonverbal events. The phonemic clause would seem to be a likely candidate for such comparisons. Dittmann and Llewellyn have already shown that the phonemic clause is useful in studying listener responses, and this work has more recently been expanded to include other classes of body movements (Dittmann, 1972). There are also some indications that the complex relationship between eye contact and speaker switching in dialogue might be illuminated by studying their occurrence relative to phonemic clause boundaries.

Neuropsychology. Lashley, in the classic essay cited earlier, drew attention to the potential importance of speech research to the understanding of brain function and specifically to the problem of temporal integration. Temporal integration refers to the brain's capacity to initiate, maintain, and control an extended behavior sequence involving a great many precisely-timed muscular innervations patterned both in series and in parallel. Typical examples are typing, juggling, and piano playing.

In a rapid arpeggio, a pianist may be executing 16 finger strokes per second. The control of speech is both faster and more complicated. Lenneberg (1967) has calculated that in normal speaking the rate of motor commands to the speech musculature may reach 1400 per second. The pace and precision of this process cannot be accounted for by traditional theories of stimulus–response and associative chaining.

Lashley approached this problem by conceptually separating the processes of planning and execution. He hypothesized that "sentences" are planned and their associated articulatory memory traces are assembled in the central nervous system and held in a state of partial activation by an opposing inhibitory process.

In the execution stage, this spatial assembly of traces is scanned by an independent execution system that transforms the spatial pattern of traces into a temporal pattern of behavior. For the computer-minded, the planning mechanism may be thought of as a program that selects relevant items from permanent memory and assembles them spatially in a temporary buffer store. The execution mechanism is a "read" system that, on command, blindly and automatically reads out to an interface the contents of the buffer store, whatever they may be.

If we substitute "phonemic clause" for "sentence" in Lashley's formulation, some of our research findings provide support for his views, which at the time he wrote them were necessarily speculative.

The American and Russian studies of pauses and the two tongue slip studies uniformly suggest that the articulatory program for a phonemic clause or syntagma is planned and executed as a unit. The tongue slip itself can be interpreted as a transient malfunction of the execution process such that, in Lashley's terms, a partially activated trace prematurely escapes the inhibitory process before it can be scanned in its proper order.

In more general terms the implications of psycholinguistics for neuropsychology can be summed up as follows: Temporal integration is a central unsolved problem in brain research, and its investigation requires that neural events be studied in relation to complex, temporally ordered behavior sequences. Speech is just such a complex temporal behavior system, with the added advantage that the output mode, language, is itself a highly structured system, the elements and organizational principles of which have been more carefully analyzed and described than those of any comparable behavioral system. The bridging discipline, psycholinguistics, has begun to work with linguistic concepts like the phonemic clause in ways that provide increasingly direct links to behavior, and ultimately, perhaps, to biology.

REFERENCES

Bolinger, D. L. Around the edge of language: intonation. *Harvard Educational Review,* 1964, **34,** 282–296.

Boomer, D. S. Hesitation and grammatical encoding. *Language and Speech,* 1965, **8,** 148–158.

Boomer, D. S., & Dittmann, A. T. Hesitation pauses and juncture pauses in speech. *Language and Speech,* 1962, **5,** 215–220.

Boomer, D. S., & Laver, J. D. M. Slips of the tongue. *British Journal of Disorders of Communication,* 1968, **3,** 2–12.

Crystal, D. *Prosodic systems and intonation in English.* Cambridge, England: Cambridge University Press, 1969.

Dittmann, A. T. The body movement–speech rhythm relationship as a cue to speech encoding. In Siegman, A. W., & Pope, B. (Eds.), *Studies in dyadic communication.* New York: Pergamon, 1972.

Dittmann, A. T., & Llewellyn, L. G. The phonemic clause as a unit of speech decoding. *Journal of Personality and Social Psychology,* 1967, 6, 341–349.

Dittmann, A. T., & Llewellyn, L. G. Relationship between vocalization and head nods as listener responses. *Journal of Personality and Social Psychology,* 1968, 9, 79–84.

Dittmann, A. T., & Wynne, L. Linguistic techniques and the analysis of emotionality in interviews. *Journal of Abnormal and Social Psychology,* 1961, 63, 201–204.

Fraisse, P. *The psychology of time.* New York: Harper & Row, 1963.

Freud, S. (1901) *Psychopathology of everyday life.* (Trans. by A. Tyson) Strachey, J. (Ed.). London: Benn, 1966.

Halliday, M. A. K. The tones of English. *Archives of Linguistics,* 1963, 15, 1–28.

Kozhevnikov, V. A., & Chistovich, L. A. *Rech: Artikulyatsia i Vospriyatiye.* Trans., *Speech: Articulation and perception.* Washington: Joint Publications Research Service, U.S. Dept. of Commerce, 1965.

Lashley, K. S. The problem of serial order in behavior. In L. A. Jeffress (Ed.), *Cerebral mechanisms in behavior.* New York: Wiley, 1951.

Lenneberg, E. H. *Biological foundations of language.* New York: Wiley, 1967.

Nooteboom, S. G. Some regularities in phonemic speech errors. *Institute for Perception Research Annual Report,* 1967, 2, 65–70.

Trager, G. L., & Smith, H. L., Jr. *An Outline of English Structure.* (Studies in Linguistics, Occasional Papers, 3.) Norman, Oklahoma: Battenberg Press, 1951.

Part IV

SPACE AND TIME

9
The Role of Space
in Social Interaction[1]

Miles L. Patterson

University of Missouri—St. Louis

The development of research in the area of nonverbal social behavior has increased rapidly over the last several years. Representative of this overall interest is a very lively concern regarding the spatial parameter in social interaction. It seems quite clear to me that the variety and sophistication of research in this area has dramatically increased since the publication of the review paper by Patterson (1968) on this topic. It is difficult to believe that it was only a little over fifteen years ago that Hall (1959) wrote, "We treat space somewhat as we treat sex. It is there but we don't talk about it [p. 147]." Conditions have certainly changed for both topics since that time. In an attempt to identify a focus for research, Hall (1963) coined the term "proxemics" to refer to the study of man's unconscious structuring of microspace. While the use of space may be generally outside of one's awareness, the increased information in this area will lead undoubtedly to greater deliberation in its use in the future. The range of issues included under Hall's definition of proxemics encompassed the use of space in social interaction, in design and architecture, and in urban planning, but the primary emphasis in research has been on the role of space in interaction. The purpose of this chapter is to review and evaluate that role.

A great deal of the research on the social use of space has developed around the concepts of territoriality and personal space. Territoriality can be defined as the demarcation and defense of a fixed geographical area. The use of the concept of territory seems to be generally consistent across animal research (Hediger, 1961) and human research (Altman & Haythorn, 1967). However, Sommer and

[1] Portions of this chapter were presented as a paper entitled, "Factors affecting interpersonal spatial proximity," at the annual meeting of the American Psychological Association, New Orleans, September, 1974.

Becker (1969) have extended the definition to include temporary territories such as chairs or tables in public settings. They note that the increasing use of public spaces often requires the marking of places with coats or other materials to insure the holding of a chair or table. Even with this extended definition of the term, territoriality is not nearly as pervasive a concern for social interaction as is personal space. Personal space may be described as the limiting distance that separates individuals when interacting with one another. Personal space has been likened to a bubble or sphere that serves to protect the individual from intrusion by others. Hall (1966, p. 119) has used a similar term, personal distance, to refer to a range from 1.5 to 4 ft. which serves to comfortably separate individuals. While one might disagree with the specific limits of such a range, the recognition of variability in this protective distance is important. Occasionally, one will encounter discussions of personal space which imply that a single fixed inter-action distance may be identified for each individual. It should become clear as we progress through this chapter that a number of factors exercise considerable influence on the interaction distances chosen in various settings, and that consequently a single estimate of personal space for an individual is not really possible.

The investigation of interaction distance has been attempted in a variety of ways. Before covering the substantive issues, it may be useful to describe some of the general techniques employed to study spatial behavior. Most frequently used is the direct or estimated measurement of individuals in live interactions, whether in a field or laboratory setting. A modification of this interaction procedure is the observation of approaches by an individual to a target person. With this technique, a subject is usually asked simply to approach another person from one or more directions until he begins to feel uncomfortable (e.g., Frankel & Barrett, 1971). Further removed from the live interaction is a type of role-playing procedure in which a person is instructed to imagine another individual in a specific location, possibly represented by a coat rack or a mannequin, and approach him assuming a posture appropriate to the situation (e.g., Mehrabian, 1968a). Another group of methods for studying interaction distance might be called representational or symbolic procedures because they are designed to approximate the live interaction. The questionnaire method as used by Sommer (1965) requires respondents to indicate their preferred seating arrangements in specific situations. A diagram of a table or set of tables allows the subject to visualize his alternative seating choices, given some limits set by the instructions. Frequent use has been made of miniaturized human figures or silhouettes which may be arranged on some background to simulate a real interaction. Usually the figures are two-dimensional cloth or cardboard cutouts (Kuethe, 1962), but three-dimensional scaled figures (Desor, 1972) have also been used. A final type of symbolic procedure is a paper-and-pencil variant of the limiting approach technique (Duke & Nowicki, 1972). A central point on a diagram is used to represent the individual. Eight radii emanate from the central point representing the angles of approach by an imaginary person. A simple mark along each radius defines the limiting approach of the imaginary person.

Because there are a variety of substantially different techniques employed in this research, the question of the validity of these procedures becomes an important one. There are several studies that have examined the validity issue, but the results are not consistent. Little (1965) has reported a very high correlation between the placement of doll figures and live actresses in the simulation of various relationships. Two studies have reported substantial correlations between a paper-and-pencil symbolic technique and actual behavioral approaches (Duke & Nowicki, 1972; Pedersen, 1973a). Dosey and Meisels (1969) found that silhouette measures were not consistently related to behavioral measures, but Haase and Markey (1973) found directly opposing results. In an examination of different techniques for studying reactions to spatial invasion, Becker and Mayo (1970) reported significant differences between several different measures. Further evidence for differences between measurement techniques was indicated in an investigation of nine different procedures, which yielded an average intercorrelation between pairs of measures of only $r = .21$ (Knowles & Johnsen, 1974).

While the evidence is conflicting, there are a couple of points which may help in coming to an evaluation of different procedures. First, most of these studies require the testing of the same subjects over different measures. Once subjects become aware of the purpose of the investigation, which is difficult to conceal, it is quite possible that they may attempt to respond consistently, even though the instructions may not direct that. If that happens, then the correlations between different measures will be artificially high, and thereby overestimate the real similarity between measures. A second concern involves the issue of generalizability or external validity, which has been extensively covered as a general methodological problem elsewhere (Campbell & Stanley, 1966; Webb, Campbell, Schwartz, & Sechrest, 1966). Because studies involving live interactions, especially those in natural settings, more closely approximate the situations to which we want to generalize, it would appear that such studies have greater utility. Regarding this point, it is interesting to note that Knowles and Johnsen (1974) found that unobtrusive approach and seating measures were among the measures least correlated with other role-playing and representational procedures. That is, the techniques apparently most representative of "real world" behavior were not substantially related to other more symbolic measures. Primarily because of this issue of generalizability greater emphasis will be placed on real rather than symbolic interactions. This caution regarding generalizability must also be extended to the potential artificiality of interactions in the laboratory.

The organization of the material on spatial behavior will be subdivided into the two basic procedures used in researching this topic. First we will examine the potential antecedents of differences in the social use of space. Among the antecedents which are most clearly identifiable and important are culture, sex, personality, interpersonal relationships, and situational factors. After discussing these variables, we will examine the consequences of varying spatial arrangements, primarily in invasion studies and in structured interaction. It might be noted that in focusing on antecedents, we are examining space as a dependent variable, while in focusing on consequences, the concern is with space as an independent variable. There are undoubtedly a variety of other ways of organizing this rapidly expanding area of research, but I feel that this method will give the reader a good perspective of the field.

ANTECEDENTS OF SPATIAL BEHAVIOR

Culture

The work of E. T. Hall has been very critical in bringing to light the importance of cultural influences on spatial behavior. Hall (1963, 1966) has suggested that the use of space, like the use of language, is culturally specific. He believes that people from dissimilar cultures not only use and structure space differently, but actually experience it differently. In fact, Hall (1968) suggests that these differences between cultures have their basis in the selective programming of sensory capacities of the individuals in each culture. Hall has personally observed considerable variety in the use of space across cultures. He has used a general contact–noncontact dimension to describe the interpersonal use of space in various cultures. At the extreme of those preferring very close contact are Arabs, who typically interact at distances close enough to permit feeling the other's breath (Hall, 1966, pp. 159–160). Hall claimed that this tendency may be the result of the Arab's appreciation of olfactory and even tactile cues in interaction. Latin American and Mediterranean people could also be described as being high-contact groups. Hall suggests that the other extreme of the contact dimension includes the English and some North European people whose aloofness and reserve is undoubtedly linked to their preference for distant interactions. In contrast to the Arab's olfactory and tactile feedback regulating interpersonal distance, the noncontact groups' regulating mechanism is at least partially related to visual feedback. This may include muscular feedback in the eyes, ease of focusing the other person, or size of the retinal image (Hall, 1968).

Hall's personal reports of substantial cultural differences in the use of space have been investigated empirically in several studies. While most of the evidence supports the hypothesis of cultural variability in the use of space, the results are not as consistent as we might hope. The close and intense interactions among Arabs, which Hall reported, have been systematically observed in a laboratory setting where pairs of male college students were brought together for discussions. The Arab pairs not only sat closer together, but had more directly confronting body orientations, greater eye contact, and spoke in louder voices than did American pairs (Watson & Graves, 1966). It is also interesting to note that the Arab pairs showed occasional—though apparently accidential—touching, which was never present among the American pairs. In a very similar study using Latin American students as representative of a contact culture, no differences were found relative to the North American students (Forston & Larson, 1968). While no differences were found in the structured sessions, the authors reported that before and after the discussion the Latin Americans appeared to stand closer together than the North American pairs did.

Additional evidence bearing on cultural differences comes from two symbolic approaches to measuring spatial preferences. Cook (1970) replicated a questionnaire study by Sommer (1965) which originally tested American students on their preferred seating arrangements. When the purpose ascribed to the hypothetical interaction was either conversation or cooperation, Cook's English subjects generally chose positions that were more distant then Sommer's American subjects. The other indirect procedure for investigating interaction distances was the use of a social schemata or figure-placing task to represent an actual interaction. Greek and Italian students, selected as representative of contact cultures, placed figures closer together than did the Scottish and Swedish subjects from the noncontact cultures (Little, 1968). To the extent that these procedures are indicative of real interactions, Hall's impressions are further supported.

These apparent differences in interaction distances as a function of national origin have implications for potential subcultural differences in a country like the United States with its diverse population. Hall's (1966, pp. 172–173) suggestion that Puerto Ricans and blacks have much greater involvement than New Englanders and Americans of Northern European stock would lead us to expect that the blacks and Puerto Ricans interact more closely than whites. However, the research is equivocal with regard to this issue. In two similar studies, black children in the first and second grades have been found to interact more closely than white children of the same age (Aiello & Jones, 1971; Jones & Aiello, 1973). Jones and Aiello (1973) found that these differences were reduced and apparently beginning to reverse themselves by the time children were at the fifth grade level. In both of these studies, it may be important to note that socioeconomic level differences were confounded with race. Further support for the hypothesis of closer interaction among blacks than whites was found in a study measuring the approaches of college students in campus settings toward a confederate of their own race and sex (Bauer, 1973). Unfortunately, no information was available on the socioeconomic levels of the subjects in this study. Bauer was rather cautious in interpreting the very close approaches by black subjects (9.8 inches versus 15.6 inches for whites) as really representing the minimal comfortable approach distance. He suggested that instructions asking subjects to "approach as close as you feel comfortable" may have been interpreted by blacks as a challenge and consequently led to closer approaches.

When socioeconomic level was equated in a study of spatial preferences in adults, no differences were found among black, Perto Rican, Italian, and Chinese groups (Jones, 1971).

With the exception of the results from the Bauer study, which may reflect more than racial differences in approach distances, the pattern of findings from the other studies might suggest that differential spatial preferences across subcultures are learned early in life, but gradually become more similar by exposure to a common cultural norm. However, Baxter (1970) has not only found differences in proxemic behavior in adults, but has evidence directly contradicting both of the Aiello and Jones' studies on children. Baxter's observations of pairs of individuals at a zoo indicated clearly shorter interaction distances for whites than for blacks, although this difference was lessened with younger children. An interesting speculation offered by Jones and Aiello (1973) in trying to resolve these inconsistencies revolved around the nature of the interaction in each of these settings. They observed that blacks, when not actually communicating, were more likely to move away from one another than whites were. Because their own distance measures were taken only during periods when children were talking, while a substantial number of Baxter's observations must have been taken during intervals when pairs were not talking, the different studies may have capitalized on situational differences between blacks and whites. That is, Jones and Aiello sampled a situation predisposing blacks to interact relatively closely, while Baxter sampled a contrasting situation in which blacks were relatively distant. The issue of potential subcultural differences will probably not be adequately clarified until a systematic consideration of developmental, situational, and socioeconomic determinants resolves the present inconsistencies.

Sex Differences

The sex of the interactants in a social situation seems to play a role in determining spatial patterning, but it is apparently not a simple, clear-cut role. In same-sex dyads, females have been found to interact more closely than do males (Dosey & Meisels, 1969; Aiello & Jones, 1971; Pellegrini & Empey, 1970). Similar patterns have been found for groups larger than dyads (Mehrabian & Diamond, 1971; Patterson & Schaeffer, 1975). Presumably, the expression of intimacy in same-sex groups has been traditionally more acceptable for females than for males, and these interaction distance differences may reflect that. The picture becomes a little more complicated in the case of opposite-sex pairings. For example, in the Dosey and Meisels (1969) study, females who approached standing males remained more distant than those who approached females. In contrast, male subjects approached males and females at very similar distances. Similarly, others have found that females typically allow closer approaches to themselves than do males (Hartnett, Bailey, & Gibson, 1970; Mehrabian & Friar, 1969; Willis, 1966). Here again, traditional sex role differences seem indicated.

Females appear to be more reserved than males not only in actively approaching someone of the opposite sex, but also in passively limiting the closer approach of such a person. This generalization is probably more representative of interactions between strangers or casual acquaintances of the opposite sex, and not of those romantically involved (or married).

The differences suggested between males and females in their preferred inter-action distances with others of the same sex are consistent with the results of two experiments on crowding. In those two studies, females reacted more positively to others of the same sex under crowded than uncrowded conditions, while males reacted in just the opposite way (Freedman, Levy, Buchanan, & Price, 1972; Ross, Layton, Erickson & Schopler, 1973). However, others have failed to clearly replicate this effect (Marshall & Heslin, 1975; Stokols, Rall, Pinner, & Schopler, 1973). The Marshall and Heslin experiment is particularly interesting because the experimenters found directly opposite results from the Freedman *et al.* (1972) and Ross *et al.* (1973) studies. Specifically, Marshall and Heslin found that for a relatively long (1.5 hr) and highly involving task, males reacted more positively to the crowded condition while females reacted more positively to the uncrowded condition. The authors suggested that, for males in the crowded condition, the combination of the longer duration and necessity for cooperation in the task reduced the initial aggressiveness and defensiveness of the males and instilled a feeling of camaraderie for accomplishing a common goal. For females in the crowded condition, the extension of a task-oriented interaction over a considerable period of time may have led to some frustration because a warm, sociable interaction was thereby prevented. Certainly results such as these suggest that much more needs to be known about the way that situational determinants affect sex differences.

The illustrations of sex differences in spatial behavior discussed up to this point have, for the most part, come from studies in which the subjects were not acquainted with one another. There is reason to believe that these patterns may be modified when the interactants are acquainted, especially for opposite-sex pairs. For example, Cook (1970) found, in both field observations and sur-veys, that opposite-sex pairs sat closer together in resturants than same-sex pairs. Given the setting of this particular study, it is likely that pairs dining together would at least be friends. A similar result has been noted in the observation of pairs of individuals visiting a zoo. Cross-sex pairs stood closer than same-sex pairs in the adolescent and adult age groupings (Baxter, 1970). Again, in this setting, it is probable that most pairs walking together would be more than casual acquaintances. Further evidence for the effect of relationship on sex differences in spacing can be found in a study by Heshka and Nelson (1972). Significantly closer approaches in outdoor settings were observed in pairs of friends or relatives than in pairs of strangers. Interaction distances in male-male dyads were similar for stranger and friend groups, but both male-female and female-female dyads indicated much closer approaches in friend pairs than stranger pairs. Thus, in these studies, which sample pairs who are likely to be well-acquainted, opposite-sex pairs typically interact more closely than same-sex pairs.

The role of the sex of the interactants is complex, but some general statements can probably be made on the basis of the research up to this point. In same sex groups, females apparently interact more closely than do males. Closer approaches by females may be a product of greater emphasis on affiliative and dependent relationships in the socialization process of females. In addition, the stigma of homosexuality, which might be inferred from very close interactions between males, probably serves to moderate approaches between males. Support for this latter factor can be seen in the similar approach distances for friend and stranger pairs among males. Females, in contrast, approach female friends much more closely than female strangers. Interaction distance in cross-sex pairs, like that in female pairs, seems to be clearly affected by degree of acquaintance. Relatively distant patterns are common for interactions between unacquainted males and females, while much closer patterns are typical between close friends or lovers. There are undoubtedly other limiting factors for which there isn't much information yet available. For example, Baxter's (1970) study suggests that sex differences in spacing may be minimal until the adolescent years, but Aiello and Jones (1971) have found differences in six to eight year olds. It is also possible, as Marshall and Heslin (1975) found, that differences in the purpose and duration of an interaction may affect the general patterns suggested as a function of sex.

Personality

It is common in much of the material written about human spatial behavior to make assumptions about individual differences in spacing. It is often suggested that such differences are a product of personality differences between individuals. It does seem clear that over time in similar situations preferred interaction distances are quite stable. The correlations between approaches in two interview sessions in one case separated by 20 min. and in another by one week, were essentially identical, $r = .96$ and $r = .97$, respectively (Patterson, 1973a). In another study using an interview format, approaches to the same interviewer separated by one or two weeks, produced correlations of approximately $r = .90$ (Daniell & Lewis, 1972). When different interviewers were employed, the correlations over similar intervals averaged approximately $r = .80$. Although situationally limited, these results certainly suggest that individual differences are temporally consistent. Given this stability, it is reasonable to try to identify specific characteristics that could be responsible for individual spatial preferences.

At a fairly general level, there is evidence suggesting that psychiatric patients may differ from normal subjects in the use of space in social interactions.

Specifically, schizophrenics have shown greater avoidance of others than normals, as indicated by greater interpersonal distances (Sommer, 1959; Horowitz, Duff, & Stratton, 1964). However, Sommer (1959) also found that following instructions to approach a seated decoy, schizophrenics tended to sit adjacent rather than opposite, as most normals did. In this case, a relatively close, but nonconfronting arrangement selected by schizophrenics may serve to minimize interaction just as avoidance does. That is, adjacent seating does not facilitate interaction as opposite seating does. Sommer suggested that these distortions in use of space also result in causing others to withdraw. Such inappropriate spatial interaction is generally consistent with the pattern of deficient social skills typically noted in schizophrenics.

Extreme interpersonal distances have been noted in another very select group of individuals—violent prisoners. A comparison between groups of violent and nonviolent inmates indicated that the violent prisoners required approximately four times as much area around themselves to feel comfortable in the presence of a male experimenter as did the nonviolent prisoners (Kinzel, 1970). This difference was particularly striking when the experimenter approached from behind. Kinzel interpreted the larger separation in violent prisoners as being an indication of a high level of homosexual anxiety. It would generally be expected, however, that violent-prone individuals would require a greater margin of safety from others, especially from behind, even if their fears did not specifically relate to homosexual assaults. Generalizations from Kinzel's small sample of 14 prisoners may be quite tenuous, but they are suggestive of a potentially useful diagnostic procedure. Very similar results have been found in a comparison of deviant and normal underachieving adolescent males. The deviant subjects, who were described as being hostile, defiant, and aggressive, required much more room from an approaching experimenter than did the normals (Newman & Pollack, 1973).

Given the rather extreme differences between psychiatric and normal groups or violent and nonviolent individuals, it is probably not very surprising that differences exist in their spatial behavior. However, the attempts to relate differential spacing behavior to personality characteristics among normal individuals have not been consistently successful. One group of personality variables, including extraversion, affiliation, and social anxiety, has indicated some predictive utility for spatial behavior. A questionnaire procedure involving the choice of seating arrangements from diagrams indicated that extraverts, in contrast to introverts, tended to not only sit closer to others, but also in positions allowing greater eye contact (Cook, 1970). The preference for closer seating with increased levels of extraversion has also been found in actual interview sessions (Patterson & Holmes, 1966). Similarly, closer comfortable approach distances have been related to higher levels of extraversion (Pedersen, 1973b). In another investigation of the relationship of extraversion to interpersonal distance, no differences were found between introverts and extraverts in their degree of approach to an interviewer (Williams, 1971). However, when the initiation of the approach was reversed, Williams found that extraverts permitted closer approaches to themselves than did introverts.

A second personality factor that may be a determinant of differential spacing behavior is social anxiety. Patterson (1973a, 1977) found marginally significant correlations between social anxiety and the subject's approach in an interview session, indicating that those scoring higher on social anxiety tended to remain more distant from the interviewer than lower scorers. Consistent with that relationship was the tendency for the more distant subjects to rate themselves as less at ease than the closer subjects (Patterson, 1973a). In a second experiment in the same study, no personality measures were taken, but again, the more distant subjects rated themselves as less at ease than the closer ones. If that is the case, it is possible that the relationship is not a simple one. That is, social anxiety might induce avoidance, but, given the avoidance, anxiety may also be produced, especially if such avoidance behavior is seen as inappropriate.

Another personality variable that should be relevant for social behavior is affiliation. Two different studies have provided data indicating that those higher on affiliation prefer greater proximity to others than do those low on affiliation. Clore (1969) examined the relationships between need affiliation of subjects and their approaches to the chair of a "stranger" whom they are about to meet. In fact, the stranger never appeared, but approaches to the chair, marked with a coat, were closer for high affiliators than for low affiliators. In one of the few studies focusing on the spatial behaviors of groups, Mehrabian and Diamond (1971) observed seating arrangements in four-person groups gathered together to supposedly evaluate some musical selections. Those scoring high on affiliation sat significantly closer to others than those low on affiliation, 5.12 ft. vs. 5.61 ft. Mehrabian has suggested elsewhere, however, that closeness of approach is not really part of a general affiliation factor for interpersonal behavior, but may be more consistent with an intimacy or liking factor (Mehrabian & Ksionzky, 1972).

The evidence relating the role of any one of these personality variables to spatial behavior is certainly not so compelling as to generate unqualified confidence. The number of studies is few and the relationships found are not particularly strong. However, regarding this weakness, it is interesting to note that there is evidence indicating very substantial correlations between test measures of extraversion, affiliation, and social anxiety (Patterson & Strauss, 1972). In fact, a majority of items from each of these three dimensions loaded on a common social approach–avoidance factor. Thus the separate results, showing that extraversion, affiliation, and a lack of social anxiety predict close approaches, may be overlapping and representative of a more general social approach–avoidance dimension.

There are several other dimensions that have been examined for their potential relationship to spatial behavior, but the evidence is not as substantial as with the social approach–avoidance variables. Some of these results indicate closer approaches may be related to high self-esteem and low authoritarianism (Frankel & Barrett, 1971), high exhibitionism and impulsivity (Sewell & Heisler, 1973), high self-concept (Stratton, Tekippl, & Flick, 1973), low test anxiety in an evaluative setting (Karabenick & Meisels, 1972), and, in mixed-sex pairs, higher levels of heterosexuality (Hartnett *et al.*, 1970). One of the more theoretically interesting findings involves results relating approach distance to the internal-external control dimension. On a symbolic approach task, both the internal- and external-control individuals approached friends and relatives at similar distances, but internals approached strangers much closer than externals (Duke & Nowicki, 1972). The authors explained these differences in terms of expectancies of the two groups in various situations. In dealing with friends and relatives, both groups acted similarly because clear expectancies were formed on the basis of adequate past experience. However, with strangers, externals, who lack confidence in their own abilities to affect situations, remained relatively distant while internals, expecting to control the situation, came much closer.

The studies reviewed which do indicate potential personality determinants of spatial behavior are by no means representative of all of the investigations focusing on individual differences. In direct contrast to other results, Patterson (1973a) and Meisels and Canter (1970) found no relationship between interaction distance and extraversion. Several other variables might intuitively be expected to influence spatial behavior in social settings. Some of the variables that have been examined and found not predictive of interpersonal distance are sensitivity to rejection (Mehrabian & Diamond, 1971), social desirability (Patterson & Holmes, 1966; Patterson, 1973a), and body image boundary and anxiety as measured by the Rorschach (Dosey & Meisels, 1969).

In evaluating the role of personality characteristics, it seems fairly clear that such individual differences, by themselves, are not primary determinants of spatial behavior. This statement should be tempered by a recognition that extreme differences, such as those between normal and psychiatric groups, may result in substantial differences in spatial behavior. However, within normal limits, the relationships between various personality characteristics and interpersonal distance are probably fairly small, and may be influenced by other factors such as the situation and the relationship between interacting individuals.

Interpersonal Relationships

The antecedents of differential spacing examined so far have focused on characteristics of the individuals involved in social interaction. In addition to such concerns, it seems obvious that the relationships between people are important determinants of social behavior. One major dimension in interpersonal relationships is the degree of attraction or liking between individuals. A great deal of research over the last decade by Byrne and his associates has linked degree of similarity in attitudes to attraction as measured by responses on rating scales (see Byrne, 1969, 1971). The generalizability of the relationship between similarity and attraction has been extended by behavioral measures of attraction, including interpersonal distance. As the degree of attraction between two individuals increases, the approach distance between them decreases. This result has been supported both in a laboratory setting where an individual was forced to sit close to either a similar or dissimilar stranger (Byrne, Baskett, & Hodges, 1971) and in an analysis of behavior following computer-dating matches (Byrne, Ervin, & Lamberth, 1970). In an interview situation, Clore (1969) found only a slight tendency for increased attraction to result in closer approaches, but he did find that with increased attraction, approaches were more directly confronting. Other studies have shown that increasing the degree of liking toward an imagined other, in a role-playing situation, produced linear decreases in distance to the imagined other (Mehrabian, 1968a; Mehrabian & Friar, 1969). Consistent with the preceding evidence are the findings that those intending to indicate disapproval to another (Rosenfeld, 1965) and those receiving disapproval from another (Mehrabian & Ksionzky, 1972) remain more distant from that person than those indicating or receiving approval.

In addition to the degree of liking or attraction, the specific type of relationship between individuals also influences their spatial interaction. However, the type of relationship and degree of attraction are obviously not independent of one another. For example, very high levels of attraction often lead to a marital relationship, given the appropriate sex combination, and conversely a specific relationship, such as that between a parent and child, usually leads to high attraction or liking. With that caution in mind, it has been observed that with more intimate relationships, especially for cross-sex pairs, individuals sit closer to one another (Cook, 1970) and stand closer to one another when initiating conversations (Heshka & Nelson, 1972; Willis, 1966). Again, as discussed in the section on sex differences, increased friendship or intimacy between male–female and female–female pairs typically leads to closer interaction distances. The absence of close approaches between males, who are even good friends, may be due to a greater concern about homosexuality among males than females. Further support for the indication of deeper relationships through closer interactions has also been found by Little (1965) who used line drawings, silhouettes, and live pairs of individuals. Across these differing methods, friends interacted at closer distances than acquaintances, who were in turn, closer than strangers.

There are a few other relationship dimensions that may influence spatial patterning. For example, approaches to others were found to be closer if the others are (1) peers rather than older (Willis, 1966), (2) of similar rather than different race (Campbell, Kruskal, & Wallace, 1966; Willis, 1966), and (3) of similar rather than different status (Lott & Sommer, 1967). Even these diverse findings may be interpreted in terms of the general framework of increased liking or attraction leading to more spatially intimate interactions. It seems quite clear, as Byrne and his associates have found, that similarity in beliefs or attitudes leads to attraction, which, in turn, is manifested behaviorally by closer interactions. However, in many situations, especially with those individuals about whom we know very little, inferences about similarity must be made on minimal information. It has been found that with little or no information about beliefs of others, evaluations may be determined by other salient characteristics of the individuals such as race (Stein, Hardyck, & Smith, 1965). Thus given little knowledge of others' beliefs, similarities in race, age, or status may serve to indicate something about the broader, more critical similarities in beliefs. That is, similarities in race, age, or status may lead to inferences of similarities in beliefs. The resulting conclusions of similarity or dissimilarity may determine attraction, and indirectly affect interpersonal distance.

The suggested dynamics for the various effects of similarities in age, race, and status is tenuous, but the general effect of interpersonal relationships on inter-action distance seems quite clear. As the degree of attraction or closeness of relationships between individuals increases, interpersonal distances are lessened. One apparently modifying factor in this prediction is the restraint typically indicated in interactions between males, even though they may be good friends or closely related. This pattern, as indicated earlier in the discussion of sex differences, may be due to the greater concern in male groups for avoiding any indication of homosexual tendencies. In spite of this concern and other potential influences, the role of interpersonal relationships on spatial behavior seems more clearly defined than the other antecedents examined up to this point.

Situation

A final antecedent may be usefully examined before looking at the various consequences of manipulating or structuring space. Situational differences, un-like the antecedents reviewed up to this point, do not relate to either individual characteristics or relationships between individuals, but focus on the constraints of different situations which may influence spatial arrangements. It can generally be assumed that the type of activity involving a group would influence the manner in which they arrange themselves. Very striking differences have been found between groups of eight individuals required to make either individual or collective decisions on a problem of judgment. The groups making collective decisions not only sat much closer together than those making individual decisions, but sat in arrangements typically circular or semicircular, which allowed greater visibility of other group members (Batchelor & Goethals, 1972).

The arrangement of pairs around a table has been investigated as a function of the general type of activity. A study by Sommer (1965) on two English samples examined questionnaire responses for seating preferences under differing conditions. Although there were some differences noted between the patterns representative of the three samples, some clear consistencies were found also. When the situation was described as one simply involving a conversation between the individual and another person, the vast majority of respondents chose positions diagonally facing one another across the corner of a rectangular table or directly opposing one another across the table. Situations involving cooperation resulted in a high proportion of adjacent choices on the same side of the table. Coaction and competion situations produced a high proportion of more distant choices than conversing or cooperating. For the competitive conditions, greater use was made of directly opposing arrangements, which apparently facilitates visually monitoring the competitor's activity. In contrast, in the coaction situations, distant, nonconfronting positions were most common, providing spatial and visual isolation from the other person.

The facilitative effect of minimizing interpersonal distance in situations of active interaction has also been noted in the placement of human figures in rooms scaled down from actual size (Desor, 1972). The specific purpose of this study was to determine the number of people who could occupy a room before it became too crowded. The largest number of people were added when the activity was described as a cocktail party, while the fewest were added when the individuals were supposed to be sitting and reading. In general, it appears that individual activities, in contrast to social activities, require greater distance between individuals in order for them to be comfortable. Conversely, as the intensity of social interaction demanded by the activity increases, approaches between individuals are likely to be not only closer, but involve more directly confronting orientations. As the orientations become more direct, the potential for visual interaction and the monitoring of facial expressions increases.

Another major situational determinant and one of obvious importance is the posture of the interacting parties. Interactions typically take place at shorter distances when individuals are standing than when seated. Desor's (1972) study of crowding indicated that a higher density of people in a given area could be comfortably accomodated if they are standing rather than seated. Although few, if any, other experiments directly compared standing versus seated interactions, the pattern of approaches clearly differs across studies focusing on one or the other posture. Average distances in seated interactions in directly confronting orientations may range from a little over 3 ft. (Forston & Larson, 1968) to 8 ft. and more (Patterson, 1973a). Intermediate distances of 5 ft. or more are not uncommon (Mehrabian & Diamond, 1971; Rosenfeld, 1965). Of course, the potential variability in interpersonal distances for seated interactions is limited by the size of the room and by the location and mobility of chairs. A much closer pattern is noted for interactions between standing individuals. In situations involving two people talking to one another in public settings, a common range of approach is between 1 and 3 ft. (Jones, 1971; Heshka & Nelson, 1972; Willis, 1966). These distances are typically based on estimated, or in some case directly measured, distance from nose-to-nose. In comparing seated and standing interactions, it should be noted that most of the data on seated interactions comes from laboratory studies involving subjects who are not well-acquainted, while most of the data on standing interactions comes from field studies of unobstrusively observed subjects. People who are interacting in natural settings probably know one another better than the typical pair of laboratory subjects, and that may exaggerate the differences described here.

A more basic factor contributing to the greater separations in seated groups than in standing groups is the area taken by the chair and legs of the interacting parties. Unless individuals are seated side-by-side, which doesn't facilitate interaction, it is unlikely that a confronting seated pair can get any closer than about 2½ or 3 ft. by a nose-to-nose measure. It is doubtful that this factor by itself would determine the full extent of the difference between seated and standing interactions in many situations. Certainly the occasional finding that seated discussions may take place at 10 (or more) ft. is not explained by adding the minimal seating distance (approximately 3 ft.) to the most extreme standing distance. At least a couple of additional factors may be operative here. First, seated interactions may be considered more formal and consequently demand greater distance. In addition, standing interactions often take place in areas where others may interfere by walking between the individuals. By standing closer together it is easier to maintain the integrity of the dyad and keep the conversation from being interrupted (Cheyne & Efran, 1972).

One final incidental concern which may be important is the influence of indoor versus outdoor settings. Baxter (1970) has found some interesting trends specific to different ethnic groups. White pairs observed at a zoo interacted at comparable distances whether indoors or outdoors. However, blacks clustered more closely when indoors, while Mexican pairs were closer outdoors. Baxter suggested that if clustering is determined at all by the perception of threat or danger, then the different interaction distances in the two settings may be a reaction to perceived vulnerability.

In general, it seems that the situational determinants exercise considerable influence over the spatial patterns in social interactions. The type of activity, the posture of the individuals involved, and the physical constraints in the setting are among some of the impersonal, situational factors that affect interaction distances. With the recent advent of interest in environmental influences on behavior, it can be expected that much more will be learned about the role of physical or structural variables on all aspects of social interaction.

MANIPULATION OF SPACE

Invasion

One method for examining the influence of space on interactions has been through varying approach distances to unsuspecting subjects. In such a study, one or more of the approaches is at a distance that would closely intrude upon an individual. Felipe and Sommer (1966) conducted an invasion study in two different locations, the grounds of a psychiatric hospital and a college library. In the closest condition, seated subjects were approached side by side so that 6 in.−1 ft. separated them from the intruder. The subjects, or victims as the case may be, were always seated by themselves, with no one nearby. In both locations, after just 10 min., approximately 50% of the invaded subjects left, while less than 10% of noninvaded controls did. Some subtle responses to the invasion, short of fleeing the situation, including turning away or blocking the presence of another through the use of a hand or elbow, were also observed. In an experiment very similar to Felipe and Sommer's, these subtle responses became the focus for observing the effects of spatial intrusion. The subjects, seated alone at tables in a library, exhibited more leaning away from the intruder and more blocking behavior as the approaches became closer (Patterson, Mullens, & Romano, 1971). With closer approaches, the frequency of gazing toward the intruder became greater, apparently in an attempt to gather more information about the intruder. Fisher and Byrne (1975) conducted an invasion study in a library, very similar to those just described, but it focused on the affective reactions of the subjects rather than their behavioral reactions. Males rated the situation most negatively when the invader sat opposite them, while females rated the situation most negatively when the invader was immediately adjacent. In a second study, Fisher and Byrne (1975) examined the placement of barriers such as books, sweaters, and coats by subjects seated alone. Consistent with the results of the first study, males placed their barriers more forward and opposite themselves, while females placed their barriers to their sides. It is interesting that not all spatial intrusions are treated as such. Fry and Willis (1971) found that five- and eight-year-old children were generally treated very positively following their intrusion of adults. However, ten year olds were generally avoided and created definite signs of discomfort in adults following comparable intrusions. Thus it seems that considerable license is granted to younger children in their approach to adult strangers.

When invasions do occur, it is likely that the flight responses and the more subtle reactions are precipitated by some anxiety or discomfort. There is some independent evidence that extremely close approaches do produce anxiety. In one study, inappropriately close interactions with an experimenter were followed by more attribution of anxiety on a projective test than were interactions at moderate distances (Baxter & Deanovich, 1970). Decreasing the distance between a subject and an approaching experimenter has been found to produce higher galvanic skin reponses in the subject (McBride, King, & James, 1965). Verbal reports of reactions to extremely close approaches to friends have included attempted avoidance, bewilderment, and acute embarrassment (Garfinkel, 1964). Efran and Cheyne (1974) found that requiring subjects to walk between a conversing pair of individuals did not affect the subjects' heart rate, but did lead to more negative facial gestures and more reported negative feelings. All of this information suggests that in order to be comfortable, some minimal separation distance is required. When this minimal distance is violated, distinct anxiety or defensive reactions often result. However, attempts at identifying very specific limits for these reactions must weigh the individual differences, interpersonal relationships, and situational factors discussed in the previous section.

It is likely that such a limiting space may be generalized beyond the individual to groups. Some research has incorporated invasion procedures to determine more about the spatial boundaries of groups. In one study, intrusion was accomplished by having the male experimenter try to walk between pairs of individuals walking down a sidewalk. Very clear differences were found in the reactions of the invaded subjects as a function of the sex type of the dyad. A total of 83% of the opposite-sex pairs moved to avoid being separated, while only half of the same-sex pairs moved to avoid being split by the intruder (Knowles, 1972). Among same-sex pairs, females avoided the intruder much more than did males.

Another study also examined the spatial integrity of dyads, but under conditions of interaction versus no-interaction (Cheyne & Efran, 1972). Rather than having someone intrude upon a pair as in the Knowles study, pairs of individuals were stationed so that naive passers-by would have to decide to intrude upon or avoid the pair. Dyads were stationed in a hallway 41 inches apart, and with 33 inches of passageway behind one of the individuals. In the interacting conditions dyads interacted verbally and visually, while in the noninteracting condition the individuals faced away from one another. Cheyne and Efran found that over 80% avoided walking between the interacting pairs, but only about 25% avoided the noninteracting pairs. Once again, mixed pairs were less permeable than same-sex pairs across both interacting and noninteracting conditions. Through the employment of a very similar procedure, it has been found that increasing group size from two to four and increasing group status decreases the number of intrusions from passers-by (Knowles, 1973).

While the results described concerning the intrusion of groups certainly suggest some validity to the concept of a group space, little information is yet available on the potential variability of such a space. Cheyne and Efran (1972) reported an increasing proportion of intrusions between interacting pairs as the distance between two individuals increased from 40 to 52 in. It is interesting to note that at a separation of 52 in., there was no difference in the proportion of people walking through the designated area with or without the stationed pair. One confounding factor here, which was apparently not a problem in this study, is that as the distance between two persons becomes greater, the room to walk around may become severely limited. Consequently in some cases, there may be no effective choice but to intrude. However, under such circumstances it might be expected that the intruder would excuse himself or at least indicate some sort of hesitancy.

The invasion studies discussed here suggest that there are some identifiable limits of comfortable approach to individuals and groups. Research involving the manipulation of very close approaches not only tells us about these limits, but also about effective avoidance behaviors in response to intrusion. That is, just as a spatial intrusion is an unwarranted nonverbal violation of intimacy, so the resulting avoidance responses are nonverbal indications of defensiveness in response to that intimacy. In addition, the nonverbal reactions of the intruded individual may effectively reduce the intimacy of the intruder. However, the manipulation of space in social settings has distinct consequences even when such extreme approaches are not involved.

Structured Interaction

The situations of structured interaction, unlike those of spatial invasion, are designed to involve direct interaction. Generally the research using this procedure either focuses on impressions and attitudes of the participants or on their behavioral reactions in differing arrangements. Usually one of the interactants is a confederate of the experimenter who is programmed to maintain a specific distance and demeanor relative to the subject. Increasing the proximity between individuals generally produces more favorable impressions of the target person. Kelly (1972) found support for this relationship in patients' judgments of photographs of therapy interactions at varying distances. Mehrabian (1968b) similarly found through the judgment of photographs that a greater interaction distance indicated a less positive attitude. In one live interaction, the addition of touch, in the form of guiding the subject to his chair as he entered the interview room, noticeably increased the effect of the confederate's initiative in self-disclosure of personal information. Those subjects who were in the self-disclosure and touch condition not only became more positive toward the confederate, but also spent more time in disclosure of information about themselves (Jourard & Friedman, 1970).

Increased proximity does not have unconditionally positive effects on impressions. Patterson and Sechrest (1970) found that ratings of a confederate on the dimensions of friendliness, extraversion, dominance, and aggression increased from 8 to 4 ft., but then decreased at a distance of 2 ft. However, there was some indication that the behavior of the confederates at the closest distance was not as consistent as that in the other conditions, which may have lead to their appearing less socially aggressive. The effect of varying interaction distances may be specific to different types of individuals. Schizophrenic patients have been found to be more attracted to an interviewer who remained distant, while alcoholic patients preferred the interviewer at a minimal separation (Boucher, 1972).

In a study examining the influence of interpersonal distance on persuasion, no effect of distance was found on the degree of liking toward the confederate (Albert & Dabbs, 1970). One particularly interesting pattern which did emerge from this study was the effect of distance on selectivity of attention by the subject. At both the close and far distances, greater attention was reportedly focused on the appearance of the confederate than at the moderate distance. Conversely, relatively more attention was directed toward the content of the confederate's message at the moderate distance than at the extremes. Similarly, in a study of the effect of distance on psychiatric interviews, a moderate separation was generally preferred over close and far ones by both patients and therapists (Lassen, 1973). The results of these two studies support Hall's contention that there are appropriate ranges for different types of interactions. Perhaps an unusual interaction distance precipitates closer scrutiny of the individual who controls the approach and thereby interferes with the attention necessary for optimal verbal communication.

The manipulation of interaction distance has more observable effects than the impression changes or facilitation of verbal interaction. Several studies have focused on the relationship between spatial behavior and a variety of other nonverbal social behaviors. For the most part, these studies may be interpreted within the framework of Argyle and Dean's (1965) equilibrium theory of social interaction. In that theory, Argyle and Dean proposed that there are approach and avoidance motives affecting social behavior, which are manifested nonverbally by the interactants. Throughout the course of an interaction, a balance is reached between these approach and avoidance forces to the mutual comfort of the individuals involved. When approach tendencies, precipitated by affiliative needs or by the necessity for feedback, balance the avoidance tendencies, due to various fears, the resulting equilibrium is identifiable in a number of behavioral dimensions. The degree of expressed intimacy between the interactants at the equilibrium or balance point is a function of interpersonal distance, eye contact, body orientation, smiling, and other related variables. Each of these behaviors contributes something to the total degree of expressed intimacy. However, once a comfortable level of intimacy has been reached, a substantial change in any one of the components requires a reciprocal or compensatory change in another component to maintain equilibrium. For example, if individuals should be forced by a particular arrangement to sit closer than they prefer, equilibrium may be possible only with a reduction in eye contact or in the directness of body orientation. The process of equilibrium can be likened to a hydraulic model in which the total pressure in a system, while remaining constant, can be differentially distributed. Thus, equilibrium theory makes directional predictions regarding behavioral changes for situations in which distance is manipulated.

The focus of the study of Argyle and Dean (1965) was the variation in eye contact as a function of altering interview distance between the subject and a confederate. As the distance between the pair increased from 2 to 6 to 10 ft., eye contact by the subject similarly increased. In addition to the reduction of eye contact with greater proximity, other signs of tension were observed at the closest distance. These included leaning backwards, looking down, scratching one's head, and shading the eyes. Conversely, at 10 ft., subjects apparently tried to compensate for the considerable separation by leaning forward. Several other studies have similarly found that the amount of eye contact increases as the distance between interactants increases (Goldberg, Kiesler, & Collins, 1969; Knight, Langmeyer, & Lundgren, 1973, Patterson, 1973a, 1977). Aiello (1972) in replicating Argyle and Dean's study, found the compensatory relationship between distance and eye contact for males, but not for females. The validity of the hypothesized relationship between eye contact and distance has been questioned on methodological grounds. Specifically, Stephenson and Rutter (1970) claimed that increased distance between interactants results in putting the observer at a greater distance from the subject whose gaze he is monitoring. By increasing observer distance, more minor deviations from eye contact are likely to be judged as eye contact. Thus Stephenson and Rutter argue that only the *judged* level of eye contact increases with distance. However, the evidence for this hypothesized observer error seems to be based on very contrived settings involving programmed directional gaze. There is good reason to believe that normal visual interaction is sufficiently distinct that observer judgments of eye contact can be made with little difficulty (Argyle, 1970; Exline, 1971). Consequently, it is not likely that observer error is responsible for the patterns of increased eye contact found over greater distances between interactants.[2]

Although eye contact may be the most fluid means of altering intimacy in response to variations in interaction distance, other behaviors may serve similar functions. For example, body orientations have been shown to be less directly confronting when interaction distances are smaller (Aiello & Jones, 1971; Felipe & Sommer, 1966; Patterson, 1977). Kleck (1970) has found that self-manipulative behaviors such as scratching or hand rubbing were more frequent at a distance of 4 ft. than at 10 ft. Kleck suggested that such behaviors may be the result of increased physiological arousal to closer approaches, which has been documented by others (McBride *et al.,* 1965). It might further be suggested that such self-manipulative behaviors are displacement activities which may lessen the intimacy in the situation by directing attention away from the other person. Other incidental data also serve to support the principle of behavioral compensation. In their study of the effect of distance on impression formation, Patterson and Sechrest (1970) observed that even practiced confederates tended to orient themselves less directly toward the subject and maintain less eye contact as they approached closer. A similar problem in standardizing the behavior of a confederate in close interactions has been found in a study of nonverbal cues as reinforcers in a projective test situation (Stewart & Patterson, 1973). The confederate in this particular study required a large number of practice trials before she could maintain the appropriate level of eye contact and degree of lean

---

[2] A more extensive discussion of this methodological issue involving eye contact and distance can be found in a recent paper (Patterson, 1975).

at the closest distance. Even though the confederate was aware of the manipulation, her own compensatory reactions were very difficult to modify.

The manipulation of space in structured interactions has provided a substantial amount of information about the role of space in social behavior. Consistent with the research indicating that increased attraction results in closer approaches, the manipulation of closer interactions generally produces more favorable impressions of others. Interactions occurring at moderate distances are generally favored by the participants and also serve to facilitate effective communication. In addition, the manipulation of distance percipitates relatively subtle, but important, behavioral changes in the interactions. Argyle and Dean's equilibrium theory, which relates a number of nonverbal social behaviors to one another, provides a framework for explaining and predicting these behavioral changes in response to varying interaction distances. A more detailed summary and evaluation of the research on this theory can be found in a recent review paper (Patterson, 1973b).

FUTURE PROSPECTS

The strategy in organizing this chapter has been essentially to provide a simple conceptual framework for presenting a relatively comprehensive view of the research on spatial behavior. Having attempted this, I would now like to chart a more precarious course in suggesting a few directions and issues for future research. First, I believe that the time has come to move beyond studies that simply focus on individual differences in the use of space, to investigations that try to identify the specific factors or processes responsible for those differences. A good example of this type of effort in identifying the intervening mechanisms responsible for different patterns of spatial behavior is Hall's suggestion of accounting for cultural differences in terms of differential use of sensory modalities. While this hypothesis has not been adequately tested yet, it is an important step in trying to explain the basis for cultural differences in the use of space.

Another general concern which deserves more attention in the future is to examine the use of space in terms of its functions. We know, for example, that, among other purposes, interpersonal space can be manipulated to communicate intimacy, to upset or threaten someone, or to achieve relative isolation or privacy. In order to understand better the influence of space in social situations, we should know what, if any, purpose is intended by the participants in differing arrangements. In addition we should try to assess how different interaction arrangements facilitate or inhibit various purposes of interactions. Sommer (1969, 1974) has noted that the physical constraints of many settings actually prohibit comfortable and meaningful interactions. Undoubtedly, there will be an accelerated concern in research to discover the interactive effects of social and environmental variables on social behavior.

A final issue which needs to be emphasized is that an understanding of the nonverbal processes in social interaction necessarily involves a multidimensional approach. Behaviors such as eye contact, body orientation, gestures, and others must be weighed with interpersonal distance in order to properly evaluate what is communicated nonverbally in an interaction. In general, it might be suggested that the spatial arrangement, in terms of distance and body orientation, is usually structured at the start of an interaction and thereby sets some limits for the expression of other behaviors. Over the course of the interaction the arrangement, particularly in seated interactions, is quite stable, and other behaviors such as eye contact, touching, gestures, or facial expressions serve to indicate momentary feedback or mood states. Discovering the manner in which these behaviors relate to one another and to the process of interaction in general will be a substantial goal for future research.

REFERENCES

Aiello, J. R. A test of equilibrium theory: Visual interaction in relation to orientation, distance and sex of interactants. *Psychonomic Science,* 1972, **27**, 335–336.

Aiello, J. R., & Jones, S. E. Field study of the proxemic behavior of young school children in three subcultural groups. *Journal of Personality and Social Psychology,* 1971, **19**, 351–356.

Albert, S., & Dabbs, J. M., Jr. Physical distance and persuasion. *Journal of Personality and Social Psychology,* 1970, **15**, 265–270.

Altman, I., & Haythorn, W. The ecology of isolated groups. *Behavioral Science,* 1967, **12**, 169–182.

Argyle, M. Eye-contact and distance: A reply to Stephenson and Rutter. *British Journal of Psychology,* 1970, **61**, 395–396.

Argyle, M., & Dean, J. Eye-contact, distance, and affiliation. *Sociometry,* 1965, **28**, 289–304.

Batchelor, J. D., & Goethals, G. R. Spatial arrangements in freely formed groups. *Sociometry,* 1972, **35**, 270–279.

Bauer, E. A. Personal space: A study of blacks and whites. *Sociometry,* 1973, **36**, 402–408.

Baxter, J. C. Interpersonal spacing in natural settings. *Sociometry,* 1970, **33**, 444–456.

Baxter, J. C., & Deanovich, B. F. Anxiety arousing effects of inappropriate crowding. *Journal of Consulting and Clinical Psychology,* 1970, **35**, 174–178.

Becker, F. D., & Mayo, C. Measurement effects in studying reactions to spatial invasions. Paper presented at the meeting of the Eastern Psychological Association, New York, April, 1970.

Boucher, M. L. Effect of seating distance on interpersonal attraction in an interview situation. *Journal of Consulting and Clinical Psychology,* 1972, **38**, 15–19.

Byrne, D. Attitudes and attraction. In L. Berkowitz (Ed.), *Advances in experimental social psychology* (Vol. 4). New York: Academic Press, 1969.

Byrne, D. *The attraction paradigm.* New York: Academic Press, 1971.

Byrne, D., Baskett, G. D., & Hodges, L. Behavioral indicators of interpersonal attraction. *Journal of Applied Social Psychology,* 1971, **1**, 137–149.

Byrne, D., Ervin, C. R., & Lamberth, J. Continuity between the experimental study of attraction and real-life computer dating. *Journal of Personality and Social Psychology,* 1970, **16**, 157–165.

Campbell, D. T., Kruskal, W. H., & Wallace, W. P. Seating aggregation as an index of attitude. *Sociometry,* 1966, **29**, 1–15.

Campbell, D. T., & Stanley, J. C. *Experimental and quasi-experimental designs for research.* Chicago: Rand McNally, 1966.

Cheyne, J. A., & Efran, M. G. The effect of spatial and interpersonal variables on the invasion of group controlled territories. *Sociometry,* 1972, **35**, 477–489.

Clore, G. Attraction and interpersonal behavior. Paper presented at the annual meeting of the Southwestern Psychological Association, Austin, 1969.

Cook, M. Experiments on orientation and proxemics. *Human Relations,* 1970, **23**, 61–76.

Daniell, R. J., & Lewis, P. Stability of eye contact and physical distance across a series of structured interviews. *Journal of Consulting and Clinical Psychology,* 1972, **39**, 172.

Desor, J. A. Toward a psychological theory of crowding. *Journal of Personality and Social Psychology,* 1972, **21**, 79–83.

Dosey, M. A., & Meisels, M. Personal space and self-protection. *Journal of Personality and Social Psychology,* 1969, **11**, 93–97.

Duke, M. P., & Nowicki, S. A new measure and social-learning model for interpersonal distance. *Journal of Experimental Research in Personality,* 1972, **6**, 119–132.

Efran, M. G., & Cheyne, J. A. Affective concomitants of the invasion of shared space: behavioral, physiological, and verbal indicators. *Journal of Personality and Social Psychology,* 1974, **29**, 219–226.

Exline, R. V. Visual interaction: The glances of power and preference. In J. K. Cole (Ed.), *Nebraska Symposium on Motivation* (Vol. 19). University of Nebraska Press, Lincoln: 1971.

Felipe, N. J., & Sommer, R. Invasion of personal space. *Social Problems,* 1966, **14**, 206–214.

Fisher, J. D., & Byrne, D. Too close for comfort: Sex differences in response to invasions of personal space. *Journal of Personality and Social Psychology,* 1975, **32**, 15–21.

Forston, R. F., & Larson, C. U. The dynamics of space: An experimental study in proxemic behavior among Latin Americans and North Americans. *Journal of Communication,* 1968, **18**, 109–116.

Frankel, A. S., & Barrett, J. Variations in personal space as a function of authoritarianism, self-esteem and racial characteristics of a stimulus situation. *Journal of Consulting and Clinical Psychology,* 1971, **37**, 95–98.

Freedman, J. T., Levy, A., Buchanan, R., & Price, J. Crowding and human aggressiveness. *Journal of Experimental Social Psychology,* 1972, **8**, 549–557.

Fry, A. M., & Willis, F. N. Invasion of personal space as a function of the age of the invader. *Psychological Record,* 1971, **21**, 385–389.

Garfinkel, H. Studies of the routine grounds of everyday activities. *Social Problems,* 1964, **11**, 225–250.

Goldberg, G. N., Kiesler, C. A., & Collins, B. E. Visual behavior and face-to-face distance during interaction. *Sociometry,* 1969, **32**, 43–53.

Haase, R. F., & Markey, M. J. A methodological note on the study of personal space. *Journal of Consulting and Clinical Psychology,* 1973, **40**, 122–125.

Hall, E. T. *Silent language.* New York: Doubleday, 1959.

Hall, E. T. A system for the notation of proxemic behavior. *American Anthropologist,* 1963, **65**, 1003–1026.

Hall, E. T. *The hidden dimension.* New York: Doubleday, 1966.

Hall, E. T. Proxemics. *Current Anthropology,* 1968, **9**, 83–108.

Hartnett, J. J., Bailey, K. G., & Gibson, F. W., Jr. Personal space as influenced by sex and type of movement. *Journal of Psychology,* 1970, **76**, 139–144.

Hediger, H. P. The evolution of territorial behavior. In S. L. Washburn (Ed.), *Social life of early man.* Chicago: Aldine Press, 1961.

Heshka, S., & Nelson, Y. Interpersonal speaking distance as a function of age, sex, & relationship. *Sociometry,* 1972, **35**, 491–498.

Horowitz, M. J., Duff, D. F., & Stratton, L. O. Body-buffer zone. *Archives of General Psychiatry,* 1964, **11**, 651–656.

Jones, S. E. A comparative proxemics analysis of dyadic interaction in selected subcultures of New York City. *Journal of Social Psychology,* 1971, **84**, 35–44.

Jones, S. E., & Aiello, J. R. Proxemic behavior of black and white first-, third-, and fifth-grade children. *Journal of Personality and Social Psychology,* 1973, **25**, 21–27.

Jourard, S. M., & Friedman, R. Experimenter-subject "distance" and self-disclosure. *Journal of Personality and Social Psychology,* 1970, **15**, 278–282.

Karabenick, S. A., & Meisels, M. Effects of performance on evaluation on interpersonal distance. *Journal of Personality,* 1972, **40**, 275–286.

Kelly, F. D. Communicational significance of therapist proxemic cues. *Journal of Consulting and Clinical Psychology,* 1972, **39**, 345.

Kinzel, A. Body-buffer zone in violent prisoners. *American Journal of Psychiatry,* 1970, **127**, 59–64.

Kleck, R. E. Interaction distance and non-verbal agreeing responses. *British Journal of Social and Clinical Psychology,* 1970, **9**, 180–182.

Knight, D. J., Langmeyer, D., & Lundgren, D. C. Eye-contact, distance, and affiliation: The role of observer bias. *Sociometry,* 1973, **36**, 390–401.

Knowles, E. S. Boundaries around social space: Dyadic responses to an invader. *Environment and Behavior,* 1972, **4**, 437–445.

Knowles, E. S. Boundaries around group interaction: The effect of size and status. *Journal of Personality and Social Psychology,* 1973, **26**, 327–331.

Knowles, E. S., & Johnsen, P. K. Intrapersonal consistency in interpersonal distance. Paper presented at the Eastern Psychological Association meeting, Philadelphia, 1974.

Kuethe, J. L. Social schemas. *Journal of Abnormal and Social Psychology,* 1962, **64**, 31–38.

Lassen, C. L. Effect of proximity on anxiety and communication in the initial psychiatric interview. *Journal of Abnormal Psychology,* 1973, **81**, 226–232.

Little, K. B. Personal space. *Journal of Experimental Social Psychology,* 1965, **1**, 237–247.

Little, K. B. Cultural variations in social schemata. *Journal of Personality and Social Psychology,* 1968, **10**, 1–7.

Lott, D. F., & Sommer, R. Seating arrangement and status. *Journal of Personality and Social Psychology,* 1967, **7**, 90–95.

Marshall, J. E., & Heslin, R. Boys and girls together: Sexual composition and effect of density and group size on cohesiveness. *Journal of Personality & Social Psychology,* 1975, **31**, 952–961.

McBride, G., King, M. C., & James, J. W. Social proximity effects of galvanic skin responses in adult humans. *Journal of Psychology,* 1965, **61**, 153–157.

Mehrabian, A. Relationship of attitude to seated posture, orientation, and distance. *Journal of Personality and Social Psychology,* 1968, **10**, 26–30. (a)

Mehrabian, A. Inference of attitudes from the posture, orientation, and distance of a communicator. *Journal of Consulting and Clinical Psychology,* 1968, **32**, 296–308. (b)

Mehrabian, A., & Diamond, S. G. Seating arrangement and conversation. *Sociometry,* 1971, **34**, 281–289.

Mehrabian, A., & Friar, J. T. Encoding of attitude by a seated communicator via posture and position cues. *Journal of Consulting and Clinical Psychology,* 1969, **33**, 330–336.

Mehrabian, A., & Ksionzky, S. Some determiners of social interaction. *Sociometry*, 1972, **35**, 588–609.

Meisels, M., & Canter, F. M. Personal space and personaltiy characteristics: A non-confirmation. *Psychological Reports*, 1970, **27**, 287–290.

Newman, R. C., & Pollack, D. Proxemics in deviant adolescents. *Journal of Consulting and Clinical Psychology*, 1973, **40**, 6–8.

Patterson, M. L. Spatial factors in social interactions. *Human Relations*, 1968, **21**, 351–361.

Patterson, M. L. Stability of nonverbal immediacy behaviors. *Journal of Experimental Social Psychology*, 1973, **9**, 97–109. (a)

Patterson, M. L. Compensation in nonverbal immediacy behaviors: A review. *Sociometry*, 1973, **36**, 237–252. (b)

Patterson, M. L. Eye contact and distance: A re-examination of measurement problems. *Personality and Social Psychology Bulletin*, 1975, **1**, 600–603.

Patterson, M. L. Interpersonal distance, affect, and equilibrium theory. *Journal of Social Psychology*, 1977, **101**, 205–214.

Patterson, M. L., & Holmes, D. S. Social interaction correlates of the MPI extraversion–introversion scale. Paper presented at the annual meeting of the American Psychological Association, New York, 1966.

Patterson, M. L., Mullens, S., & Romano, J. Compensatory reactions to spatial intrusion. *Sociometry*, 1971, **34**, 114–126.

Patterson, M. L., & Schaeffer, R. E. Effects of size and sex composition on interaction distance, participation, and satisfaction in small groups. Paper presented at the annual meeting of the Rocky Mountain Psychological Association, Salt Lake City, May 1975.

Patterson, M. L., & Sechrest, L. B. Interpersonal distance and impression formation. *Journal of Personality*, 1970, **38**, 161–166.

Patterson, M. L., & Strauss, M. E. An examination of the discriminant validity of the social-avoidance and distress scale. *Journal of Consulting and Clinical Psychology*, 1972, **39**, 169.

Pedersen, D. M. Relations among sensation seeking and simulated and behavioral personal space. *Journal of Psychology*, 1973, **83**, 79–88. (a)

Pedersen, D. M. Correlates of behavioral personal space. *Psychological Reports*, 1973, **32**, 828–830. (b)

Pellegrini, R. J., & Empey, J. Interpersonal spatial orientation in dyads. *Journal of Psychology*, 1970, **76**, 67–70.

Rosenfeld, H. M. Effect of an approval-seeking induction in interpersonal proximity. *Psychological Reports*, 1965, **17**, 120–122.

Ross, M., Layton, B., Erickson, B., & Schopler, J. Affect, facial regard, and reactions to crowding. *Journal of Personality and Social Psychology*, 1973, **28**, 69–76.

Sewell, A. F., & Heisler, J. T. Personality correlates of proximity preferences. *Journal of Psychology*, 1973, **85**, 151–155.

Sommer, R. Studies in personal space. *Sociometry*, 1959, **22**, 247–260.

Sommer, R. Further studies in small group ecology. *Sociometry*, 1965, **28**, 337–348.

Sommer, R. *Personal space: The behavioral basis of design*. Englewood Cliffs, New Jersey: Prentice-Hall, 1969.

Sommer, R. *Tight spaces: Hard architecture and how to humanize it*. Englewood Cliffs, New Jersey: Prentice-Hall, 1974.

Sommer, R., & Becker, F. Territorial defense and the good neighbor. *Journal of Personality and Social Psychology*, 1969, **11**, 85–92.

Stein, D. D., Hardyck, J. A., & Smith, M. B. Race and belief: An open and shut case. *Journal of Personality and Social Psychology*, 1965, **1**, 281–289.

Stephenson, G. M., & Rutter, D. R. Eye-contact, distance and affiliation: A re-evaluation. *British Journal of Psychology*, 1970, **61**, 385–393.

Stewart, D., & Patterson, M. L. Eliciting effects of verbal and nonverbal cues on projective test responses. *Journal of Consulting and Clinical Psychology*, 1973, **41**, 74–77.

Stokols, D., Rall, M., Pinner, B., & Schopler, J. Physical, social and personal determinants of the perception of crowding. *Environment and Behavior* 1973, **5**, 87–115.

Stratton, L. O., Tekippl, D. J., & Flick, G. L. Personal space and self-concept. *Sociometry*, 1973, **36**, 424–429.

Watson, M. O., & Graves, T. D. Quantitative research in proxemic behavior. *American Anthropologist*, 1966, **68**, 971–985.

Webb, E. J., Campbell, D. T., Schwartz, R. D., & Sechrest, L. *Unobtrusive measures: Nonreactive research in the social sciences.* Chicago: Rand McNally, 1966.

Williams, J. L. Personal space and its relation to extraversion–introversion. *Canadian Journal of Behavioral Sciences*, 1971, **3**, 156–160.

Willis, F. N. Initial speaking distance as a function of the speakers' relationship. *Psychonomic Science*, 1966. **5**, 221–222.

10

Conversational Control Functions of Nonverbal Behavior

Howard M. Rosenfeld

The University of Kansas

INTRODUCTION

The scientific study of human social interaction recently has undergone dramatic changes. Interpersonal behavior, like other natural phenomena, is being analyzed in ever-increasing detail. Just as the invention of the microscope permitted the identification of intricate physical processes, the recent development of sophisticated apparatus for the recording and analysis of social behavior has enabled the exploration of previously undetected interpersonal processes. While the behaviors involved in social interaction must be perceived at some level by the persons who are affected by them, they often are too complex in structure and too rapid in occurrence to be adequately recorded through direct observation. However, through detailed analysis of audio-visual records and with the aid of high-speed computers, the structures and functions of many fleeting interpersonal events now can be analyzed objectively and efficiently. Although such explorations still are in an early stage, some consensual discoveries are beginning to emerge. Thus, this is an opportune time to pull together some of the results of research, evaluate its progress and suggest promising directions for future study.

Participants in social interaction must manage a wide variety of interpersonal tasks (Goffman, 1967). In larger social assemblies, persons who wish to converse with each other give signals of orientation by which to initiate a focused relationship (Kendon, 1970). Once oriented, the participants typically must go through certain phases such as the semiritualistic exchange of greetings, which may determine the possibilities of further phases (Kendon & Ferber, 1973, Schegloff, 1968), the conduct of the major items of business that constitute the main body of the interaction (Bales, 1955), and an exchange of farewells, which permits them to terminate the encounter to their mutual satisfaction (Knapp,

291

Hart, Friedrich, & Shulman, 1973; Schegloff & Sacks, 1973). Particularly throughout the more central phases of interaction, the participants are faced with the persistent problem of how to facilitate the virtually continuous flow of information.

The successful conversant must be skillful in the management of all of these requirements. Thus, a comprehensive theory of social interaction ultimately must integrate the diverse findings that are being generated, rather piecemeal, by research on the various subproblems. There also is a need for more thorough understanding of circumscribed aspects of the total conversational process. In this chapter we focus our attention on the fundamental problem of how conversants use nonverbal behavior to regulate the flow of information throughout the main body of their interaction. We will refer to this particular usage of nonverbal behavior as its "conversational control function". First, we outline a perspective that is intended to incorporate current conceptions of the process. In subsequent sections we review and evaluate research that bears upon the perspective.

A PERSPECTIVE ON
CONVERSATIONAL CONTROL PROCESSES

We are particularly concerned with face-to-face interactions of pairs of persons in which a major purpose of the participants is to exchange information that is encoded primarily through spoken language, and in which both participants are relatively free to select their means of accomplishing this task. Perhaps the most common variety of such interactions is the problem-oriented discussion. More constricted forms are structured interviews and psychotherapy sessions. Activities excluded by this emphasis are highly ritualistic or ceremonial exchanges in which reactions are preprogrammed, and occasions in which a person is concerned only with showing off in the presence of an audience and not with their reaction to his particular behaviors. Emotional aspects of communication (Dittmann, 1972b), while they may be informative, are dealt with only tangentially in our analysis.

No precise method has been devised for categorizing and quantifying the information exchanged throughout natural conversations. Yet it is commonly assumed that conversational behavior does consist of units of information that are at least informally or indirectly definable. We colloquially refer to such units as "ideas," "facts," and "opinions," and we assume that the flow of "new" information in an interaction sequence is at least grossly detectable. Even though we may not yet be able to confidently quantify the rates at which information is exchanged in conversations, recent research indicates that we now are able to identify reliably behavioral units into which information is organized by participants.

Our basic proposition is that conversations can productively be viewed as orderly structures of informational units. The orderly structure itself is the result of a collaborative exchange of signals by the participants that function to regulate the flow of informational units. While the presentation of complex information in human interactions is most efficiently carried out via the verbal–linguistic channel (speech), we will argue that the orderly flow of verbal information is influenced in large part by simpler signals carried in the nonverbal channels. Of particular importance in this control process are the vocal and kinesic channels, which refer to nonlinguistic properties of vocal behavior and to observable bodily activities, respectively.

Our emphasis on nonverbal behavior is not meant to imply that a substantial amount of control is not also carried out by verbal–linguistic behavior. Spoken language is clearly better suited for the provision of complex, differentiated commentaries upon specific items of information and thus for the control of the content of subsequent informational units. Psycholinguists, sociolinguists, and social psychologists, among others, are making progress toward the analysis of the ways in which conversants process information. However, they have not reached consensus on ways of determining the content and quantity of information transmitted in natural conversations. In addition, their work has proceeded substantially in isolation from research on nonverbal aspects of communication. Ultimately, this artificial separation of the communication process will have to be integrated.

The tendency for conversations to be structured into orderly sequences of units can be attributed primarily to the widely recognized necessity for conversants to alternate in speaking turns if they are to understand each other. It is difficult, if not impossible, for a pair of persons to exchange complex information if they are both talking at the same time. Somehow they must manage to coordinate complementary roles, analogous to the need for pedestrians or drivers approaching each other from opposite directions on a narrow road to avoid a collision (cf. Goffman, cited in Duncan, 1972). Specifically, they must assume reciprocal roles for periods of time, during which one participant is primarily the conveyor of verbal information and the other primarily the receiver.

To understand how the above role-complementarity is accomplished throughout conversation, it is necessary to detect the exchange of two kinds of control signals. We must recognize the signals that indicate when it is appropriate and those that indicate when it is inappropriate for the participants to switch speaker–listener roles. These two kinds of controlling signals do not occur at random in the conversational process, for they are intimately connected to the process of information exchange. They occur primarily at the ends of coherent units of verbal information. At the junctures terminating these units, the speaker typically seeks some indication of his success in conveying information. The reaction sought from the listener may be simply a brief signal of attention, or perhaps a further indication of whether or not the listener has understood the message or agrees with it. Or a more elaborate reaction may be called for, in which case the listener and speaker may have to signal an impending switch in speaker–listener roles.

Certain nonverbal cues at natural junctures in speech are important components of the responses that indicate whether speaker–listener roles should continue versus whether they should switch, and whether or not the listener is satisfied with the prior utterance of the speaker. The nonverbal cues can occur singly or in combinations, and with or without verbal accompaniment. Some different-appearing cues are functionally equivalent or substitutable, while some similar-appearing cues serve separate functions.

Although our focus will be upon nonverbal processes that control the orderly flow of information in conversations, we know that not all conversations proceed smoothly. One reason is that participants do not always agree about when speaker–listener roles should shift. Thus, they may give conflicting signals or they may even choose to ignore clear signals. Another possible reason is that the participants fail to interpret each other's signals in the same way. The latter may be the result of mental retardation or deficient socialization experiences. It may also occur when the participants are normal members of different cultural groups, each of which has its own signaling system.

If participants are from different linguistic communities, it is obvious that they will have difficulties understanding messages transmitted by the verbal–linguistic channel. But what is the likelihood of comparable difficulties in the exchange of nonverbal controlling signals? We review a body of evidence that indicates there should be considerable commonality in the performance of nonverbal controlling signals across linguistic communities. This commonality should result from the involvement of certain physiological mechanisms in speech processing. Even though there is increasing evidence that virtually any physical response may be modifiable through experience with the environment (Miller, 1969), the occurrence of common innate dispositions in humans may function to limit variability in the actual distribution of controlling cues across social groups.

SEGMENTATION AND CLASSIFICATION
OF CONVERSATIONAL BEHAVIOR

The analysis of conversational control functions of nonverbal behavior requires that conversations be segmented into certain classes of units. First the flow of verbal–linguistic behavior must be divided into successive periods in which one subject is considered to be in the speaker role and the other subject simultaneously in the listener role. Within each of these complementary role periods, the utterances of the speaker must be subdivided into informational units. The informational units, in turn, must be classified into those whose endings indicate that the participants should shift speaker–listener roles, and those that indicate that the present role-relationship should continue. Listener signals at the ends of the speaker's informational units also must be classified into those that indicate a desire to maintain versus switch roles, as well as those that indicate satisfaction or dissatisfaction with the preceding speech unit.

Units of Complementary Verbal Participation

We have noted that there is consensus that participants in a conversation must segment their time into complementary speaker–listener roles. This may appear at first glance to be a simple distinction to make. However, there is much disagreement about what constitutes a speaking turn. Definitions and procedures for determining turns have ranged from dependence upon simple physical criteria to complex judgmental criteria. Part of the problem appears to be that as one approaches a more intuitively meaningful definition, the efficiency and reliability of its implementation decreases. The ideal definition would be both reliable and comprehensive. Inasmuch as consensual decisions about how to define speaker-listener periods are critical to progress in the understanding of conversational control functions, we will now review different approaches in some detail.

In the most objective approach (Feldstein, 1972; Jaffe & Feldstein, 1970), speaking turns are defined on the basis of the automated measurement of who is vocalizing, beyond a specified threshold of intensity, at each moment in time. It should be noted that the vocalizations of the participants are recorded in situations in which vocal responses can reasonably be assumed to be primarily linguistic, in contrast to humming, grunting, and the like. Also the threshold of intensity for each speaker's voice is set at a level at which the voice is intelligible to a normal listener. Speaker–listener roles are determined with the aid of a computer that assesses whether or not each participant is vocalizing in each successive, brief time interval (for example, .3 sec.).

In this automated method of analysis, a person may be considered to maintain the speaker role until the other person becomes the sole vocalizer. Thus, occasional occurrences of simultaneous speaking, and more common occurrences of simultaneous silence, would be considered part of the turn of the preceding sole speaker. We will have relatively little to say in this chapter about the interesting processes by which "contests" for gaining or rejecting the speaker role occur and are resolved. Rather, we will emphasize the processes by which smooth turn-taking is accomplished. However, it should be noted that automated measures of relative intensity of vocalization of participants during periods in which simultaneous speech occurs have been utilized to determine how the outcome is resolved (Morris, 1971). It also should be noted that periods of rapid alternation of vocalization between speakers might be considered to constitute contests for the floor. In such a case, a switch in speaker–listener roles might not be considered to occur until the computer detects that a certain minimal duration of speech occurs by the prior listener only.

Verbal Responses of Listeners

A more significant problem in the determination of speaker–listener periods concerns the classification of brief verbal responses by the listener following an informational unit by the speaker. By the automated criterion we have just discussed, the brief verbalization would be considered a shift in the speaker–listener role. However, other investigators hold that certain minimally informative verbal and vocal responses should be considered as continuations of the listener role. From this latter perspective, the brief utterances by listeners are interpreted as methods by which they help maintain the speaker in his role. A familiar example is the "mm-hmm," which commonly is considered functionally equivalent to the silent head nod as a signal not to change speaker–listener roles.

The differentiation of verbal responses into those that constitute speaker responses and those that constitute listener responses presents some serious problems for reliability of measurement. Still, it has considerable intuitive appeal. Yngve (1970) has proposed that a participant in a conversation "holds the floor" as long as he maintains primary responsibility for presenting a body of information. During this period the listener may occasionally engage in "back-channel" verbalizations that function to aid the floor-holder in the communication of his position. However, we have argued that satisfactory measures of the content of information in conversation have not been devised. Thus, how can we determine the conditions under which a verbal response should be defined, paradoxically, as a listener response?

Researchers have varied in criteria for identifying verbal listener responses. The most common basis is the judgment by the coder that the content of the verbal response indicates that the responder wishes to remain in a listener role. Many simple verbalizations are assumed to indicate that the responder is simply attending to the speaker or acknowledging the occurrence of the speaker's prior utterance (Rosenfeld, 1966a; Snyder, 1945). The most notorious examples are the "mm-hmm", or "uh-huh." These "vocal identifiers" (Pittenger & Smith, 1957) have been viewed linguistically as members of a larger class of common nonlexical "vocal segregates" (Bateson: see Trager, 1958, p. 6.). Attentional functions also have been attributed to brief lexical terms such as "yeah" and "I see."

Some researchers have proposed that certain more evaluative or informative messages also should be categorized as listener responses. For example, Kendon (1967) gave the examples of "mm yes" and "that's true" as point granting or assenting signals by listeners, and contrasted them with the simple attentional usage of "mm-hmm." However, his tentative classification scheme also took into account the degree to which the prior speaker appeared to be trying to elicit assent by the listener. Thus, it is not clear whether or not the form of the verbal listener response is in itself a sufficient basis for making the distinction, or if further verbal context is necessary. In addition, the intonational qualities of such responses may or may not confirm their substantive implications.

Another argument for the inclusion of brief verbal responses within the listener role is that their brevity itself excludes them from consideration as substantive informational units. Research on the temporal properties of speech indicates that informative utterances of greater complexity require more time for preparation and production (Goldman-Eisler, 1968). On the basis of such evidence, Kendon (1967) included among listener responses speech that lasted less than an arbitrary minimum of 5 sec. While the wisdom of selecting this particular length may be argued, length of utterance, in contrast to judged meaning of utterance, does have the current advantage of being assessable with high reliability.

One additional set of criteria that should be considered in determining whether a verbal response should be categorized as speaker or listener behavior is the kinesic accompaniments of the utterance. In general, speakers avert gaze more than do listeners in dyadic interaction (Exline, 1963; Nielsen, 1962). In particular it has been found that more complex utterances, which supposedly require both more concentration for their formulation and absence of interruption for their performance, tend to be initiated with orientation of the speaker's eyes away from the listener (Day, 1964; Duke, 1968; Kendon, 1967). Conversely most brief vocal–verbal responses, including attention signals, laughs, short questions, and exclamations, were observed by Kendon to be accompanied by gaze directed toward the other person. (Exceptions were verbal assenting signals, which typically were accompanied by a brief dropping of the eyelids, thereby interrupting gaze, and negative exclamations.) Furthermore, the initiation of more complex units of speech tends to be accompanied by gesticulatory activity (Dittmann & Llewellyn, 1969). In contrast, gestural activity rarely occurs as an accompaniment of brief listener verbalizations (Gunnell & Rosenfeld, 1971). Rosenfeld and Hancks (in preparation), as part of an ongoing study to be described more fully later, compared the nonverbal accompaniments of brief listener verbalizations with the nonverbal concomitants of the first two words of the speaker's next utterance. The relative frequencies of speech-related nonverbal signals of listeners and speakers obtained from 250 such comparisons representing 20 independent conversational dyads were as follows: movements of the head away from the other person, 5/25; movements of the eyes away from the other person, 22/104; initiations of gesticulations of the hand or arm, 2/14. In contrast, the comparable frequencies for head nodding were 188/6. Thus, longer utterances initiated with gaze avoidance and gesticulation are especially indicative of the speaker role.

The use of length of utterance and kinesic concomitants as criteria for defining listener verbalizations may not be applicable if complex utterances are included within the definition of listener responses. Rosenfeld and Hancks found that only 6% of listener responses that were composed of simple segmentals or simple lexical items were accompanied by shifts in gaze away from the speaker, whereas 25% of listener responses consisting of multiple lexical items (for example, "that's very very true") were associated with gazes away. Duncan and Niederehe (1974) have reported some difficulty in distinguishing between speaker and listener responses when applying the broad conception of listener behavior suggested by Yngve, which includes asking questions, making comments, and filling in information initiated by the speaker.

In the present writer's view, progress in understanding conversational control processes requires greater attention to the reliability of definitions of verbal listener responses. It is necessary to give as complete a specification of defining criteria as possible. These might profitably include audio or visual tape-recorded examples that serve as models of subtle paralinguistic and kinesic qualifications of content. Of course, the ultimate criterion for validating a verbal act as a listener response should be evidence of its role in the process of conversational control. This will be considered in a later section, along with nonverbal aspects of listener behavior.

INFORMATIONAL UNITS WITHIN SPEAKER ROLES

Now that we have a general idea about how conversations can be segmented into complementary speaker–listener periods, we can turn our attention to the task of subdividing those periods into informational units of speech. Recall the conception of the conversational process as organized to facilitate the flow of such units. It was proposed that nonverbal control processes will be activated primarily around the junctures that separate the units. At such junctures the participants should transmit nonverbal information that indicates whether they should switch or maintain speaker–listener roles, as well as what general form of informational content is needed in subsequent utterances. We now face the problem of deciding what criteria should be used for segmenting speaker periods into informational units. Once again, we review some of the major options that have been proposed.

Semantic and Quantitative Analysis of Information

Ideally, we would like to describe conversational units in terms of the substantive information they convey. In particular it would be advantageous to determine how much of a total body of information to be transmitted from one participant to another actually is conveyed in each unit. From the formal perspective of information theory, this decision depends upon both the message sent (encoded) by the speaker and its reception (decoding) by the listener. The communication engineer has a precise definition of the transmission of information. The basic unit *H,* refers to the receiver's uncertainty about a message prior to its successful transmission by the sender (Shannon & Weaver, 1949). Unfortunately, we do not know how to apply the measure of information to the flow of natural conversational behavior. To do so would require prior knowledge of what the participants initially do and do not know about a topic, how they encode their informational repertoires into measurable units of speech, and the degree to which their knowledge is affected by each other's utterances (Haas & Wepman, 1972; MacKay, 1972).

It is possible to track *roughly* the flow of information in conversations by artificially controlling the ideational input available to participants, assessing its subsequent verbal performance, and testing for its acquisition following the interaction (Rosenfeld & Sullwold, 1969). However, the validity of inferences about the amount of information that is transmitted during the conversation is limited by the possibility of covert, higher level integration by the participants of the discrete units of informational input.

More precise records of informational flow can be obtained through restricting conversations by means of structured "referential communication" tasks (Glucksberg, Krauss, & Higgins, 1975; Rosenberg, 1972). Such paradigms allow one to keep better track of informational production of speakers and its effects upon listeners by placing rather severe constraints upon not only the contents available for discussion, but also upon the occasions for performing them. Within the restricted range of response opportunities available to participants, this research has indicated that lack of comprehension by listeners affects the subsequent informational output by speakers. For example, experimentally induced noncomprehension by listeners has resulted in substantive descriptions by speakers that were more slowly spoken, lengthier, and more redundant (Longhurst & Siegel, 1973). While such research procedures seldom have been employed for detecting the effects of nonverbal signals upon the flow of information in conversations, they might productively be adapted for that purpose.

Using transcriptions of speech in unconstrained conversations, various efforts have been made to define information on the basis of the linguistic content. For example, the "type–token" ratio–the number of different kinds of words divided by the total number of words spoken over a specified sample of speech–has been widely applied as a general index of amount of information or nonredundancy. Distinctions between the contents of words, individually as well as in phrases and sentences, within a corpus of speech have been used for differentiating classes and amounts of information by means of automated computer analysis (Stone, Dunphy, Smith, & Ogilvie, 1966; Psathas, 1969). More subjective definitions have been used in the designation of subtle variations in informational content, such as changes in ideas (Horowitz & Newman, 1964) or topic (Ervin-Tripp, 1969), the occurrence of subordinate "side sequence" phases of conversation (Jefferson, 1972), as well as more elaborate listings of varieties of substantive units (Pace & Boren, 1973). Different scoring systems have been designed for application to different structures or purposes of conversation, such as interviews (Hawes, 1972), psychotherapy (Snyder, 1945), and conferences (Bales, 1955).

Particularly promising have been recent efforts to incorporate the larger conversational context and the task requirements of participants in the interpretation of messages (Carswell & Rommetveit, 1971; Glucksberg, Trabasso, & Wald, 1973), and to compare sequences of syntactic utterances on the basis of their fundamental ideational correspondences (Schank, 1972). Some common forms of sequential relations between the contents of utterances of alternating speakers in conversation have been identified, such as question–answer sequences, elliptical references to prior utterances, and extensions of the other person's utterance (Speier, 1972). However, at this time it seems safe to conclude that less progress has been made in semantic bases for constructing conversational units than in grammatical approaches.

Syntax and Pausing

A problem with all of the above semantically based measures of information when applied to natural conversations is that they provide no valid basis for segmenting a speaker's behavior into functional communicative units. There is increasing evidence that minimally meaningful units of conversational information are structured in units larger than single words (Goldman-Eisler, 1972), but determination of the appropriate size of unit remains a problem. Definitions of minimal units of utterance commonly have been based upon the criteria of grammatical completion and subsequent pausing (Davis, 1937, p. 44). However, a minimal functional requisite for validating a definition of a unit* of spoken information in conversation should be that noticeable changes in listener behavior typically occur near the boundaries of the units. Both grammatical phrase endings and pauses contribute to the predictability of speaker switching (see Jaffe & Feldstein, 1970, pp. 49–50). Yet, these measures are insufficient for defining a conversational speech unit. Kendon (1967) reported that only 49% of verbal "accompaniment" signals by listeners occurred at "phrase boundary pauses", leaving 51% unaccounted for. Similar results were presented in a case study by Yngve (1970). While the occurrence of grammatical junctures, especially when followed by pauses, is a better predictor of listener reactions than are nonjunctural locations or hesitation pauses within phrases, none of these appears to be an adequate basis for unitization of conversation.

The Phonemic Clause

A promising minimal unit is the "phonemic clause," a rhythmic segment of speech consisting of short strings of words, identified by a single primary stress which is followed by a slowing or stretching of speech (Boomer, Chapter 8;

Dittmann & Llewellyn, 1967; Trager, 1962; Trager & Smith, 1951). The stressed word typically is the highest "information" word, in contrast to "function" words which serve to hold the information words together. Listener responses rarely occur at locations other than the junctures that separate phonemic clauses. The association between junctures and such listener responses as "mm-hmm's" and head nods has been statistically significant in virtually every individual conversation in which it has been tested.

Phonemic clauses that terminate with a rising or falling pitch change—called "final" junctures (Dittmann, 1972a)—regularly precede verbal and nonverbal listener responses (Dittmann & Llewellyn, 1967, 1968). Compared to sustained-pitch junctures, final junctures increased the predictability of brief verbal listener responses by 21% in the 1967 verbal interaction study. Postjunctural pauses accounted for 18% of the listener responses, but when juncture type was held constant, the juncture pauses were found to contribute only an additional 10% to the predictability of the verbal listener responses. Final junctures terminated half of the phonemic clauses scored in the 1968 face-to-face inter-action study. With an average of five words per clause such junctures should have occurred an average of once every 10 words in their data.

Most smooth speaker switches also occur in the junctures that follow pho-nemic clauses (Duncan, 1972, 1973). Duncan included some sustained as well as final junctures in his predictive units, but only when the sustained junctures were accompanied by such additional cues as head turning toward the listener, termination of movement or relaxation of the hand, unfilled pause, drawl, and drops in pitch or loudness. Of the 2,481 phonemic clauses he scored, 885 (36%) met his criteria for predictive units. With an average length of 2.8 clauses, we would estimate his selected speech units to average about 14 words in length. Although the junctures that separate phonemic clauses are not sufficient for the prediction of major listener responses in free conversations, they do appear to be virtually necessary. Thus, the phonemic clause meets a major requisite for a minimal information unit, even though its definition does not identify the amount or content of information contained in the unit. It is apparent that phonemic clauses are related to semantic and syntactic properties of conversa-tional speech, but the precise nature of the relationship is not yet clear.

Kinesic Concomitants

We mentioned earlier that common nonverbal orientational and gesticulatory behaviors can aid in discriminating between speaker and listener verbal re-sponses. Similarly, gaze avoidance and gesticulation constitute criteria for iden-tifying the initiation of separate speaking units *within* a speaking turn.

On the basis of preliminary observations of normal speakers of American English, Birdwhistell (1970, pp. 110–143) has proposed that kinesic activities serve to demarcate, distinguish between, and interrelate grammatical and seman-tic units of speech ranging from sublexical components to strings of sentences.

Units comparable to phonemic clauses, which we have found to meet the functional requisites of minimal communicative units, were observed by Birdwhistell to be regularly accompanied by kinesic stress and juncture markers involving the head, eyes, hands, and feet of the speaker.

Observations of sound films of conversations between psychotherapists and their clients led Scheflen (1964) to emphasize higher order units. The "point," which may be roughly defined as a coordinated set of phonemic clauses that correspond to colloquial notions of "making a point," was characterized by persistent head and eye activities. Different individuals were found to utilize small and sometimes idiosyncratic kinesic repertoires, but with variations within the repertoires demarcating adjacent points. Examples of activities associated with points were the tilting, turning, cocking, and extension of the head. Some correspondence also was noted between the nonverbal characteristics of a point and the substantive content of its verbal component. The next higher level, the "position," comprising a sequence of points, was marked by a gross shift in posture, and typically lasted from .5 to 6 min. Finally, the "presentation" consisted in all positions of a speaker in a continuous discourse and was marked by a complete change in location.

Kendon (1972; 1973) performed a comprehensive microanalytic analysis of speech rhythms and body movement on a sound film of a 1.5-min segment of informal conversation in a group setting. He identified a five-level hierarchy of intonationally defined speech units (see Crystal, 1969) which appeared to correspond to levels of substantive complexity. The units, in ascending order of size, are the "prosodic phrase" (compare the phonemic clause), the "locution" (similar to the written sentence), the "locution group," the "locution cluster" (similar to the written paragraph), and finally the entire "discourse" or total verbal participation of the speaker. Speech units both within and between levels were differentiated by kinesic activities.

Larger movements, involving more body parts, were associated with more comprehensive verbal structures. Smaller and more rapidly changing movements accompanied the simpler, faster changing levels. In the example described by Kendon, movements of the face (eyes, brows, mouth) occurred at higher rates than did head movement; the wrists and fingers moved more frequently than did the forearms; and the forearms more than the upper arms. Distinctive movements characterizing each phrase appeared to be predominantly organized—that is, to "peak"—around the major stressed syllable, which we previously noted is typically located in the highest information word of a phonemic clause. Each speech unit was preceded by a form of nonverbal "speech preparatory" activity (cf. Dittmann & Llewellyn, 1969), and the latency of speech following the preparatory movements increased with the comprehensiveness of the unit. Within a level of speech complexity, similar body parts were employed across units, but with distinctive patterns per unit.

If these limited but promising observations prove to be characteristic of conversations in general, they should lead to a much more elaborated and exact system for the segmentation of informational units of speech than currently is available. From the present perspective, it is particularly important to determine the ways in which the different kinds of speaker units affect the responses of listeners.

NONVERBAL LISTENER RESPONSES

We have defined the role of listener as the total period of time during which the other person is the dominant speaker. If there are no periods of role-indeterminacy or floor-negotiation, then the listener period is bounded by the listener's own speaker roles. At the verbal level, the listening period is characterized primarily by substantive verbalizations of the speaker and silence by the listener, with possible segments of silence by the speaker and brief verbalization by the listener. We already have discussed vocal and verbal aspects of listener responses. Throughout the listening period the listener can engage in a wide range of kinesic responses that are capable of serving conversational control functions. Junctures between phonemic clauses of speakers are particularly critical occasions for the performance of major listener reactions.

Just as the speaker provides responses that can be conceptually separated into information-encoding and listener-controlling functions, so too might the listener provide both decoding cues and speaker-controlling cues. On the basis of the observation that movements of listeners are synchronized somewhat independently with the vocal and the visible behavior of speakers, Kendon (1970) has speculated that listeners may provide distinctive nonverbal cues that they are decoding the speaker's utterances at various hierarchical levels of organization. Dittmann (1972c) similarly has suggested that listener responses may reflect not only a social reaction to the speaker, but also energy expended in the decoding process—analogous to the kinesic activity of speakers that is associated with the encoding of utterances (Dittmann & Llewellyn, 1968; Moscovici, 1967).

There is no standard lexicon of nonverbal listener responses, and the literature on listener behavior varies widely in the range of responses that have been included in the concept. However, there is an emerging consensus about what components are most centrally involved in the control process. One of the most widely utilized kinesic response by listeners is the head nod. We will discuss the functions of its variations as well as the implications of its occurrence alone versus with verbal concomitants. As is the case with speakers, listeners also can exert control by means of visual orientation and gesticulation, although they do so at a lower rate. We will pay less attention to a variety of less common kinesic listener reactions, such as postural changes, small head movements, frowns, eyebrow flashes, and small smiles. Finally, we will consider the conversational control functions of the failure of listeners to provide distinctive responses at clear junctures in the speaker's behavior.

NONVERBAL CONTROL PROCESSES

The behaviors by which conversants influence each other's orderly participation and their progression toward substantive goals fall within a more general class of interpersonal control signals referred to as "regulators" or "integration signals" (Scheflen, 1963, 1968). According to Ekman and Friesen (1969), "Régulators are acts which maintain and regulate the back-and-forth nature of speaking and listening. . . . They tell the speaker to continue, repeat, elaborate, hurry up, become more interesting, less salacious, give the other a chance to talk, etc. They can tell the listener to pay special attention, to wait just a minute more to talk, etc. [p. 82]." From common experience it is not difficult to conjure up familiar nonverbal responses by which these respective outcomes are solicited. For example, the listener could communicate the above sequence of reactions by silent visual attention or small periodic nods, a cocking of the head while cupping an ear, a puzzled expression, speech-accompanying head nods that recycle beyond the rate of stresses of the speaker, yawning, opening the mouth and raising a hand, and so on. And we can imagine the speaker communicating his respective desires by tapping the listener with a finger, raising a hand in an emblem of "wait", and so forth. In fact, as Scheflen as well as Ekman and Friesen have pointed out, virtually any category of nonverbal behavior can serve as a regulator in some circumstances.

Thus, to provide a comprehensive list of nonverbal regulators virtually would require a complete dictionary of nonverbal communication. Even if such a horrendous task were possible, the accompanying inference that "all nonverbal behavior is regulatory behavior" is too general to be of value. The solution chosen by Ekman and Friesen (1969) was to limit regulators to those nonverbal behaviors that did not fit into their four other major categories of nonverbal usage—emblems, affect displays, illustrators, and adaptors. From their perspective, which implicitly emphasizes the interpretive—communicative functions of nonverbal behavior more than its social—behavioral consequences, this was a sensible decision. However, it left the category of nonverbal regulator impoverished with little more than the listener head nod as an entry, except under special circumstances (See Ekman & Friesen, 1972, p. 359, regarding overlap between regulators and speech-illustrative movements).

From the present perspective there is another solution. While recognizing that all elementary nonverbal acts may have multiple social meanings or usages, their specific functions as regulators may be identified through the addition of contextual cues. By contextual cues we refer to the larger array of behavior of conversants within which a specific nonverbal act is performed. For example, a smile initiated by a listener in the middle of a phonemic clause may differ in function from one emitted after a final-sounding juncture. Another way of utilizing the concept of context in the identification of regulators is to include configurations of multiple nonverbal activities that occur in close temporal association. Thus, we are suggesting that the nonverbal behaviors that serve different social functions be viewed not as mutually exclusive, but rather as imbedded in mutually exclusive contexts or behavioral configurations.

It should be noted that the degree to which the *forms* of common classes of nonverbal responses might subtly vary with the *contexts* in which they are performed is not yet well-understood. Birdwhistell (1970) has described extremely wide variations in the forms of head nods (pp. 158–166) and smiles (pp. 29–39). Gunnell and Rosenfeld (1971) found that smiles typically differ contextually from head nods and brief verbal listener responses in that only the last two occurred predominantly in listening periods. Yet Dittmann (personal communication) has observed that listeners occasionally give brief smiles at junctures, which differ in form from speech-associated smiles by their smallness and quickness of termination. Also Rosenfeld and McRoberts (in preparation) found that positivity ratings of head nods were predictable from such features as initial direction and duration, as well as presence of concomitant smiles.

THE DATA BASE

Conversational control functions of nonverbal behavior have been referred to, at least in passing, in numerous studies. However, only a few studies have been oriented primarily toward their analysis. For the present chapter, we will emphasize available studies that have been dedicated to a temporal analysis of interpersonal control processes within face-to-face conversations. The studies we review generally fall into two classes: extensive behavioral measurement of small numbers of subjects, and limited behavioral measurement of larger numbers of subjects. Possibly because of limitations in the time available to investigators, some tradeoff has occurred between comprehensiveness of behavioral assessment and breadth of sampling of subjects.

The studies, taken as a whole, are a rather fragmentary assortment. Yet the consensual findings that have emerged from them attest to the robustness of certain processes of conversational control. On the other hand, the very limited sampling of subject populations and situations clearly indicates a need for much more research in the area. The research has been based almost exclusively upon polite conversations among American or English adults of the middle or upper-middle class. Thus, the scholar seeking definitive documentation of conversational control processes may well be disappointed. However, the discovery-oriented researcher may be encouraged by the range of territory remaining to be explored.

One of the most detailed analyses was performed upon sections of a 16 mm sound motion picture of a multiperson conversation in an English pub. Portions of the film were analyzed by Kendon (1970, 1972), frame by frame, for all changes of movements of the head, hands, arms, and trunk, and for the correspondence of these movements with the phonetically transcribed speech of the participants. Another comprehensively analyzed set of data, coded by more molar and eclectic categories, consisted of two videotaped 19-min conversations among adults, with one person in common in the two dyads (Duncan, 1972, 1973, 1974; Duncan & Niederehe, 1974). These painstaking studies required years of analysis to reach their present state of completion. In addition to deriving important heuristic hypotheses about the variables involved in conversational control, their authors were able to aid future researchers by indicating which miniature behaviors are unlikely to be implicated.

More selective nonverbal measurements have been applied to larger samples consisting of college students. The relationship of interpersonal visual orientation to molar categories of verbal behavior was studied in 5-min samples of coordinated audiotape and film (two frames per second) records of seven dyads in which the participants were getting acquainted (Kendon, 1967). Unfortunately, in none of the publications identified so far in this section on the data base was any assessment of intercoder reliability coefficients reported for the various behavioral categories. However, it is evident that meticulous attention was required for the detailed, temporal scoring of these studies and that multiple coders were involved, who at least resolved disagreements through discussion.

The relationship of phonemic junctures to verbal listener responses and head nods was investigated in 20 dyads by Dittmann and Llewellyn (1968). Automated procedures were employed to aid in the objective detection of head nods and their coordination with reliably assessed units of speech. All of the studies mentioned so far in this section consisted of descriptive analyses of relatively unrestricted conversations. A relatively comprehensive molar analysis also has been performed on nonverbal behaviors reliably assessed from videotapes of six college students in a more restricted condition (Gunnell & Rosenfeld, 1971; Rosenfeld, 1972). Each student spent about 45 min interviewing the same actress—confederate who was trained to perform fluent and disfluent utterances on a random schedule and to terminate her utterances with clear junctures at which she gazed at the listener and paused. Rates of each category of nonverbal behavior by interviewers were compared at junctures versus between junctures of the interviewee.

While we have arbitrarily decided to emphasize the role of body motion and, to a lesser extent, brief verbal listener responses in conversational control, it should be mentioned that thorough analyses have been performed on another important dimension of nonlinguistic behavior. The structure of the purely temporal properties of vocal behavior in conversations has been extensively analyzed in repeated samples (Feldstein, 1972; Jaffe & Feldstein, 1970; also see relevant chapters in this book). Automated measurement assured high reliability.

Finally, it should be noted that relatively comprehensive analyses of nonverbal control processes have been initiated on larger samples of subjects and situations. For example, Duncan (personal communication) is replicating his study on six additional dyads. Twenty-six videotapes of half-hour conversations also are being analyzed in the present author's laboratory. All conversants were carefully selected for their mutual involvement in the topic of their discussion. High-resolution videotape records were obtained, with split-screen full-face images of each participant, permitting the scoring of such details as gaze direction, in addition to head movement. Pam Gunnell is comparing nonverbal behavior in samples of speaker switching and "mm-hmm" listener responses from twenty of the conversations. Rosenfeld and Margaret Hancks are studying the same tapes to compare the nonverbal concomitants and consensually judged functions of several levels of complexity of verbal listener response, including vocal segregates (for example, "mm" or "mm-hmm"), simple lexical items (for example, "yeah" or "I see"), and multiple lexical items (for example, "yeah, okay").

The other six half-hour videotapes, collected by Rosenfeld and Diane Beecher, have one person in common to the six dyads. In two conversations he was predominantly in a learner role, in two a teacher, and in two others a co-discussant. The study was designed to include some control over individual differences in interpreting different control functions of nonverbal behavior. Because these studies were accessible to the writer, completed analyses from some of them will be mentioned in this chapter. Any omissions of other relevant research is unintentional.

CONTROL FUNCTIONS OF NONVERBAL BEHAVIORS

Speakers and listeners probably monitor each other's behavior regularly, if not continuously, throughout most conversations. Thus, any clear behavioral change by one participant at any point in the interaction could produce a noticeable effect on the behavior of the other. In the typical polite conversation, however, the relationship between speaker and listener behavior *prior* to junctures probably reflects little more than their coordinated effort to mutually track the subphrase elements of the speaker's utterance and to signal each other that they are doing so. Such "synchrony" has been noted between nonverbal movements of listeners and the phonic, syllabic, and lexical units of speakers (Condon & Ogston, 1966).

However, on the basis of very limited numbers of thoroughly analyzed interactions, Kendon (1970) has described ways in which synchronization prior to the juncture may lead to more molar variations in the conversational process. For example, synchronization of the listener's movements with the elements of the speaker's utterance near the end of a phonemic clause may serve to signal the speaker that the listener has comprehended the speaker's meaning prior to the completion of the speaker's utterance. Such prejunctural signaling by the listener may indicate that the speaker should either provide new information or else let the listener take on a more dominant role in the conversation.

The role of prejunctural head nodding in this process has been suggested and illustrated by Birdwhistell (1970), Dittmann and Llewellyn (1968), and Rosenfeld (1972). If such prejunctural signaling should prove to be common, then the assumption of discrete alternation in turns, which typifies theories of conversation, may convey an oversimplified perspective. In fact, the nature of most of the conversations that have been analyzed indicates a bias toward an overemphasis on polite, cooperative social encounters.

In current analyses at our laboratory, Gunnell has found significantly more smooth speaker switches among dyads who were given complementary conversational goals than among those given less compatible tasks. Also, Duncan and Niederehe (1974) report that nonverbal efforts by listeners to gain control of the floor sometimes are initiated prior to the completion of the speaker's utterance, and that such listener behaviors affect the likelihood of disruptive versus smooth transitions between speaking turns. In larger data samples reported by Jaffe and Feldstein (1970), more simultaneous speech occurred in conversations based on attitudinal discrepancies than in interviews. Also, within the attitude discrepancy study simultaneous speech varied with changes in partner and topic. Finally, it is noteworthy that both simultaneous speech and pauses were shorter in duration among conversants in their study between whom a visual barrier had been inserted than between those who conversed face to face. One might speculate that the screen eliminated nonverbal cues that otherwise would have perpetuated conflicting floor claims and would have allowed a speaker to hold the floor for longer pause durations.

Speaker Elicitation of Listener Behavior

First let us consider how the speaker signals that he does *not* wish to switch speaking roles at the juncture. Inasmuch as speakers tend to look away from listeners when formulating or initiating complex speech units, we would expect gaze avoidance to inhibit listener responses. Kendon (1967) investigated this process in two conversations. He reported that when the speaker ended his utterance without looking at the listener, 71% of the time the listener either gave no subsequent speech or else "delayed" his speech. When the speaker ended with an extended look at the listener, the listener followed with no speech or delayed speech only 29% of the time.

Duncan (1972, 1973) found one speaker behavior that was particularly effective in preventing the listener from taking over the floor, even after the listener signaled a wish to do so. This cue was a hand gesticulation by the speaker that was maintained or not returned to resting state through the juncture. Of 361 junctures that contained the gesticulation plus at least one additional cue that otherwise tended to predict turn switching, only two of the junctures resulted in speaker switching. Of 416 junctures containing a turn-switching cue but which lacked the gesticulation, 86 resulted in changes in speaking turn. It will be recalled that gesticulation, like gaze avoidance, also is characteristic of the initiation of complex utterances. The possibility of its intentional use as a switch-suppressing signal may derive from its natural usage in speech formulation (Dittmann & Llewellyn, 1969) and illustration (Ekman & Friesen, 1972).

How does a speaker indicate that he wants, or is available for, a listener reaction? We previously noted that a "final" pitch ending of the speaker's phonemic clause itself is a predictor of listener responses. Dittmann and Llewellyn (1968) compared falling, rising, and sustained endings for their prediction of listener head nods and brief vocalizations. One or both of these listener responses occurred after 37% of falling, 26% of rising, and only 6% of sustained junctures. Similarly Duncan (1972, 1973) listed rising or falling pitch, but not sustained pitch, as one of six speaker behaviors at the juncture that predicted the occurrence of speaker switches.

Dittmann and Llewellyn (1968) also compared the probability of occurrence of head nods or verbal listener responses at junctures versus at nonjuncture locations of speech. The ratio between the two was 15:1 (50:1 for head nods alone), indicating that performing the body of the phonemic clause in itself is a major inhibitor of listener responses. Inasmuch as pausing is more common after final than sustained junctures, one might expect that pausing itself accounts for listener responses. However, while pausing after the final juncture increases the probability of listener responses, pausing within the juncture (hesitation) has little if any effect. In telephone-type conversations studied by Dittmann and Llewellyn (1967), the ratio of the probabilities of verbal listener responses after juncture pauses versus after hesitation pauses was 20:1.

Dittmann and Llewellyn (1968) showed that final junctures, in contrast to sustained junctures, almost always preceded head nods or brief vocalizations by listeners. However, the occurrence of final junctures was not sufficient for predicting *when* the listener responses would occur. The listener responses occurred after only 37% of falling junctures and 26% of rising junctures.

Comparable results were found by Duncan, who used an overlapping but more complex definition of junctures at which cues permitting listener reactions were provided by speakers. His study indicated that a maximum of only 29% of the speaker signals were followed by listener responses (Duncan, 1974), and that only an additional 11% were followed by floor switches (Duncan, 1972). Thus, a liberal estimate of the degree to which all possible opportunities for reaction provided by speakers are responded to by listeners is about 40%.

Duncan identified several speaker cues, in addition to the junctures that terminate phonemic clauses, which preceded listener responses and speaker switching. His major finding was that the greater the *number* of speaker cues at the juncture, the greater was the probability of the listener taking over the speaker role. Six cues were involved. We already have noted that one cue was the final ending of the juncture (rising or falling pitch). Duncan's other five speaker cues at junctures that preceded switching included only one kinesic variable—the termination of any hand gesticulation or the relaxation of a tensed hand position used in the prior speech unit. This cue, of course, would include the termination of the hand gesticulation that serves as a turn-suppressing signal. Another of the cues was grammatical completion; but inasmuch as the same cue also predicted the occurrence of listener responses, it was not uniquely either a turn-predicting cue or a listener response cue. Rather, it enabled either response. The remaining three cues were drawl on the final or stressed syllable of the phonemic clause, the occurrence of a verbal "sociocentric sequence" (for example, "and so on" or "you know"; see the reassurance-seeking "sympathetic circularity" sequence described by Bernstein, 1962), or a combination of a sociocentric sequence and a drop in pitch or loudness below the levels characteristic of the clause.

None of the six cues was found to be more predictive than the others. The correlation between number of speaker cues at the juncture and the probability of floor switching was .96. However, the size of this rank-order correlation should be interpreted with caution because the occurrence of more than four cues was too infrequent to be reliable. A more accurate picture of the effect of number of cues is reflected in the substantial increases in prediction occurring between one and two cues and between two and three cues. Both zero cues and one cue were followed by switching only 10% of the time. With two cues, the prediction increased to 17%; and with three or four cues it was about 33%.

Duncan's results and interpretations imply that the final juncture occurring *alone* (one turn-offering cue) is no more predictive than a sustained juncture alone (zero turn cues). Yet, in the telephonelike conversations studied by Dittmann and Llewellyn (1967) final junctures predicted listener responses substantially better than did sustained junctures. Reconciliation of the two studies would seem to require than in Dittmann and Llewellyn's study final junctures had to be associated with additional cues in the vocal or linguistic channels. While the latter authors did find that postjunctural pausing was confounded with finality of juncture and that it added modestly to the prediction of listener responses, pauses were not included in Duncan's set of speaker cues. Other vocal—verbal possibilities from Duncan's list include grammatical completion, drawl, sociocentric sequence, and decreasing loudness.

Also, as one would expect, the *fewer* the speaker's eliciting cues the more likely it was that an attempt by the listener to speak would result in simultaneous talk—a breakdown in the turn-taking mechanism. But in this case the critical numbers of cues were not quite the same as for the prediction of smooth switches. Listener attempts at speaking resulted in simultaneous talk 100% of the time after zero cues, 17% after one cue, 8% after two or three cues, and not at all after four or more cues.

Duncan (1974) also claimed that two nonverbal cues by speakers at junctures additively predicted listener responses (to be discriminated from floor-switching responses or no response at all). The cues were grammatical completion of clauses and turning of the speaker's head toward the listener. However, neither of these cues is capable of differentially predicting whether a listener response or a turn-switch is more likely to result. Grammatical completion also was one of the six cues that predicted switches. The head-turning cue was not included as a predictor of switches by Duncan because it did not differentiate between smooth versus contested varieties of speaker switching, and apparently not because it failed to differentiate speaker continuation versus switching at the juncture.

On the basis of Duncan's data let us assume that visual orientation and grammatical completion by speakers at junctures indicate that the listener should make *some* kind of response, but does not specify whether it should be a listener response or a switch from the listener to the speaker role. The decision, then, must be left up to the listener. The option the listener selects should depend upon its relative potential for facilitating the flow of information in the conversation. If the speaker is generating new information at an adequate rate the listener should be expected to signal the speaker to continue via a simple listener response. If the listener wishes to give a more complicated commentary on the information he has been receiving than could be provided by a listener response, he would be expected to attempt to take over the speaking role. In other words, we are proposing that the decision of the listener whether or not to give a listener response depends upon his success in processing information, which in turn is affected by variables outside of the scope that we have been considering.

Still, the *form* of the listener response, if it occurs, may be affected by nonverbal cues of the speaker. Earlier we suggested that nonverbal listener responses can provide various simple messages to the speaker, including degree of attentiveness, understanding, and agreement. In the next section we will review evidence concerning the nonverbal composition of these different messages and how their occurrence may be selectively influenced by nonverbal signals from the speaker. We have reviewed evidence that several kinds of speaker cues apparently are functionally equivalent, or substitutable, in their capacity to evoke some form of listener behavior. Is it also true that different forms of listener responses are functionally equivalent? The most readily available evidence by which to answer this question involves head nods and brief verbal responses.

First there is clear evidence from two studies that the two kinds of listener response occur together at junctures more often than would be expected from chance combinations of their individual occurrences. Dittmann and Llewellyn (1968) found that their co-occurrence constituted 22% of listener responses, compared to 60% for vocalizations alone and 18% for head nods alone. The significant proportion of cooccurrences was upheld within the responses of each of 14 subjects for whom it was testable. Gunnell and Rosenfeld (1971) found the same result in four of five subjects on whom it was testable. The significant cooccurrences indicate that the combination of nods and verbal responses have a communicative function that is not served by the individual components.

Next, it should be noted that while nods and brief verbal responses typically occurred at or near junctures in both studies, the two forms of response differed in time of occurrence relative to the juncture. In both studies, when the two responses occurred at the same juncture, the nod typically preceded the verbal portion of the listener response. Dittmann (personal communication) found that 23% of listener nods versus only 6% of "mm-hmms" preceded phonation stops of the speaker. He also found that the average latencies of the two responses after junctures were 10 versus 30 msec, respectively. Similar results were obtained by Rosenfeld (1972) in an analysis of head nodding from the Gunnell and Rosenfeld (1971) videotapes. A sample of 126 listener nods from the six dyads was studied in detail. Seven of the 31 nods that occurred in conjunction with verbal listener responses and an additional 31 nods that occurred alone were initiated prior to the completion of the speaker's terminal clause. Verbal listener responses, on the other hand, rarely occurred prior to the juncture. The difference may be attributable to the likelihood that a verbal listener response, in contrast to a nod, would disrupt the utterance of the speaker.

Finally, there was evidence in Rosenfeld's analysis that particular speaker behaviors evoked the nods prior to the junctures. Most of the listener nods that preceded the speaker's juncture were themselves preceded by the initiation of one of the following speaker behaviors: a filled hesitation pause ("ah" type) accompanied by a hand gesticulation, a filled pause accompanied by a head movement (usually a nod or shake), or a phrase whose content was redundant with the preceding phrase. Several other listener nods started during sociocentric sequences (especially "y'know") by the speaker. Dittmann and Llewellyn (1968) also found that nods were elicited by "y'know." They also observed that the joint occurrence of nods and brief verbalizations tended to be preceded by speaker behaviors requiring a relatively vigorous type of listener response. For example, the joint listener responses occurred after the speaker asked a question but before the listener gave a reply, or after the speaker answered a brief question previously asked by the listener. Dittmann and Llewellyn estimated that simple attentional functions were performed by only 30% of the joint responses, compared to 51% of the single responses. Thus, it would appear that the joint listener response tends to indicate understanding or agreement, whereas the individual occurrence of the head nod or "mm-hmm" is more likely to indicate simple attention.

Rosenfeld and Hancks sought to determine the degree to which nonverbal behaviors of speakers accounted for the "complexity" of subsequent verbal listener responses ("mm-hmm" or other segmentals, simple lexical responses and more elaborate forms). Although only accounting for about 18% of the variance in the complexity of 250 verbal listener responses from 20 dyads (using a hierarchical analysis of variance statistic), they found the following speaker behaviors to contribute: pointing of the head or initiating low-amplitude head nods prior to the juncture, and raising the head after the juncture. Again, it would appear that the noticeability of a listener response is at least partly attributable to elicitations by the speaker. This interpretation is enhanced by the further finding that more complex verbal listener responses, compared to simpler ones, tended to be louder and were more likely to be accompanied by eyebrow flashes and repetitive nods.

A variety of examples of possible nonverbal signals were given earlier in this chapter to illustrate the diversity of controlling messages that may be given by the speaker and listener. Rosenfeld and Hancks attempted to determine which nonverbal behaviors of listeners were indicative of attention, understanding, and agreement, and how these behaviors were affected by speakers. Five independent observers of the audio–video records were asked to take the role of the speaker and to rate the 250 listener responses on each of the three dimensions using a four-point scale. Certain nonverbal activities of both listener and speaker were found to be associated with each of the averaged judgments.

Behaviors of the listener that were associated with judgments of "agreement" were complex verbal listener responses and multiple head nods. The agreeing-type listener response was found to predictably follow the speaker's pointing of his head in the direction of the listener. In contrast, judgments that the listener was indicating understanding were associated with repeated small head nods by the listener prior to the speech juncture, and did not involve any apparent speaker signals. Thus, signals of understanding, in contrast to agreement, appear to be more subdued in form and more likely to be initiated by the listener than elicited by the speaker. Finally, judgments of listener attention were associated with forward leaning of the listener prior to the speaker's juncture, audibility of verbal listener response after the juncture, and initiation of gesticulation by the speaker after the juncture but prior to resuming speech. While the implications of the judgment study should be taken only as suggestive, they support the contention that distinctive configurations of nonverbal listener responses communicate different types of feedback to speakers, some of which are elicited by the speakers and some of which are initiated by the listeners.

Effects of Listener Responses on Speaker Behavior

It is the listener's responsibility to aid the speaker in conveying verbal information as well as to collaborate in the process of speaker switching. We will deal with the latter problem first. To the degree that the speaker provides the turn-switching cues we have discussed, the listener merely has to decide whether or not to take advantage of the opportunity. If he does, he thereby contributes to putting the former speaker into a listener role. However, the listener may wish to take over the speaking role in the absence of such "permission" by the speaker. In such cases, the listener can engage in turn-claiming cues, which, if acknowledged by the speaker, will lead to a smooth switch.

Duncan and Niederehe (1974) detected four such turn-claiming cues by listeners in the two conversations they studied. Two were nonlinguistic vocal cues: overloudness and a sharp, audible inhalation. The other two were kinesic: a shift of the head away from the speaker and the start of a gesticulation. The two kinesic cues were more effective than the two vocal cues. Their usage should be familiar to the reader by now; the head-away cue and the gesticulation were previously found to be associated with the preparation and initiation of speech. In one of the two dyads at least one of the four turn-claiming cues was found to precede 95% of the smooth turn switches, but only 19% of the listener response junctures. In the other dyad, the comparable percentages were 72 and 9%. The cues were even more strongly involved in the resolution of simultaneous talking. There were 18 occasions of simultaneous speech in the study in which the number of turn-claiming cues minus the number of turn-yielding cues favored one participant over the other. Each participant was favored in a substantial number of the occasions. In all 18 cases, the favored participant took over the speaking role at the end of the simultaneous talking.

Duncan (1974) also found that when listener responses occurred prior to the completion of speaking units, the speaker was more likely to emit floor-retaining cues. On 63% of such occasions the speaker turned his head away or gesticulated, in contrast to only 24% of the occasions in which the listener response had followed the completion of the speech unit. Presumably, the early listener response indicates that the listener has already comprehended the speaker's information prior to the completion of the utterance within which it was encoded. This could be threatening to the speaker in two ways—by inferring that the speaker has been unnecessarily slow or overly redundant in presenting information and by increasing the probability that the listener intends to take over the speaker role before the speaker is ready to give it up. This could explain why the early listener response leads the speaker to insert a floor-retaining signal that otherwise would have been omitted.

It is likely that rather minor variations in the timing of brief listener signals, as well as in their content, can function as "feedback," indicating a need for the speaker to modify his flow of information. Nonverbal feedback signals, especially in the context of the verbal content of speech, can provide the speaker with more or less specific information about what modifications are needed.

Consider the possible variants of the head nod. Its general form has been technically defined (McGrew, 1972): "The head is moved forward and backward on the condyles resting on the atlas vertebra, resulting in the face moving down and up [p. 57]." Variations in performance of the act occur along such dimensions of velocity, amplitude, and frequency of cycles (Birdwhistell, 1970, pp. 160–165). Birdwhistell has proposed that different forms of the head nod are involved in different control functions. He differentiated functional classes of head nods by normal listeners in terms of the number and timing of repetitions and their relationship to speaker behavior. What we have referred to as a simple attentional signal was attributed to brief single head nods by listeners that occur repeatedly during the speaker's utterance. Longer lasting single nods were claimed to result in disruption of the flow of speech and justification of prior substantive points. Double head nods were said to either modify the vocalization rate of the speaker upward or downward, or else to evoke an elaboration of the substance of the speaker's prior utterance. Triple head nods at nonprimary-stress points in a phonemic clause were claimed to produce hesitations and, if the cycles were very brief, to result in termination of speech or an inquiry into the listener's problem. These interesting observations should be verified in formal research on larger samples.

The possible feedback implications of less common listener movements at nonswitching junctures also should be further explored. For example, in an ethological approach to the analysis of interviews, Grant (1968) identified a cluster of correlated nonverbal responses that were associated with point-making by speakers and attention by listeners. This "contact" cluster included the head bob and flashing and raising of the eyebrows. Wiener, Devoe, Rubinow, and Geller (1972) claimed that the raised eyebrow or frown of a listener typically leads the speaker to reiterate or correct his message (p. 208). They also asserted that the listener's smile, when accompanied by eye contact, signals comprehension but with an unwillingness to speak. Even the horizontal head shake, recognized as a common multicultural emblem of negation by Darwin (1872/1965), has been attributed the function of reassurance in certain social contexts (McGrew, 1972).

The effects of another kind of listener state at nonswitching junctures also deserves greater attention—the absence of a noticeable listener response at the juncture. Occasions in which the listener fails either to "comment" or take over the floor are likely to be bothersome to the speaker. According to Wiener *et al.* (1972) the speaker will either give a louder repetition of his message, make an attention-eliciting sound, or quit talking altogether. However, we have noted that most junctures are not followed by verbal listener responses or head nods (Dittmann & Llewellyn, 1968; Duncan, 1972). Perhaps the absence of additional reaction by the listener is aversive to the speaker to the degree that it is preceded by speaker signals which normally evoke more active listener responses.

Our general proposition is that *a listener response which is insufficient relative to the level of evocation by the speaker will be interpreted by the speaker as a negative response.* Experimental research on learning by children has shown that they interpret the absence of response by the experimenter as meaning the opposite of the typical kind of response provided by that experimenter (Crandall, Good, & Crandall, 1964). If the experimenter's mode of operation had been to reward the child after a correct response, then the subsequent occurrence of no response was reacted to as if it were a punishment. The opposite reaction occurred if the experimenter had previously only punished the child for poor responses.

Negative interpretations of videotapes of neutral face–head behaviors of teachers occurred in a developmental study of judge reactions only among judge groups beyond the first grade of elementary school (Rosenfeld, Shea, & Greenbaum, 1975). This finding has been replicated in nonnormal populations as well. There is evidence that persons are more likely to give positive reactions to desirable behavior than negative reactions to undesirable behavior in polite social situations (Rosenfeld, 1966a) and elsewhere (Boucher & Osgood, 1969). Thus, as children become increasingly exposed to social evaluations, they are more likely to interpret nonreactions as the opposite of the positive reactions to which they have become accustomed.

Rosenfeld (1972, pp. 433–434) has described a microanalysis of a videotaped episode in which a listener failed to reciprocate the smile initiated by a speaker at three consecutive junctures, responding instead with a head turn and side glance toward the speaker. Following each successive juncture the speaker modified the substance of his comment (which apparently was unintentionally insulting to the listener) into an increasingly less offensive form and also produced a weaker and briefer smile. Finally, the listener gave a strong smile. The speaker then smiled broadly and quickly suggested that they discuss a different topic. A more extreme example of the disruptive effects of insufficient responsiveness is the actual awkward exodus of speakers from a conversational setting in which the listener was an operant conditioner preprogrammed to shift into a strict extinction period (Ulrich, 1962).

We end our discussion of short-term nonverbal controlling processes in face-to-face interaction by noting that many general rules governing conversational participation in such situations can be generated from the linguistic channel alone (Sacks, Schegloff, & Jefferson, 1974). However, given the considerable independent and interactive effects of the nonverbal channel it is quite clear that both channels of communication must be integrated into a comprehensive theory of conversational structure and process.

LONGER-TERM EFFECTS OF LISTENER RESPONSES

Thus far, our conception of control processes has emphasized the immediate or short-term consequences of a specific signal. We have viewed conversations as if control processes operate independently at each juncture. But there are also likely to be longer term effects as a result of the pattern of signals given over extended time periods. The important problem of how speakers and listeners cumulatively influence the structure of their interaction has been approached from a variety of perspectives. Thus far, however, the comprehensive temporal analyses needed for clear understanding of this process have not been performed.

There is abundant evidence that participants in conversations tend to become more similar in their nonverbal behaviors over time. Most of this evidence has consisted of correlations between behaviors that have been summarized over large blocks of time. Thus, it is difficult to determine what specific social influence mechanisms might have contributed to the obtained relationships. At the vocal level significant similarity between members of dyads has been found in pause length (Jaffe & Feldstein, 1970) as well as loudness, articulatory precision, and duration of utterance (see review in Webb, 1972). At the kinesic level, interpersonal gazing has been found to be significantly correlated in amount (Argyle & Ingham, 1972; Kendon, 1967) and in mutuality beyond that expected on the basis of amount of gazing by each participant (Stephenson, Rutter, & Dore, 1972).

The time required for nonverbal correspondences to develop varies between response categories. Rosenfeld (1966b) found that smile rates were significantly related within the first 5 min of casual get-acquainted sessions among pairs of college students; however, head nod rates were not significantly correlated between the participants until the third 5-min session, which was held two weeks later. In the case of smiling, the degree of correlation was consistently so high that one might expect smiling to have strong effects on the control of conversation only when nonreciprocated.

In an example described earlier we noted how the repeatedly nonreciprocated smile was followed by reformulations of a substantive statement into increasingly more agreeable forms. There is more extensive evidence that repeated failure to reciprocate nonverbal elicitations is upsetting and disruptive to the recipient. In a study by Rosenfeld (1967) adult experimenter-interviewers of young teenagers repeatedly withheld smiles, head nods, and brief verbal listener responses at the junctures following the subjects' responses. This resulted not only in a significant reduction of subject smiles and nods, but also in an increase in self-stimulatory responses and non-"ah" types of verbal disfluencies. Other research has shown that rates of verbal and kinesic attentional responses are among the strongest determinants of positive impression formation (Rosenfeld, 1966a). Perhaps also relevant in this vein is the finding by Argyle, Lalljee, and Cook (1968) that speech is disrupted when a subject is put into a condition in which he can be seen by the other conversant but cannot see the latter. These studies are consistent with our proposition that nonresponses are viewed as negative responses, especially when they occur in reaction to cues that normally evoke positive responses.

The cumulative effects of negative nonverbal responses and neutral responses of listeners on the reduction of nonverbal responses of speakers are interpretable within an operant conditioning paradigm as instances of punishment and extinction. Similarly, the modification of the content of speaker utterances in response to differential evaluative reactions by listeners could be attributable to selective reinforcement. Insufficient research has been done by which to determine the degree to which differential reinforcement processes can account for the cumulative effects of nonverbal control processes on conversational content or on the nature of the control process itself. However, existing data are compatible with the hypothesis that the behaviors involved in interpersonal control tend to become more simplified and efficient throughout interaction (MacKay, 1972; Ruesch, 1973; Scheflen, 1963; Vine, 1970).

There is substantial experimental evidence that nonverbal reinforcement processes can affect verbal behavior in face to face interaction. Rates of occurrence of arbitrarily designated classes of verbal response have been increased by providing such listener consequences as head nods, smiles, and leaning forward (Krasner, 1958, p. 152). Early efforts to apply operant conditioning principles, that were initially developed in animal laboratories, to human conversations led to some oversimplified conclusions. Later research, in which certain structural features of conversation were taken into account, has corrected some of the earlier misconceptions. Matarazzo and his colleagues (1964a, b) found that more or less continuous head nodding or "mm-hmming" by interviewers resulted in substantial increases in utterance duration. However, in similar studies in which the interviewee was permitted to state when he had completed his utterance and in which kinesic cues were not transmitted, no such effects of noncontingent "mm-hmms" were found (Siegman, 1973). In fact, there was a tendency for nonresponsiveness to lead to an increase in utterance length, possibly because it signaled that the speaker's response was incomplete.

From an operant conditioning perspective, it is critical to establish both that one has an effective reinforcer and that it is made contingent upon the occurrence of a particular class of response. In future research on the conditioning of conversational content more attention should be payed to evidence that the content and intonation of verbal responses have different reinforcing capacities in different demographic groups (Brooks, Brandt, & Wiener, 1969; Stevenson, 1965). Also, the occurrence of junctures and other natural configurations of speech should be considered in defining a unit of response. In semicontrolled two-person interactions, subtle verbal conditioning of the lexical content of brief utterances has been established (Rosenfeld & Baer, 1969, 1970). However, it subsequently was found that such conditioning is less likely to work if an attempt is made to modify the normal usage of established communicative habits (see Rosenfeld, 1972). Subtle modifications in the contents of utterances can be conditioned within the range of normal usage, but it is difficult to subtly influence a normal conversant into uttering meaningless messages.

THE ORIGINS OF CONVERSATION CONTROL SIGNALS

Inasmuch as the nonverbal behaviors we have found to be involved in conversational control processes were assessed in studies of primarily middle class American and English subjects, we have not established the degree to which they are characteristic of other social and linguistic groups. If the behavioral codes by which control functions are carried are as arbitrary as linguistic codes, then we would expect little similarity across linguistic communities. If, on the other hand, the control code is inherently related to universal requisites for human verbal communication, then there may be common usages across linguistic communities. This is not to deny the increasing evidence that most if not all human behavior is subject to modification through experience. Yet a natural linkage between a particular behavior form and the requisites of effective conversation should give that form a higher likelihood of usage than arbitrarily encoded forms. Similarity in conversational control signals across linguistic communities could be of great advantage in promoting understanding between members of the different groups.

Probably the most regularly employed nonverbal control signal is visual orientation—toward or away from the person with whom one is conversing. The high proportion of conversational time in which listeners look at speakers is attributable to more than signaling attention and observing kinesic activity of the speaker. It also is explainable in terms of an acoustic orienting reflex characteristic of humans and other species. When not directly facing a speaker (or other generator of vocal signals), a sound shadow at the far ear can block or alter many high-tone inputs. Binaural balance is achieved by means of a reflexive "noncompensatory nystagmus which moves the eyes toward the locus of the perceived sound source" (Diebold, 1968, p. 555). In this way the visual–kinesic and vocal–auditory systems become linked early in the developmental process. Significant "coupling" between the gaze of infant and mother appears early in the infant's first year (Jaffe, Stern, & Peery, 1973; Stern, 1974), as does the connection of gaze with the turn-taking pattern of vocalization (Bateson, 1971).

Periodic gaze avoidance also may reflect more than the conventional signaling of floor-maintaining or floor-taking interests, or of covert verbal encoding processes. In several species the head is oriented away from a threatening animal. This "cut-off" posture (Chance, 1962; see Hutt & Ounsted, 1966) has been interpreted as a means of preventing excessive stimulation which could inhibit the threatened animal from taking adaptive action. In primates, "cut-off" behavior may take a variety of forms all of which decrease visual input. These forms include facing at an oblique angle, head turning, lowering of eyes, partially closing the eye lids, or covering the eyes with the hand.

Ellsworth and Ludwig (1972) and Coss (1973) have reviewed evidence that adults increase in autonomic arousal when stared at, which may relate to the widespread cultural "taboos" on staring and to the flight reactions that often follow staring episodes. In the conversational process we have noted that there is considerable mutual gazing, controlled mainly by changes in gaze orientation of the speaker. Perhaps the ability of speaker gazes (particularly when accompanied by feedback eliciting cues) to evoke listener responses or speaker switching is partially explainable as the product of escape or avoidance conditioning. By engaging in listener responses or speaker-switching cues, the listener thereby sets the occasion for at least one of the participants to avert gaze and thereby to terminate the uncomfortable pressure of the speaker's coercive visual signals.

An additional impetus to the development of the visual—attentional behaviors that characterize conversation is the apparently innate attention-evoking function of eyelike stimuli in many animals and in humans (Ahrens, 1954; Hindmarch, 1973). Once the attention of the developing child is thereby drawn to the face area, the varied stimulus properties associated with the face (movements, and later, structural configurations) become increasingly attractive (Walters & Parke, 1965). Vine (1970) has further argued that the evolution of the head and face area as a dense source of a variety of nonverbal signals, such as cross-culturally common displays of emotion, may be associated with the fact that the human visual apparatus can only focus upon a limited area of the visual field.

Perhaps the next most strongly implicated kinesic activity in the conversational control processes we have discussed is the gesticulation—particularly whether or not hand motion is in process versus returned to a resting state. There are wide individual differences in the form and quantity of gesticulation in the conversational process, indicating that it may not have a strong inherent relationship to conversational control.

The role of cultural factors in the acquisition of gesticulatory habits was clearly demonstrated by Efron (1941/1972). Large differences in gestural style were observed by Efron and his associates in New York City between unassimilated members of two European cultures—Southern Italian and Eastern European Jewish. Many of these cultural differences were related to the conversational control process. For example, the traditional Jews characteristically conversed at very close distances. This proximity was associated with a high degree of gesturing, often via head movements because of the restricted opportunities for arm motion. Manual contact between conversants was common both as an attention-eliciting device by speakers and as a means of gaining the speaking turn by listeners. One humorous observation was reported of a speaker actually gesticulating in a berating manner with the arm of the listener. Simultaneous gesturing was common and was associated with simultaneous talking. The traditional Italian displayed more fluid and controlled gesticulatory habits, and tended to use termination of gestural movement as a floor-seeking signal. Comparisons of assimilated Jews and Italians in New York City, from the same European ancestry as the unassimilated groups, revealed virtually no differences in gestural style.

In addition to arm movements, Dittmann and Llewellyn (1969) found that head and foot movements of speakers were most common at the initiation of phonemic clauses in conversation. The occurrence of *some* kind of noticeable kinesic activity at the beginning of complex speech units is likely to be common cross-culturally. This would be expected on the basis of the hypothesis that the process of speech encoding involves tension or energy expenditure which tends to be manifest in kinesic activity (Dittmann, 1972c; Kendon, 1970), as well as by the turn-regulating capacity of such responses. Hand and arm movements provide a convenient, although not necessary, means of engaging in such activity.

Certain components of facial affect displays that are optionally employed in conversational regulation—for example, eyebrow flashes, small smiles, or frowns—have been considered to have derived from related functions in pre-human primates and other mammals (see McGrew, 1972; Vine, 1970). If so, they are likely to be correctly interpretable across many linguistic communities, even though there are substantial cultural differences in display rules (Ekman, 1972). It also has been argued that the head nod and head shake occur too frequently across cultures as signals of affirmation and negation to be considered arbitrary signals (Darwin, 1872/1965). Spitz (1957) has offered developmental evidence to support the theory, previously proposed by Darwin, that the affirmative function of the head nod derives from the reciprocating horizontal motion of the head of the infant in the reflexive sucking process, while the head shake derives independently from the infant's rejection of attempts to feed him.

LaBarre (1964), on the other hand, has argued that variations in the ways that affirmation and negation are expressed cross-culturally are inimical with a universalistic interpretation. For example, he noted that in the Punjab and Sind, affirmation is expressed by "throwing the head back in an oblique arc to the left shoulder, one time, somewhat 'curtly' and 'disrespectfully' to our taste"; and in Ceylon it is expressed by "curving the chin in a downward leftward arc . . . , often accompanied by an indescribably beautiful parakineme of back-of-right-hand cupped in upward-facing-palm of the left hand, plus-or-minus the additional kineme of a crossed-ankle curtsey [p. 198]." Other societies are even reputed to use the horizontal head shake as a sign of affirmation.

While no extensive efforts are here being made to provide sufficient evidence to resolve the controversy over how much nature and nurture contribute, we will retain the conservative proposition that *the nonverbal signals involved in conversational control are less arbitrarily coded than are the linguistic contents with which they are associated.* In this context we will add that there is considerable evidence indicating that in the communication of positivity and negativity, the visual–kinesic channel typically dominates the verbal–auditory channel (Bugental, Kaswan, & Love, 1970a; Burns & Beier, 1973; Levitt, 1964; Zaidel & Mehrabian, 1969). Finally, if it may be assumed that the major messages involved in conversational control consist of binary opposites (speak–listen, approve–disapprove, etc.), then even arbitrary forms may be easily learned by observers through brief exposure to their contextual usages as suggested by Leach (1972).

Little is known about the contribution of developmental processes in the acquisition of conversational control skills. We have noted that elementary school children begin to recognize the communicative functions of neutral and subtle negative facial reactions (Rosenfeld *et al.,* 1975). This, and additional evidence that the dominance of nonverbal over verbal cues of positivity and negativity increases with age among linguistically competent persons (Bugental, Kaswan, Love, & Fox, 1970b) may be attributable to the effect of gradual social learning of the referential meanings and normative social reactions to subtle nonverbal signals in conversation. An initial descriptive study of young children in conversations indicated that their listener responses are more latent and less common than are those of adults (Dittmann, 1972a). Experimental research also indicates that younger children are less likely to reformulate their utterances in response to nonverbal or minimal verbal expressions of noncomprehension (Peterson, Danner, & Flavell, 1972). The degree to which the deficiencies in nonverbal control of conversation in children can be attributed to less well-developed information processing skills (cf. Glucksberg, Krauss, & Higgins, 1975) and to less well-established social habits has not been determined.

SUMMARY AND CONCLUSIONS

The era of serious research on conversational control functions of nonverbal behavior is well under way. A small number of limited studies has produced encouraging results. Some of the results have been replicated sufficiently to be considered confirmed. These include the role of phonemic clause endings as major occasions for the occurrence of nonverbal controlling activities and the use of head and eye orientation and of gesticulation in the maintenance and change of speaker roles. It also is evident that nonverbal control signals by listeners may or may not occur in conjunction with verbal listener responses and that combinations of listener activities have stronger or different effects than do isolated activities. In addition, evidence was offered in favor of the proposition that nonverbal listener reactions that are insufficient relative to the nonverbal evocations of speakers are similar in function to active negative reactions. Research also was reviewed in support of the proposition that there are some physiological reasons for the widespread, if not inevitable, occurrence of certain nonverbal controlling cues in the conversational process.

Other discoveries concerning the roles of a variety of small movements of the head and face need further confirmation. More research also is needed on the determination of functional equivalences and differences in the usage of various forms of nonverbal response. Progress in this rapidly developing field of inquiry should be particularly enhanced by efforts to overcome certain methodological limitations of much of the current body of evidence. These requisites include the wider sampling of subject populations and situations, greater attention to the production of comprehensive coding systems that are reliably communicable; and the precise temporal analysis of multivariate data for short-term and cumulative effects. Finally, progress toward the understanding of the role of nonverbal activities in the exchange of information requires greater integration with new developments in the area of verbal information processing.

REFERENCES

Ahrens, R. Beitrag zur entwicklung des physiognomie-und mimikerkennens. *Zeitschrift fur Experimentelle und Angewandte Psychologie,* 1954, **2,** 412–454.

Argyle, M., & Ingham, R. Gaze, mutual gaze, and proximity. *Semiotica,* 1972, **6,** 32–49.

Argyle, M., Lalljee, M., & Cook, M. The effects of visibility on interaction in a dyad. *Human Relations,* 1968, **21,** 3–17.

Bales, R. F. How people interact in conferences. *Scientific American,* 1955, **192,** 31–35.

Bateson, M. C. Epigenesis of conversational interaction. Paper presented to the Society for Research in Child Development, Minneapolis, April 4, 1971.

Bernstein, B. Social class, linguistic codes, and grammatical elements. *Language and Speech,* 1962, **5,** 221–240.

Birdwhistell, R. L. *Kinesics and context: Essays on body motion communication.* Philadelphia: University of Pennsylvania Press, 1970.

Boucher, J., & Osgood, C. W. The Pollyanna hypothesis. *Journal of Verbal Learning and Verbal Behavior,* 1969, **8,** 1–8.

Brooks, R., Brandt, L., & Wiener, M. Different responses to two communication channels: Socioeconomic class differences in response to verbal reinforcers communicated with and without tonal inflection. *Child Development,* 1969, **40,** 453–470.

Bugental, D. E., Kaswan, J. W., & Love, L. R. Perception of contradictory meanings conveyed by verbal and nonverbal channels. *Journal of Personality and Social Psychology,* 1970, **16,** 647–655. (a)

Bugental, D. E., Kaswan, J. W., Love, L. R., & Fox, M. N. Child versus adult perception of evaluative messages in verbal, vocal and visual channels. *Developmental Psychology,* 1970, **2,** 367–375. (b)

Burns, K. L., & Beier, E. G. Significance of vocal and visual channels in the decoding of emotional meaning. *Journal of Communication,* 1973, **23,** 118–130.

Carswell, E. A., & Rommetveit, R. (Eds.), *Social contexts of messages.* New York: Academic Press, 1971.

Chance, M. R. A. An interpretation of some agonistic postures: The role of "cutoff" acts and postures. *Symposia of the Zoological Society of London,* 1962, **8,** 71–89.

Condon, W. S., & Ogston, W. D. Sound film analysis of normal and pathological behavior patterns. *Journal of Nervous and Mental Disease,* 1966, **143,** 338–347.

Coss, R. G. The cut-off hypothesis: Its relevance to the design of public places. *Man—Environment Systems,* 1973, **3,** 417–440.

Crandall, V. C., Good, S., & Crandall, V. J. Reinforcing effects of adult reactions and *nonreactions on children's achievement expectations; A replication study.* Child Development, 1964, **35,** 485–497.

Crystal, D. *Prosodic systems and intonation in English.* London: Cambridge University Press, 1969.

Darwin, C. *The expression of the emotions in man and animals.* Chicago: The University of Chicago Press, 1965. (Originally published London: Murray, 1872.)

Davis, E. A. *The development of linguistic skill in twins, singletons with siblings, and only children from five to ten years.* Minneapolis: University of Minnesota Press, 1937.

Day, M. E. An eye movement phenomenon relating to attention, thought and anxiety. *Perceptual and Motor Skills,* 1964, **19,** 443–446.

Diebold, R. A., Jr. Antropological perspectives: Anthropology and the comparative psychology of communicative behavior. In T. A. Sebeok (Ed.), *Animal communication: Techniques of study and results of research.* Bloomington: Indiana University Press, 1968.

Dittmann, A. T. Developmental factors in conversational behavior. *The Journal of Communication,* 1972, **22,** 404–423. (a)

Dittmann, A. T. *Interpersonal messages of emotion.* New York: Springer, 1972. (b)

Dittmann, A. T. The body movement–speech rhythm relationship as a cue to speech encoding. In A. W. Siegman & B. Pope (Eds.), *Studies in dyadic communication.* New York: Pergamon Press, 1972. (c)

Dittmann, A. T., & Llewellyn, L. G. The phonemic clause as a unit of speech decoding. *Journal of Personality and Social Psychology,* 1967, **6,** 341–349.

Dittmann, A. T., & Llewellyn, L. G. Relationship between vocalizations and head nods as listener responses. *Journal of Personality and Social Psychology,* 1968, **9,** 79–84.

Dittmann, A. T., & Llewellyn, L. G. Body movement and speech rhythm in social conversation. *Journal of Personality and Social Psychology,* 1969, **11,** 98–106.

Duke, J. D. Lateral eye movement behavior. *Journal of General Psychology,* 1968, **78,** 189–195.

Duncan, S. Jr. Some signals and rules for taking speaking turns in conversations. *Journal of Personality and Social Psychology,* 1972, **23,** 283–292.

Duncan, S., Jr. Toward a grammar for dyadic conversations. *Semiotica,* 1973, **9,** 29–46.

Duncan, S., Jr., On the structure of speaker–auditor interaction during speaking turns. *Language in Society,* 1974, **2,** 161–180.

Duncan, S., Jr., & Niederehe, G. On signaling that it's your turn to speak. *Journal of Experimental Social Psychology,* 1974, **10,** 234–247.

Efron, D. *Gesture, race, and culture.* The Hague: Mouton, 1972 (Originally published as *Gesture and environment.* New York: King's Crown Press, 1941).

Ekman, P. Universals and cultural differences in facial expressions of emotion. In J. K. Cole (Ed.), *Nebraska Symposium on Motivation,* (Vol. 19). Lincoln: University of Nebraska Press, 1972.

Ekman, P., & Friesen, W. V. The repertoire of nonverbal behavior: Categories, origins, usage, and coding. *Semiotica,* 1969, **1,** 49–98.

Ekman, P., & Friesen, W. V. Hand movements. *The Journal of Communication,* 1972, **22,** 353–374.

Ellsworth, P. C., & Ludwig, L. M. Visual behavior in social interaction. *The Journal of Communication,* 1972, **22,** 375–403.

Ervin-Tripp, S. Sociolinguistics. In L. Berkowitz (Ed.), *Advances in experimental social psychology* (Vol. 4). New York: Academic Press, 1969.

Exline, R. V. Explorations in the process of person perception: Visual interaction in relation to competition, sex, and need for affiliation. *Journal of Personality,* 1963, **31,** 1–20.

Feldstein, S. Temporal patterns of dialogue: Basic research and reconsiderations. In A. W. Siegman & B. Pope (Eds.), *Studies in dyadic communication.* New York: Pergamon Press, 1972.

Glucksberg, S., Trabasso, T., & Wald, J. Linguistic structures and mental operations. *Cognitive Psychology,* 1973, **5,** 338–370.

Glucksberg, S., Krauss, R., & Higgins, E. T. The development of referential communication skills. In F. D. Horowitz, M. E. Hetherington, S. Scarr-Salapatek, & G. M. Siegel (Eds.), *Review of Child Development Research,* Vol. 4. Chicago: University of Chicago Press, 1975.

Goffman, E. *Interaction ritual: Essays on face-to-face behavior.* Garden City, New York: Doubleday, 1967.

Goldman-Eisler, F. *Psycholinguistics: Experiments in spontaneous speech.* New York: Academic Press, 1968.

Goldman-Eisler, F. Segmentation of input in simultaneous translation. *Journal of Psycholinguistic Research,* 1972, **1**, 127–140.

Grant, E. C. An ethological description of non-verbal behaviour during interviews. *British Journal of Medical Psychology,* 1968, **41**, 177–184.

Gunnell, P., & Rosenfeld, H. M. Distribution of nonverbal responses in a conversational regulation task. Paper presented to Western Psychological Association, San Francisco, California, April, 1971.

Haas, W. A. & Wepman, J. M. Information theory measures of grammatical goodness of fit. *Journal of Psycholinguistic Research,* 1972, **1**, 175–181.

Hawes, L. C. Development and application of an interview coding system. *Central States Speech Journal,* 1972, **23**, 92–99.

Hindmarch, I. Eyes, eye-spots and pupil dilation in nonverbal communication. In M. von Cranach & I. Vine (Eds.), *Social communication and movement: Studies of interaction and expression in man and chimpanzee.* New York: Academic Press, 1973.

Horowitz, M. W., & Newman, J. B. Spoken and written expression: An experimental analysis. *Journal of Abnormal and Social Psychology,* 1964, **68**, 640–647.

Hutt, C., & Ounsted, C. The biological significance of gaze aversion with particular reference to the syndrome of infantile autism. *Behavioral Science,* 1966, **11**, 346–356.

Jaffe, J., & Feldstein, S. *Rhythms of dialogue.* New York: Academic Press, 1970.

Jaffe, J., Stern, D. N., & Peery, J. C. "Conversational" coupling of gaze behavior in prelinguistic human development. *Journal of Psycholinguistic Research,* 1973, **2**, 321–329.

Jefferson, G. Side sequences. In D. N. Sudnow (Ed.), *Studies in social interaction.* New York: Free Press, 1972.

Kendon, A. Some functions of gaze-direction in social interaction. *Acta Psychologica,* 1967, **26**, 22–63.

Kendon, A. Movement coordination in social interaction: Some examples described. *Acta Psychologica,* 1970, **32**, 100–125.

Kendon, A. Some relationships between body motion and speech: An analysis of an example. In A. W. Siegman & B. Pope (Eds.), *Studies in dyadic communication.* New York: Pergamon Press, 1972.

Kendon, A. The role of visible behaviour in the organization of social interaction. In M. von Cranach & I. Vine (Eds.), *Social communication and movement: Studies of interaction and expression in man and chimpanzee.* London: Academic Press, 1973.

Kendon, A., & Ferber, A. A description of some human greetings. In R. P. Michael & J. H. Crook (Eds.), *Comparative ecology and behaviour of primates.* London: Academic Press, 1973.

Knapp, M. L., Hart, R. P., Friedrich, G. W., & Shulman, G. M. The rhetoric of goodbye: verbal and nonverbal correlates of human leave-taking. *Speech Monographs,* 1973, **40**, 182–198.

Krasner, L. Studies of the conditioning of verbal behavior. *Psychological Review,* 1958, **55**, 148–170.

LaBarre, W. Paralinguistics, kinesics, and cultural anthropology. In T. A. Sebeok, A. S. Hayes, & M. C. Bateson (Eds.), *Approaches to semiotics.* The Hague: Mouton, 1964.

Leach, E. The influence of cultural context on nonverbal communication in man. In R. A. Hinde (Ed.), *Non-verbal communication.* Cambridge: Cambridge University Press, 1972.

Levitt, E. A. The relationship between abilities to express emotional meanings vocally and facially. In J. R. Davitz (Ed.), *The communication of emotional meaning.* New York: McGraw-Hill, 1964.

Longhurst, T. M., & Siegel, G. M. Effects of communication failure on speaker and listener behavior. *Journal of Speech and Hearing Research,* 1973, **16,** 128–140.

MacKay, D. M. Formal analysis of communicative processes. In R. A. Hinde (Ed.), *Nonverbal communication.* Cambridge, England: Cambridge University Press, 1972.

Matarazzo, J. D., Saslow, G., Wiens, A. N., Weitman, M., & Allen, B. V. Interviewer head nodding and interviewee speech durations. *Psychotherapy: Theory, Research and Practice,* 1964, **1,** 54–63. (a)

Matarazzo, J. D., Wiens, A. N., Saslow, G., Allen, B. V., & Weitman, M. Interviewer mm-hmm and interviewee speech durations. *Psychotherapy: Theory, Research and Practice,* 1964, **1,** 109–114. (b)

McGrew, W. C. *An ethological study of children's behavior.* New York: Academic Press, 1972.

Miller, N. E. Learning of visceral and glandular responses. *Science,* 1969, **163,** 434–445.

Morris, W. N. Manipulated amplitude and interruption outcomes. *Journal of Personality and Social Psychology,* 1971, **20,** 319–331.

Moscovici, S. Communication processes and the properties of language. In L. Berkowitz (Ed.), *Advances in experimental social psychology,* Vol. 3. New York: Academic Press, 1967.

Nielsen, G. *Studies in Self Confrontation.* Copenhagen: Munksgaard, 1962.

Pace, R. W., & Boren, R. R. *The human transaction: Facets, functions, and forms of interpersonal communication.* Glenview, Illinois: Scott, Foresman, 1973.

Peterson, C. L., Danner, F. W., & Flavell, J. H. Developmental changes in children's response to three indications of communicative failure. *Child Development,* 1972, **43,** 1463–1468.

Pittenger, R. E., & Smith, H. L., Jr. A basis for some contributions of linguistics to psychiatry. *Psychiatry,* 1957. **20,** 61–78.

Psathas, G. Analyzing dyadic interaction. In G. Gerbner, O. R. Holsti, K. Krippendorff, W. J. Paisley, & P. J. Stone (Eds.), *The analysis of communication content: Developments in scientific theories and computer techniques.* New York: Wiley, 1969.

Rosenberg, S. The development of referential skills in children. In R. L. Schiefelbusch (Ed.), *Language of the mentally retarded.* Baltimore: University Park Press, 1972.

Rosenfeld, H. M. Approval-seeking and approval-inducing functions of verbal and nonverbal responses in the dyad. *Journal of Personality and Social Psychology,* 1966, **4,** 597–605. (a)

Rosenfeld, H. M. Instrumental affiliative functions of facial and gestural expressions. *Journal of Personality and Social Psychology,* 1966, **4,** 65–72. (b)

Rosenfeld, H. M. Nonverbal reciprocation of approval: An experimental analysis. *Journal of Experimental Social Psychology,* 1967, **3,** 102–111.

Rosenfeld, H. M. The experimental analysis of interpersonal influence processes. *The Journal of Communication,* 1972, **22,** 424–442.

Rosenfeld, H. M. & Baer, D. M. Unnoticed verbal conditioning of an aware experimenter by a more aware subject: The double-agent effect. *Psychological Review,* 1969, **76,** 425–432.

Rosenfeld, H. M., & Baer, D. M. Unbiased and unnoticed verbal conditioning: The double-agent robot procedure. *Journal of the Experimental Analysis of Behavior,* 1970, **14,** 99–107.

Rosenfeld, H. M., & Hancks, M. The association of nonverbal behaviors of speakers and listeners with judgments of listener attention, understanding, and agreement (in preparation).

Rosenfeld, H. M., & McRoberts, R. Effects of topographical features and nonverbal context on ratings of teacher head nods. (in preparation)

Rosenfeld, H. M., Shea, M., & Greenbaum, P. Developmental trends in the recognition of normative facial emblems of "right" and "wrong" by normal children from grades 1 to 5. Paper presented to Society for Research in Child Development, Denver, April 1975.

Rosenfeld, H. M., & Sullwold, V. Optimal informational discrepancies for persistent communication. *Behavioral Science,* 1969, **14,** 303–315.

Ruesch, H. *Therapeutic communication.* New York: Norton, 1973.

Sacks, H., Schegloff, E. A., & Jefferson, G. A simplest systematics for the organization of turn-taking for conversation. *Language,* 1974, **50,** 696–735.

Schank, R. C. Conceptual dependency: A theory of natural language understanding. *Cognitive Psychology,* 1972, **3,** 552–631.

Scheflen, A. E. Communication and regulation in psychotherapy. *Psychiatry,* 1963, **26,** 126–136.

Scheflen, A. E. The significance of posture in communication systems. *Psychiatry,* 1964, **27,** 316–331.

Scheflen, A. E. Human communication: Behavioral programs and their integration in interaction. *Behavioral Science,* 1968, **13,** 44–55.

Schegloff, E. A. Sequencing in conversational openings. *American Anthropologist,* 1968, **70,** 1075–1095.

Schegloff, E. A., & Sacks, H. Opening up closings. *Semiotica,* 1973, **8,** 289–327.

Shannon, C. E., & Weaver, W. *The mathematical theory of communication.* Urbana: University of Illinois Press, 1949.

Siegman, A. W. Effect of noncontingent interviewer mm-hmms on interviewee productivity. *Proceedings, 81st Annual Convention, American Psychological Association,* 1973, **8,** 559–560.

Snyder, W. U. An investigation of the nature of non-directive psychotherapy. *Journal of General Psychology,* 1945, **33,** 193–223.

Speier, M. Some conversational problems for interactional analysis. In D. N. Sudnow (Ed.), *Studies in social interaction.* New York: Free Press, 1972.

Spitz, R. A. *No and yes: On the genesis of human communication.* New York: International Universities Press, 1957.

Stephenson, G. M., Rutter, D. R., & Dore, S. R. Visual interaction and distance. *British Journal of Psychology,* 1972, **64,** 251–257.

Stern, D. N. Mother and infant at play: The dyadic interaction involving facial, vocal and gaze behaviors. In M. Lewis & L. Rosenblum (Eds.), *The effect of the infant on its caregiver.* New York: Wiley, 1974.

Stevenson, H. W. Social reinforcement of children's behavior. In L. P. Lipsitt & C. C. Spiker (Eds.), *Advances in child development and behavior,* Vol. 2. New York: Academic Press, 1965.

Stone, P. J., Dunphy, D. C., Smith, M. S., & Ogilvie, D. M. *The general inquirer: A computer approach to content analysis.* Cambridge, Massachusetts: M.I.T. Press, 1966.

Trager, G. L. Paralanguage: A first approximation. *Studies in Linguistics,* 1958, **13,** 1–12.

Trager, G. L. Some thoughts on 'juncture'. *Studies in Linguistics,* 1962, **16,** 11–22.

Trager, G. L., & Smith, H. L., Jr. *An outline of English structure.* (Studies in Linguistics: Occasional Papers, 3). Norman, Oklahoma: Battenberg Press, 1951. (Republished: New York: American Council of Learned Societies, 1965).

Ulrich, R. Conversational control. *Psychological Record,* 1962, **12,** 327–330.

Vine, I. Communication by facial–visual signals. In J. H. Crook (Ed.), *Social behaviour in birds and mammals: Essays on the social ethology of animals and man.* London: Academic Press, 1970.

Walters, R. H., & Parke, R. D. The role of the distance receptors in the development of social responsiveness. In L. P. Lipsitt & C. C. Spiker (Eds.), *Advances in child development and behavior,* Vol. 2. New York: Academic Press, 1965.

Webb, J. T. Interview synchrony: An investigation of two speech rate measures. In A. W. Siegman & B. Pope (Eds.), *Studies in dyadic communication.* New York: Pergamon Press, 1972.

Wiener, M., Devoe, S., Rubinow, S., & Geller, J. Nonverbal behavior and nonverbal communication. *Psychological Review,* 1972, **79,** 185–214.

Yngve, V. H. On getting a word in edgewise. In M. A. Campbell *et al.* (Eds.), *Papers from the sixth regional meeting, Chicago Linguistic Society.* Chicago: University of Chicago Department of Linguistics, 1970.

Zaidel, S. F., & Mehrabian, A. The ability to communicate and infer positive and negative attitudes facially and vocally. *Journal of Experimental Research in Personality,* 1969, **3,** 233–241.

11

A Chronography
of Conversation: In Defense
# of an Objective Approach

Stanley Feldstein

University of Maryland Baltimore County

Joan Welkowitz

New York University

Conversational interaction is increasingly being viewed as a singularly intriguing and rich interpersonal process. Consider the astonishing variety of behaviors that can occur within the confines of even a single conversation. Mouths open narrowly or widely; voices emerge to utter sounds, grow loud and soft, and high and low; lips curl and stretch; teeth grind; nostrils twitch; eyes blink; pupils dilate; eyebrows lift; foreheads crease; heads nod; shoulders shrug; arms wave; hands turn; fingers flex; legs cross; feet shuffle; bodies shift, and—through it all perhaps—eyes may watch; ears may listen; noses may sniff. The list is not exhaustive. But amidst such a bustle of activity, it is relatively easy to overlook one of the basic dimensions of conversational interaction, that is, the temporal organization of its sounds and silences. It is this temporal organization, indexed by the chronography of conversation, with which the present chapter is concerned.

The importance of time as a psychologically meaningful dimension of human behavior cannot seriously be questioned. Time as a succession, time as duration, time as rhythm, are aspects of all the ventures of human existence (e.g., Fraser, 1966). Formal studies of the perception of time form a body of psychological literature that is probably smaller than it ought to be. But studies of the time it takes to do or say something, or to begin doing or saying something represent a quite sizable portion of the literature of psychology. Nonetheless, although the formal investigation of the time patterns of verbal interaction began several decades ago, it has only recently begun to develop in ways that are of more general psychological interest. It is probably fair to say that this development was stimulated in large part by the coupling of a markedly increased concern about the details of interpersonal behavior with, as Rosenfeld (Chapter 10) suggests, a technological sophistication that made the adequate recording and analysis of such behavior possible. That this concern has focussed, in part, upon conversation implies two basic and related notions. The first is that conversation might usefully be considered a microcosm of social interaction; the second, that characteristic patterns of individual behavior are most clearly displayed in social interactions.

The working expectations that underlie much of the research in conversation chronography have to do with the possibilities that the pacing of a conversational exchange not only modifies (along with other coverbal behavior) the lexical message embedded in it, but in part communicates and is determined by aspects of the participants' personalities and by dimensions of their relations with each other. These possibilities are enhanced by the fact that such pacing is not ordinarily under deliberate control. On the other hand, the adequacy with which the possibilities can be explored very much depends upon the adequacy with which the pacing is described. This chapter is concerned primarily with some of the major issues involved in such a description. To that end, it reviews the temporal classifications that initiated the area of conversation chronography and an alternative classification preferred by the authors. It then compares, in some detail, the implications of recent definitions of turn-taking behavior (which is viewed as the behavior that centrally characterizes conversation) and briefly describes some investigations of talking in and out of turn. Finally, the chapter presents a series of studies that have to do with the tendency of conversational participants to match each other's speech patterns during the course of one or more conversations.

INITIAL APPROACHES

To what does the "chronography" of a conversation refer, that is, exactly what aspects of a conversation are timed? The earliest answer was provided by Norwine and Murphy (1938): "In the simplest case of conversational interchange each party speaks for a short time, pauses, and the other party replies. The time intervals are then simply the lengths of time each party speaks and the lengths of the pauses between speeches" [p. 282]. They called the speeches *talkspurts* and defined a single *talkspurt* as the "...speech of one party, including his pauses, which is preceded and followed, with or without intervening pauses, by speech from the other party perceptible to the one producing the talkspurt" [p. 282]. They also noted that there are instances in which, instead of alternating, the speakers engage in simultaneous talkspurts, which they named *double talking*. Their recognition of the fact that there are pauses within talkspurts was formalized by labeling such pauses *resumption times*. However, the pauses that separated the talkspurts of different speakers were called *response times*.

Norwine and Murphy worked for the Bell Telephone System and the data they used to formulate a description of conversational time patterns were recorded telephone interactions. The apparent clarity of their categories was marred by the ambiguity they introduced into their discussion of *response time,* which, they asserted, ". . . ordinarily occurs at the end of a talkspurt but may be a pause followed by a resumption of speech by the first talker" [p. 282]. The qualification implies that either an arbitrary duration must be set beyond which a resumption time becomes a response time, or the classification of silences must be a matter of judgment. Either way, the objectivity of the talkspurt and silence categories are compromised.

A quite different method of timing conversational interactions was offered by the anthropologist, Eliot Chapple, who was concerned with cross-cultural comparisons. Chapple (1939, 1940) asserted that the timing of the "acts" of one individual in interaction with another could provide psychology with an objective and reliable method of assessing personality. To examine the assertion, he constructed the Interaction Chronograph (Chapple, 1949), which is simply an instrument used by an observer to record the occurrences and durations of the "actions" and "inactions" of each participant in an interaction, as well as "interruptions (when both act)" and "failures to respond (when both are silent)." Although the method utilized verbal behavior as its primary data, it included all gestural behavior that was judged by the observer to be part of the interaction. Average scores of 12 presumably different measures could be derived from the record of the Interaction Chronograph, although it might be noted that of the 66 coefficients obtained by intercorrelating the measures, only 17 were nonsignificant and 14 were ±.70 or above; no one of the measures was statistically independent of all the others (Matarazzo, Saslow, & Hare, 1958, p. 421). Nevertheless, they were thought to be conceptually different from each other.

It must be stressed that Chapple was concerned with interpersonal action rather than interpersonal verbal behavior. The Chronograph was intended for the study of "action" units rather than speech units, and observers were instructed to score an action as finished only when "all facial (and other) muscle activity" had ceased (Chapple, 1939). Theoretically, an action could include the occurrence of speech but does not necessarily imply it. In point of fact, however, Chapple and his colleagues used as their interactional contexts interviews and, occasionally, somewhat less constrained types of conversations (e.g., Chapple & Harding, 1940). Moreover, the action units served as the basis for scoring "utterance" and "silence" durations. It seems quite appropriate, therefore, to regard Chapple's research as embodying a model of conversational time patterns. The research that, in fact, took this position with respect to Chapple's work was begun in 1954 by Matarazzo and his colleagues (Matarazzo & Wiens, 1972). They used the Chronograph to describe the temporal patterning of interviews as a method of examining the "emotional, attitudinal, or motivational state" of the interviewees.

Originally, Matarazzo and his associates utilized the measures devised by Chapple, but they then discovered that most of the variance associated with the 12 measures could be accounted for by just two variables, namely *speech* and *silence* (Matarazzo *et al.,* 1958). To facilitate obtaining the values of these variables directly, they designed a system (Johnston, Jensen, Weitman, Hess, Matarazzo, & Saslow, 1961) that recorded and automatically scored sequences of verbal interactions. As does the Chronograph, the system, called the Interaction Recorder, requires a human observer. However, the observer is not required to view the interacting individuals but simply to hear them. In 1966, Wiens, Molde, Holman, and Matarazzo reported that the exclusion of all bodily gestures from the decisions involved in the unitizing of verbal behavior yielded utterance durations that differed very little from those that included gestural behavior. Thus, they characterize the verbal interactions in an interview in terms of four measures: *utterances, interruptions, reaction time latencies,* and *initiative time latencies.* According to Matarazzo and Wiens (1972), ". . . *an utterance (or speech unit) is recorded as the total duration of time it takes a speaker to emit all the words he is contributing in that particular unit of exchange (as this would be judged by common social standards)*" [p. 6, original italics] . *Interruptions* are defined as instances of simultaneous speech. A *reaction time latency* is the interval of silence between the end of one person's utterance and the beginning of the other person's utterance. Finally, an *initiative time latency* is the silence that occurs between two consecutive utterances of the same speaker. They are silences that ". . . precede the introduction of new ideas or thoughts by the same individual *without an intervening comment by the other interview participant* . . ." [p. 8, original italics] .

These four parameters are less ambiguous than the earlier measures used by Matarazzo and his colleagues by virtue of the fact that their delineation is not dependent upon gestural information. According to its definition, however, an utterance is still determined by an observer's judgment about the semantic content of what a speaker says. The observer probably also uses the pitch and intensity contours of the speaker's voice to make his determination. At the same time, Matarazzo and Wiens indicate that, in practise, an utterance that can be judged incomplete by virtue of its content is recorded as completed if it is interrupted by the comment of another speaker.

Note that the labels, *reaction time latency* and *response time,* while they may not necessarily imply a strict stimulus-response model of interactional behavior, do assign responsibility for the silence indicated to the person whose speech follows the silence. The assumptions that underlie the assignment may or may not characterize interviews; in the absence of systematic evidence, they cannot be said to characterize conversations in general.

Judgmental variables are problematical. They can, of course, be shown to be reliable in the sense that the same judge, given the same data and sufficient training, will tend to make the same judgment from one time to the next. Moreover, different judges can usually be trained to make the same, or similar judgments about the same data. Nevertheless, judgments are rarely as satisfying as objective measurements if only because it is never clear how the various sorts of information used to make judgments are weighted, or whether all of the available information is even used.

AN EMPIRICAL CLASSIFICATION

In 1963, Jaffe and Feldstein began to explore the possibility of using interaction chronography to study psychopathological communication. They made two decisions, however, which determined the course of their research and differentiated it from previous chronographic research. The first decision was to describe a set of temporal categories that carried no inferential baggage, was concerned only with verbal behavior, and could be obtained automatically from live or audiotaped dialogues (or multilogues). The second was based upon the realization that to learn anything about the relation of dialogic time patterns to psychopathology, they would need to know much more than was known about the patterns of nonpathological interactions. Thus, they decided to examine the temporal structure of conversations by individuals not considered psychologically disturbed.

The decision to study the temporal patterns of verbal interactions empirically was also made—at about the same time—by a number of other investigators. Brady (1965, 1968, 1969) developed a completely automated system for detecting what he calls the "on-off patterns" of speech. His concern, as had been that of Norwine and Murphy, was with the patterns of telephone conversations rather than with face-to-face interactions. Nevertheless, the care and sophistication of his approach to the area and particularly to aspects of instrumentation design that affect the interpretation of the on-off patterns have been instructive. Similarly, Hayes and Meltzer and their associates approached the empirical analysis of conversational time patterns as a way of studying the details of social behavior (e.g., Hayes, 1969; Meltzer, Hayes, & Shellenberger, 1966). They have been sufficiently impressed with the usefulness of the approach and the importance of physicalistic cues (e.g., amplitude, duration) in social interaction to propose that the study of such cues warrants the formation of a subdivision of social psychology called "social psychophysics" (Meltzer, Morris, & Hayes, 1971).

The AVTA System

An empirical analysis of conversational time patterns can be accomplished most easily by an electronic system capable of automatically detecting and recording the presence and absence of speech. The investigators mentioned above have developed their own instruments for the purpose. Only one system, the Automatic Vocal Transaction Analyzer, or AVTA (Cassotta, Feldstein, & Jaffe, 1964; Jaffe & Feldstein, 1970), will be described here, firstly because it broadly illustrates the type of system needed, and secondly because the description will clarify the nature of the data used by Jaffe and Feldstein to categorize conversational time patterns.

AVTA does not require the use of a human observer.[1] It includes a component[2] that "perceives" the verbal behavior of each participant in an audiotaped or ongoing conversation simply as a sequence of sounds and silences. The component is essentially an analogue-to-digital converter with voice relays and a cancellation network that electronically cancels the spill of each speaker's voice into the other speaker's microphone. It functions by "inquiring" about the state of the relays associated with each speaker at a predetermined rate that can range from 100 to 1000 msec. The initial studies (Jaffe & Feldstein, 1970) used an inquiry rate of 300 msec., that is, the state of the relays were monitored 200 times per minute. Subsequent studies have used inquiry rates of either 100 or 300 msec. Comparisons have indicated that the two inquiry rates yield results that, in terms of average values per time interval, are not markedly different (Jaffe & Feldstein, 1970). The information obtained from the relays is transmitted to a computer component of the system which provides a computer-readable record of the digitized sound–silence sequences and descriptive statistics summarizing the parameter values derived from them.

One other technical point should be made clear. Although no one is required to monitor the verbal interactions processed by ATVA, a person with unimpaired hearing is needed to determine the level of vocal intensity that AVTA is to accept as a speech sound, thereby enabling AVTA to decide which behavior is to be assigned to what temporal category. The purpose of this procedure is to generate a description of the time patterns of verbal interactions as perceived by a human listener and, presumably, by the speakers themselves.

---

[1] Welkowitz and Martz (unpublished data) recently completed a software version of AVTA for use with the PDP/12 computer (Digital Equipment Corporation). The hardware version uses a PDP/8.

[2] Another component analyzes the amplitude, or intensity level, of the voices in a conversation.

Parameters of Conversational Time Patterns

Jaffe and Feldstein (1970) segmented the conversational speech stream into five empirically defined categories or parameters: *speaker switches, vocalizations, pauses, switching pauses,* and *simultaneous speech.* The intervals of time between successive speaker switches were rather awkwardly called "floor times." It is more convenient—and consistent with other parameter definitions—to consider "speaker switches" and "floor times" two aspects of a single parameter that may be called *speaking turns,* or more simply, *turns.* Speaker switches index the frequency of turns, and floor times their durations. A *turn* begins the instant one participant in a conversation starts talking alone and ends immediately prior to the instant another participant starts talking alone.[3] It is, in other words, the time during which a participant has the floor. The parameter, *turns,* is the crux of the temporal classification inasmuch as it indexes the feature that defines a conversation, that is, the fact that its participants alternate, or take turns speaking. It is also the superordinate member of the classification in that the other parameters represent events that occur during each participant's turn. Thus, a *vocalization* is a continuous (i.e., uninterrupted) segment of speech (sound) uttered by the person who has the floor. A *pause* is an interval of joint silence bounded by the vocalizations of the person who has the floor and is, therefore (as are the vocalizations), credited to him. A *switching pause* is an interval of joint silence bounded by the vocalizations of different participants, that is, it follows a vocalization by the participant who has the floor and is terminated by the vocalization of another participant who thereby obtains the floor. Thus, the switching pause is a silence that marks a switch of speakers or, alternatively, the end of one turn and beginning of another. Since it occurs during the turn of the person who relinquished the floor, it is credited to him.

Simultaneous speech is speech uttered by a participant who does *not* have the floor during a vocalization by the participant who does have the floor. On the basis of its outcome, simultaneous speech may be divided into two types: interruptive and noninterruptive (Feldstein, BenDebba, & Alberti, 1974). *Noninterruptive simultaneous speech* begins and ends while the participant who has the floor is talking. *Interruptive simultaneous speech* is part of a speech segment that begins while the person who has the floor is talking and ends after he has stopped. Only that portion of the segment uttered while the other person is still talking is considered interruptive simultaneous speech. The remaining portion, inasmuch as it is a unilateral utterance, marks the beginning of a turn for the participant who initiated the simultaneous speech and is considered, therefore, his vocalization. Thus, interruptive simultaneous speech culminates in a change

---

[3] Although the parameters have, to date, been utilized only for the analysis of dialogues, the wording used here to define them is intended to indicate their applicability, in principle, to the temporal analysis of multilogues.

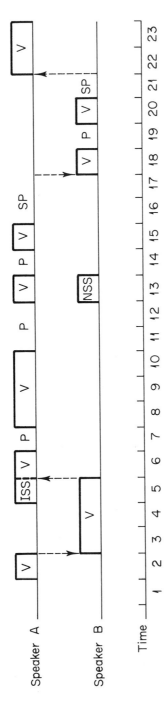

FIG. 1. A diagramatic representation of a conversational sequence. The numbered line at the bottom represents time in 300-msec units. V stands for *vocalization*, P for *pause*, and SP for *switching pause* (the silence that frequently occurs immediately prior to a change in the speaking *turn*). The arrows that point down denote the end of speaker *A*'s turns; the arrows that point up denote the end of speaker *B*'s turns. ISS and NSS stand for *interruptive* and *noninterruptive simultaneous speech*, respectively. (Adapted from Figure II-2 of Jaffe and Feldstein, 1970).

of which participant has the floor while noninterruptive simultaneous speech does not.[4] Figure 1 graphically illustrates the five temporal parameters.

Parameter Characteristics

Inasmuch as the parameters were quite different from those involved in previous classifications of interactional time patterns, studies were conducted to investigate the extent to which they are independent of each other and reliable. The studies are described in detail elsewhere (e.g., Jaffe & Feldstein, 1970) and their results need only be reviewed briefly here. It should be noted, however, that these results are concerned primarily with the average durations of pauses, switching pauses, and vocalizations. Only later were more extensive analyses of the characteristics of speaking turns and simultaneous speech conducted, and the results of those analyses are reported in greater detail.

Most of the results presented here are from one study, both for the sake of brevity and because the study was the one best suited to examine the interrelationships and reliabilities of the parameters. However, the results are representative of those obtained in previous and subsequent investigations. The study (Marcus, Welkowitz, Feldstein, & Jaffe, 1970) examined the verbal exchanges of 24 female college students who had been divided into six equal groups. The design required that each subject meet individually with each of the three other subjects in her group for half an hour a day for eight consecutive weekdays. She was told that the purpose of the study was to provide information about how

---

[4] The distinction between interruptive and noninterruptive simultaneous speech is identical to that made by Meltzer et al. (1971) between successful and unsuccessful interruptions. The difference in terminology, which may seem to make for an unnecessary proliferation of names for the same events, appears to reflect a basic difference in approach. The names *interruptive simultaneous speech* and *noninterruptive simultaneous speech* are purely descriptive; the occurrence of simultaneous speech either terminates in an interruption (the participant who has the floor stops talking) or does not. Such names communicate no preconceptions that are likely to bias inquiries about the events they describe and/or needlessly complicate the ways in which the results of the inquiries can be interpreted. On the other hand, the names *successful interruptions* and *unsuccessful interruptions* are meaningful only when viewed as abbreviations of *successful-* and *unsuccessful-*interruption attempts. But the name *interruption attempts* implies knowledge about the intentions of those participants who happen to speak simultaneously. Indeed, Meltzer and his colleagues frame the paper in words and phrases (for example, win, lose, defender, contest for the floor, wrest the floor away) that assume that the intentions of the speakers play a motivational role in the occurrence of simultaneous talking. They even speculate about whether such brief utterances as "yes" and "uh-huh" should be classified as "interruptions" (when they occur as simultaneous speech) inasmuch as they ". . . are obviously not attempts to take over the floor . . ." (Metzler et al., 1971, p. 395). Since they provide no evidence for such a position, it can only be considered to reflect their preconceptions about a possibly important but still unexplored dimension of the issues they investigated. The point here is not to denigrate an otherwise excellent paper, but to suggest that the meaning of parameters might better be established by research than by fiat.

people get to know each other through conversation, and she was asked to use the half-hour periods with each partner to talk about whatever might further that goal. Thus, the subjects engaged in 36 dialogues on each of eight occasions. (Inasmuch as the groups each consisted of four subjects, they were called quartets while the study was being conducted, and the informal name, *quartet study,* will be used here as a convenient reference label.)

Pauses, switching pauses, and vocalizations. The first question that had to be answered was whether the parameters—although they clearly represent different events—could be considered distinct aspects of the time structure of conversation. The results of the quartet study and previous studies (Cassotta, Feldstein, & Jaffe, 1967; Feldstein, Jaffe, & Cassotta, 1967) indicated that only pauses and switching pauses are significantly related to each other and then only within the context of relatively unstructured conversations; the comparisons of pauses and switching pauses yielded product-moment rs of .60 and .66 for the conversations and .23 for interviews. That the magnitude of their relationship distinguished two different types of dialogue seemed to justify maintaining their separate identities. Subsequent studies (to be discussed later) have confirmed the usefulness of that decision.

Several types of reliability were examined. One that need only be mentioned is the reliability of the AVTA system. Research (Cassotta *et al.,* 1964) demonstrated not only the capability of the system to replicate accurately the analysis of a given conversation, but also the superiority of its performance to that of a human observer. The remaining types of reliability involve the consistency of the parameter values within single conversations and their stability from conversation to conversation.

The following types of reliability were evaluated: (a) the consistency of the parameter values from the first to the second 15 min. of a conversation; (b) the stability of the parameter values from one conversation to another involving the same participants; and (c) the stability of the parameter values from one conversation to another in which only one of the participants is the same. For the first type of reliability, the evaluation yielded average estimates of .71 for pauses, .72 for switching pauses, and .76 for vocalizations. For the second type, it yielded average estimates of .65 for pauses, .66 for switching pauses, and .68 for vocalizations. Assessment of the third type yielded average estimates of .33 for pauses, .33 for switching pauses, and .72 for vocalizations. The estimates suggest that the ways in which individuals time their verbal participation in conversational exchanges remain quite consistent during the course of a conversation and, with the same partners, stable from one conversation to the next. However, when the different conversations involve different partners, only the average durations of their vocalizations remain stable. A possible explanation for the unreliability of the average silence durations in such a context will be offered later.

TABLE 1

Means (M) and Standard Deviations (SD) of the Frequencies and Average Durations of Interruptive and Noninterruptive Simultaneous Speech (ISS and NSS, respectively) and Speaking Turns within and across the Eight Occasions of the Quartet Study

Parameter			1	2	3	4	5	6	7	8	Average
						Occasions					
Frequency	ISS	M	24.6	27.3	28.2	27.6	29.3	30.6	29.4	29.0	28.3
		SD	13.8	15.0	15.0	13.3	15.2	14.7	14.5	15.0	14.7
	NSS	M	43.1	45.0	44.6	48.8	48.4	45.8	42.5	41.6	45.0
		SD	29.7	29.5	22.8	36.6	25.0	19.2	21.2	19.5	26.0
Duration	ISS	M	.416	.422	.422	.461	.425	.436	.425	.419	.428
		SD	.062	.059	.048	.236	.059	.077	.069	.065	.084
	NSS	M	.397	.403	.398	.425	.410	.403	.412	.407	.407
		SD	.047	.049	.048	.166	.050	.043	.053	.061	.065
Turn frequency		M	188.9	193.4	187.8	185.5	192.9	191.2	191.6	198.9	191.3
		SD	41.5	32.8	35.6	38.5	45.0	40.6	42.1	46.2	40.3
Turn duration		M	4.983	4.749	4.958	5.008	4.877	4.938	4.893	4.708	4.889
		SD	2.045	1.707	1.797	1.776	1.819	2.160	1.952	1.931	1.898

Note: The durations are given in seconds. The quartet study (Marcus et al., 1970) is described in the text.

Speaking turns and simultaneous speech. Information about the descriptive characteristics of speaking turns and simultaneous speech (as defined earlier) has, for the most part, not yet appeared in print. It may be useful, therefore, to present such information before going further. Table 1 lists the means and standard deviations that were derived from the conversations obtained in the quartet study. Note again that the conversations were relatively unconstrained and might be expected to differ in frequencies and durations of turns and simultaneous speech from other types of dialogues. Indeed, in the interviews examined by Cassotta *et al.* (1967), too little simultaneous speech occurred to warrant its analysis.

Initially, it seemed a potentially fruitful strategy to explore both the frequencies and durations of turns and simultaneous speech, if only to obtain the sort of descriptive statistics presented in Table 1. There is, of course, a necessary and inverse relation between the average duration of an individual's turns and the number of turns he has taken within a given unit of time. In the quartet study, the correlation of turn frequencies and turn durations yielded an average coefficient of $-.54$. On the other hand, there is no necessary relation between the number of times people engage in simultaneous speech and the durations of their engagements. It may well be that the two aspects of simultaneous speech reflect different processes and/or person characteristics. The extent of the relation between the frequencies and durations of simultaneous speech (in the quartet study) is indexed by correlation coefficients of .22 for noninterruptive simultaneous speech (NSS) and .11 for interruptive simultaneous speech (ISS). It may be more likely, though, that the magnitude of these coefficients is primarily a function of the inconsistency of the NSS and ISS durations. The consistency with which the women who took part in the quartet study utilized NSS and ISS durations during the course of a conversation was examined by comparing the first and second 15 min. of their conversations on each occasion. As can be seen in Table 2, the consistency estimates for the durations of NSS and ISS are markedly lower than are those for the frequencies of NSS and ISS; indeed, the estimates for the ISS durations hover about zero. It is not clear why the durations are unreliable. The durations used in the study ranged (given the constraint of the AVTA inquiry period) from one 300-msec. unit to three 300-msec. units. Most of the women engaged in one- and two-unit segments; whether they used one or the other was apparently fortuitous. Similarly, assessments of the stability of NSS and ISS durations over time yielded low, nonsignificant coefficients[5] of .20 for the NSS segments and .06 for the ISS

---

[5] Remember that each dyad conversed once each day for eight days. Thus, the study permitted an examination of stability over varying time intervals, the shortest being that between two consecutive conversations and the longest between the first and last conversation. The eight occasions allow for 28 "between-occasions" comparisons, and they were made by means of product-moment correlations. The resulting coefficients were transformed to z's before being averaged.

TABLE 2

Reliability Estimates for the Comparison of the First and Second Fifteen
Minutes Within each Occasion of the Quartet Study for the Frequencies
and Average Durations of Interruptive and Noninterruptive Simultaneous
Speech (ISS and NSS, respectively) and Speaking Turns

Parameter						Occasions				
		1	2	3	4	5	6	7	8	Average
Frequency	ISS	.70	.59	.78	.65	.63	.64	.66	.70	.67
	NSS	.82	.66	.79	.64	.69	.53	.64	.51	.67
Duration	ISS	.17	.02	.06	.29	.32	−.06	−.02	.35	.15
	NSS	.17	.38	.25	.53	.22	.26	.31	.36	.31
Turn Frequency		.69	.56	.54	.54	.75	.57	.64	.69	.63
Turn Duration		.74	.63	.58	.51	.59	.60	.77	.56	.63

Note: The reliability estimates are zero order product-moment correlation coefficients.
The df for each comparison is 22. A coefficient of .40 is needed for significance at the .05
level (two-tailed).

segments. Thus, the amount of time spent in each occurrence of simultaneous
speech varied inconsistently not only within single conversations but also from
conversation to conversation (in which the same participants were involved).

A comparison of the mean durations of the NSS and ISS segments (averaged
over the eight occasions) indicated that there is neither a significant relationship nor an appreciable difference between them. This lack of a difference
seems to suggest that the duration of simultaneous speech does not determine its
outcome, that is, whether it becomes interruptive or noninterruptive. This
suggestion, as well as the fact that the average durations of the NSS and ISS
segments obtained in the quartet study are brief and indistinguishable, are at
variance with the findings of Meltzer *et al.* (1971). They obtained simultaneous
speech segments that lasted as long as 6 sec. Moreover, their report seems to
imply that the durations of the ISS and NSS segments they obtained (the
"successful" and "unsuccessful" interruptions, to use their own words) were
different. This difference in the results of the two studies may be a function of
gender and/or task; Meltzer, Morris, and Hayes used male as well as female
participants, and asked them to engage in problem-solving discussions. It seems
likely, however, that the nature of the conversation is the more important
determinant. Apparently, social conversations that are essentially not task oriented do not elicit sustained instances of simultaneous speech. In any case, that
the studies obtained different results argues for a systematic look at the duration
of simultaneous speech as a function of different conversational contexts and
structures.

The frequency with which simultaneous speech occurred in the quartet study was both consistent within conversations (Table 2) and stable across conversations; the stability estimate for NSS is .48 and for ISS is .61. It is particularly interesting to note the considerable variation in the frequencies with which individuals engaged in the two types of simultaneous speech. NSS was initiated by one of the participants only three times during the course of a conversation and by another, 201 times. The frequencies with which the participants initiated ISS ranged from 1 to 87 per conversation. In other words, there was one person who initiated NSS on an average of about every 9 sec. and another person who actually interrupted her partner at an average rate of approximately once every 21 sec.! A comparison of the NSS and ISS frequencies, averaged over the eight occasions, yielded a correlation coefficient of .62 (Feldstein, BenDebba, & Alberti, 1974), indicating that those persons who tended to initiate NSS often also tended to initiate ISS often and vice versa. The magnitude of the relationship raises some questions about the viability of differentially categorizing segments of simultaneous speech simply on the basis of their consequences. But that, after all, is the basis upon which pauses and switching pauses are distinguished; they are silences which have different outcomes. It has yet to be demonstrated clearly, however, that the distinction between NSS and ISS is more than topographical, although some efforts relevant to the issue will be explored later.

Intercorrelations between the two types of simultaneous speech and pauses, switching pauses, and vocalizations yielded the coefficients presented in Table 3. It is worth noting that, although all of the coefficients are low, the majority are

TABLE 3

Comparisons of the Frequencies and Average
Durations of Interruptive and Noninterruptive
Simultaneous Speech (ISS and NSS,
Respectively) with the Average Durations
of Pauses (P), Switching Pauses (SP) and
Vocalizations (V)[a]

		P	SP	V
Frequency	ISS	−.39	−.37	.01
	NSS	−.32	−.24	−.24
Duration	ISS	−.18	−.26	.34
	NSS	−.23	−.29	.19

[a]Note: The values in the table are zero-order product-moment correlation coefficients averaged (using z transformations) over the eight occasions of the quartet study. The df for each comparison is 22. An coefficient of .40 is required for significance at the .05 level (two tailed).

negative, and especially that those participants who tended to initiate ISS more frequently tended also to have shorter pauses and switching pauses.

Not only is it interesting to note the wide range of frequencies with which individuals initiate simultaneous speech, but also the markedly different frequencies with which turns are initiated (or relinquished) in relatively unrestrained conversations. (It is necessarily the case that the number of turns taken by one participant in a dialogue cannot differ from that taken by the other participant by more than 1. On the other hand, the average amount of time a participant keeps the floor once he has acquired it can be very different from that of the other participant.) The one 30-min. conversation of the quartet study that had the fewest number of turns had 96; the one with the most had 312. The average duration of turns within a single conversation ranged from approximately 1.5 sec. to 15 sec. As can be seen in Table 1, however, the average (over eight occasions) number of turns initiated during the course of a conversation was approximatly 191, and the average duration of each turn was about 5 sec. It is, moreover, clear from Table 2 that the frequencies with which the women of the study took the floor and the lengths of time they held it were quite consistent within conversations. Indeed, they also remained stable from one conversation to another; the stability estimates are .61 for turn frequencies and .64 for turn durations.

Pauses, switching pauses, and vocalizations are the events of which most speaking turns are comprised, although it should be clear that a turn may consist of a single vocalization, a vocalization and a switching pause, or only vocalizations and pauses. Nevertheless, one might suppose that the average durations of the three events account for much of the variability associated with the average durations of turns. Comparisons between turn durations and the durations of vocalizations, pauses, and switching pauses, using the data from the quartet study, yielded zero-order correlation coefficients of .44, .34, and .12, respectively. However, the multiple correlation (R) of the three parameters with turns is .66 $(F_{3,20} = 17.32; p < .001)$ indicating that, in the quartet study, the three parameters accounted for 43% of the variability of turns. Of the 43%, vocalizations contributed 19%, pauses 22%, and switching pauses only 2%. (The relation between pauses and switching pauses yielded an R of .66.) Notice, then that the *duration* of turns does not appear to be entirely accounted for by durations of its components; indeed, a good bit of its variability remains unexplained. The finding tends to support the notion, implicit in the empirical classification of time patterns, that the parameter, speaking turns, carries information that is not fully shared by the other parameters.

Not surprisingly, the contribution of the durations of pauses, switching pauses, and vocalizations to the *frequency* of turns was much smaller. The coefficients indexing the relations between turn frequency and the durations of the three parameters are −.08 for vocalizations, −.31 for pauses, and −.40 for switching pauses. Together, they account for 19% of the variability of turn frequencies

$(F_{3,20} = 5.43; p < .05)$ but of that, switching pause durations are responsible for 16%. The more active the interaction in a dialogue (the larger is its number of turns), the more likely it is that the participants will have shorter switching pauses.

Simultaneous speech is not a component of the turn. However, the strong relation between the frequencies of turns and of interruptive simultaneous speech ($r = .75$) is not unexpected. By definition, the more interruptive simultaneous speech individuals engage in, the more frequently they obtain the floor. The addition of noninterruptive simultaneous speech frequencies to this relationship is inconsequential in its effect. On the other hand, the frequencies of both ISS and, particularly, NSS are highly related to the *duration* of turns. NSS frequencies account for 38% of the variability of turn durations in the data from the quartet study, and ISS frequencies account for an additional and significant 6%. There does not appear to be a necessary relation between the frequency with which people initiate NSS and the average duration of their turns, but the analysis indicates that the more the participants of the study did initiate NSS the shorter were the average durations of their turns. Similarly, the more ISS they initiated, the shorter were their turns on the average.

Turn durations were also significantly related to the *durations* of both NSS and ISS, but given the unreliability of simultaneous speech durations, it is not clear that the relationship is meaningful.

TURN-TAKING BEHAVIOR: DISAGREEMENTS AND DIRECTIONS

A growing number of investigators have become interested of late in the fact that people alternate—take turns—speaking when they engage in conversation. (Even the participants in a conversation recognize the importance of such alternation and will occasionally comment on its absence with the observation, "This seems to be a one-sided conversation.") Schegloff (1968) asserted that the phenomenon be considered a basic rule of conversation and, more than a decade ago, Miller (1963) suggested that the taking of turns in conversation may warrant the status of a language universal.

Definitional Differences

Offhand, one would think it easy to know who in a conversation has the turn and who does not. It is, therefore, surprising to find so little agreement about not only what a turn is, but when it occurs and who has it. "Difficult as it might be to realize, a major hurdle to research on human speech (whether involving content or noncontent approaches) has been the lack of agreement among investigators on how to define the basic unit or units to be studied" (Matarazzo & Wiens, 1972, pp. 3–4). As was said earlier, the turn in the pivotal unit in conversation. The fact that different investigators define the unit in different ways *but refer to it by the same name* can only make for an increasing amount of confusion and noncomparable research findings. The position taken here is (as might be expected) that the turn is best defined empirically and the fact that turn-taking behavior is receiving increased research attention justifies a comparison of some recent definitions of the turn with that presented earlier.

Semantic information and gestural behavior as unitizing criteria.   As Rosenfeld (Chapter 10) notes, the definitions of a turn vary from those that rely heavily upon the judgments of the investigators to that determined solely by the objective measurement of speech onset and termination. However, the issue is not sufficiently clarified by labeling one approach subjective and the other objective. One position within the former approach views the turn as a unit the boundaries of which are determined primarily by gestural information. What the gestures are, however, and the precise delineation of their characteristics as well as of the points at which they need to occur in the speech stream in order to serve as turn signals, are decisions currently based upon investigators' judgments. Another, not entirely independent position, views conversation as a vehicle for the exchange of "information" and a turn as the mechanism for ordering the flow of information in a way that will insure maximum comprehensibility. It must be said that the latter view of a conversational exchange appears intuitively reasonable, and not necessarily subjective. The approach, however, further assumes that if, indeed, turns serve such an end, their delineation must be determined primarily by the semantic content of the exchange and, to some degree, the "amount" of information implied by the content. However, the differentiation of content and amount of information can, at this point, only be subjective. Thus, for example, Yngve (1970) suggests three structural categories to which utterances can be assigned: "back-channel" messages, "having the turn" and "having the floor". A participant has the floor when his utterances represent a substantive amount of information, a "topic" appears to be Yngve's term. Having the turn involves the communication of less informative messages, perhaps "subtopics." Yngve (1970) states that ". . . dialogue appears to be organized by topics which they [the participants] take turns pushing forward by means of subtopics . . ." [p. 575]. Back-channel messages are remarks made by the person who does not have the floor and, perhaps, not even the turn. Yngve does not make the latter distinction clear. Nor does he clearly indicate whether back-channel messages are less informative than those communicated by turns. He does say that back-channel activity is "quite varied" and includes gestural and vocal behavior, and that the vocal comments range from vocal segregates to short remarks and questions. However, his report represents an initial and somewhat informal inquiry into the structure of conversation.

Duncan (1972), who is concerned with the signals that regulate the "turn system" (Duncan, 1973, 1974; Duncan & Niederehe, 1974), asserts that a back-channel remark constitutes neither a turn nor a claim for a turn. He notes that back-channel communication includes gestural activity, vocal segregates and other short utterances, and suggests that it may also include many other conversational control signals. He proposes that the back channel be expanded to include, among other things, requests for clarification, brief restatements by one participant of immediately preceding statements by the other participant, and completions by one participant of sentences begun by the other participant. Implied in his discussion of back-channel communication, however, is that it is less informative than communication by turns. Duncan's position allows him to divide simultaneous speech into two categories: *simultaneous talk* and *simultaneous turns.* Simultaneous talk occurs when the person who does not have the turn utters a back-channel remark while the person who has the turn is talking. If, however, the remark uttered by the person who does not have the turn can be considered a turn or a claim for a turn, the resulting simultaneous speech is classified as simultaneous turns. Whether or not the remark is consigned to the back channel, or designated a turn or claim for a turn, seems to depend upon the appearance or nonappearance of "turn-yielding" and/or "attempt-suppressing" signals sent by the participant who has the turn. Here, the amount of information conveyed by the remark may be secondary; the point is not explicated.

It is Rosenfeld (Chapter 10) who most explicitly combines the notion that conversation is structured in terms of informational units with the suggestion that the flow of such units is regulated by nonverbal signals. He is, however, very much aware of the definitional problems involved in such a position. In his discussion of these problems he makes the point that utterance duration as a criterion of amount of information (the longer the utterance the greater the amount of information) has the advantages of being precisely and reliably measurable. But the basic question is not whether duration of utterance and amount of information are related; it is whether, for the purpose of describing the semantic content of natural conversation, the term "information" can be defined in a way that renders it both meaningful and measurable. If the answer is negative, as it is at the present time, then unitizing the time patterns of a conversation in terms of something that cannot be adequately defined does not seem likely to be very useful.

None of this is meant to deny the probable value of viewing conversation as an information exchange process. To be sure, the study of conversation from such a perspective would be tellingly facilitated were a technique devised for objectively assessing the informational characteristics of a conversational exchange. But the important point is that, given such a perspective, it is not surprising that the units that are used to describe the exchange are primarily informational and only secondarily temporal. A turn cannot simply be taken; it has to be earned. Or to put it another way, one takes a turn not by talking but by saying something! (It is only half jesting to comment that long experience in listening to casual conversations suggests that if informativeness were the criterion that identified a turn then most conversations involve people who do a great deal of talking without ever having a turn!)

Speaker switching as the sole criterion.   Consider, instead, the possibility that the (speech) sounds and silences of a conversational exchange have a coherent structure of their own that can be described without recourse to information from other dimensions of the exchange, such as the words or body movements. The only information needed for the description that is extrinsic to the sounds and silences is the knowledge of their source, that is, knowing by whom they were generated. Thus, no preconceptions are incorporated into the description about the "meaning" of its components or parameters. Initially, at least, a sound is just a sound, a silence just a silence. Only source and structure are used to differentiate categories of sound and/or silence, or configurations of sounds and silences.

The approach makes no assumptions about the function of conversational interaction, nor is it designed to facilitate the study of a particular function. It seems quite likely that conversation serves a variety of ends, and may even satisfy more than one at the same time. Its most apparent function, for example (although not necessarily its most frequent), is to communicate cognitive and affective information. It is probably also used, and perhaps frequently, as simply a form of interpersonal contact in which the participants attend primarily to the sound of each other's voice and minimally to the words that are uttered—a sort of auditory stroking. There is even some indication (Cobb, 1973) that persons who know each other and are together in an appropriate situation tend to engage in conversation at predictably regular intervals of time. That conversational interaction should exhibit such periodicity was recently suggested by Chapple (1970), who views it as controlled by endogenous factors. The position argues that the mere occurrence of conversational behavior satisfies a biologically programmed need.

The approach translates a conversation into a string or sequence of sounds and silences, each of which is identified by its source. The knowledge of their sources allows for the formulation of a rule that provides the string with a coherent structure. This "alternation rule" is that a participant takes a turn by vocalizing alone and loses it when another participant begins to vocalize alone. The rule thus unambiguously assigns the turn and transforms the string into a chain of concatenated events. One way to describe the structure of these "events" is in terms of the classification presented earlier.[6] But how seriously are these events, these segments of speech sounds and silences and their combinations, to be taken? They are indexed by their durations and/or frequencies. Are their durations (and therefore their frequencies) primarily a function of their having been processed by a "threshold device" such as AVTA (Hayes, Meltzer, & Wolf, 1970)? Are the durations, in other words, arbitrary and their fluctuations random with respect to the durations of the preprocessed events? It seems unlikely. As pointed out earlier, the threshold intensity of the AVTA system is

---

[6] Models have been presented elsewhere which attempt to account for the structure mathematically (Jaffe, 1970; Jaffe & Feldstein, 1970) and recursively (Feldstein, 1972).

determined by a person of unimpaired hearing in order to enable AVTA to "hear" what presumably would be heard by all persons with unimpaired hearing. The event durations generated by AVTA are intended to be their "perceived" durations rather than their "true" durations. Moreover, the average duration of each of these events (other than that of simultaneous speech) has been shown to reliably characterize individuals in the sense that different individuals tend to use consistently different average durations in their conversational interactions. Finally, it has been shown thus far (Jaffe & Feldstein, 1970) that the average durations of vocalizations, pauses, and switching pauses, and even the frequency of vocalizations (BenDebba, 1974), can be systematically modified. At the very least, these findings argue that the components of the classification offered here—an objectively temporal description of the verbal interaction of a conversation—are very much worth further investigation.

In this approach, then, a turn is taken by the participant who begins to talk while the other participant is silent. It does not matter what he talks about, or whether the talk is informative or uninformative. Nor does it matter whether he speaks only very briefly or at length. A vocal segregate can serve as a turn even though it takes only a fraction of a second to utter. It would be easy to exclude it; AVTA (or any similar automated data processor) could be instructed to not classify as turns utterances that meet the other criteria but are shorter than a specified duration. But there is no adequate reason to do so at present, certainly none that has any convincing evidence to support it. On the contrary, if the having of discernible consequences were considered a reasonable justification, there is evidence to support the inclusion of such a turn. Not only have segregates such as "mm-hmm" been shown to serve as effective reinforcers in the control of certain syntactical classes of words (e.g., Greenspoon, 1955; Salzinger, Portnoy, Zlotogura, & Keisner, 1963), but BenDebba (1974) has demonstrated that "mm-hmm" can be used, in a way that renders it a turn, to increase a participant's rate of vocalizations in a verbal exchange. In short, the categorization of very brief utterances as turns is troublesome only if the turn is considered an informational unit rather than a temporal unit.

One other issue deserves mention. It seems to be assumed by many of those concerned with identifying the nonverbal signals that function as conversational control mechanisms that the alternation that occurs in a conversation is one that involves the roles of "speaker" and "listener" or "auditor." The roles are not meant just to indicate who is speaking and who is silent. An "auditor" may speak and remain an auditor if what he says is judged to be a back-channel communication (Duncan, 1972) or a "listener response" (Dittmann & Llewellyn, 1968). And although he may not be talking at any particular moment, a participant can remain the "speaker" for as long as he has the turn. The "speaker," then, is the participant who conveys information and the "listener" is the one who receives it (Rosenfeld, Chapter 10). The attribution of such roles implies, of course, the position that conversation is an information exchange system. But, if the participant who is judged to be conveying information is thereby considered to be having a turn (or the floor), it is not clear that anything more is gained by also considering him to be the "speaker." In other words, the essential characteristics of the role of "speaker" are talking (much of the time) and conveying information. However, the essential characteristics of the state of "having the turn" are also talking and conveying information. Thus, the state of "having the turn" and the role of "speaker" are equivalent. But is the role of "listener" the same as the state of *not* "having the turn?" The participant who, at a particular time in the conversation, does not talk much and does not convey much information even when he does talk cannot, presumably, be considered to have the floor. Thus, he is the participant who does not have the floor. To say, however, that he is not talking much and not conveying information does not appear to be the same as saying that he is listening and receiving information, both of which are the essential characteristics of the "listener" role. Attributing the role of "listener" to the participant who does not have the turn implies that instead of simply not being engaged in one set of activities he is engaged in another set of activities, that he is, if you will, taking a turn at listening and receiving information. The distinction, then, between not having the turn and being a "listener" appears to be substantive, but it is also problematic. While it may not be clear, in many if not most ordinary conversations, that when a "speaker" is talking he is conveying information, it is obvious at least that he is talking. It is frequently not at all clear, however, that a "listener" is either listening or receiving information! In any case, the position holds that the participants in a conversation alternate in the taking of the roles. Thus, the roles are considered to be temporal units as well as informational units. Unfortunately, given the lack of reliable criteria for evaluating amount of information, it becomes more than occasionally difficult to determine which participant is filling which role at which moment.

The alternation rule simply determines who has the floor in a conversation. It does not allot roles to the participants such that the one who has the floor is the "speaker" and the other is the "listener." The total amount of time a participant spends in not having the floor is, of course, equivalent to the sum of the durations of the other participant's turns and is, therefore, not separately indexed. The use of the descriptive category of simultaneous speech rather than "listener response" to take into account the speech of the participant who does not have the floor entails considerably fewer assumptions.

It may well be that the attribution of a listener role, or alternatively, the categorization of time spent not having the floor, is a necessary (or useful) step in accounting for the temporal structure of verbal interaction. Jaffe (1970), for example, proposed a Markov-based model of dialogic time patterns that posits two silence "states" and one sound "state." The silence states are pausing and "listening." He demonstrated that, given the three parameters that index these states for each participant, one can quite nicely approximate the actual transition probabilities generated by the sound–silence sequences of the two participants. The assumption of a listening state (in addition to the pausing and sound states for each participant) not only reduces the eight parameters of an alternative model to six parameters, but also markedly reduces the sizes of the discrepancies between actual transition probabilities and those predicted by the alternative model. However, it seems clear that, apart from the substantive issues involved in combining certain of the original parameters to make possible the reduction, the posited listening *state* is not meant to approximate the listening *role* discussed above. It accounts only for the time spent in silence while not having a turn. Moreover, the model dictates that the likelihood that one of the participants will remain silent during the time he does not have a turn is almost wholly dependent upon the behavior of the other participant.[7]

In short, the disagreements about what constitutes a turn reflect different approaches to the study of conversational time patterns. The positions that comprise one approach assume, implicitly or explicitly, that the primary function of conversation is to exchange information, and that the characteristics of, and interrelations among, the various dimensions of a conversation are determined by that function. The other approach assumes that the dimensions of a conversational exchange can be defined and examined independently of each other and without regard to the function of the conversation. It does not imply that the dimensions are unrelated to each other or that their characteristics are not influenced by the function, but that such relationships and influence must be demonstrated rather than assumed. It does imply that a particular dimension may be subject to influences other than that wielded by the function of a conversation and may carry information different from and even contradictory to that carried by other dimensions.

Research Directions

To date, few studies of turn-taking behavior have been concerned with much more than the relations between turns (defined in various ways) and types of nonverbal behaviors and initiation strategies (Schegloff, 1968). Fewer still have investigated turns and simultaneous speech as they are defined in this chapter. These few are worth reviewing if only to demonstrate that the parameters,

---

[7] In Chapter 2, Jaffe talks about "speaker" and "listener" in ways that seem to imply that the two are role behaviors. He even talks about the "listener's response" and "listeners' interjections." He does, however, regard the interjection as a speaker switch, that is, a change in who has the speaking turn. On the other hand, the following remarks make his position vaguely reminiscent of Yngve's (1970) distinction between "having the turn" and "having the floor": "To pursue the metaphor of parliamentary procedure, the listener has been briefly recognized by the chairman, *but the longer term sending-receiving configuration is preserved*" (italics mine).

although empirically defined, bear consistent and meaningful relationships to other behaviors of interest.

A preliminary study by Alberti (1974) explored the notion that the amount of interaction in a dialogue may be related to the time, or time frame, to which the semantic content of the dialogue refers. He therefore compared the frequency of turns per minute, which he used as an index of amount of interaction, with the frequencies of past, present, and conditional verbs, which he used as estimates of referred time. The conversations used in the study were four task-oriented dialogues (involving college students) that were randomly selected from a much larger number of recorded dialogues. Analyses of the data indicated that the use of the present tense was positively related to the frequency of turns per minute. The frequencies with which past and conditional tenses were used were not found to be related to the frequency of turns. Thus, while a rapid exchange in a dialogue may mean that the discussion is referring to what, for the participants, can be considered the present time, a slow interaction may not necessarily imply a discussion of the past or future.

A most imaginative experiment by Martindale (1971) examined the effects of territorial dominance on turn-taking behavior in a simulated legal bargaining situation. Martindale used as his subjects 60 male college students who lived in dormitories on their campus. The students were randomly divided into equal numbers of "defense attorneys" and "prosecuting attorneys." Each defense attorney was asked to meet for half an hour with a prosecuting attorney to argue—out of court—the prepared case of a defendent known to be guilty. The attorneys were instructed to negotiate a prison term for the defendent, with the prosecuting attorneys arguing for the maximum allowed by law and the defense attorneys arguing for the minimum. The critical experimental manipulation was that half of the 30 dialogues were conducted in the dormitory rooms (home territory) of the defense attorneys and half in the rooms of the prosecuting attorneys! It was hypothesized that when attorneys are negotiating on their own territory they (a) hold the floor longer and (b) are more successful than the attorneys with whom they are negotiating. It should also be mentioned that the students were given, prior to their negotiating sessions, the Dominance Scale of the California Personality Inventory.

The results supported both hypotheses. The average turn durations of those students who negotiated the case on their own territory (in their own rooms) were significantly longer than were the turn durations of the students with whom they negotiated, regardless of which role they were playing. They were also the students whose negotiations were more successful. The average prison term agreed upon by the two attorneys on the territory of the defense attorney was 22 months; the average term agreed upon on the territory of the prosecuting attorney was 60 months!

The correlation between territory and the average turn durations statistically controlled for the scores the students received on the Dominance Scale of the

CPI. Interestingly, however, the personality characteristic presumably indexed by the scores did not markedly affect how long on the average, the students kept the floor each time they took it, although it was related to the total amount of time the students held the floor during their negotiations.

Talking out of turn.   Talking at the same time as a speaker who has the floor is talking (i.e., simultaneous speech) is, in effect, talking out of turn. It seems perfectly appropriate that such behavior be discussed within the context of talking about turns.

If, as Schegloff (1968) suggested, the taking of turns is considered a basic conversational rule, then talking out of turn, is a violation of the rule. It is a violation that often disrupts the flow of an interaction. Yet the frequencies with which individuals engage in such behavior, that is, initiate simultaneous speech, have been shown earlier to be characteristic of their conversational styles, which suggest, at the least, that they merit further exploration.

Meltzer *et al.* (1971), in the study mentioned earlier, concern themselves with the question of what determines the outcome of a segment of simultaneous speech. Why do some segments terminate in a change of which speaker has the floor while others do not? The investigators explored the possibility that vocal amplitude (intensity) plays a role in determining outcome. To obtain their data, they randomly selected one participant in each of 60 problem-solving dialogues as the target and identified all instances in which the target person initiated simultaneous speech. They then computed the proportion of these instances that were "successful interruptions," that in the classification preferred here would be considered instances of interruptive simultaneous speech (ISS). These proportions of ISS for the target persons were used as the dependent variable in a stepwise multiple regression analysis in which 10 vocal amplitude variables were used as the predictors. The analysis revealed that only two of the 10 predictors were significantly related to the proportions of ISS and together accounted for 62% of their variance, although they were unrelated to each other. One predictor variable was the average difference between the vocal amplitudes of each target person and his conversational partner while they were engaged in simultaneous speech; the larger the difference and louder the partner's voice, the less likely it was that the simultaneous speech of the target person would interrupt his partner. The other variable was the mean difference between the amplitude of the partner's voice immediately prior to the occurrence of simultaneous speech and its amplitude during the simultaneous speech. The relation indicated that the greater the increase in amplitude from before to after the onset of simultaneous speech, the less likely was it that the latter would culminate in an interruption.

The investigators suggest that most instances of simultaneous speech are of too short a duration for their outcomes to be determined by the semantic content of what is being said, hence, the importance of physicalistic cues. They did, however, find instances of simultaneous speech that lasted for as long as 6 sec. They therefore examined the comparative utility of the two amplitude variables in predicting the outcome of simultaneous speech segments of various durations. As had been expected, they found that both variables became less effective in predicting outcome as the durations of the segments increased. The decline in effectiveness, however, was much less marked for the variable indexing the average amplitude differential between the voices of the two speakers during simultaneous speech than for that indexing the change in vocal amplitude following the onset of simultaneous speech made by the speaker who had the floor.

Although the results are excitingly provocative, Meltzer, Morris, and Hayes point out that the study leaves unsettled the question of whether semantic content plays any role in determining the outcome of brief segments of simultaneous speech. That is, amplitude may function as a mediating factor that allows speakers to respond quickly to content, or it may be so highly related to content (e.g., the greater the semantic information, the higher the amplitude) that its role in determining outcome is artifactual. The position of the investigators is that amplitude operates independently of content. The results seem to justify the position although the correlational method of the study might be viewed as limiting their conclusiveness. An experimental verification of part of these results was provided by another excellent study conducted by Morris (1971).

Working within the conceptual framework of the earlier study (Meltzer *et al.*, 1971), Morris views the participant in a conversation who initiates simultaneous speech as the "interrupter" and the participant who had the floor prior to its initiation as the "defender." His experiment tested three hypotheses. The first is that amplitude is causally related to the outcome of simultaneous speech such that increases in vocal amplitude by the defender during occurrences of simultaneous speech ". . . significantly increase his ability to successfully defend the floor" (Morris, 1971, p. 320). Put more empirically, the causal relationship is such that the more likely it is that a participant who has the floor raises his voice during the occurrence of simultaneous speech, the more likely he is to have the floor at the end of its occurrence. The second hypothesis is that, whereas amplitude increments by the defender during simultaneous speech are effective in helping him keep the floor, amplitude increments by the interrupter during simultaneous speech do not affect the likelihood of his obtaining the floor. The implication here is that the determination of who *will* have the floor is influenced primarily by the behavior of the participant who *does* have the floor. Finally, the study posits that those participants who initiate simultaneous speech that tends to terminate noninterruptively (without their having obtained the floor) tend, over time, to increase the amplitude of their voices upon the initiation of simultaneous speech by their partners and are, thereby, more likely over time to retain the floor following occurrences of simultaneous speech.

The study utilized two experimental and one control condition with 11 dyads in each condition. The discussions of the control dyads were allowed to proceed without experimental intervention. In one experimental condition, the vocal amplitude of one of the participants in each dyad was electronically increased, prior to its reception (via earphones) by the other participant, during 50% of the instances in which the *other* participant initiated simultaneous speech. In the other experimental condition, the vocal amplitude of one of the participants in each dyad was increased during 50% of the instances in which *he* initiated simultaneous speech. To use the investigator's terms, the former experimental condition was one in which the defender's amplitude was boosted whereas the latter was one in which the interrupter's amplitude was boosted.

The results appear to support the first two hypotheses fully and the third only partially. That is, the increase in amplitude during simultaneous speech over time described by the first half of the third hypothesis is only significant (at the .05 point) when evaluated by a one-tailed test (the use of which is no more justified in evaluating this result than it would have been in evaluating the other results). The results confirm the basic findings of the Meltzer, Morris, and Hayes study (although not the interaction of amplitude and duration), and make clear that vocal amplitude, or intensity, operates as a critical interpersonal cue in determining the outcome of a majority of instances of simultaneous speech. Although Morris concedes that semantic content may play some role in such determinations, he justifiably points out that the role cannot be considered decisive.

It is also of interest that amplitude is effective as a determinant primarily when it is used by the participant who has the floor. One of the suggestions Morris offers to account for its asymetrical effectiveness is that the amplitude increase by the participant who has the floor forces the participant who initiated the simultaneous speech to recognize that he is violating a conversational rule, that is, that he is being rude, and thereby it decreases the likelihood of his persisting. Morris also assumes that the amplitude increase expresses the intention of the participant who has the floor to continue talking, and that it is so interpreted by the violator. It is not clear that the assumption is either warranted or necessary. The amplitude increment may well be an automatic response to a competing acoustical input and serve to maintain the previous signal-to-noise ratio. It is conceivable that the increment is viewed as a reminder of the violation rather than as a statement of intent.

In any case, the results of both of the two studies described above are important, and the studies themselves suggest research paradigms that may be useful in exploring other aspects of temporal behavior and its correlates. As both studies indicate, however, the outcome of simultaneous speech is not wholly determined by change in vocal amplitude. Semantic content is not completely ruled out as a determinant. But more important, perhaps, are personality characteristics.

It may be inferred from the reliability data presented earlier that there are consistent differences among individuals in the extent to which they initiate ISS and NSS in conversations. The inference raises two questions: Do personality characteristics play a role in the initiation of simultaneous speech, and do they influence its outcome? Although there have been few speculations about what "kinds" of people tend to talk while someone else is talking, it has been suggested that the outcome of such simultaneous speech may be a function of dominance and submissiveness (Gallois & Markel, 1975). Meltzer *et al.* (1971) do, in fact, wonder whether ". . . the *outcome* of an interruption (who "wins" the floor) may be a more valid indicator of dominance than the occurrence of an interruption" [p. 393].

Using the data from the quartet study described earlier, Feldstein, Alberti, BenDebba, and Welkowitz (1974) compared the frequencies with which the participants initiated simultaneous speech with those of their personality characteristics indexed by the Cattell Sixteen Personality Factor Questionnaire or the 16PFQ (Cattell, Eber, & Tatsuoka, 1970). The 16PFQ was completed by the subjects (along with Witkin's (1950) form of Embedded Figures Test, of which more will be said later) prior to their participation in the experimental conversations. The study asks three questions. Do personality characteristics influence the frequencies with which individuals initiate simultaneous speech? Are the frequencies with which individuals initiate simultaneous speech influenced by the personality characteristics of their conversational partners? Are the two possible outcomes of simultaneous speech (ISS and NSS) differentially related to personality characteristics?

The relations between the simultaneous speech frequencies and the 16 personality factors were compared by means of 16 hierarchical multiple regression analyses. Each regression equation used the initiation frequencies as its dependent variable and had seven independent variables, the order of which was specified in advance by the investigators (Cohen & Cohen, 1975). The first variable to enter the equation identified which of the frequencies of the dependent variable were ISS and NSS. The second variable consisted of the factor scores of the participants, and the third, those of their conversational partners. The remaining four variables are product variables which, as a function of their order in the equation, examined possible interaction effects among the participants, their partners, and the outcome of simultaneous speech.

The analyses indicated that it was the participant who received low scores on factors L, O, and Q_4, and high scores on Factor I, who more frequently initiated simultaneous speech. According to the *Handbook* of the 16PFQ (Cattell *et al.,* 1970), persons who obtain low scores on the first three factors can be characterized as easygoing, relaxed, conciliatory, complacent, secure, and relatively insensitive to the approbation or disapprobation of others. The interpretations of Factor I are discussed shortly.

The analyses also indicated that the participants who initated more simultaneous speech had partners who received high scores on Factors A, C, and F and low scores on Factor Q_2, who, in other words, could be described as good-natured, cooperative, attentive to people, emotionally mature, realistic, talkative, cheerful, and socially group-dependent. They were partners who also received high scores on Factor H. However, the analyses revealed that the participants' initiation of simultaneous speech was also influenced by interactions among certain aspects of their personalities with those of their partners. The interactions involve Factors H, I, and M. The *Handbook* describes persons who score high on Factor H as adventurous, "thick skinned," genial, and socially bold, whereas persons who score low are described as shy, timid, restrained, and sensitive to threat. The results show that although in general, the participants initiated more simultaneous speech while talking to partners who scored high on Factor H than to partners who scored low, the initiation frequencies of participants who received low scores—the shy, timid, restrained participants—were considerably more affected by how their partners scored on Factor H than were those of participants who received high scores.

Those participants who scored low on Factor I—participants described as "tough minded," unsentimental, self-reliant, and practical—initiated, on the average, *less* simultaneous speech than did participants with high scores on Factor I—those described as sensitive, dependent, insecure, attention seeking, and imaginative. However, the initiation frequencies of participants who scored high on the factor were apparently unaffected by the factor scores of their partners, whereas those of participants who scored low on the factor show a significant positive relation to the factor scores of their partners.

Finally, the analysis of Factor M indicates that those participants who scored high on the factor—characterized by the *Handbook* as imaginative, unconventional, absent-minded, absorbed, and fanciful—initiated more simultaneous speech when talking to partners who scored high than to partners who scored low. On the other hand, those participants with low scores on the factor—subjects characterized as "down-to-earth," conventional, prosaic, earnest, and concerned with immediate interests and issues—initiated more simultaneous speech with partners who had low scores.

Of considerable interest is the fact that the results provide no evidence that those personality characteristics of the participants and their partners that are measured by the 16PFQ had any influence on the outcome of their simultaneous speech!

One further regression equation was computed which included all those factors shown by the previous analyses to be related to the initiation of simultaneous speech. The solution yielded a significant multiple correlation of .55, indicating that the personality factors in the equation accounted for approximately 30% of the variability in the frequencies with which simultaneous speech was initiated. The personality characteristics of the participants contributed 8% of the variance, those of their partners accounted for 16% of the variance, and the interactions among these two sets of characteristics accounted for 6%. Each of these contributions is significant.

Obviously, the study needs to be cross-validated and extended to men. The results do suggest, however, that the extent to which a woman initiates simultaneous speech in a conversation—the extent to which she talks out of turn—is not only influenced by aspects of her own personality, but also by those of her conversational partner. Women who are relaxed, complacent, secure, and not overly dependent upon the approval of others tend to initiate more simultaneous speech than women who are generally apprehensive, self-reproaching, tense, and frustrated. But apart from their own characteristics, women tend to initiate more simultaneous speech when they converse with others who are cooperative, attentive, emotionally mature, and talkative than with others who are aloof, critical, emotionally labile, introspective, silent, and self-sufficient.

What is surprising is that none of the 16 personality factors were related to the *outcome* of simultaneous speech. It seems so much more likely that the outcome, rather than simply the initiation of simultaneous speech, would be influenced by personality characteristics. It may be the case, however, that the presumed relation between personality and outcome is dependent upon contextual, or situational, variables. One such variable might be the stated purpose of a discussion. The dialogues of the study were casual and unconstrained. It is possible, however, that only task-oriented and/or argumentative dialogues permit personality dimensions to influence the outcome of simultaneous speech. The implication here is that there is an interaction of outcome, personality, and conversational demands such that personality is differentially related to ISS and NSS only in certain types of conversations.

Gallois and Markel (1975) conducted a study of the relation between turn-taking behavior and "social personality." Inferring from the other research that the personality of a bilingual individual varies according to which of his languages he is using, they requested each of 13 bilingual men to converse (on separate occasions) with two friends, one who primarily spoke English and the other Spanish. Although the investigators defined turns as they are defined in this chapter, their analyses involved not the durations of turns but the amount of speech in the turns. They did, however, use the frequency of turns and the frequency of turns following simultaneous speech in examining another aspect of the study. Frequency of turns following simultaneous speech sounds very like an estimate of ISS.

For their analyses, the authors segmented each conversation into the first 5 min., the last 5 min. and 5 min. from the exact center of the conversation. In comparing these three "sections" of the dialogues, they found turns occurred more frequently during the opening section than during the closing section. In addition, a higher frequency of turns following simultaneous speech occurred in the middle section than in either the first or last sections. They conclude that people are more interactive at the beginnings of conversations and more interruptive during the middle of conversations. They speculate that obtaining the floor by means of simultaneous speech may reflect ". . . heightened involvement in the conversation" [p. 1139].

CONVERSATIONAL CONGRUENCE: CORRELATES AND CONCERNS

It was noted earlier that comparisons of successive conversations involving the same individuals have indicated that the stability of their average silence durations depended upon whether their partners were the same in the different conversations; the participation of different partners resulted in markedly lower stability. The loss of stability appears, at least in part, to be a function of the propensity of conversational participants to vary the time patterns of their verbal contributions such that their patterns became increasingly similar during the course of a conversation. This mutual influence apparently exerted by speakers upon one another seems to reflect the more general tendency, on the part of interacting individuals, to develop orientations and interpersonal behavior that become more similar the more frequently the individuals interact (e.g., Homans, 1950; Newcomb, 1953). The expression of this tendency in terms of a variety of the dimensions of verbal interaction has been observed by a number of investigators (e.g., Feldstein, 1968; Jaffe, 1964; Jaffe & Feldstein, 1970; Kendon, 1967; Lennard & Bernstein, 1960; Marcus et al., 1970; Matarazzo, 1965; Welkowitz & Feldstein, 1969). The phenomenon has been variously labeled *synchrony* (e.g., Webb, 1972), *symmetry* (Meltzer et al., 1971), *pattern matching* (Cassotta et al., 1967), and *congruence* (Feldstein, 1972). In his discussion of synchrony, Webb (1972) reviews some mechanisms that may account for its occurrence and asserts that synchrony exists ". . . when intensity, frequency, or durational characteristics of one's behavior rhythmically agree with similar characteristics of ambient stimuli, whether personal or impersonal in origin" [p. 125]. Although the definition is general, Webb confines his discussion to what he calls "verbal synchrony" and is concerned with speech rates within interview contexts.

Congruency (or pattern matching) can be defined much like synchrony but is more restricted in its reference. It is used to describe the occurrence, within the span of one or more conversations, of similar intensity, frequency, or durational values for the participants on one or more of the parameters that characterize temporal patterning. Almost all of the studies conducted thus far by the authors and their associates have indicated that the parameters are, in one way or another, susceptible to the type of interspeaker influence reflected by congruence.

The first study (Feldstein *et al.*, 1967) to examine the occurrence of congruence in conversations rather than interviews involved task-oriented conversations. Thirty-two men and 32 women participated in the study, and each engaged in one conversation with each of two different members of his or her own sex and one with a member of the opposite sex. The dyad participants were asked to resolve differences in their answers to an attitude questionnaire. (The study is more fully described by Jaffe & Feldstein, 1970, as Experiment 2.) Comparisons of the average durations of pauses and switching pauses of the dyad participants yielded congruence coefficients[8] of .56 and .55, respectively. However, a comparison of the average durations of their vocalizations yielded a coefficient of −.04. Whereas the conversational participants were apparently able to influence the durations of each other's silences, they were unable to influence the durations of each other's vocalizations. These findings were confirmed by subsequent studies. In the quartet study described earlier, for example, the congruence coefficients obtained by comparing the mean durations of the pauses and switching pauses of the conversational participants, averaged over the eight occasions of the study are .43 and .62, respectively; that for their mean durations of vocalizations is .08. A preliminary study conducted by Welkowitz and Feldstein (1969) also indicated that durations of vocalizations used by each participant in the dialogues were not markedly affected by those of the other. Interestingly, however, a trend analysis of the absolute differences between the average durations of the members of participant pairs did show that their average durations were more similar by the end of their third conversation than by the end of their first. That is, the duration of their vocalizations had converged by the end of the third conversation. Perhaps durations of vocalizations simply take longer to influence than do those of pauses and switching pauses. The finding needs to be replicated.

Although the durations of vocalizations do not appear to be readily susceptible to interspeaker influence, the intensity levels of vocalizations do. Vocal intensity, measured in terms of the average amplitude of speech for a given time unit, roughly corresponds to what is subjectively perceived as the "loudness" of speech. There is both anecdotal and systematic evidence to suggest that intensity congruence occurs in unconstrained conversations. Try, for example, to begin a conversation by speaking very softly or whispering. As likely as not, the person you speak to will respond in an equally soft voice. And it will probably take a few minutes before he realizes what the two of you are doing (given that the

---

[8] Degree of congruence has been frequently indexed by an intraclass correlation coefficient (Haggard, 1958) that, when so used, has been called for convenience, a congruence coefficient. For the purpose of explication, consider one participant of a dialogue the speaker and the other participant the partner. Then, for a particular parameter and group of dialogues involving different participant pairs, the appropriate values of the speakers (e.g., their average pause durations) are correlated with those of their partners. The intraclass correlation assesses the similarity of not only the shapes of the distributions under scrutiny but also their means. The significance of an intraclass correlation coefficient is indexed by its associated F ratio.

circumstances do not appear to call for it) and requests an explanation. There is a body of observational and experimental studies that indicates that speakers adjust the intensity of their voices according to the amount of noise present in the situations in which they find themselves talking (e.g., Charlip & Burk, 1969; Gardner, 1966; Hanley & Steer, 1949; Kryter, 1946; Webster & Klump, 1962) and to the intensity levels of their own voices and those of people talking to them (e.g., Baird & Tice, 1969; Black, 1949a,b; Jacobson, 1968; Lane & Tranel, 1971). None of the latter studies had to do with conversational interactions. Of particular relevance to the issue of mutual interspeaker influence of vocal intensity is the finding reported by Meltzer et al. (1971) in a footnote (p. 396) of what they call *symmetry,* that the correlation of one person's amplitude in a conversation with that of the other person yielded a coefficient of .57. This incidental discovery that conversational participants tend to match the intensity levels of their voices was confirmed in a subsequent, independent exploration of the issue (Welkowitz, Feldstein, Finkelstein & Aylesworth, 1972). Whereas the former study involved problem-solving discussions, the latter study asked the participants to talk about anything they wished. The latter study was also concerned with the effects of interpersonal perception upon intensity congruence. Specifically, one group of participants was informed that its members had been paired on the basis of having similar personality characteristics while the other group was told that its members had been randomly paired. Intensity congruence occurred in the conversations of those who presumably perceived each other as similar. However, it occurred only in the second conversation in which the participant pairs engaged. It is worth noting that the study also demonstrated that the average intensity levels used by speakers remain quite consistent during the course of conversation.

A more thoroughgoing investigation of the congruence of vocal intensity in conversations was conducted by Natale (1975b). Two experiments were involved. The first one used a modified standardized interview to test the expectation that the vocal intensities of interviewees would match the experimentally controlled changes in the vocal intensity of the interviewer. The second experiment examined the notions that (a) the degree to which the vocal intensity levels of participants in unconstrained conversations become congruent is directly related to their "social desirability" (measured by the Marlowe-Crowne Scale), and (b) the vocal intensity levels of the participants converge over the course of three conversations. The results support the three expectations. Of importance is the fact that the dialogue participants were in separate booths and could not see each other. While such a procedure may make the generalizability of the results to "ordinary face-to-face conversations" somewhat precarious, it serves the purpose of controlling for the possible influence of nonverbal cues. Together with the findings of Meltzer et al. (1971) and Welkowitz and her associates (1972), the Natale study establishes the viability of vocal intensity as a behavior systematically susceptible to interpersonal (or interspeaker) influence.

Some Correlates and Questions

Early research on durational congruence (Cassotta *et al.*, 1967) and the recent research on intensity congruence (Natale, 1975b; Welkowitz *et al.*, 1972) strongly suggest that there are notable differences in the extent to which conversational pairs achieve congruence. It may then be that the degree to which their pauses and switching pauses become mutually modified is dependent upon certain of their personality characteristics, on their perceptions of themselves and each other, or on some aspect of their relationship to each other. A number of studies have concerned themselves with these possibilities.

Interpersonal perception. There is a considerable history of research concerned with the role of interpersonal perception in attitude change (e.g., Berscheid, 1966; Brock, 1965; Dabbs, 1964), in facilitating communication (e.g., Runkel, 1956), in interpersonal attraction (e.g., Byrne, 1961; Byrne, Griffitt, & Stefaniak, 1967; Griffitt, 1966), and in self-perception (e.g., Stotland, Zander, & Natsoulas, 1961; Burnstein, Stotland, & Zander, 1961). Dabbs (1969) has also briefly reported two experiments that examined the effects of gestural similarity on interpersonal perception. The experiments, in which confederate interviewees mimicked the gestures of interviewing subjects, yielded results that indicated that those subjects who were mimicked tended to view the confederates as more persuasive, better informed, and more similar to themselves than did subjects who were not mimicked. Even apart from the experimental evidence, it is difficult to imagine how many of the ways in which people behave toward each other could *not* be influenced by the ways in which they perceive each other. Welkowitz and Feldstein (1969), in an exploratory study, examined the possibility that the degree to which interacting speakers achieve temporal congruence depends upon whether they perceive each other's "personality" as similar or dissimilar.

The subjects of the study were asked to complete a battery of personality tests and were then randomly assembled into 40 same-sex dyads, or pairs, with one of the following explanations: The members in each of 15 of the dyads were told that they had been paired with each other because their performances on the personality tests indicated that they were very much alike. Those in 15 other dyads were informed that they were paired because the tests indicated that they were different from each other. The subjects in the remaining 10 dyads were told that they had been randomly paired. The subjects were also informed that the purpose of the experiment was to attempt an assessment of "how people who are similar (dissimilar, or randomly paired) get to know each other." The dyads met for an hour a week for three consecutive weeks. Prior to each conversation, each member of a dyad was placed in a separate room which allowed him only verbal communication with the other member of his dyad. The recorded conversations were processed by AVTA and the average durations of pauses, switching pauses, and vocalizations were subjected to separate statistical analyses.

The analyses confirmed the consistency and stability of the parameters. In addition, they also confirmed the finding of previous studies that the vocalization durations of conversationalists do not become similar within the course of single conversations although, as was noted earlier, they did become more similar by the end of the third conversation. The coefficients that indexed the congruence of the vocalizations, averaged over the three occasions on which the subjects conversed, were .24 for the "similar" group, .22 for the "different" group, and .25 for the "random" group. The averaged congruence coefficients for pauses and switching pauses were .58 and .53, respectively, for the "similar" group, .45 and .48 for the "different" group, and .29 and .33 for the "random" group. Although only the .58 is significant, it seems very likely, on the basis of prior and subsequent research, that the magnitude of the coefficients are at least in part a function of the small number of dyads in each group (with its resulting low statistical power). It may well be, however, that the low coefficients of the group of randomly paired dyads are not as much a result of the number of dyads as of an actual lack of congruence. Analyses of variance of the absolute differences between the average durations of pauses, switching pauses, and vocalizations of the dyad members indicate the average difference of the "random" group is almost four times as large as those of the other groups for pauses, almost three times as large for switching pauses, and about twice as large for vocalizations. The average intradyad differences of the "similar" and "different" groups are not significantly different for any of the parameters.

That the randomly paired dyads did not achieve congruence becomes intriguing when one considers that in subsequent correlational studies the dialogue participants were almost always randomly paired but did achieve congruence. Somehow, the explicit knowledge of having been randomly paired seems to have made the difference. The results begin to suggest that not only are the silence durations of a conversationalist capable of being modified by those of his partner in the conversation, but that the extent of the modification is capable of reflecting their interpersonal perceptions.

One other finding of the study may be worth mentioning as a possible source of future research. The analyses of pauses and switching pauses yielded significant interactions among the groups and occasions. Whereas the average intradyad differences associated with the two parameters decreased from the first to the second conversation (occasion) for both the "different" and "random" groups, those for the "similar" group increased. Could it have been that the dyad members in the similar group discovered by the end of their first conversation that they were not as similar as they were led to expect, and that the discovery was responsible for the increased differences of their second conversation? What, to put it more generally, is the effect on congruence of a marked change in an

individual's perception of his conversational partner? A postexperimental inquiry might have shed some light on the question, but none was conducted.

Psychological differentiation. It seems hardly likely that the occurrence of
congruence is fully explained by conversationalists' perceptions of each other. If
congruence can be viewed as reflecting susceptibility or sensitivity to interpersonal influence, then it may be related to personality characteristics that presumably measure such sensitivity. The first study to pursue this possibility was
the quartet study described earlier and referred to so often. The major purpose
of the quartet study was not, in fact, to confirm the occurrence of congruence,
but to investigate the relation of congruence to the personality characteristic
that has been called *psychological differentiation* (Witkin, Dyk, Faterson,
Goodenough, & Karp, 1962). Although the construct, *psychological differentiation,* is presumably quite similar to that labeled *field dependence* it is not clear
that they are identical. Both, however, basically refer to the differential responsiveness of individuals to internal and external cues. More psychologically
differentiated individuals have been found to be more responsive to internal and
less responsive to external cues than are less differentiated individuals. (Psychological differentiation is inversely related to field dependence.) However, the
justification for examining the relation between psychological differentiation
and congruence is that a host of studies (e.g., Bieri, Bradburn, & Galinsky, 1958;
Crutchfield, Woodworth, & Albrecht, 1958; Fitzgibbons, Goldberger, & Eagle,
1965; Konstadt & Forman, 1965; Wallach, Kogan, & Burt, 1967) have shown
that less psychologically differentiated persons are the more responsive to,
interested in, and aware of others in interpersonal contacts, and are more likely
to be influenced by others. The general hypothesis of the quartet study was that
there is an inverse relationship between the degrees of psychological differentiation of participants in dialogues and the extent to which their dialogues exhibit
temporal congruence.

Degree of psychological differentiation was estimated by the individual form
of the Embedded Figures Test (Witkin, 1950), or EFT.[9] The score used to index
the degree of congruence that occurred in a dialogue was the absolute difference
between the average parameter duration of one conversational participant and
that of her conversational partner. Thus, the higher the score (that is, the greater
the difference), the less the congruence. Such *congruence scores* were obtained
for the parameters of pauses and switching pauses. Since the durations of the
participants' vocalizations tended not to become congruent during the course of
a conversation, the relation of their differences to psychological differentiation

[9] Inasmuch as Witkin and his associates (Witkin *et al.,* 1962) found that the correlation of
the EFT with the Block Design subtest of the WAIS yielded an *r* of .80, the EFT scores of
the subjects in the quartet study were statistically adjusted for the subjects' performance on
the BD subtest. That is, the subjects' BD scores were covaried out of their EFT scores.

was not investigated. The general hypothesis was tested in terms of the congruence of pauses and switching pauses by means of separate hierarchical multiple regression analyses in which the order of the entering independent variables was specified in advance (Cohen & Cohen, 1975). The independent variables (in the order in which they entered the regression equation) were the EFT scores of the subjects, the EFT scores of their conversational partners, and the products of the two sets of scores. By dint of their position in the equation, the product scores indexed the interaction of the subjects' and partners' scores.

In effect, the results of the analyses supported the hypothesis, although not quite in the way anticipated. One analysis indicated that the degrees of psychological differentiation of the subjects and of their partners separately and significantly affected the congruence of their pauses such that the greater the differentiation of the subject or her partner, the less similar did their pause durations become. Presumably, then, dyads in which both participants are highly differentiated achieve less pause congruence in their conversations than do dyads in which only one of the participants is highly differentiated, and considerably less pause congruence than do dyads in which neither of the participants is highly differentiated. The other analysis, however, indicated that only the interaction of the subjects' and partners' EFT scores was effectively related to the congruence of their switching pauses. In other words, the level of psychological differentiation of one or the other conversational participant was not, in itself, sufficient to influence the extent to which their interaction achieved congruence. Instead, the congruence they achieved depended upon the joint effect of both their levels of differentiation. Specifically, the relation was such that although the degree of congruence achieved by the more differentiated subjects and their partners was not markedly affected by their partners' levels of differentiation, the less differentiated subjects achieved a greater degree of congruence with partners who were less differentiated.

In view of the findings of others that persons who are more sensitive to interpersonal cues tend to be less psychologically differentiated, the relation of the construct to congruence makes sense. It also makes sense that the congruence of switching pauses is related only to configurations of *both* participants' levels of differentiation since switching pauses are primarily *inter*personal silences whereas pauses are primarily *intra*personal silences. The results, then, do suggest that temporal congruence is more likely to occur during the conversations of persons who are interpersonally responsive, or sensitive, than during the conversations of persons who are not. But is it simply the greater awareness of interpersonal cues that makes for congruence? Might it be that other interpersonal dynamics either enhance the effectiveness of such awareness in bringing about congruence or independently contribute to its occurrence? At the present time, there are no proper answers to these questions, although a tentative indication, again from the quartet study, suggests that they may be worth investigating.

Social contact. At the end of their participation in the quartet study, the subjects were asked to rate each of their three conversational partners on a seven-point scale which had to do with whether or not they liked the contact they had with their partners. The seven statements of the scale proceeded from "I disliked the contact with her very much." to "I enjoyed the contact with her very much." The scales provided four scores for each subject. Three of the scores indicated the degree to which she enjoyed her contact with each of her partners and were called *contact enjoyment* scores. The fourth, a *general contact enjoyment* score, was the sum of the three contact enjoyment scores.

The analyses of the scores revealed that the extent to which the average switching pause durations of the conversational participants became similar depended, in part, upon the interaction of their contact enjoyment scores. It should be noted that almost all the participants tended to enjoy their contacts with their partners. However, those participants who expressed greater enjoyment achieved congruence with partners who expressed greater enjoyment than with partners who expressed less enjoyment. The degrees of congruence achieved by the dialogues of those who tended to enjoy their contacts less were not materially affected by the extent of enjoyment claimed by their partners. Interestingly, the levels of psychological differentiation of the subjects were not related to the extent to which they claimed to enjoy their contact with each of their partners, although they were positively related to the general levels of enjoyment they expressed. Apparently, psychological differentiation and contact enjoyment as measured in the quartet study independently contribute to the occurrence of switching pause congruence. Can the same be said of psychological differentiation and interpersonal perception? Another pilot study was conducted (Welkowitz & Feldstein, 1970) to examine the relation of *perceived* differences and similarities of personality to the congruence of pauses and switching pauses after *actual* differences and similarities of psychological differentiation are taken into account. The design of the study replicated that of the Welkowitz and Feldstein (1969) study described earlier. However, the battery of personality tests included the individual form of the EFT. In addition, the "similar," "different," and "random" groups each had 20 dyads. Finally, each dyad met for only two 60-min. conversations spaced one week apart. Multiple regression analyses were performed in which the levels of psychological differentiation of the subjects and their conversational partners (and the product scores for the interaction) were entered into equations prior to entering the variables that assessed the contributions to pause and switching pause congruence of the three groups.

Coefficients of congruence were computed and found to be significant for the pauses and switching pauses of the "similar" and "different" groups only. No significant relations, however, were found between the levels of psychological differentiation of the participants and either pause or switching pause congruence. There were much larger differences (congruence scores) between the average pause and switching pause duration of conversational participants in the "random" group than in the other two groups and those of the "different" group were larger than those of the "similar" group. The vocalization congruence scores of the "random" group were larger than those of the similar group only. As with the earlier study, the results should be viewed as no more that suggestive. Although, for example, there were both male and female dyads, the analyses did not take gender into account. Could it be that differences between the levels of psychological differentiation of males and females were responsible for the failure to find a relationship between psychological differentiation and the congruence scores?

Social desirability. A correlational study published by Natale (1975a) attempted to explore the relation between social desirability and the congruence of pauses and switching pauses. Marlowe and Crowne (1960) originally thought that their Social Desirability Scale measured a need for social approval, which they considered indicative of a readiness to engage in socially conforming behavior and responsiveness to social influence. Natale, suggesting that congruence can be viewed as an instance of conforming behavior, reasoned that persons who score high on the Social Desirability Scale contribute more to the occurrence of congruence than those who score low.

The subjects were college students who were assembled into eight male and five female dyads each of which was asked to engage in two half-hour dialogues scheduled a week apart. To test the expectation of the study, the social desirability scores of the participants were subjected to multiple regression analyses in which the congruence scores of pauses and switching pauses were entered as the dependent variables. The results of the analyses seem[10] to support the expectation only with respect to the congruence of switching pauses and only for the second occasion on which the participants conversed. As noted earlier, switching pauses are interpersonal silences and might be expected to be more sensitive to interpersonal processes than pauses. The results make sense whether the Marlowe-Crowne estimate of social desirability is viewed as indexing a need for social approval or a need to avoid feelings of rejection (Crowne & Marlowe, 1964) if the latter need makes for socially compliant behavior. The results are seemingly at variance, however, with an interpretation of the estimate

[10] Natale reports what may be considered a significant main effect that indexes the relation between the subjects' social desirability and the congruence scores for switching pauses. However, the relationship is apparently modified by an interaction of the social desirability of the subjects with that of their conversational partners, although it is not clear from the degrees of freedom associated with the F ratio he reports for the interaction effect, that Natale entered the partners' social desirability scores as a variable in the regression equation. Assuming, however, that he did (and in the proper order), he misinterprets the meaning of the interaction effect. It seems likely, from the information given, that the interaction indicates that, compared to subjects with low social desirability scores, those with high scores achieved much more congruence with partners who had high social desirability scores than with partners how had low scores.

as reflecting a defensiveness that, as it increases, is expressed in the avoidance of interpersonal contact (Jacobson & Ford, 1966; Jacobson, Berger, & Millham, 1970). It may well be, of course, that individuals whose defensiveness leads them to ordinarily avoid interpersonal situations are compliant when they find themselves within the context of such situations. However complex the psychodynamic correlates of high scores on the Marlowe-Crowne Scale may be, such scores do appear to be positively associated with the congruence of switching pause durations and vocal intensity (Natale, 1975b).

Interpersonal warmth.   The greater sensitivity of switching pauses to interpersonal processes emerged in still another study conducted by Welkowitz and Kuc (1973). One of the aims of the study was to examine the relation of temporal congruence to the extent to which conversational participants rate each other as "warm," "genuine," and "empathic" *and* the extent to which independent observers so rate them. Extrapolating from the position that such qualities enhance effectiveness and communication within therapeutic dyads (e.g., Rogers, 1958, 1961; Truax & Carkhuff, 1967), the authors suggest that the same qualities should make for mutual satisfaction in ordinary interpersonal exchanges, and they note that temporal congruence was found to be related to mutual satisfaction (Marcus *et al.,* 1970).

College students were assembled into 16 male and 16 female dyads and the members of each dyad were asked to talk to each other about whatever interested them. The dyads met once for a 45-min. conversation. Following their conversations the participants were requested to complete a number of scales which included the rating of their conversational partners on items (Truax & Carkhuff, 1967) related to empathy, warmth and genuineness as defined by Rogers (1961). The same items were used by three independent observers who rated each participant after listening to the recorded conversations.

Appropriate multiple regression equations were used to evaluate the relations between the ratings and temporal congruence. In addition, the ratings made by the dyad members abour each other were compared with those made by the independent observers and found to be unrelated. The only significant result of the regression analyses that is of interest here indicates that the participants who received higher ratings of warmth *from the independent observers* contributed more to the congruence of switching pauses than did those who received lower ratings.

One of the questions raised by the results is why congruence was not related to the participants' rating of each other. Earlier explorations (Welkowitz & Feldstein, 1969, 1970) suggest that congruence is, in part at least, a function of interpersonal perception, although the perception was global and experimentally induced. In this study, the participants had to formulate their own perceptions of each other and do so in terms of specific characteristics. However, their perceptions were solicited *after* the conversations had taken place and it may very well be that it was the inquiry that made the participants aware of their impressions of each other. Is it possible that interpersonal perceptions affect the time patterns of a conversation only if the participants are aware of them?

Socialization level. At the very least, the occurrence of congruence implies that the participants in the dialogues have heard each other. It might be argued, however, that its occurrence is a consequence not simply of the participants having heard each other, but also of their ability to attend to each other, to take each other's contribution into account. What Piaget (1955) in his discussion of children's language, calls *socialized* speech, can be viewed as an aspect of this ability. *Socialized* speech, in contrast to *egocentric* speech, indicates that the child is capable of taking his listener into account to the extent of recognizing his point of view and engaging in an exchange of ideas. Note that the difference between the two types of speech is in terms of their semantic content. Welkowitz, Cariffe, and Feldstein (1976) suggest that the distinction can also be related to temporal congruence. They assert that the distinction made by Piaget reflects a difference in degree of socialization, and they posit that the emergence of congruence in children's conversation parallels the progression from an egocentric to a sociocentric orientation. Thus, they hypothesize that for children the occurrence of congruence is positively related to age.

Two groups of children participated in the experiment. Each consisted of 10 same-sex dyads. The younger group involved children whose ages ranged from 5.4 to 6.1 years, the older children whose ages ranged from 6.4 to 7.2 years. Each pair of children met on two occasions, spaced one week apart and, on each occasion, engaged in a 20-min. dialogue.

The average durations of the children's pauses were found to be both consistent during the course of each conversation and stable from one conversation to the other. Interestingly, the consistency of the younger group increased significantly from the first to the second conversation. The average durations of switching pauses were consistent only for the older group on the first occasion but for both groups on the second occasion. On the other hand, it was only the switching pause durations that yielded significant congruence coefficients for both groups on both occasions. The younger group did not achieve pause congruence on either occasion.

That the pause durations of the younger group were not susceptible to interpersonal influence provides partial support for the hypothesis that the emergence of congruence in children's conversations is a function of age. The findings also suggest that switching pause durations reflect interpersonal influence earlier than do pause durations. It is apparent, however, that to test more adequately the general notion that the occurrence of congruence is related to level of socialization requires a look at the verbal interactions of children younger than those who took part in this study and, more importantly perhaps, a direct comparison of the occurrence of congruence in children's dialogues with the semantic content of the dialogues classified in terms of the Piagetian categories. Even more telling would be a comparison of the occurrence of congruence with estimates of the children's levels of socialization, although it is not at all clear how the latter might be formulated.

Garvey and BenDebba (1974) assembled middle-class children between the ages of about 3.5 and 5.7 years into 12 triads and had each child talk to each other member of his triad. Three of the resulting dyads were male, nine were female, and 24 were mixed. The children in the dyads were previously acquainted with each other.

The authors examined the relation of the ages of the children to the numbers of utterances they produced within a 5-min. period and to their average numbers of words per utterance. Of interest is the finding that the sex of the dyad was not related to either variable. Of greater interest are the findings that (1) a comparison of the numbers of utterances produced by the members of the dyads yielded a significant intraclass (congruence) coefficient, and (2) the absolute differences between the numbers of utterances produced by the dyad members are significantly and negatively related to their ages. The latter finding suggests that older children more closely match the frequencies of their utterances to those of their conversational partners than do younger children.

One problematical aspect of the study is that its definition of an "utterance" makes it an ambiguous unit. An utterance is considered to be any segment of the speech of one person that is bounded on each end by *either* the speech of another person or a silence of one or more seconds. Thus, an utterance is a speech sound, or a sequence of speech sounds separated by one or more silences each of less than one second duration, embedded in one of four possible boundary configurations. The use of another person's speech as a boundary condition is difficult to argue with. But using a duration of 1 sec. as the criterion that distinguishes between boundary and nonboundary silences seems to imply that silences of 1 sec. or more have correlates and/or functions that differ from those of briefer silences. The more general implication is that there are "long" and "short" silences that reflect different states and/or processes. The possibility has been explored by Siegman and his associates (Siegman, Chapter 7). They, however, have used silences of 2 or more seconds as their "long" silences. On the other hand, it may be recalled from the brief review presented earlier, that Matarazzo and his colleagues also use silence as an utterance boundary. They call such silences *initiative time latencies,* and report (Matarazzo & Wiens, 1972, p. 42) that their durations tend to range between 1 and 2 sec. Presumably, however, it is not the duration of the latencies that defines them but semantic (and perhaps paralinguistic) characteristics of the surrounding utterances. In any case, given the seemingly arbitrary duration of the silences that Garvey and BenDebba use to help define an utterance unit, it is difficult not to consider the unit an at least partially arbitrary segment.

The study cannot be directly compared with that reported by Welkowtiz *et al.* (1976). The results of the two studies, however, make more credible the notion that the extent to which children match the temporal patterns of each other's speech in their interactions is related to their levels of socialization.

Some Issues of Concern

At least two further issues about congruence merit discussion. One has to do with its measurement and the other with its mechanism. In most of the studies reviewed above, the occurrence of congruence was indexed by an intraclass correlation coefficient. The coefficient is, however, computed for a group of dyads and says little about the extent to which each dyad has achieved congruence. A somewhat more direct tack has been taken by Natale (1975b) in his investigation of vocal intensity. The first experiment he reports examined the effect of systematic changes in the vocal intensity level of an interviewer upon the average intensity level of not only a group of interviewees but each of the interviewees in the group. He found a significant and positive relation between the vocal intensity level of the interviewer and that of 17 of the 21 interviewees. Similar investigations involving free dialogues and the analyses of other aspects of the temporal parameters would be valuable.

The notion that dyads "achieve" congruence implies, in part, that the parameter values of their members not only become increasingly similar during the course of a conversation, but that they become more similar to each other than to the values of other dyads. These kinds of similarity are indexed by the intraclass correlation coefficient. Part of the implication, then, is that the parameter values of the participants in conversations are, at the start of the conversations, different from and relatively unrelated to those of their partners. But what are the parameter values of participants who have not yet begun to converse? They can be the parameter values obtained by the participants in previous conversations with other persons. Marcus *et al.* (1970) used such parameter values to examine the notion that the parameter values of persons who have not yet begun their first conversations tend not to exhibit the similarities indexed by a significant congruence coefficient. The average durations of the pauses, switching pauses, and vocalizations obtained by the 24 women who participated in the quartet study were assembled into 36 random pairs for each of the eight occasions. That is, the average parameter durations obtained by each participant were randomly paired with those of three other participants such that none of the pairs were drawn from persons who had actually conversed together. Moreover, the random pairs were different in the different occasions.

The reason for replicating the design of the original study (with regard to the number of pairs per occasion) was to make possible at least an inspectional comparison of the congruence coefficients yielded by the randomly paired durations with those by the appropriately paired durations. Intraclass analyses of the random pairs yielded coefficients (averaged over the eight occasions) of −.14

for pauses, $-.03$ for switching pauses, and $-.04$ for vocalizations. None of the coefficients on any of the occasions was significant; those for pauses and switching pauses ranged from $-.25$ to $.15$. Recall that the average congruence coefficients for pauses, switching pauses, and vocalizations obtained in the original study were $.43$, $.62$, and $.08$, respectively. Thus, the results seem to provide some indirect evidence in support of the notion.

Perhaps more direct evidence could be obtained by dividing dialogues into several segments, calculating for each dyad a congruence score per segment, and computing a trend analysis of the congruence scores from the first to last segment. Such a procedure has been used to study the *convergence* of parameter values over successive conversations by the same dyads (Welkowitz & Feldstein, 1969). One should expect a general decrease in congruence scores (that is, an increase in congruence) from the first to last segment. The shape of the trend may even help to answer the question—raised by the notion of achieving congruence—of whether there is a particular point in time at which congruence occurs in conversations. One difficulty is raised by the possibility that both participants begin with durations that are relatively similar. Another difficulty with the procedure is deciding what ought to be the duration of the segments. Should each one be 5 min., 10, 15? Jaffe and Breskin (1970) assert that 5-min. speech samples seem to characterize the temporal parameters reliably, but should reliability be the sole basis for such a decision? Should the duration of the segments vary according to the type of dialogues that are to be examined? It is not clear, for example, that the duration of the speech sample needed for reliable estimates of the parameters is independent of the type of dialogue being examined. One probably useful consideration is that the segments be long enough to allow for a trend analysis of the segment means of individual dyads.

It is conceivable, of course, that dialogues can be divided into segments that consist, for instance, of only a single turn. The analysis of this kind of moment-to-moment tracking involves a correlation of the turn durations of one participant in a dyad with those of the other. While it is certainly possible that such momentary influence occurs between participants, the little evidence now available (Feldstein, 1968; Ray & Webb, 1966) suggests otherwise.

The mechanism or mechanisms that make for congruent behavior are still unknown. None of the models proposed thus far convincingly accounts for its occurrence. Webb (1972) notes the inadequacies of the reinforcement paradigm offered by Matarazzo (1965) and the more recent suggestion by Matarazzo and Wiens (1967) that temporal synchrony may be viewed as an outcome of "modeling" (Bandura, 1965) on the parts of one or both participants. His preference is for an activation-level approach (Fiske & Maddi, 1961) which assumes that organisms have characteristic levels of activity that respond in kind to the varying impacts of both interpersonal and impersonal stimuli. Since it is difficult to believe that the physiological activity level of an organism does not play some role in all or most of its interactions with its environment, the appeal of the model is understandable. However, it views the occurrence of interpersonal congruence as the outcome of a more or less automatic response of each individual to the impact of the particular aspect of the other individual's behavior that is being matched. Such a position seems too simplistic to be useful.

Natale (1975b) claims that synchronous behavior can be explained by a "communication model" he adopted from Lane and Tranel (1971). The latter authors theorized that the autoregulation of vocal intensity in the direction of matching the vocal intensity level of another voice represents a speaker's attempt to achieve or maintain intelligibility. Natale speculates that the model accounts equally well for the congruence of the temporal aspects of verbal interaction, although his argument in support of the assertion is not entirely convincing. Nonetheless, the model is most promising and deserves serious investigation. Its implications are perhaps more complex than is immediately apparent.

One implication of the model is that a speaker anticipates (although without necessarily being aware of it) that a failure on his part to match the temporal and/or intensity patterns of the speech of his conversational partner will render his message less intelligible. What is the basis for such an expectation? Is it actually likely that the intelligibility of a verbal exchange is noticeably enhanced by the presence or diminished by the absence of congruence? That one participant in a dialogue speaks loudly, for example, and the other speaks softly does not, at first glance, seem likely to affect the intelligibility of either speaker's message unless both talk at the same time. If the pauses of one speaker are very long and those of the other quite short, will they fail to understand each other adequately? Or fully?

In point of fact, no reliable data are available that could help answer such questions. It seems possible that noncongruous interactions are less communicative than they might be, or that their messages are in some way distorted. It is conceivable, for example, that noncongruent patterns elicit attitudes and/or affective responses that interfere with message reception. Or it may be that congruence (or the lack of it) serves as a form of metacommunication, especially perhaps in those cases in which the verbal message is not the *raison d'etre* of the exchange. And the metacommunication may be as much concerned with the sustaining of a conversation as with the maintaining of its intelligibility. All of these possibilities are empirically testable.

CONCLUDING COMMENTS

The chapter has tried to make two major and, to some extent, related points. The first is that it is possible to consider the temporal patterning of a conversation a dimension in its own right, one that is not dependent upon the other dimensions of the conversation for the definitions of its parameters. The second point is that the parameters of a chronography of conversation should be defined such that they empirically describe the behaviors they are supposed to tag, and incorporate no presumptions about the intentions of the participants that are based primarily upon the expectancies and intuitions of the investigator. In short, the parameters ought to be defined as objectively as possible. The reason for making these points is that the investigation of conversation chronography can still be considered a relatively new area of study, and its development ought not to be hampered—as is the case with so many other areas of psychology—by measurement procedures and a terminology that include by definition unnecessary and unwarranted preconceptions. As was said earlier in the chapter, the importance and utility of a temporal classification of dialogue should be established by research rather than by fiat.

On the other hand, one reason for studying the various channels of communication is to provide a more complete picture of their separate and combined contributions to the total communicative act. It is an ambitious goal and there are no well-defined ways to accomplish it. The work of Duncan, Kendon, Rosenfeld, Yngve, and others who explore the simultaneous interplay of several channels represents a seemingly more direct, perhaps richer, approach to the goal than that advocated in this chapter. It is an approach that demands very careful and exceedingly detailed analyses of the data and is not, therefore, undertaken lightly. It may well be the more fruitful approach.

The chapter has also presented some of the directions researchers have taken in their efforts to examine the relevance of conversation chronography to issues and events of more traditional psychological interest. In doing so, the chapter raised questions that were intended to serve as markers of possible paths for further inquiries.

The statement of the authors' position presented in this chapter may appear to be unnecessarily strong. After all, it is, in essence, a reiteration of the familiar argument that objectivity and precision are among the characteristics usually considered fundamental to a scientific investigation. It is not clear, however, that the familiarity of the argument makes its emphasis less useful.

ACKNOWLEDGEMENT

The authors gratefully acknowledge the computing assistance of Mary June Fowler, the extended discussions with Mohamed BenDebba, and the generous amount of computer time provided by the Statistics Center of UMBC. They are particularly indebted to Dr. Sherry Rochester for her constructively critical reading of a prepublication draft of the chapter.

REFERENCES

Alberti, L. Some lexical correlates of speaker switching frequency in conversation. Paper read at the Eighteenth International Congress of Applied Pyschology, Montreal, July, 1974.

Baird, J. C., & Tice, M. Imitative modeling of vocal intensity. *Psychonomic Science,* 1969, **19**, 219–220.

Bandura, A. Behavior modification through modeling procedures. In L. Krasner & L. P. Ullman (Eds.), *Research in behavior modification.* New York: Holt, Rinehart & Winston, 1965.

BenDebba, M. Vocalization rate as a function of contingent "mm-hmms." Paper presented at the annual meeting of the Eastern Psychological Association, Philadelphia, April, 1974.

Berscheid, E. Opinion change and communicator-communicatee similarity and dissimilarity. *Journal of Personality and Social Psychology,* 1966, **4**, 670–680.

Bieri, J., Bradburn, W. M., & Galinsky, M.D. Sex differences in perceptual behavior. *Journal of Personality,* 1958, **26**, 1–12.

Black, J. S. The intensity of oral responses to stimulus words. *Journal of Speech and Hearing Disorders,* 1949, **14**, 16–22. (a)

Black, J. S. Loudness of speaking: The effect of heard stimuli on spoken responses. *Journal of Experimental Psychology,* 1949, **39**, 311–315. (b)

Brady, P. T. A technique for investigating on-off patterns of speech. *Bell System Technical Journal,* 1965, **44**, 1–22.

Brady, P. T. A statistical analysis of on-off speech patterns in 16 conversations. *Bell System Technical Journal,* 1968, **47**, 73–91.

Brady, P. T. A model for generating on-off speech patterns in two-way conversation. Paper presented at the annual meeting of the Acoustical Society of America, Philadelphia, April, 1969.

Brock, T. C. Communicator-recipient similarity and decision change. *Journal of Personality and Social Psychology,* 1965, **1**, 650–653.

Burnstein, E., Stotland, E., & Zander, A. Similarity to a model and self-evaluation. *Journal of Abnormal and Social Psychology,* 1961, **62**, 257–264.

Byrne, D. Interpersonal attraction and attitude similarity. *Journal of Abnormal and Social Psychology,* 1961, **62**, 713–715.

Byrne, D., Griffitt, W., & Stefaniak, D. Attraction and similarity of personality characteristics. *Journal of Personality and Social Psychology,* 1967, **5**, 82–90.

Cassotta, L., Feldstein, S., & Jaffe, J. AVTA: A device for automatic vocal transaction analysis. *Journal of Experimental Analysis of Behavior,* 1964, **7**, 99–104.

Cassotta, L., Feldstein, S., & Jaffe, J. *The stability and modifiability of individual vocal characteristics in stress and nonstress interviews.* Research Bulletin No. 2. New York: William Alanson White Insitute, 1967.

Cattell, R. B., Eber, H. W., & Tatsuoka, M. M. *Handbook for the Sixteen Personality Factor Questionnaire.* Champaigne, Illinois: Institute for Personality and Ability Testing, 1970.

Chapple, E. D. Quantitative analysis of the interaction of individuals. *Proceedings of the National Academy of Sciences,* 1939, **25**, 58–67.

Chapple, E. D. "Personality" differences as described by invariant properties of individuals in interaction. *Proceedings of the National Academy of Sciences,* 1940, **26**, 10–16.

Chapple, E. D. The Interaction Chronograph: Its evolution and present application. *Personnel,* 1949, **25**, 295–307.

Chapple, E. D. *Culture and biological man: Explorations in behavioral anthropology.* New York: Holt, Rinehart and Winston, 1970.

Chapple, E. D., & Harding, C. F., III. Simultaneous measures of human relations and emotional activity. *Proceedings of the National Academy of Sciences,* 1940, **26**, 319–326.

Charlip, W. S., & Burk, K. W. Effects of noise on selected speech parameters. *Journal of Communication Disorders,* 1969, **16**, 267–270.

Cobb, L. Time series analysis of the periodicities of casual conversations. Unpublished doctoral dissertation, Cornell University, 1973.

Cohen, J., & Cohen, P. *Applied multiple regression/correlation analysis for the behavioral sciences.* Hillsdale, New Jersey: Lawrence Erlbaum Associates, 1975.

Crowne, D. P., & Marlowe, D. *The approval motive.* New York: Wiley, 1964.

Crutchfield, R. S., Woodworth, D. G., & Albrecht, R. E. *Perceptual performance and the effective person.* Lackland Air Force Base, Texas: Personnel Laboratory, WADC-TN-58-60, ASTIA Doc. No. AD 151 039, 1958.

Dabbs, J. M., Jr. Self-esteem, communicator characteristics, and attitude change. *Journal of Abnormal and Social Psychology,* 1964, **69,** 173–181.

Dabbs, J. M., Jr. Similarity of gestures and interpersonal influence, *Proceedings of the 77th Annual Convention of the American Psychological Association,* 1969, **4,** 337–338.

Dittmann, A. T., & Llewellyn, L. G. Relationship between vocalizations and head nods as listener responses. *Journal of Personality and Social Psychology,* 1968, **9,** 79–84.

Duncan, S., Jr. Some signals and rules for taking speaking turns in conversations. *Journal of Personality and Social Psychology,* 1972, **23,** 283–292.

Duncan, S., Jr. Toward a grammar for dyadic conversations. *Semiotica,* 1973, **9,** 29–46.

Duncan, S., Jr. On the structure of speaker-auditor interaction during speaking turns. *Language in Society,* 1974, **3,** 161–180.

Duncan, S., Jr., & Niederehe, G. On signaling that it's your turn to speak. *Journal of Experimental Social Psychology,* 1974, **10,** 234–247.

Feldstein, S. Interspeaker influence in conversational interaction. *Psychological Reports,* 1968, **22,** 826–828.

Feldstein, S. Temporal patterns of dialogue: Basic research and reconsiderations. In A. W. Siegman & B. Pope (Eds.), *Studies in dyadic communication.* New York: Pergamon, 1972. Pp. 91–113.

Feldstein, S., Alberti, L., BenDebba, M., & Welkowitz, J. Personality and simultaneous speech. Paper presented at the annual meeting of the American Psychological Association, New Orleans, August, 1974.

Feldstein, S., BenDebba, M., & Alberti, L. Distributional characteristics of simultaneous speech in conversation. Paper presented at the Acoustical Society of America, New York, April, 1974.

Feldstein, S., Jaffe, J., & Cassotta, L. The effect of mutual visual access upon conversational time patterns. *American Psychologist,* 1967, **23,** 595. (Abstract)

Fiske, D. W., & Maddi, S. R. A conceptual framework. In D. W. Fiske & S. R. Maddi (Eds.), *Functions of varied experience.* Homewood, Illinois: Dorsey, 1961. Pp. 11–56.

Fitsgibbons, D. L., Goldberger, L., & Eagle, M. Field dependence and memory for incidental material. *Perceptual and Motor Skills,* 1965, **21,** 743–749.

Fraser, J. T. (Ed.). *The voices of time: A cooperative survey of man's views of time as expressed by the sciences and by the humanities.* New York: Braziller, 1966.

Gallois, C., & Markel, N. N. Turn taking: Social personality and conversational style. *Journal of Personality and Social Psychology,* 1975, **31,** 1134–1140.

Gardner, M. B. Effect of noise, system gain, and assigned task on talking level in loud-speaker communication. *Journal of the Acoustical Society of America,* 1966, **40,** 955–965.

Garvey, C., & BenDebba, M. Effects of age, sex and partner on children's dyadic speech. *Child Development,* 1974, **45,** 1159–1161.

Greenspoon, J. The reinforcing effect of two spoken sounds on the frequency of two responses. *American Journal of Psychology,* 1955, **68,** 409–416.

Griffitt, W. Interpersonal attraction as a function of self-concept and personality similarity-dissimilarity. *Journal of Personality and Social Psychology,* 1966, **4,** 581–584.

Haggard, E. A. *Interclass correlation and the analysis of variance.* New York: Dryden, 1958.

Hanley, T. D., & Steer, M. Effect of level of distracting noise upon speaking rate, duration, and intensity. *Journal of Speech and Hearing Disorders,* 1949, **14**, 363–368.

Hayes, D. P. The Cornell datalogger. *Administrative Science Quarterly,* 1969, **14**, 222–223.

Hayes, D., Meltzer, L., & Wolf, G. Substantive conclusions are dependent upon techniques of measurement. *Behavioral Science,* 1970, **15**, 265–269.

Homans, G. C. *The human group.* New York: Harcourt Brace, 1950.

Jacobson, L. I., Berger, S. E., & Millham, J. Individual differences in cheating during a temptation period when confronting failure. *Journal of Personality and Social Psychology,* 1970, **15**, 48–56.

Jacobson, L. I., & Ford, L. H., Jr. Need for approval, defensive denial, and sensitivity to cultural stereotypes. *Journal of Personality,* 1966, **34**, 596–609.

Jacobson, R. *Child, language, aphasia, and phonological universals.* The Hague: Mouton, 1968.

Jaffee, J. Computer analysis of verbal behavior in psychiatric interviews. In D. Rioch & E. A. Weinstein (Eds.), *Disorders in communication: Proceedings of the Association for Research in Nervous and Mental Diseases,* Vol. 42. Baltimore, Md.: Williams & Wilkens, 1964. Pp. 389–399.

Jaffe, J. Linked probabilistic finite automata: A model for the temporal interaction of speakers. *Mathematical Biosciences,* 1970, **7**, 191–204.

Jaffe, J., & Breskin, S. Temporal patterns of speech and sample size. *Journal of Speech and Hearing Research,* 1970, **13**, 667–668.

Jaffe, J., & Feldstein, S. *Rhythms of dialogue.* New York: Academic, 1970.

Johnston, G., Jansen, J., Weitman, M., Hess, H. F., Matarazzo, J. D., & Saslow, G. A punched tape data preparation system for use in psychiatric interviews. *Digest of the International Conference on Medical Electronics,* 1961, p. 17.

Kendon, A. Some functions of gaze direction in social interaction. *Acta Psychologica,* 1967, **26**, 22–63.

Konstadt, N., & Forman, E. Field dependence and external directedness. *Journal of Personality and Social Psychology,* 1965, **1**, 490–493.

Kryter, K. D. Effects of ear protective devices on the intelligibility of speech in noise. *Journal of the Acoustical Society of America,* 1946, **18**, 412–417.

Lane, H. L., & Tranel, B. The Lombard reflex and the role of hearing in speech. *Journal of Speech and Hearing Research,* 1971, **14**, 677–709.

Lennard, H. L. & Bernstein, A. *The anatomy of psychotherapy.* New York: Columbia University Press, 1960.

Marcus, E. S., Welkowitz, J., Feldstein, S., & Jaffe. J. Psychological differentiation and the congruence of temporal speech patterns. Paper presented at the meeting of the Eastern Psychological Association, Atlantic City, April, 1970.

Marlowe, D., & Crowne, D. P. A new scale of social desirability independent of psychopathology. *Journal of Consulting Psychology,* 1960, **24**, 349–354.

Martindale, D. A. Effects of environmental context in negotiating situations: Territorial dominance behavior in dyadic interactions. Unpublished doctoral dissertation, City University of New York, 1971.

Matarazzo, J. D. The interview. In B. B. Wolman (Ed.), *Handbook of clinical psychology.* New York: McGraw-Hill, 1965. Pp. 403–450.

Matarazzo, J. D., Saslow, G., & Hare, A. Factor analysis of interview interaction behavior. *Journal of Consulting Psychology,* 1958, **22**, 419–429.

Matarazzo, J. D., & Wiens, A. N. Interviewer influence on durations of interviewee silence. *Journal of Experimental Research in Personality,* 1967, **2**, 56–69.

Matarazzo, J. D., & Wiens, A. N. *The interview: Research on its anatomy and structure.* Chicago: Aldine-Atherton, 1972.

Meltzer, L., Hayes, D. P., & Shellenberger, D. Consistency of vocal behavior in discussions. Paper presented at the meeting of the American Psychological Association, Chicago, September, 1966.

Meltzer, L., Morris, W., & Hayes, D. Interruption outcomes and vocal amplitude: Explorations in social psychophysics. *Journal of Personality and Social Psychology,* 1971, **18**, 392–402.

Miller, G. A. Speaking in general. Review of J. H. Greenberg (Ed.), *Universals of language. Contemporary Psychology,* 1963, **8**, 417–418.

Morris, W. N. Manipulated amplitude and interruption outcomes. *Journal of Personality and Social Psychology,* 1971, **20**, 319–331.

Natale, M. Social desirability as related to convergence of temporal speech patterns. *Perceptual and Motor Skills,* 1975, **40**, 827–830. (a)

Natale, M. Convergence of mean vocal intensity in dyadic communication as a function of social desirability. *Journal of Personality and Social Psychology,* 1975, **32**, 790–804. (b)

Newcomb, T. M. An approach to the study of communicative acts. *Psychological Review,* 1953, **15**, 393–404.

Norwine, A. C., & Murphy, O. J. Characteristic time intervals in telephonic conversation. *Bell System Technical Journal,* 1938, **17**, 281–291.

Piaget, J. *The language and thought of the child.* New York: World, 1955.

Ray, M. L., & Webb, E. J. Speech duration effects in the Kennedy news conferences. *Science,* 1966, **153**, 899–901.

Rogers, C. A process conception of psychotherapy. *American Psychologist,* 1958, **13**, 142–149.

Rogers, C. *On becoming a person.* Boston: Houghton Mifflin, 1961.

Runkel, P. Cognitive similarity in facilitating communication. *Sociometry,* 1956, **19**, 178–191.

Salzinger, K., Portnoy, S., Zlotogura, P., & Keisner, R. The effect of reinforcement on continuous speech and on plural nouns in grammatical context. *Journal of Verbal Learning and Verbal Behavior,* 1963, **1**, 477–485.

Schegloff, E. A. Sequencing in conversational openings. *American Anthropologist,* 1968, **70**, 1075–1095.

Stotland, E., Zander, A., & Natsoulas, T. Generalization of interpersonal similarity. *Journal of Abnormal and Social Psychology,* 1961, **62**, 250–256.

Truax, C. B., & Carkhuff, R. R. *Toward effective counseling in psychotherapy.* Chicago: Aldine, 1967.

Wallach, M. A., Kogan, N., & Burt, R. B. Group risk taking and field dependence-independence of group members. *Sociometry,* 1967, **30**, 323–338.

Webb, J. T. Interview synchrony: An investigation of two speech rate measures. In A. W. Siegman & B. Pope (Eds.), *Studies in dyadic communication.* New York: Pergamon, 1972. Pp. 115–133.

Webster, J. C., & Klump, R. G. Effects of ambient noise and near-by talkers on a face-to-face communication task. *Journal of the Acoustical Society of America,* 1962, **34**, 936–941.

Welkowitz, J., Cariffe, G., & Feldstein, S. Conversational congruence as a criterion of socialization in children. *Child Development,* 1976, **47**, 269–272.

Welkowitz, J., & Feldstein, S. Dyadic interaction and induced differences in perceived similarity. *Proceedings of the 77th Annual Convention of the American Psychological Association,* 1969, **4**, 343–344.

Welkowitz, J., & Feldstein, S. Relation of experimentally manipulated interpersonal perception and psychological differentiation to the temporal patterning of conversation. *Proceedings of the 78th Annual Convention of the American Psychological Association,* 1970, **5**, 387–388.

Welkowitz, J., Feldstein, S., Finkelstein, M., & Aylesworth, L. Changes in vocal intensity as a function of interspeaker influence. *Perceptual and Motor Skills,* 1972, **35,** 715–718.

Welkowitz, J., & Kuc, M. Interrelationships among warmth, genuineness, empathy, and temporal speech patterns in interpersonal interaction. *Journal of Consulting and Clinical Psychology,* 1973, **41,** 472–473.

Welkowitz, J., & Martz, M. J. WELMAR: Computer programs to analyze dialogic time patterns. Unpublished manuscript, New York University, 1975.

Wiens, A. N., Molde, D., Holman, D., & Matarazzo, J. D. Can interview interaction measures be taken from tape recordings? *Journal of Psychology,* 1966, **63,** 249–260.

Witkin, H. A. Individual differences in ease of perception of embedded figures. *Journal of Personality,* 1950, **19,** 1–15.

Witkin, H. A., Dyk, R. B., Faterson, H. F., Goodenough, D. R., & Karp, S. S. *Psychological differentiation.* New York: Wiley, 1962.

Yngve, V. H. On getting a word in edgewise. In M. A. Campbell *et al.* (Eds.), *Papers from the Sixth Regional Meeting, Chicago Linguistic Society.* Chicago: University of Chicago Department of Linguistics, 1970. Pp. 567–578.

Author Index

Numbers in *italics* refer to the pages on which the complete references are listed.

Subject Index